John

Maya Subsistence

Studies in Memory of Dennis E. Puleston

Dennis E. Puleston, Maya archaeologist (photo by Peter D. Harrison).

Maya Subsistence

Studies in Memory of Dennis E. Puleston

Edited by

KENT V. FLANNERY

Museum of Anthropology
University of Michigan
Ann Arbor, Michigan

ACADEMIC PRESS

A Subsidiary of Harcourt Brace Jovanovich, Publishers

New York London
Paris San Diego San Francisco São Paulo Sydney Tokyo Toronto

Cover and part opening art by F. E. Smiley.

This is a volume in

Studies in Archaeology

A complete list of titles in this series appears at the end of this volume.

ACADEMIC PRESS, INC.
111 Fifth Avenue, New York, New York 10003

United Kingdom Edition published by
ACADEMIC PRESS, INC. (LONDON) LTD.
24/28 Oval Road, London NW1 7DX

Library of Congress Cataloging in Publication Data
Main entry under title:

Maya subsistence.

(Studies in archaeology)
Papers presented at a conference, organized by the University of Minnesota Dept. of Anthropology, which was held at the university in Oct., 1979.
Includes bibliographies and index.
1. Mayas--Agriculture--Congresses. 2. Mayas--Economic conditions--Congresses. 3. Indians of Mexico--Agriculture--Congresses. 4. Indians of Central America--Agriculture--Congresses. 5. Indians of Mexico--Economic conditions--Congresses. 6. Indians of Central America--Economic conditions--Congresses. 7. Puleston, Dennis Edward, 1940-1978--Congresses. I. Puleston, Dennis Edward, 1940-1978. II. Flannery, Kent V. III. University of Minnesota. Dept. of Anthropology. IV. Series.
F1435.3.A37M39 338.1'0972 81-17620
ISBN 0-12-259780-X AACR2

PRINTED IN THE UNITED STATES OF AMERICA

82 83 84 85 9 8 7 6 5 4 3 2 1

The studies in this volume are dedicated to the memory of Dennis E. Puleston. All royalties from the sale of this book accrue to the Dennis E. Puleston Memorial Fund, Department of Anthropology, University of Minnesota.

Contents

10

11

12

Contributors

Numbers in parentheses indicate the pages on which the authors' contributions begin.

PIERRE P. ANTOINE* (227), Department of Soil Sciences, University of Minnesota, St. Paul, Minnesota 55108

EPIFANIO JIMÉNEZ ÁVILA (327), Instituto Nacional de Investigaciones sobre Recursos Bióticos, Jalapa, Veracruz, México

JULIO JIMÉNEZ ÁVILA (327), Instituto Nacional de Investigaciones sobre Recursos Bióticos, Jalapa, Veracruz, México

PAUL R. BLOOM (227), Department of Soil Sciences, University of Minnesota, St. Paul, Minnesota 55108

GEORGE A. COLLIER (345), Department of Anthropology, Stanford University, Stanford, California 94305

WILLIAM M. DENEVAN (181), Department of Geography, University of Wisconsin, Madison, Madison, Wisconsin 53706

LAWRENCE H. FELDMAN (295), Museum of Anthropology, University of Missouri, Columbia, Missouri 65211

DAVID A. FREIDEL (131), Department of Anthropology, Southern Methodist University, Dallas, Texas 75275

ARTURO GÓMEZ-POMPA (327), Instituto Nacional de Investigaciones sobre Recursos Bióticos, Jalapa, Veracruz, México

PETER D. HARRISON (119), Department of Anthropology, University of New Mexico, Albuquerque, New Mexico 87131, and Middle American Research Institute, Tulane University, New Orleans, Louisiana 70118

*Present address: National Agronomic Institute of Yangambi, Yangambi, Zaire.

GRANT D. JONES (275), Department of Anthropology, Hamilton College, Clinton, New York 13323
JOYCE MARCUS (239), Museum of Anthropology, University of Michigan, Ann Arbor, Michigan 48109
RAYMOND T. MATHENY (157), Department of Anthropology, Brigham Young University, Provo, Utah 84602
FRANK C. MILLER (349), Department of Anthropology, University of Minnesota, Minneapolis, Minnesota 55455
HECTOR LUIS MORALES (327), Instituto Nacional de Investigaciones sobre Recursos Bióticos, Jalapa, Veracruz, México
CARSON N. MURDY (19), Department of Anthropology, Pennsylvania State University, University Park, Pennsylvania 16802
MARION MARSHALL NIMIS† (313), Department of Animal Science, University of Minnesota, St. Paul, Minnesota 55108
MARY POHL (295), Department of Anthropology, Florida State University, Tallahassee, Florida 32306
DENNIS E. PULESTON‡ (353), Department of Anthropology, University of Minnesota, Minneapolis, Minnesota 55455
WILLIAM T. SANDERS (19), Department of Anthropology, Pennsylvania State University, University Park, Pennsylvania 16802
VERNON SCARBOROUGH (131), Department of Anthropology, Southern Methodist University, Dallas, Texas 75275
PAYSON D. SHEETS (99), Department of Anthropology, University of Colorado, Boulder, Colorado 80309
ALFRED H. SIEMENS (205), Department of Geography, University of British Columbia, Vancouver, British Columbia, Canada V6T1W5
RICHARD L. SKARIE§ (227), Department of Soil Sciences, University of Minnesota, St. Paul, Minnesota 55108
BARBARA VOORHIES (65), Department of Anthropology, University of California, Santa Barbara, Santa Barbara, California 93106
GORDON R. WILLEY (1), Peabody Museum of Archaeology and Ethnology, Harvard University, Cambridge, Massachusetts 02138

†Present address: 801 Iowa West, St. Paul, Minnesota 55117.
‡Deceased.
§Present address: Box 29, Rt 1, Audobon, Minnesota 56511.

Preface

In the autumn of 1978, returning from the isolation of a field season in southern Mexico, I was met with very sad news: Mesoamerican archaeology had lost one of its nice guys. Dennis Puleston—a gentle person, a born naturalist, a fearless explorer, and a superb field-worker—had been taken from us prematurely. A chance bolt of lightning—unpredictable, completely unlikely, a truly one-in-a-million accident—had robbed us of one of the most colorful and delightful of all our colleagues.

I remember asking myself, why does it always happen to the good guys? Surely archaeology has had more than its share of bright young people who were taken before their time—Robert Barlow, George Vaillant, David Clarke, Jack Ladd, and Jim Gifford are among those who come quickly to mind. At such times, it does indeed seem that the good die young, while, as the Mexicans say, "*cosa mala nunca muere.*"

Then came a telephone call from the University of Minnesota, where the Anthropology Department was organizing a conference in Denny's memory. Would I chair the conference and edit the resulting volume, they wondered? I replied that nothing would give me greater pleasure than to do something positive for Denny.

The conference, held at the University of Minnesota in October 1979, was entitled "The History and Development of Maya Subsistence." It was felt that this topic, which had been one of Denny's major interests, would be the most appropriate choice to integrate the efforts of his many friends who were invited to contribute papers or ideas. Those friends came in great numbers and arrived in an extraordinarily good mood. All seemed to sense that, although the circumstances leading up to the conference were sad ones, the man we were there to honor was not a sad person. Maya archaeology had been a joyful celebration for

Denny, and such was the mood of the participants that on the final day of talks one of them whispered to me, "This has been the Woodstock of all Maya conferences."

One of the reasons for the success of any conference is the group of people organizing it, and I can barely begin to thank all of them. Chairman Elden Johnson and the Anthropology Department of the University of Minnesota planned everything so well that there was little for me to do. William L. Rowe, Skip Messenger, and Phyllis Messenger orchestrated all the sessions, lunches, receptions, slide presentations, and coffee breaks. Olga Stavrakis Puleston, who knew better than anyone else who Denny's tried and true friends were, played a major role in the selection of speakers. The costs of the conference were underwritten by the Archaeological Institute of America; the Dennis E. Puleston Memorial Fund; the Lucille P. Wellington Trust; and the College of Liberal Arts, Department of Anthropology, Graduate School, and Office of International Programs of the University of Minnesota. Finally, I would like to thank the contributors to this volume for allowing all royalties to accrue to the Dennis E. Puleston Memorial Fund in order that similar conferences may be held in the future.

This volume begins with Gordon R. Willey's analysis of Dennis Puleston's career, a chapter in which Willey reviews the history of inquiry into Maya subsistence and places Denny's contributions in their intellectual context. Following this, the volume is organized into four groups of chapters dealing with Maya subsistence from the earliest Preclassic period up to the present day. Topics include agriculture, hunting, wild plant collecting, animal husbandry, and trade. A pervasive theme throughout the volume, however, is the question of the role of intensive agricultural systems in the rise of ancient Maya civilization.

We know relatively little about the origins of agriculture in the Maya region. Quite simply, most research into the beginnings of agriculture has taken place in the semiarid highlands of Mexico, where plant preservation is better. Bottle gourds are among the oldest plants for which we have any evidence—not much of a surprise when we consider that Mexico's earliest farmers had no pottery. The primitive ancestors of today's squashes and pumpkins came under domestication prior to 7000 B.C. in areas as widely separated as the Sierra Madre de Tamaulipas and the eastern Valley of Oaxaca. Wild runner beans were used during the same period over the same area, and common beans were domestic by 4000 B.C. Actual cobs of maize dating to 5000 B.C. were recovered by MacNeish at Coxcatlán Cave in the Tehuacán Valley of Puebla; domestic chile peppers appeared in the same cave by 4000 B.C. (MacNeish 1964; Cutler and Whitaker 1967; Kaplan 1967). (For a summary, see Flannery 1973: Table 2, pp. 287–301.)

As this book goes to press, however, we may be on the verge of finding out a lot about the origins of agriculture in the Maya region. Richard S. MacNeish and S. Jeffrey K. Wilkerson have embarked on the investigation of a whole series of preceramic sites on the coast of Belize. Their discoveries could fill in an enormous gap in our knowledge of early Maya subsistence.

One of the problems on which MacNeish and Wilkerson may be able to shed some light is the role of manioc among the peoples of lowland Mesoamerica. Ever since Bronson (1966) suggested that the Classic Lowland Maya might have cultivated manioc, the number of manioc "groupies" has grown steadily until we now have people convinced that the Olmec grew manioc, the Preclassic farmers of Tehuantepec grew manioc, and Maya civilization rose and fell on manioc. We even have people ready to argue that there were two forms of early Mesoamerican civilization—a highland culture based on maize and a lowland culture based on root crops. All of this, of course, must be believed on faith because there is no archaeological evidence to support it.

There are at least 5–10 species of wild *Manihot* in the Maya region, but it cannot yet be shown that any one of them is the ancestor of domestic manioc (*Manihot esculenta*). The two most closely related Mexican and Central American species, *M. gualanensis* and *M. aesculifolia,* have stouter and more many-branched inflorescences than *M. esculenta;* on the other hand, the northeastern South American species *M. saxicola* will produce fertile hybrids with *M. esculenta* (Rogers 1963). For this and other reasons, many botanists see northern South America as a possible center for early domestication. Also, the fact that many of the terms used for manioc in Mesoamerica are of Carib or Arawak origin (Marcus present volume, see Chapter 10) may even suggest that the plant is a relatively recent arrival from Central America or the Antilles.

Potentially, archaeology could solve this problem. It is simply not true, as some have claimed, that it is impossible to find archaeological evidence for manioc in the lowlands. Alejandro Martínez (1978) proved this by floating ash from bell-shaped pits at the Protoclassic Don Martín site in the Grijalva Depression of Chiapas. Carbon is preserved even in the tropics, and Martínez recovered two carbonized seeds of *Manihot* sp. out of a sample of hundreds of identifiable plants (Martínez 1978:Figure 17a). Note, however, that his *Manihot* sp. is *not* identified to species; hence, it would be a mistake to leap to the conclusion that it is cultivated manioc rather than one of the numerous wild species that are native to Chiapas and were undoubtedly used for food. The situation is similar to that of the *Manihot* sp. seed recovered by MacNeish (1958) from one of his Tamaulipas caves, which has frequently been cited as evidence for cultivated manioc. According to C. Earle Smith, Jr. (personal communication), the seed is from a wild species native to Tamaulipas.

With evidence for manioc so scanty at present, it is not surprising that archaeologists have turned to circumstantial evidence. Several have argued for Preclassic manioc cultivation on the basis of small, anomalous obsidian chips, which are said to resemble those used in manioc graters in South America. There are several problems with this idea, however, which have recently been summarized by Zeitlin (1978:188–189). First, the type of manioc currently grown in Mesoamerica does not even need to be grated to make it edible. Second, the obsidian chip argument would be convincing only if such chips were present at tropical lowland sites where manioc growing is possible, but absent at highland sites where frost conditions would rule out manioc growing. The fact is, there is virtually no Preclassic site lacking in small obsidian chips; they occur even at 2,400 m in the Valley of Mexico. Third, there is no ethnographic or other evidence that manioc graters were ever used in Mesoamerica, since the "sweet" variety of manioc used there does not need to be grated.

Belize, lying as it does on the frontier between Mesoamerica and the Caribbean region where manioc was so important, may well be one corridor through which the plant entered the Maya region. I suspect, therefore, that MacNeish and Wilkerson's work may go a long way toward resolving this interesting issue in Maya subsistence. I also suspect that, whether manioc arrived relatively early or relatively late, it is maize that was the key to Classic Maya civilization.

In Part I of this volume, contributions by William T. Sanders, Carson N. Murdy, and Barbara Voorhies are featured. Sanders and Murdy trace cultural development in the Valley of Guatemala from 1500 B.C. to the Spanish Conquest. In the process, they model the relationship between growing populations, their agricultural strategies, and the environmental changes they bring about. Voorhies examines the resources of the tropical lowlands and presents a model for their use and exchange by the early Maya. The enormous diversity of products undermines old notions that the Petén was a resource-poor environment with little to offer the neighboring highlands.

Part II consists of four chapters dealing with archaeological investigations of Preclassic and Classic Maya subsistence. Payson Sheets examines actual prehistoric cornfields miraculously preserved by volcanic ashfall in El Salvador. Peter Harrison considers the possibility of raised-field agriculture at Belize's Pulltrouser Swamp (my candidate for the best archaeological site name since the Booger Bottom Mound [Caldwell *et al.* 1952]). David Freidel and Vernon Scarborough investigate a possible irrigation canal system along Belize's New River. In a regionally wide-ranging chapter, Ray Matheny discusses the evidence for Maya soil and water conservation over the entire area from Yucatán to Chiapas and central Guatemala.

Geographers and soil scientists have also made important contributions to our understanding of Maya subsistence, and three such studies make up Part III. William Denevan provides an overview of hydraulic agriculture in the American tropics, including the Maya region. When one considers how recently it was believed that the tropical lowlands had only slash-and-burn agriculture, the number of intensive (or "hydraulic") systems currently known is impressive. Focusing on one such area, Alfred Siemens discusses Maya use of the northern Belizean wetlands. This was an area, and a research project, dear to Denny Puleston's heart. Three more of Puleston's colleagues—Pierre Antoine, Richard Skarie, and Paul Bloom—critically reexamine the possible raised fields of northern Belize and come to conclusions different from those that archaeologists have drawn previously.

It will be clear from Parts I through III that most of the critical issues of early Maya subsistence are far from settled: We do not know when maize agriculture began in the area; we do not know when (or if) root crops became important; we do not know how widespread intensive or hydraulic agricultural systems were; we do not know what the role of possible "export crops," such as cotton or cacao was; and we do not know how much of the apparent patterning seen in the landscape is natural and how much is artificial, although ground-truth studies of the aerial-radar-detected patterns recently found by R.E.W. Adams and T. Patrick Culbert will help to answer this question. As for the Classic Maya "collapse" of A.D. 900, we do not know whether agriculture ceased because the political system failed, or the political system ceased because agriculture failed. Opinions on this issue have varied. Theories range from Thompson's (1954) notion of a "peasant revolt" to Brewbaker's (1979) suggestion that maize mosaic virus could have wiped out the crops of the Petén.

If the Preclassic and Classic are obscure, however, the outlines of Maya subsistence become somewhat clearer with the written documents of the sixteenth-century Spaniards. Part IV begins with this early European contact period and moves forward, through a series of five chapters, into the modern era. Joyce Marcus attempts to reconstruct aboriginal Maya farming, complete with field sizes and Indian classifications of land and vegetation, from the earliest available Spanish documents. The arrival of the Spaniards had a great impact on Maya subsistence, however, and Grant Jones shows the way changing patterns of regional trade in the Colonial period affected both subsistence products, such as maize, and export crops, such as cacao.

Two chapters focus on the economic role of women in Maya subsistence. Mary Pohl and Lawrence Feldman consider the raising of wild and domestic animals for subsistence and ritual, tracing the pattern back from today's Maya to the sacrifices of deer and turkeys seen in the Postclassic codices. Marion Marshall Nimis also focuses on the role of women in livestock production in the Maya Lowlands today, an activity that contributes to women's economic independence as well as to the overall productivity of the region.

What lessons can modern agronomists learn from the ancient Mesoamerican farmer? According to Arturo Gómez-Pompa, Hector Luis Morales, Epifanio Jiménez Ávila, and Julio Jiménez Ávila, a great many. Disillusioned by modern "development" practices, which frequently destroy more environments than they improve, Gómez-Pompa and his colleagues created a series of experimental raised fields or *chinampas* in swampy areas of Tabasco, Veracruz, and Hidalgo, Mexico. Should these experiments succeed in raising local productivity, while making more use of unskilled labor than modern machinery, they may cause developers to rethink their philosophy. The chapter by Gómez-Pompa *et al.*, which received a standing ovation in Minnesota, makes the intensive agriculture of the ancient Maya relevant to today's problems.

In his overview of the symposium, George Collier examines all these contributions from the perspective of an ethnologist concerned with Maya farmers, and takes archaeology politely to task for spending insufficient time on the social organization of agriculture.

The volume concludes with two appendices. The first is a tribute to Denny Puleston, delivered by his colleague Frank C. Miller on behalf of the entire

Anthropology Department of the University of Minnesota. The second is a previously unpublished paper by Puleston, himself. In this paper, completed shortly before his death, Denny takes a retrospective look at the ramón-tree issue, which was one of his many intellectual contributions to the literature.

It is more than Denny's intellectual contribution, however, that will be missed. His energy, enthusiasm, and fearlessness were like a shot of adrenalin for the whole field. It was all these qualities that drew hundreds of his friends to the Minnesota conference that produced this volume.

References

Brewbaker, James L.
1979 Diseases of maize in the wet lowland tropics and the collapse of Classic Maya civilization. *Economic Botany* 33(2):101–118.

Bronson, Bennet
1966 Roots and the subsistence of the ancient Maya. *Southwestern Journal of Anthropology* 22:251–279.

Caldwell, Joseph R., Charles E. Thompson, and Sheila K. Caldwell
1952 The Booger Bottom Mound: A Forsyth period site in Hall County, Georgia. *American Antiquity* 17(4):319–328.

Cutler, Hugh C., and Thomas W. Whitaker
1967 Cucurbits from the Tehuacán caves. In Environment and Subsistence, edited by Douglas S. Byers, pp. 212–219. *The Prehistory of the Tehuacán Valley,* Vol. 1. Austin, Univ. of Texas Press.

Flannery, Kent V.
1973 The origins of agriculture. *Annual Review of Anthropology* 2:271–310.

Kaplan, Lawrence
1967 Archaeological *Phaseolus* from Tehuacán. In Environment and Subsistence, edited by Douglas S. Byers, pp. 201–211. *The Prehistory of the Tehuacán Valley,* Vol. 1. Austin, Univ. of Texas Press.

MacNeish, Richard S.
1958 Preliminary archaeological investigation in the Sierra de Tamaulipas, Mexico. *Transactions of the American Philosophical Society,* new series 48(6). Philadelphia.
1964 Ancient Mesoamerican civilization. *Science* 143:531–537.

Martínez, Alejandro
1978 *Don Martín, Chiapas: Inferencias económico–sociales de una comunidad arqueológica.* Unpublished M.A. thesis, Department of Anthropology, Escuela Nacional de Antropología e Historia, Mexico City.

Rogers, David J.
1963 Studies of *Manihot esculenta* Crantz and related species. *Bulletin of the Torrey Botanical Club* 90(1):43–54.

Thompson, J. Eric S.
1954 *The Rise and Fall of Maya Civilization.* Norman, Univ. of Oklahoma Press.

Zeitlin, Robert N.
1978 Long-distance exchange and the growth of a regional center: An example from the southern Isthmus of Tehuantepec, Mexico. *Prehistoric Coastal Adaptations,* edited by Barbara L. Stark and Barbara Voorhies, pp. 183–210. New York, Academic Press.

Dennis Edward Puleston (1940–1978): Maya Archaeologist

Gordon R. Willey

THIS is an account of the life and especially the career of a gifted young archaeologist. In less than a score of years, during which time he devoted his interests and energies to the field of Maya archaeology, Dennis Edward Puleston made a significant impact on and a substantial contribution to that branch of the discipline.

In any consideration of achievement it is important to know the individual. Dennis Puleston was born on June 19, 1940, in New York City, the son of Dennis and Betty Puleston. His father was formally trained as an architect, but much of his career was spent as a naturalist. In Dennis' early years, he lived on eastern Long Island, an area that was close to the metropolis and yet in some ways distant as well, an environment where it was possible for a young boy to grow up with some understanding of the nature of the countryside. Dennis attended Antioch College in Ohio, graduating from there with a degree in biology in 1964; but prior to and during his college years, he had opportunities to spend time in more distant parts of the world, including a year in Tahiti, a year of study in Wales, during which he was able to gain some archaeological experience, and several archaeological field seasons in Guatemala. The time he spent in Guatemala was to prove determinative in his choice of a professional career, and in 1964, he entered graduate school at the University of Pennsylvania under the guidance of the archaeologists who had been his field mentors at the famed Maya archaeological site of Tikal in Guatemala. He held fellowships at Pennsylvania, taught briefly at Temple University, joined the staff of the Department of Anthropology at the University of Minnesota as an Instructor in 1969 and rose to Assistant Professorship there in 1974. His Ph.D. in anthropology was granted by Pennsylvania in 1973. In 1965, Dennis Puleston married Olga Stavrakis, a fellow graduate student at Pennsylvania, and they have two children, Cedric Owen and Lyda Lowrie. From his early student field seasons in the 1960s

ISBN 0-12-259780-X

through the 1970s, Dennis Puleston was constantly active in the Maya area of Mexico and Central America. It was during a trip there at Chichén Itzá in Yucatán, that he met his death suddenly and unexpectedly in an electrical storm in the summer of 1978.

These are, of course, the bleakest of vital statistics. I hope I can give you a fuller sense of Dennis Puleston as we examine his career and accomplishments. Achievement must always be measured and appraised in context, and in speaking of the achievements of Dennis Puleston, it behooves us to consider the context of Maya archaeology in order to better appreciate his contribution.

Of all of the fields of New World archaeology, the Maya field, more than any other, is surrounded by a kind of special mystique, a penumbra of tradition and myth, of actuality and fancy. This does not pertain to the realities of the subject, which can be dealt with in as straightforward a manner as any other, but to attitudes which have grown up about it. These attitudes are important to anyone entering upon Maya archaeology for the first time, for they have conditioned much of the research in this field. I say this neither approvingly nor disapprovingly, but with a degree of fascination. For, let us face it, the Precolumbian Maya past is romantic in the formal definition of that term—that is to say, it is "fantastic, extravagant, quixotic, and goes beyond what is rational or practical." Today, even with the vocabulary of social science, which produces one of the dreariest forms of discourse, we cannot altogether dispel these romantic feelings. It is interesting to speculate on just how this came about.

At the time of the European discoveries of the Americas, some of the Maya ruins of Mexico and Central America were explored and described in rather matter-of-fact ways by Spanish Crown officials. Then, for two centuries and more, they virtually dropped out of sight. They were rediscovered in the nineteenth century by John Lloyd Stephens and Frederick Catherwood and brought to the attention of an emerging middle-class reading public in two now famous books of travel (Stephens 1841, 1843) and a portfolio of brilliant drawings (Catherwood 1844). These were readers who had been nurtured on the romantic tradition by Horace Walpole and Sir Walter Scott. In America, Edgar Allan Poe wrote an enthusiastic review that touched off the great popularity of Stephens's first book. Van Wyck Brooks evokes the attitude of the 1840s at Stephens's revelations.

> One marvelled at these remains of a people who had reached their golden age and perished, entirely unknown, for there were no associations connected with these cities like those that hallowed Greece and Rome. The links were severed and broken that related them to the human family, and these were the only monuments of their people on earth; yet, wherever one moved, one saw evidence of a taste and skill that indicated one of the world's great races. Architecture, sculpture, and painting flourished in these forests, and orators, warriors, and statesmen; ambition and beauty had once lived there and passed away, and one could imagine scenes of splendour there that realized the most brilliant visions of the oriental poets (Brooks 1944: 375–376).

A certain mood for Maya studies was thus set at the beginning.

To this romantic mood was added another element to make Maya archaeology "special." The early field explorers brought back information on the Maya hieroglyphs and calendrics, and these evidences of the intellectual attainments of a "lost civilization" attracted first-class minds and scholarship, men like Ernst Forstemann, the director of the Dresden Library, and the gifted American amateur, J. T. Goodman, who were the two individuals most responsible for the initial partial decipherments of the hieroglyphs and an understanding of the Maya calendar. Goodman effected a correlation of the ancient Maya calendrical inscriptions with the Christian calendar, an accomplishment that indicated that many of the Maya cities were abandoned 500 years or more before the arrival of the Spaniards, and thus deepened even further the mystery surrounding the Maya.

These two factors, the romantic setting of "lost cities" in the jungle and the high-quality, esoteric scholarship of early Maya studies, gave the field a special status in Americanist archaeology. The decades that followed did little to change this; if anything the separateness increased. Maya studies of the period of 1914 through the 1950s were dominated by the archaeologists of the Carnegie Institution (Adams 1969). They did excellent work, and much of what we know about the Maya today must be attributed to them. Nevertheless, I think it fair to characterize Maya archaeology of the time as a formidable establishment in the full sense of that term. To a degree, it was a "closed establishment"—or so it would have appeared to a fledgling archaeologist confronting it for the first time. The complexity, richness, and tradition of the field held its practitioners enthralled and presented a rather fearsome aspect to the uninitiated.

The late Sir Eric Thompson, a principal Carnegie staff member, was the foremost synthesizer of Maya archaeological knowledge for this era (Thompson 1954); indeed, he was the Maya "high priest." He was, without a doubt, the greatest Maya scholar of all time; his research accomplishments were wide-ranging, and his knowledge was encyclopedic. Yet, he had his own definite interpretations about the Maya, interpretations in keeping with the traditions of the profession and of his time. His view of Maya life was heavily weighted on the ritualistic side. He saw its leaders as priest–intellectuals who carried a vision of an ordered cosmos and set down these otherworldly thoughts in their hieroglyphic texts. The great material feats of the Maya were, according to this view, achieved against overwhelming odds on a meager and precarious technological and subsistence base. The temple–palace sites were not true cities, but precincts of the elite, visited by a humble and loyal peasantry only as logistical supporters or on special religious occasions. Above all, the Classic Maya lived in splendid isolation. This high-minded world came to an end only when this isolation was broken by vulgar ideas and men from the outside.

In the 1950s some new researches began to nibble at the foundations of this reconstruction. New and younger archaeologists began to enter the Maya field. Classic Maya isolationism was challenged both by Olmec discoveries and a consideration of the role of Teotihuacán in the rise and growth of Maya civilization. Settlement pattern studies in the Maya Lowlands called for reappraisals of population estimates as well as a reconsideration of the urban nature and functions of Maya centers. This and other revisionist trends were to characterize the decades that followed, and it is at this point, in the early 1960s, that Dennis Puleston entered the Maya field.

By now you may be understandably impatient with me for this long prologue about Maya archaeology, but I think it necessary in order that you may put Dennis Puleston's achievements in proper perspective. I would like to preface a description of these achievements by affirming that Dennis Puleston's stance and behavior as an archaeologist were in the best traditions of the profession. He was, to be sure, something of an iconoclast in a part of his work. Perhaps all young men are, or should be, with respect to the opinions of their elders; indeed, how else would the whole business advance? Yet, at the same time, he was a traditionalist in that he respected and believed in the solid scholarly accomplishments that preceded his. Indeed, on the strength of two of his last, and most brilliant, papers, I like to think that Sir Eric would have admitted him to the inner sanctum of the temple as a fellow member of the "priesthood."

Puleston's first assignments at the Tikal excavations and explorations, carried out by the University of Pennsylvania in the Petén Department of Guatemala, were the mapping and excavation of house mounds. Tikal, like all great Maya centers, had a heart or core of massive pyramids and platforms, faced with stone masonry and topped with handsome stone temple and palace buildings. We use these terms "temple" and "palace" rather freely in Maya archaeology, considering we have no very precise knowledge of the functions of these imposing buildings, but it can be assumed that they were essentially public edifices, places of worship, or residences for the elite of Old Maya society. Prior to about 1950, we had relatively little knowledge about the residential clustering in and around these large buildings, and the surveys directed toward this problem at Tikal, headed by W. A. Haviland, who was assisted by Puleston and other graduate students, were among the first such investigations in the Maya Lowlands.

As a result of these seasons of mapping and exploring, Puleston and his colleagues became impressed by the number and density of small-mound (or household-residential) units in the immediate vicinity of Tikal. While these were not found packed in street-to-street arrangements, there were literally thousands of them within a 5-km radius of what one might think of as "downtown" Tikal. There was a gradation in these assumed residences; some were of modest size, and others approached the palace norm in size and elaboration. Excavations in many of the units demonstrated their domestic functions. Puleston was one of the first to notice that there were just too many of these small-mound complexes that had been occupied contemporaneously to explain the support of the populations who had lived in them on a subsistence base of *milpa,* or shifting slash-and-burn maize farming. This realization, which was brought home with particular force at Tikal, but which was also dawning on other Maya archaeologists engaged in similar settlement pattern work in other parts of the Maya Lowlands, was to effect a major change in our attitudes about the Maya. In brief, there was just too much Classic period settlement (which is also indicative of too many people) to sustain the traditional notions of Maya subsistence. More productive subsistence practices must have been followed in ancient times. What were they?

Dennis Puleston was one of the first to look for evidences of these more productive subsistence modes. It was a simple but sensible application of the principles of the new archaeology of the 1960s: the formulation of an hypothesis about past behavior and the testing of this hypothesis. It seemed to Puleston that the close spacing of the residential households precluded extensive growing of maize in the immediate vicinity, that is, within the dispersed urban pattern of the Tikal city. There was, however, sufficient space between the house groups for "infield" or "kitchen-type" gardens. Another young colleague, Bennet Bronson (1966), who was also unsatisfied with the traditional notion of the strict maize diet as the means by which the Maya sustained themselves, argued that root crops, especially manioc, could have been grown in "infield" garden plots next to the houses. Puleston, while admitting this possibility, continued looking for other food sources. It is common knowledge among old Petén "hands"—muleteers, chicleros, and mahogany workers—that certain trees seem to grow in profusion around Maya ruins. While this probably has something to do with microenvironmental adaptations—most Maya centers occupy relatively high, well-drained spots in the rain forests—the high incidence of occurrence of some species would seem to be due to more than this. The *cohune* palm with its abundant and nutritious oily nuts is one of these; another is the *ramón* tree (*Brosimum alicastrum)* or breadnut tree. A good many years earlier, C. L. Lundell, the botanist, had called attention to the density of this tree around old Maya sites and suggested that they were relic populations of a former Maya cultigen. This suggestion, however, had not been followed up further by Mayanists; Puleston proceeded to do so.

A 12-km-long transect survey was run through the Tikal zone, plotting the occurrences of present-day *ramón* trees with respect to ancient Maya structures of both the large, ceremonial types and the smaller, residential types. The results indicated a statistically high correlation between *ramón* trees and settlement. After carefully considering various nonhuman factors that could have contributed to this correlation, Puleston was convinced that it did, indeed, result from man's former activities. He then turned his attention to the *ramón* nut, or breadnut, as a food source.

The *ramón* tree is highly productive. It takes less phosphorus but much more calcium from the soil than maize. Phosphorus is in short supply in Maya Lowlands soils, but calcium is abundant and generally ubiquitous. Puleston noted that, under wild conditions, a single Tikal *ramón* tree yielded 33 kg (72 lb) of farinaceous seeds in a season, and under plantation conditions, the yield can go up to as much as 75 kg/year (165 lb/year) (Puleston 1968). Projecting such figures to an area basis, he concluded that the *ramón* productive capacity, measured in terms of edible foodstuff, was 10 times as great as that of maize; moreover, the crop is an annual and, therefore, the fallow periods necessary for the growing of maize in the tropical forest environment are not necessary with the *ramón* tree. *Ramón* harvesting also demands little labor. Working 8 hours a day, one woman and two small children could gather a 1,360-kg (3,000-lb) crop in less than 20 days (Puleston 1968). This is in striking contrast to labor-intensive maize cultivation. The *ramón* nut is also highly nutritious, having a higher protein content than maize or root crops and a substantial vitamin content as well. Finally, these *ramón* seeds have a low moisture quotient, a factor that is a favorable one for their longtime storage.

With his systemic outlook, Puleston was to follow up this last consideration with an intensive study of Tikal subsurface pits, or *chultuns.* At the time, however—and this was 1968—he consolidated his *ramón* argument in a Master's thesis at Pennsylvania, "*Brosimum alicastrum* as a Subsistence Alternative for the Classic Maya of the Central Southern Lowlands" (Puleston 1968). Most Mayanists will remember, however, that even before this, Puleston vigorously defended his *ramón* tree views in several papers on the subject presented at archaeological meetings.

Not all of us were convinced then of the high economic importance that Puleston wished to place on breadnut cultivation by the Classic Maya. For one thing, although admittedly there is a strong case for his arguments at the great metropolis of Tikal, there are Lowland Maya sites and regions that lack the *ramón* tree. In the long view, I think that the greatest impact of Puleston's *ramón* tree research lay in the fact that it was an entering wedge into the sealed-up assumptions held by most of us that the Old Maya lived by maize alone. Other investigators began to look for other food sources. The whole concept of the "kitchen garden" plot was examined, both in terms of its agricultural potential and from a cross-cultural perspective of the way such farming functioned in other societies under similar social and natural environmental conditions. Robert Netting (1977) has written of this as have others in the recent volume, *Prehispanic Maya Agriculture* (Harrison and Turner 1978), and this theme of variation, of alternatives in Maya agriculture and food procurement has been expanded to subsume not only variation in the products themselves, but variation in their use from region to region and from period to period.

Puleston's study of the Tikal *chultuns,* mentioned briefly before, was a nicely coordinated approach, combining archaeological, ethnographical, and experimental data. Maya archaeologists had long noted pitlike excavations in the underlying limestone at many sites. In the northern Lowlands, where surface water is scarce, it was reasoned that deep, bottle-shaped pits with plaster linings were used to catch and store rainwater; the situations of these *chultuns* with respect to drainage and runoff seemed to support this reasoning. On the other hand, subsurface pits in the damper southern Lowlands appeared to have had a different function. They were not well suited for water storage since they were unlined and considerably smaller than those of the north. Most of them were also double-chambered or consisted of a vertical pit excavated down from the surface of the ground with a side chamber excavated back from one face of the initial pit, the two often being separated by a ridge of unexcavated limestone. Earlier archaeologists had speculated on their use for food storage, for garbage disposal, and as small mines for obtaining limestone for building, but these theories were open to doubt. Acting on a lead suggested by the writings of O. F. Cook, Puleston experimented with the *chultuns* at Tikal. He dug one out of the soft limestone and used it for food storage. It proved too damp for long-term storage for maize, beans, or root crops, all of which mildewed and rotted in a relatively short time. *Ramón* nuts, on the other hand, remained edible after 13 months under such conditions, a circumstance apparently relating to their low water content, as mentioned previously. This experimental archaeology, the results of which are quite convincing in the Tikal setting, not only strengthened the case for the *ramón* seed dietary hypothesis, but, if accepted, offered an archaeological dating for such subsistence practices. Not only had the Tikal *chultuns* been made and used throughout the Classic period, but some could be dated back to as early as the Late Preclassic as well (Puleston 1971).

During this *ramón* and *chultun* research, Puleston also continued his surveys and examinations of the Tikal settlement in all of its aspects. His doctoral dissertation, "Ancient Maya Settlement Patterns and Environment at Tikal, Guatemala: Implications for Subsistence Models," was accepted in 1973, and in a paper published in 1974, "Intersite Areas in the Vicinity of Tikal and Uaxactún," he addressed a topic about which little is known, settlement densities between major centers. A number of Mayanists had speculated on this matter, but there was little hard information.

Tikal and Uaxactún are 18 km apart if one measures from site center to site center. At Tikal, as noted, there is a high density of residential small mounds for a radius 5–6 km out from the center. An *emic* definition of the city is suggested by a defense wall 6 km out from the Tikal center on its north side in the direction of Uaxactún. The Uaxactún circumambient settlement has not been as thoroughly surveyed as that of Tikal, but, presumably, there are some "hinterlands" intermediate between the two sites. Puleston found that while the house-mound density within the Tikal wall—presumably a defensive feature—was 197/km^2, the count beyond the wall was only 88/km^2. In making these surveys, he was also able to come up with some interesting chronological information. The Preclassic intersite occupation was thin, the Early Classic was quite heavy, and the Late Classic, again, was thin. This certainly suggests that there was a Late Classic process of centralization and urbanization going on at Tikal that was not entirely related to overall regional population growth.

With the Tikal field explorations behind him, Dennis Puleston—in the midst of teaching, writing, and continued reading in Maya archaeology—began to contemplate some of the larger questions about ancient Maya civilization—the whys and wherefores of the rise and decline of Classic Maya civilization. Two papers were written in conjunction with his wife, Olga Stavrakis Puleston, on these subjects (Puleston and Puleston 1971, 1974). It is interesting to note that in these papers, in keeping with his regard for the basic data as well as his ever-present desire to weave all parts into the whole, he anchored his ideas in the *ramón* and subsistence investigations.

It was the Pulestons' thesis in these papers that the Maya Lowlands were settled initially by riverine peoples moving into the heartland of the Petén from its margins. These early immigrants were not slash-and-burn farmers but intensive river levee agriculturalists. Once these people settled in the interior Petén, where the riverine adaptation was no longer possible, they shifted to a subsistence dependency on *ramón* seed harvests. Moreover, in their struggle to provide adequate water supplies, the immigrants moved on to a nonegalitarian sociopolitical footing, which led to the complexities of Maya civilization. The reconstruction was ingenious, and, at the time, archaeological dates from various Maya Lowland regions seemed to back it up; however, our knowledge of the Maya has continued to expand over the last few years, and the argument is less appealing now.

More significantly, however, in terms of Puleston's own development of further ideas, one aspect of the scheme, that of raised or artificial cultivation plots, was to help open up new vistas. In his discussions of Preclassic river levee agriculture, the presence of artificial modifications of these levees was mentioned in passing. This information had come from an air and ground survey of the Río Candelaria region of southwestern Campeche Puleston made with the geographer, Alfred H. Siemens, in 1969 to 1970. This Campeche region is on the northwestern border of the Guatemalan Petén. Here, Siemens and Puleston had found a series of rectilinear, artificially constructed ridges or embankments which were very similar to constructions in several parts of South America where they were apparently used as garden plots (Siemens and Puleston 1972). These raised fields, constructed in alluvial flatlands along sluggish, meandering, and seasonally flooding rivers, provided proper drainage and sufficient moisture for intensive agricultural cropping. In form and principles of operation, they are quite similar to the *chinampas,* or "floating gardens," in the lake region south of Mexico City today. Here was another mode of farming that had been available to the ancient Maya, a mode that, presumably, would have been much more productive than that of shifting slash-and-burn fields. The total territory of the Candelaria River raised fields was not large. Nevertheless, this occurrence does lead us to question whether the method had been used elsewhere in the Maya Lowlands, and, if so, during what periods it was used. Subsequent explorations by Siemens, Puleston, and their colleagues revealed similar constructions along the Río Hondo in northern Belize (Olson *et al.* 1975); and since that time, other archaeologists have reported comparable constructions in many places in the lowlands. Some of these were riverine and some were in seasonal swamps or *bajos* (see Puleston 1978; Harrison 1978). It is still too early to define the overall importance of this raised-field cultivation to the Maya Lowlands and to the rise—and perhaps the subsequent fall (see Harrison 1977)—of Maya civilization. It is clear, however, that in some places such fields have a considerable antiquity, reaching back to Middle or Early Preclassic times, and it would seem fairly certain that many of them were in use throughout the Classic period.

Puleston's boundless energy and his love of getting to know the feel of things by doing them led him to experiment once more. With the help of local workmen, and by making every effort to duplicate aboriginal conditions in tools and work methods, he constructed a raised field in northern Belize by working waist deep in the river swamps to pile up marl, vegetation, and muck in the approved fashion. He experimented further by planting a variety of native crops on the raised field—maize, beans, cotton, and cacao—and observing the results.

The raised cultivation fields investigation was to lead him in another direction, however, and, in so doing, he produced, in 1977, one of the most seminal and brilliant papers in Maya archaeology, "The Art and Archaeology of Hydraulic Agriculture in the Maya Lowlands." In this paper, Puleston drew on his knowledge of raised-field cultivation techniques as well as his general knowledge of Maya Lowland ecology and combined these with a new analysis of Classic Maya iconography to effect a closure, as it were, of Maya subsistence with Maya ideological systems. Puleston reasoned that if Maya raised fields had a respectable antiquity, were fairly widespread throughout the Lowlands (both of which appear to be true), then they must have had an important place in Maya life, and they must have been deeply imbedded in Maya thought.

In examining Maya art and iconography with this in mind, he found that subsistence themes were not confined to representations of the rain gods, or *Chacs*. Instead, they were replete with a different kind of aquatic symbolism. Water birds, fish, turtles, snails, crocodiles, and water lilies abound. These are all creatures or plants of an aquatic nature; their habitat is in sluggish riverine settings, ponds, or swamplands. In brief, what is depicted are the forms of life that characterize the settings of the raised agricultural fields, such as those found along the Candelaria or in the Petén bajos. Puleston noted that the water lily is a part of the Maya glyph which stands for the first of the 20 day names, and in Maya mythology, it is both a sign for abundance and frequently associated with maize symbols. The lily is also associated with Itzamna, the dragonlike, or crocodilian, creator god of the Mayas. This same Itzamna, in Maya cosmology, was conceived of as the earth itself, floating in a pond. Puleston asks the question: Are the ridges of the crocodilian back symbolic of the ridges of the raised cultivation fields and, therein, symbolic of the source of life? Farfetched? Perhaps, but there is better evidence linking much of this together. On an altar at Copán, a crocodile is shown with water lilies tied to its wrists, fish are nibbling at the lilies, and maize sprouts from the beast's temples. Is not all of this a fitting diagram of the Mayas' comprehension of the importance of the ecological setting in which they lived? As Puleston states:

> The discovery of the importance of raised fields provides us with a rationale for this seemingly unlikely assemblage. With successful crop production tightly interwoven with the complex, manipulated interrelationships between canals and their fish, piscivorous birds and reptiles, the transport of upland marls and the field surfaces themselves, it is not hard to see how these elements became incorporated into Maya religion and iconography. In short, the Maya were deeply involved in flood plain ecology socially, economically, and intellectually (Puleston 1977: 463).

Both the power and the charm of this article derive from the fact that its author has come full circle in Maya studies and that he is now aware of their truly holistic nature. He began by questioning the Maya subsistence system as had been reconstructed by his predecessors. This led him into several years of explorations for alternatives to this reconstruction. From the very materialist base of his findings in this direction—the revelation of an agricultural system of great productive potential—he turned to one of the strongholds of traditional Maya archaeology, the corpus of a rich and complex iconography, and, with imaginative insight, gave us a whole new slant on Maya ideology and world view. It is an essay that I wish I had had the research vision to have written myself.

Dennis Puleston had many of the qualities of a mystic, in the most classic definition of that term, one who is concerned with the spiritually allegorical or symbolical. Would this point of view in a man who is also a scientist, a careful seeker of the facts and their place in the natural order of things, provoke a tension or a conflict? I think that it would, but such a conflict is not to be derogated. True creativity does not flow easily from stable conventional perspectives; more often it is the result of a resolution of tensions. This is not a direct quote, but I believe that the novelist F. Scott Fitzgerald once said that a genius is a person who can carry two conflicting ideas in his head and still retain the ability to operate. This does not mean, in this instance, that the Maya world of the material and the Maya world of the mind were in irreconcilable opposition; but there is always a dialectic between matter and spirit, and ideas and great art are born in this dialectic. In the same manner, an understanding of these creations grows out of an ability to comprehend underlying unity beneath apparent polarity.

This mystical side of Dennis' nature is evident in one of the last papers that he published, "An Epistemological Pathology and the Collapse, or Why the Maya Kept the Short Count" (Puleston 1979). For those not fully versed in Maya history and prehistory, the "collapse," which I mentioned earlier, refers to the rapid decline and cessation of Maya great architecture, art, and intellectual life in the ninth century A.D. Within a span of 100 years, in the many thriving cities of the southern lowlands, the construction of temples, palaces, and monumental arts and the erection, carving, and dedication of their hieroglyphic stelae, which celebrated the reigns of important rulers and the passage of time, ceased. Most of these cities were deserted by all or most of their populations. This failure of the elite segment of Old Maya society was also, at least in many regions, paralleled by drastic general population declines. As can be imagined, there has been no dearth of speculative explanations about the causes for the collapse. These have ranged from rather simple, catastrophic, monocausal solutions, such as sudden epidemics and earthquakes, to theories concerning ecological imbalances or sociopolitical events, such as foreign invasions and revolution at home. None of these seems consistently supported by the archaeological evidence. Lately, in keeping with general trends in archaeological thinking, multicausal, systemic explanations have come more to the fore. These may be reviewed in the symposium volume, *The Classic Maya Collapse* (Culbert 1973). While there seems to be little doubt that these systemic views do recapitulate and describe many of the things that must have happened to the Lowland Maya in the ninth and tenth centuries, the elucidation of what might be called a "triggering cause" remains elusive. In "An Epistemological Pathology and the Collapse, or Why the Maya Kept the Short Count," Puleston addresses this issue.

In his readings of the *Books of the Chilam Balam,* texts of legendary history and prophecy that were set down in Latin script by Maya priest–intellectuals after the Spanish Conquest, Puleston was impressed by the sense of doom and fatality that the Maya expressed over the passage of the 13-*katun* or short count periods of time. This was a form of calendrical continuity brought forward from the more ancient long count calendrical system of the Maya. A *katun* was a day count of 7,200 days. Thirteen such *katuns,* or 93,600 days, approximates 256 years of the Christian calendar. The *Chilam Balam* prophecies associated the 13-*katun* ending dates with the disasters of the Postclassic period that involved Maya cities and polities of northern Yucatán. The prophecies also referred to dire happenings and disasters in the more remote past, going back as far as the sixth century A.D.

In the Maya world view, there was a very definite cyclical conception of history. The Maya did not believe that events would necessarily repeat themselves in all their specificity, but rather they believed that there was a foreordained configuration through time of the rise of great rulers and of success, peace, and prosperity and that such an interval would be followed by another of war, famine, and disaster.

Puleston noted that the disasters of the sixth century A.D. correlated remarkably well with a period we have referred to as the "hiatus." The "hiatus" lasted for about 50 years, or somewhat longer in some cities, during which time there was very little major architectural reconstruction and virtually no stelae dedications. At Tikal, the "hiatus" has been identified with a period of troubled times, weak rulers, and internal strife. Following this period, in the seventh and eighth centuries A.D., Maya Classic civilization at Tikal and elsewhere enjoyed a renaissance; indeed, the zenith of Tikal's greatness was in the Late Classic period. Counting ahead from the "hiatus," 13 *katuns,* or 256 years, later, the Maya again enter into a slump. And this slump was to continue into the great collapse of the southern lowland cities. There was to be no real recovery from this slump, although in the far northern part of the lowlands there was some renaissance—as indicated by the prophecies of *Chilam Balam* and as is also indicated in the archaeological record of the Postclassic period. Again, afterward, the cycle of fall and rise repeats itself in the abandonment of Chichén Itzá, the founding and hegemony of Mayapán, and the subsequent decline and abandonment of Mayapán shortly prior to the Spanish Conquest.

To return to the subject of Puleston's paper, the great collapse, he writes:

> The hypothesis to be presented here is that whatever other factors may have been involved, the collapse . . . was an event fully anticipated by ancient Maya scholars and priests, who by means of consultations with their books and prophecies were well aware of their impending fall (Puleston 1979:63).

That Maya traditions, and recorded histories, contained the seeds of this idea is expressed not only in the known events of the previous "hiatus"; counting back from this disastrous time, one arrives at another low point in Maya fortunes in the third century A.D. This was the Protoclassic period for which the archaeological record shows a time of little construction following the impressive building of the Late Preclassic period—at least insofar as this can be documented by the excavations at Tikal.

Concerning the great collapse of the ninth century, Puleston concludes his article with the following:

> What were at first minor disruptions in the system gained momentum; changes that had a negative effect on the stability of the system as a whole could only be taken as evidence for the truth of the central assumption; and in a very real sense the prophecies of the *katun* were self-fulfilling. In this case, however, unlike that of the previous cycle, there was essentially no recovery. The survival of the system and of the population that sustained it was too dependent on established patterns to maintain itself without them. The disruption of social mechanisms that maintained control affected production and the maintenance of vital services, including perhaps the reservoir system, the distribution of food, even the tasks and behavior directly linked to the maintenance of public health. It is not difficult to imagine how a combination of factors might have resulted in increased mortality in a system that was already under stress. Essential to the argument here is that every step, in this vortex of possible feedback relationships, confirmed the predictions of prophecy and the general sense of fatalism. In the social and economic holocaust that followed, the fundamental epistemological error was the only thing left of the old system of order that could be believed in. Stability was not achieved, as in a great forest fire, until virtually everything was consumed (Puleston 1979:70–71).

I would not like to insist that this gives a final solution to the "collapse problem." As to that, there will probably never be a solution that is satisfying to all Mayanists. At the time when I first read Puleston's paper, I remarked that it was "enough to set a good materialist's teeth on edge" (Willey and Hammond 197:xv). But that is all right; we are dealing with a very complex nexus of human events; and I, for one, would be unwilling to concede that "epistemological error" (that lovely term for self-destructive predispositions of the mind) has no bearing on human events, even very large human events. I feel certain, too, that Puleston would not have insisted that his idea was immutably right. This was not his way. He was exploring, as he had always done, moving now into the depths and complexities of the Maya mind, at least insofar as it is possible for any of us to do so across alien barriers and reaches of time.

Puleston was to continue his explorations in this direction. He was as aware as any anthropologist of the profound gulf between the *etic* (the viewpoint of the outside observer) and the *emic* (the insider's view of a culture), and yet he wanted to sense the "feel" or the "texture" of cultural experiences different from ours. His wife, Olga, tells me that his last interests were in Maya religion, and that his last work was an explanation of the cave as a passage into the underworld. Characteristically, he was not satisfied with the word alone in these interests.

In March, 1978, he descended into one such Maya Lowland limestone cave. As Olga Puleston says, "his story of that descent serves as a good example of his love for physical experience and his belief that experience leads to intellectual understanding." She gave me the following passage from Dennis Puleston's journal, previously published by Harrison and Messenger (1980:274), in which he recounts his experiences in the cave and on its underground river:

> I tied my pack to the inner tube, debating putting out my lamp and putting in more carbide, but rejected the idea as I knew I would have trouble lighting it again. At last I pushed off with everything loaded. Then moving out of the tributary channel into the main river, I made up my mind to go back without a light at all. A faint patch of luminescence, [which] I knew must be light, reflected down from the gravel bar breakout. I blew out the lamp and was soon paddling my way upstream into thick darkness. I was facing backwards so I could watch the fading of the junction entrance. Soon I could see my pack, when it was directly behind me, blocking out the junction entrance light. Blacker and blacker it became. My only fear was running into a *fer de lance* . . . or losing the pack inner tube and not finding it. I imagined the effect of darkness on Maya initiates; how would they react? Probably with some fear, although I did not myself feel particularly terrified now. I was simply experiencing the inky blackness, the feel of the water and the feeling of the tunnel as a passage through the earth. A wind now stirred, blowing from the gravel bar breakout downstream. Gradually it got lighter.
>
> It was at this point that I began to toy with the idea that Xibalbá (the lowest level of the underworld) as described in the Popol Vuh . . . was a land reached via such underground rivers as these.

It is evident that Dennis Puleston was a remarkable and highly creative young man. The achievements of the years of his short career augured for him still greater accomplishments; but fate ruled otherwise, and these were not to be. Still, in the time that was allotted to him, he showed us how the varied aspects of the Old Maya life—from their economic interface with nature to their reconciliation with destiny and the gods—could be appreciated as an holistic entity—the creation of a great people. This will stand as the not inconsiderable contribution to Mayanist archaeology of Dennis Edward Puleston.

References

Adams, Richard E. W.
1969 Maya archaeology 1958–1968, a review. *Latin American Research Review* 4(2):3–45.
Bronson, Bennet
1966 Roots and the subsistence of the ancient Maya. *Southwestern Journal of Anthropology* 22(3):251–279.
Brooks, Van Wyck
1944 *The World of Washington Irving.* New York, E. P. Dutton.
Catherwood, Frederick
1965 *Views of Ancient Monuments in Central America, Chiapas and Yucatán.* Barre, Massachusetts, Barre. (Reprint of the first edition of 1844.)
Culbert, T. Patrick (editor)
1973 *The Classic Maya Collapse.* Albuquerque, Univ. of New Mexico Press.
Harrison, Peter D.
1977 The rise of the bajos and the fall of the Maya. In *Social Process in Maya Prehistory,* edited by Norman Hammond, pp. 470–509. New York, Academic Press.
1978 Bajos revisited: Visual evidence for one system of agriculture. In *Prehispanic Maya Agriculture,* edited by Peter D. Harrison, and B. L. Turner II, pp. 247–254. Albuquerque, Univ. of New Mexico Press.
Harrison, Peter D., and Phyllis E. Messenger
1980 Dennis Edward Puleston, 1940–1978. Obituary in *American Antiquity* 45(2):272–276.
Harrison, Peter D., and B. L. Turner II (editors)
1978 *Prehispanic Maya Agriculture.* Albuquerque, Univ. of New Mexico Press.
Netting, Robert McC.
1977 Maya subsistence: Mythologies, analogies, possibilities. In *The Origins of Maya Civilization,* edited by Richard E. W. Adams, pp. 299–334. Albuquerque, Univ. of New Mexico Press.
Olson, G. W., A. H. Siemens, D. E. Puleston, G. Cal, and D. Jenkins
1975 Ridged fields in British Honduras. Mimeograph available from author.
Puleston, Dennis E.
1968 Brosimum alicastrum *as a subsistence alternative for the Classic Maya of the Central Southern Lowlands.* Unpublished M.A. thesis, Department of Anthropology, Univ. of Pennsylvania. Univ. Microfilms (Order No. M-3977), Ann Arbor, Michigan.
1971 An experimental approach to the function of Classic Maya chultuns. *American Antiquity* 36(3):322–335.
1973 *Ancient Maya settlement patterns and environment at Tikal, Guatemala: Implications for subsistence models.* Unpublished Ph.D. dissertation, Department of Anthropology, Univ. of Pennsylvania. Univ. Microfilm (Order No. 74–14, 128), Ann Arbor, Michigan.
1974 Intersite areas in the vicinity of Tikal and Uaxactún. In *Meso-American Archaeology: New Approaches,* edited by Norman Hammond, pp. 303–311. London, Duckworth.
1977 The art and archaeology of hydraulic agriculture in the Maya Lowlands. In *Social Process in Maya Prehistory,* edited by Norman Hammond, pp. 449–479. New York, Academic Press.
1978 Terracing, raised fields, and tree cropping in the Maya lowlands: A new perspective on the geography of power. In *Prehispanic Maya Agriculture,* edited by Peter D. Harrison and B. L. Turner II, pp. 225–246. Albuquerque, Univ. of New Mexico Press.
1979 An epistemological pathology and the collapse, or why the Maya kept the short count. In *Maya Archaeology and Ethnohistory,* edited by Norman Hammond and G. R. Willey, pp. 63–74. Austin, Univ. of Texas Press.
Puleston, Dennis and Olga Stavrakis Puleston
1971 An ecological approach to the origins of Maya civilization. *Archaeology* 24(4):330–336.
Puleston, Olga Stavrakis, and Dennis E. Puleston
1974 A processual model for the rise of Classic Maya civilization in the southern lowlands.

Proceedings of the XLth International Congress of Americanists, Rome, 1972, pp. 119–124. Geneva, Tilgher.

Siemens, Alfred H., and Dennis E. Puleston

1972 Ridged fields and associated features in southern Campeche: New perspectives on the Lowland Maya. *American Antiquity* 37(2):228–239.

Stephens, J. Lloyd

1841 *Incidents of Travel in Central America, Chiapas and Yucatán*, 2 vols. New York, Harper.

1843 *Incidents of Travel in Yucatán*, 2 vols. New York, Harper.

Thompson, Sir Eric S.

1954 *The Rise and Fall of Maya Civilization.* Norman, Univ. of Oklahoma Press.

Willey, Gordon R., and Norman Hammond (editors)

1979 Introduction. In *Maya Archaeology and Ethnohistory,* pp. xi–xvii. Austin, Univ. of Texas Press.

I
Ecological Models for Early Maya Adaptations

1

Cultural Evolution and Ecological Succession in the Valley of Guatemala: 1500 B.C.–A.D. 1524

William T. Sanders and Carson N. Murdy

Introduction

IN this chapter, we will summarize some of the results of the Pennsylvania State University Kaminaljuyú Project. Most particularly, we will focus on the interactive relationships among a set of variables: population growth, agricultural intensification, environmental deterioration, and sociopolitical evolution.

The highlands of Guatemala contrast with the Maya Lowlands in a number of features. First, the highlands offer much greater diversity per square kilometer in terms of rainfall, temperature, topography, and soils. Second, large portions of the area have been subject to recent volcanic activity, and much of the region offers a very different soil pattern from that characteristic of the limestone shelf of the Yucatán Peninsula. Generally, the highlands are characterized by abundant rainfall, a feature which contrasts with much of the Mesoamerican highlands and approximates the conditions over most of the Maya Lowlands.

Highland Guatemala generally consists of three major mountain masses running east–west across the country. To the north, is a series of limestone hills and mountains formed during the Cretaceous period; the middle ranges are more recent, are of volcanic origin, and date from the Cenozoic period; and finally, in very late Cenozoic and Pleistocene times, the southernmost range, a string of much younger volcanoes, formed, fronting the Pacific Coast. This

ISBN 0-12-259780-X

southern range includes a number of still-active volcanoes, such as Pacaya, Agua, and Fuego. Most of the valleys and plateaus in highland Guatemala lie below the frost line at elevations of 1,300 to 1,800 m above sea level, but a number of upland surfaces extend to about the 2,000 m contour, one of the largest being the Valley of Quezaltenango. There is a striking contrast in soil characteristics in highland Guatemala between the older limestone valleys of the north and the younger volcanic-ash-filled basins of the south, differences that particularly affect the productivity of maize. Our test case, the Valley of Guatemala, is a young volcanic basin with soils of exceptional fertility.

Geologically, the Valley of Guatemala is a volcanic-ash-filled graben, limited by the Santa Catarina Pinula and Mixco fault scarps to the east and west, respectively. Late Tertiary orogeny may have dropped the graben floor as much as 300 m while at the same time partially diminishing relief through fissure eruptions of lavas and tuffaceous sediments (Williams 1960). Subsequent quaternary volcanic activity, particularly from Volcán Pacaya immediately to the south, filled the graben with 90 to 150 m of waterlaid and airborne pumice and ash which has produced a complex stratigraphy of interbedded tephras, ash-flow tuffs, fluvial and lacustrine sediments, and paleosols (Koch and McLean 1975).

Topographically, the valley is better described as a dissected plateau surface, with three great terraces. The upper terrace has an elevation of 1,800 m above sea level (the Canchón plateau) and lies to the east; the middle terrace occupies the central and western parts of the valley and ranges from 1,400 to 1,550 m above sea level; and finally, a lower terrace lies to the south, situated at an elevation of 1,200 m above sea level, and includes Lake Amatitlán. Although most of the drainage flows from the terraced plateau into the Pacific, drainage in the northern section joins the Motagua River, ultimately emptying into the Caribbean Sea. This complex and abundant drainage system has incised deep, canyonlike structures over much of its surface; the terraces actually consist of small zones of flatland interrupted by deep canyons. The only area of truly mountainous topography defines the southern boundary of the survey region, a boundary formed by the great volcanoes of the southern volcanic range, Agua and Pacaya. The west boundary is a steeply sloping escarpment of the central terrace, and to the north, is a series of low hills and plateau surfaces around Chinautla that initiate the descent to the Motagua. Because the Valley of Guatemala does not form a neat topographic or hydrographic unit, our definition is somewhat arbitrary.

Between 1968 and 1970, the senior author, with Joseph Michels, directed an intensive study of the large archaeological site of Kaminaljuyú (Figure 1) on the western edge of Guatemala City along with an intensive settlement survey of an arbitrarily defined 600-km^2 region around that site (the valley survey was supervised by Michael Davis). Of this designated area, approximately 50% was actually covered by the survey. These survey data, as well as excavation data from Kaminaljuyú, provide the basis for this analysis. Finally, a number of areas to the east and north were spot-surveyed, providing data from an additional 400 km^2.

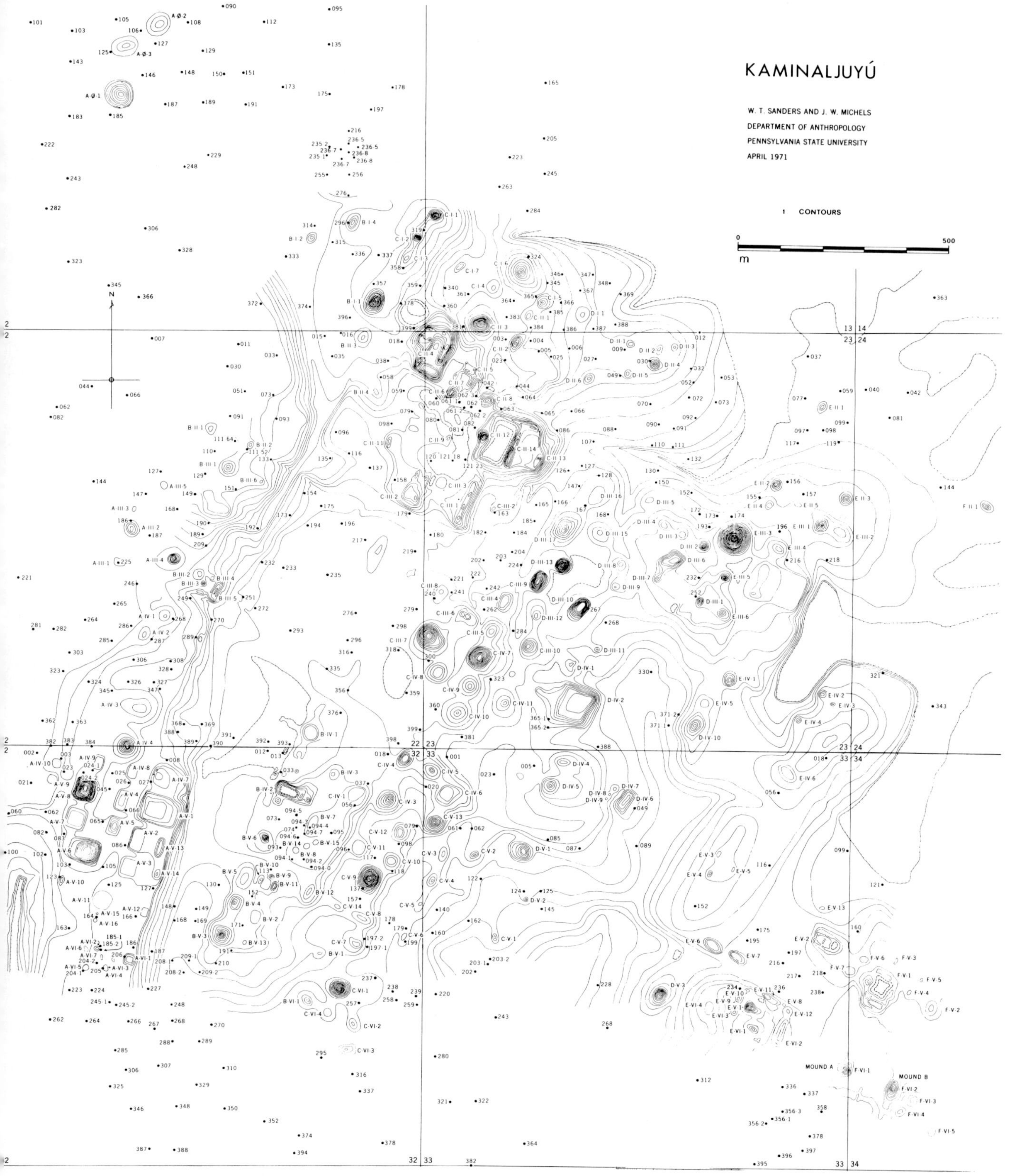

FIGURE 1. *Map of Kaminaljuyú.*

FIGURE 2. *Map of south central highlands of Guatemala showing site distribution and locations of survey squares.*

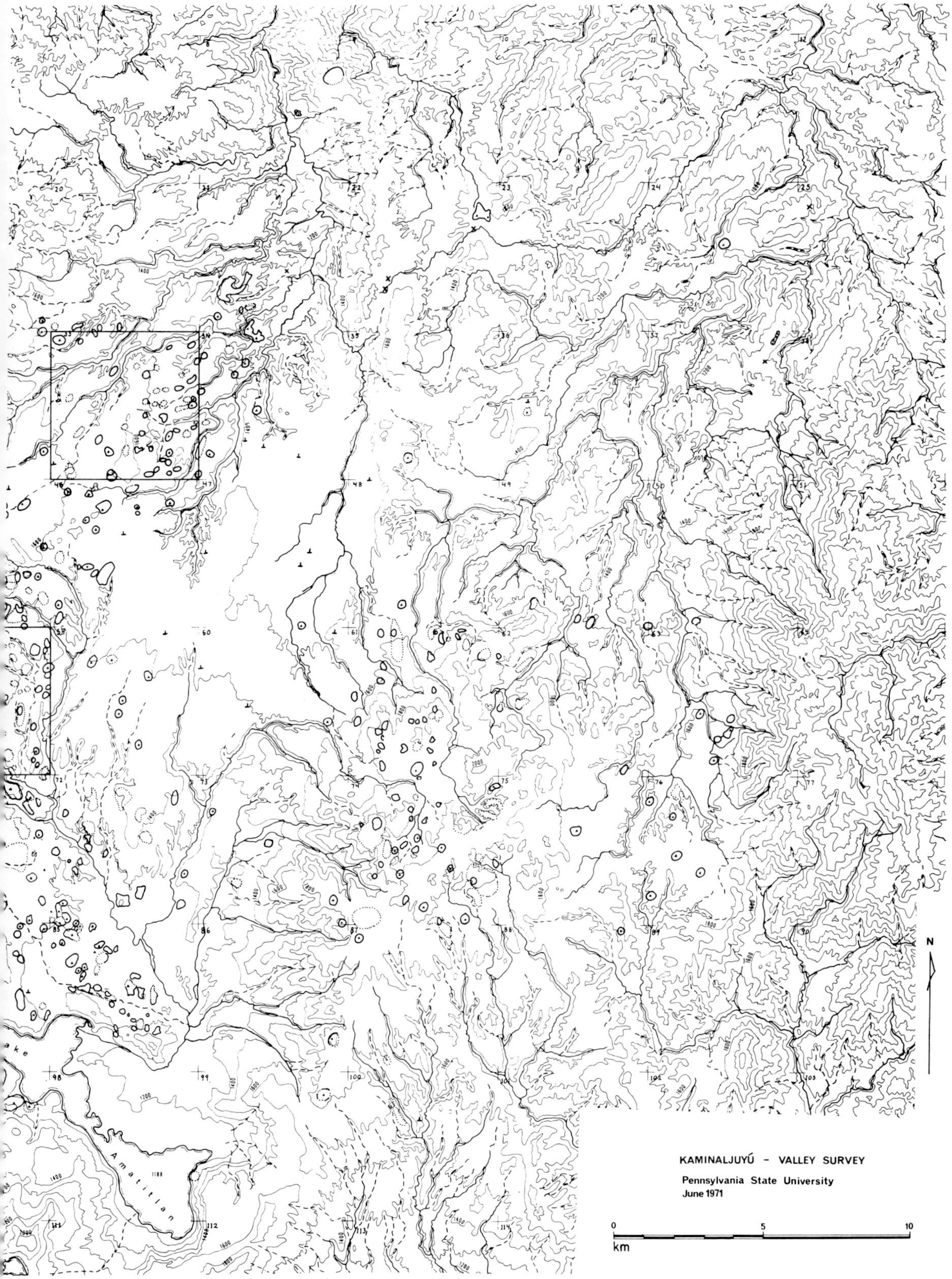

KAMINALJUYÚ - VALLEY SURVEY
Pennsylvania State University
June 1971
0
5
10
km
N
Amatitlan
1200
1188

An additional 25-km^2 square, surveyed in the Chimaltenango Valley west of the Valley of Guatemala, is not included in this analysis. We also collected information on contemporary peasant agriculture to provide ourselves with guidelines for the interpretation of the prehistory of the region (these latter data were collected by Michael Logan).

The 1,000-km^2 survey area (Figure 2) can be divided into six clearly defined ecological zones, each of which presented somewhat different problems to the prehistoric farming population. Three of these zones, the tops of the noted three terraces, are relatively level surfaces. The largest and most important one, the area around Guatemala City with a mean elevation of 1,500 m above sea level, is the key zone of the 1,000-km^2 area in terms of agricultural potential. A second zone is the Canchón plateau, a gently undulating surface that is 1,800 m above sea level. The third and lowest zone is the Lake Amatitlán basin, with a mean elevation of about 1,300 m above sea level. Zone 4 is the rugged, heavily dissected terrain around Chinautla, an elevation of about 1,300 to 1,400 m. The fifth and sixth zones are the steep escarpments that lie east and west of Zones 1 and 3.

Rainfall values over this area are rather uniform, ranging from an annual average of 1,200 to about 1,500 mm. Virtually all of this rain falls during the period from May 1 to November 1, and the subsequent months are almost rainless. The abundant seasonal rainfall, along with the fact that most of the soils in the area have excellent water retentive abilities, means that crop security levels are unusually high in comparison with the Mexican highlands.

The most significant factors that promote variety in agricultural utilization of the area are topography and soils. The formation of volcanic ash soils, or Andisols (Soil Survey Staff 1975:230; Smith 1977), in humid climates, such as the Valley of Guatemala, is principally carried out by two basic processes: the abundant accumulation of humus on the surface and A horizons and the extensive leaching of silica and bases throughout the profile. These two processes rather rapidly define an A and a C horizon within the soil, following which continued eluviation and leaching of humus from the A horizon may form an AC horizon. This, plus the occasional new eruption of the parent volcano, which buries the developing profile beneath fresh deposits of ash, account for the many paleosols seen in the stratigraphic profiles of areas such as the Valley of Guatemala (cf. Bryan 1945).

The A horizons of Andisols are generally thick (35–90 cm) and brownish black to black with 10% to 30% humus, texture varies from clay to fine sandy loam, and structure is weakly to moderately developed granular to subangular blocky (in an A2); A horizons are very friable, and the boundary is gradual. The AC, or occasionally B2, horizons are generally dark brown to yellowish brown, clay loam to loam, moderately developed coarse to very coarse angular blocky, fine porous with low bulk density, and friable. These horizons are generally very light yellowish brown to brown, fine sandy loam to clay, with moderately to strongly developed angular blocky structure.

Of the various minerals and clays found in Andisols, distinctive and most important in terms of agricultural capability is the amorphous hydrous silica of low base status and high anion exchange capacity known as allophane. Allophane appears to be responsible for two of the most prominent characteristics of volcanic ash soils: the high adsorption of polyphosphates over orthophosphates, resulting in a deficiency of phosphorus usable by plants, and the high accumulation of organic matter. Although Andisols may present problems of low mineral–nutrient content, high phosphate adsorption capacity, and close packing of glass particles in the C horizon, which impedes root penetration, as well as the fact that fresh ash falls may cause considerable crop damage with soluable sulphates and chlorides, they are generally considered excellent agricultural soils due to the high organic content in the A horizon, and concomitant water retention capacity, and the low bulk density, which makes them easily workable. These, coupled with fertilization with night soil to maintain essential phosphorous, should make for a highly productive neolithic agriculture.

To date, the best information available on the soils of the valley, from an agronomic viewpoint, comes from a reconnaissance survey of Guatemala by Simmons *et al.* (1959). Based on this study, we have prepared Table 1 and Figure 3. A number of summary statements can be derived from Table 1. Over 66% of the surface consists of soils weathered from young volcanic materials, and all but 9%, or 55% of the total surface of the area, have soils of high fertility. The remaining 9% of volcanic soil is rated as of moderate fertility. Adding the 2.1% of the area with limestone-derived soil and the 6.3% of alluvial soils (the latter found primarily on the edge of Lake Amatitlán), 63% of the surface of the area is rated as having soils of high fertility, which is an extremely high percentage for any geographic area of this size. Slightly less than 15% consists of lake and rocky areas classifiable as noncultivable lands. Virtually all of the soils have a texture that varies only slightly from the "*franca*" category—a soil with an even balance of sand, loam, and clay—which are ideal for agricultural exploitation in terms of water retention ability, friability, and fertility. In general, this area would seem to be ideal for both extensive and intensive agriculture.

The one unfavorable characteristic of the area is that a high percentage of the soils is susceptible to erosion. Only two soil types, a total percentage of only 37% of the surface area (the Guatemala and the alluvial soils), are characterized by a low susceptibility to erosion. The alluvial soils vary considerably in terms of characteristics related to agricultural exploitation—the capacity to store water and the nature of the parent materials. The Guatemala-type soils, because of the substantial area occupied by them and because of their quality (good drainage, excellent water storage capacity, friable texture, depth, low susceptibility to erosion, and high fertility) represent the most favorable component of the survey area. One unfavorable feature of the Guatemala soil is that the areas in which these soils are found are also areas of abundant surface drainage. During the history of agricultural use of the area there has been a progressive deepening and widening of these streams, attributable to increased stream flow caused by

Table 1
Soils and Agricultural Potential in the Valley of Guatemala

Soil type	Percent	Soil source	Drainage	Texture	Mean depth (cm)	Mean slope angle (degrees)	Water storage capacity	Erosion risk	Fertility
Morán	22.0	Volcanic rock	Good	Loam	40–50	8–15	High	High	High
Cauque	12.0	Volcanic rock	Good	Loam	20–40	15–19	High	High	High
Guatemala	31.0	Volcanic rock	Good	Clay loam	30–50	0–2	Very high	Low	High
Guatemala Quebrada	.3	Volcanic rock	Good	Sandy loam	Deep	0–2	Very high	Low	High
Guatemala Pendiente	1.9	Volcanic rock	Good	Loam	Shallow	Steep	High	Very high	High
Fraijanes	2.5	Volcanic toba	Good	Loam	20–30	40–60	Moderate	Very high	Moderate
Jalapa	2.5	Volcanic rock	Good	Sandy loam	10–15	15–25	Very low	High	Moderate
Pinula	4.0	Volcanic toba	Good	Loam	20–30	10–20	Moderate	High	Moderate
Chinautla	1.1	Granite	Regular	Loam	10–20	20–50	Low	Very high	Low
Subunal	2.1	Limestone	Good	Clay	10–25	10–30	Low	High	High
Tierra Fragosa	13.0	—	—	—	—	—	—	—	—
Alluvial plain	6.0	Variable	Variable	Sandy loam	Deep	Flat	Variable	Low	Variable
Lake	1.6	—	—	—	—	—	—	—	—

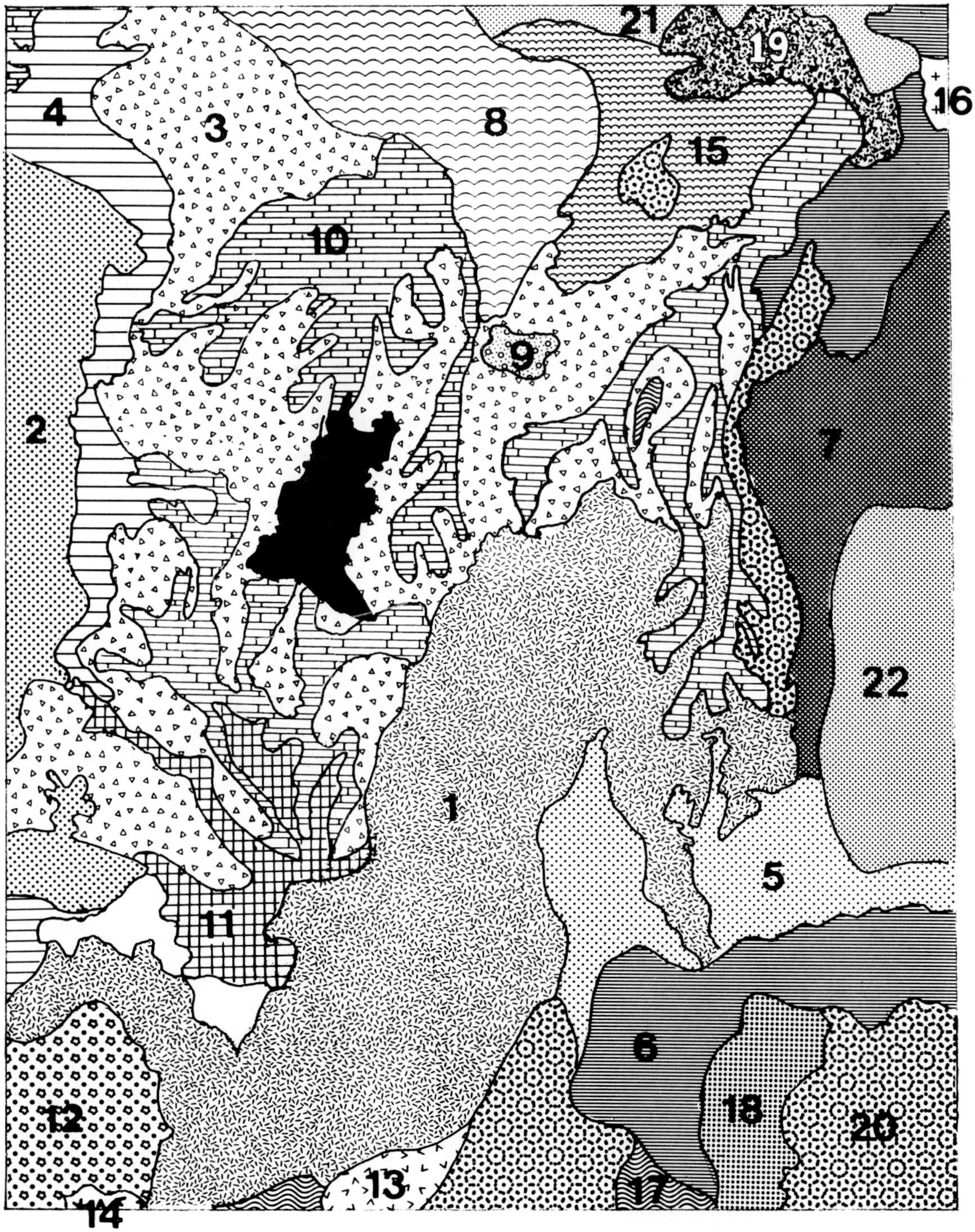

FIGURE 3. *Soil map of the Valley of Guatemala. Soil types: Morán (1), Cauque (2), Guatemala (3), Guatemala Pendiente (4), Fraijanes (5), Jalapa (6), Pinula (7), Chinautla (8), Subunal (9), Tierra Fragosa (10), alluvial plain (11), Alotenango (12), Barberena (13), Cimas Volcánicas (14), Jigua (15), Mongoy (16), Pacaya (17), Salamá (18), Salamá Quebrada (19), Suelos de los Valles (20), Chuarrancho (21), and Camanchá (22). Black area, Guatemala City; white areas, lakes. (Redrawn from Simmons* et al.*)*

increasing erosion of the neighboring slopes. This process has affected all the flatland of the drainage basin and has resulted in a gradual reduction and fragmentation of cultivable land surfaces. We suggest the very strong probability that much of this hydrographic patterning is anthropogenic.

Chronology

On the basis of Michels and Wetherington's reorganization of the Carnegie chronological sequence, the following periods have been defined: Early Formative (Arévalo) 1500–1000 B.C., Middle Formative (Las Charcas) 1000–500 B.C., Late Formative (Providencia–Sacatepéquez) 500–200 B.C., Terminal Formative A (Verbena) and B (Miraflores–Arenal) 200 B.C.–A.D. 200, Early Classic (Aurora) A.D. 200–400, Middle Classic (Amatle I–Esperanza) A.D. 400–600, Late Classic A (Amatle II) A.D. 600–800, and B (Pamplona) A.D. 800–1000, Early Postclassic (Ayampuc) A.D. 1000–1200, Late Postclassic (Chinautla) A.D. 1200–1524, (Wetherington 1978; Michels and Wetherington 1979).

The Test Squares

Final analysis has now been completed on 3 of the 12 intensively surveyed squares (or an area of 75 km^2). We also have complete data on Kaminaljuyú itself within the 5-km^2 area of a fourth square. First, we will present, in considerable detail, an analysis of the 3 study units. The data from this analysis will then be used to extrapolate for the balance of the survey area. It should be noted, however, that we also have a fairly clear picture from preliminary examination of the data as to the archaeological situation in the remaining nine intensively surveyed squares (an area of 225 km^2) as well as from data collected by Shook in previous surveys of the entire 1,000-km^2 region of the Valley of Guatemala. The 3 squares, 33, 43, and 58, and their occupational history are probably fairly representative of the region as a whole, particularly when one compares their environmental features with those of the balance of the area.

Because of the severely eroded conditions of much of the surface pottery in the valley, it was necessary to create an absolute chronology for the archaeological sites in question using obsidian hydration dating coupled with and checked against the data provided by ceramics and architecture (see Table 2). In the pragmatic interests of producing the most reliable chronology possible in a reasonable amount of time, a random sample of obsidian artifacts, stratified according to catalog lot numbers, were selected from each site for dating. At least 4 dates were calculated for each small site, and at least 12 dates were calculated for each site with ceremonial architecture. The obsidian samples were processed according to the laboratory procedures detailed by Michels and Bebrich (1971), and dates were calculated according to formulae and conversion tables provided

Table 2
Comparison of Obsidian Dates and Ceramic Phasing[a]

Site number	Obsidian dates[b]	Ceramic phases
33-00-204	LTF	Preclassic?
33-01-012	*EPC,* LLC	Amatle II
33-01-069	*MC,* EPC	Terminal Formative, Amatle II
33-04-214	*LPC,* EC, LLC	Late Classic–Postclassic
33-11-219	*ETF,* EC, LLC, LPC	Verbena–Arenal
33-13-130	*EC,* LLC, EPC	Chinautla
33-13-204	*LPC,* LF, LTF	*Postclassic,* Amatle II, Late Classic
33-14-170	*ELC,* LF	Early Classic, Postclassic
33-14-188	*ELC,* MC, EPC	Postclassic
33-23-030	*LLC,* EPC	Amatle II
33-23-322	*LLC,* LTF, MC	Amatle II
33-24-007	ELC, LLC	Postclassic
33-24-175	*ELC,* LTF, MC	Terminal Formative, Late Postclassic[c]
33-24-285	*ELC,* LF, LTF	Amatle I?
33-33-385	*EPC,* LF, EC	Post Classic, Las Charcas[c]
33-34-059	*LLC,* ELC	Terminal Formative
33-34-213	*LLC,* LF, EC	Amatle II
33-34-222	*EPC, LTF,* EC, MC, ELC, LLC	Amatle II
33-41-118	*LLC, LPC, EPC,* LTF, EC	Amatle II
33-43-139	*ELC, LTF,* MF, ETF, EC,LLC, EPC, LPC	Arévalo, Amatle I, Late Postclassic?, Historic
33-43-194	*LPC,* ELC, EPC	Classic
33-43-237	*LTF,* ELC, EPC	Chinautla or Late Classic
33-43-364	*LPC,* MC, ELC	Amatle I–II
33-44-119	*LPC,* LTF, EC, EPC	Amatle II, Chinautla
33-44-305	*MC,* EPC	Terminal Formative–Amatle I
33-44-360	*EC*	Historic
43-00-003	*ELC,* EC, LLC, EPC	*Amatle II*
43-00-019	*ELC,* ETF, LLC, LPC	Amatle II
43-00-069	*EPC,* EC, ELC	*Amatle II,* Classic trade
43-00-212	*LLC, ELC,* LTF	*Amatle II, Las Charcas,* Preclassic
43-01-211	*MC,* EC, EPC	Preclassic, Amatle II
43-01-245	*ELC,* EC, LPC	Preclassic, Amatle II
43-01-358	*ELC, EC,* MC	Amatle I–II
43-02-203	*LLC,* ELC	Preclassic, Amatle I–II
43-10-057	*ELC, LPC,* MC	Amatle II
43-10-088	*ELC, EPC, EC, MC,* EF	*Amatle II, Amatle I, Preclassic,* Sacatepéquez, Aurora
43-10-310	EC, MC, Colonial	*Amatle II,* Sacatepéquez, Amatle III, Chinautla
43-10-399	*EC,* ELC	Postclassic
43-11-021	*MC,* LLC, Colonial	Sacatepéquez, Chinautla
43-11-163	*MC,* EC, ELC	Amatle II
43-12-030	*LTF, EC,* LF	*Amatle II,* Aurora

(*Continued*)

Table 2 (*Continued*)

Site number	Obsidian dates[b]	Ceramic phases
43-13-217	*ELC, LF, LTF,* ETF, MC, LPC	*Amatle II, Preclassic, Sacatepéquez, Amatle I*
43-20-063	*ELC, LLC*	Amatle II, Chinautla
43-20-289	*LLC,* ELC	Chinautla
43-21-315	*MC, LLC*	Amatle I–II
43-21-327	*EPC, LPC,* MF, ELC, LLC	*Amatle I–II,* Las Charcas, Chinautla
43-23-131	LF, ELC, LLC	Arenal, Amatle II
43-23-286	*MC, EC, LTF, LLC,* ETF	*Amatle II, Preclassic, Amatle I Verbena, Sacatepéquez, Arenal, Classic,* Las Charcas, Chinautla
43-23-290	*LPC,* EF, ETF, EC	Late Classic–Chinautla
43-31-115	*MC,* LF, ELC	*Amatle I,* Amatle II
43-33-003	*LTF, MC, EC, LLC,* EPC	Preclassic, Amatle II
43-33-239	*ELC,* EC	*Amatle II, Amatle I,* Preclassic? Postclassic?
43-33-369	*LLC,* EPC	*Amatle II,* Sacatepéquez
43-44-179	*ELC, LF,* LTF, EC, MC	*Verbena,* Sacatepéquez, Arenal, Aurora
58-03-245	*EC,* LF, EPC	*Verbena, Sacatepéquez, Preclassic, Las Charcas, Amatle II, Amatle I,* Arenal, Aurora
58-14-179	*MC,* LF, LTF	Amatle I
58-21-036	*ELC,* ETF, EC	Amatle II

[a] Only those sites for which ceramic identifications are available are included.

[b] Phases of major occupation are italicized and placed in order of importance; otherwise, the order is chronological. EF = Early Formative; MF = Middle Formative; LF = Late Formative; ETF = Early Terminal Formative; LTF = Late Terminal Formative; EC = Early Classic; MC = Middle Classic; ELC = early Late Classic; LLC = late Late Classic; EPC = Early Postclassic; LPC = Late Postclassic.

[c] According to Shook (1952).

by Michels (1973) and Hurtado de Mendoza (1977). The sites were then phased into the Valley of Guatemala chronology in the following manner: For any rural site, if at least two of the four dates obtained fell within the same phase, the site was dated to that phase at its maximum population and extent. Dates falling outside the phase assignment of the site, either earlier or later, were regarded as representing trace occupations during the given phase of no more than 1 ha in extent (cf. Michels 1979). For sites with architecture, at least three dates were deemed necessary for assignment of a major occupation with architecture to the phase indicated; otherwise, the dates were considered to represent hamlets or trace occupations. Those phases into which the largest number of dates fell were considered as the phases of maximum extent and population of the site. The results of this procedure can be seen in the accompanying site distribution maps for each phase in each zone.

In this chapter, two different systems of classification of the land are given and used, each of which is useful for different purposes. The first, based upon a reconnaissance soil survey by Simmons *et al.* (1959) summarized previously, is a classification by which each soil is categorized as a "series," based upon characteristics such as the parent material, color, texture, consistence, structure, pH reaction, and special formations within each horizon of the soil classified. Based upon such a description and classification of a soil, certain properties of the soil may be inferred, such as internal drainage, rooting depth of plants, water retention capability, and tilth potential, that have important implications regarding the major land uses, cropping system, tillage methods, protection, water control and use, use and conservation of organic matter, reaction control, and fertilization of the particular soil series.

The land-use capability classification, on the other hand, is based on and is essentially interpretive of the soil series classification, giving the potential for cultivated crops or permanent vegetation based on such factors as the slope, erosion hazard, excess water, and climate as well as the soil itself. Generally, Classes I–IV are considered arable, whereas Classes V–VIII are not.

More specifically, the land-use potential maps, which have been elaborated for each zone, are based on the land-use capability classification of Klingebiel and Montgomery (1961), but with emphasis on factors of slope and drainage, as used by the Instituto Geográfico Nacional de Guatemala (IGN) (C. Sierra, personal communication). The maps are based upon preliminary studies and information supplied courtesy of the IGN and C. Lemmerhofer. The eight classes of land are briefly described as follows:

Class I soil deeper than 90 cm; medium textured; permeable; maximum slope of 4%; flat or slightly undulating relief; granular or subangular blocky structure; imperceptible erosion with less than 12.5% of the A horizon removed; well-drained with subparallel or developed dendritic runoff pattern; salinity less than .2%; water table below 150 cm; high fertility and water retention.

Class II soil 50–90 cm deep; slightly fine or somewhat coarse texture; permeable; less than 8% general slope; inclined or undulating relief; subangular to angular blocky structure; light to moderate erosion with up to 35% of the A horizon removed by sheetwash or runnels; external drainage generally intermittent in developed dendritic and subparallel runoff patterns; less than .5% salinity above 90 cm; water table between 90 and 150 cm; moderate organic content, fertility, and water retention.

Class III soil 25–50 cm deep; loose sand or permeable clay texture, slowly or rapidly permeable, 8%–12% slope; strongly inclined or strongly undulating relief; subangular blocky or prismatic structure; moderate to severe erosion with an average 60% of A horizon removed; may have hardpan; moderate salinity below 60 cm but less than .5%; water table between 60 and 90 cm; low organic content, fertility, and water retention; may be rocky.

Class IV shallow soil less than 50 cm deep; sandy, clayey, or silty clay texture; very slowly or rapidly permeable; 12%–16% slope; sharply undulating or gullied relief; prismatic, columnar, or degraded structure; severe erosion with moderate gullies and 60%–80% of the A horizon removed; very developed dendritic surface drainage, which may be inundated regularly in the winter; may have hardpan below 25 cm; moderately saline below 50 cm and pH may be greater than 8.5; water table between 25 and 50 cm; medium to very low organic content; low fertility and water retention.

Class V soil 25–90 cm deep; generally fine texture; generally impermeable or slowly permeable; may be almost flat or with a slope of up to 24%; flat, inclined, or undulating relief; blocky, columnar, or degraded structure; little erosion; very poorly drained and very susceptible to inundation; may have hardpan below 50 cm; pH less than 6.5 or more than 8.0; water table permanently less than 25 cm; medium to low organic content; medium to low fertility retention; excessive water retention; may be rocky.

Class VI soil very shallow, less than 25 cm deep, may be stratified in compact layers; impermeable or rapidly permeable; 24%–32% slope; sharply undulating or broken relief; structure weakly developed; severe to very severe erosion with 80%–100% of the A horizon removed through runnels and severe gullies; very poorly drained and subject to inundations or torrents; may have hardpan below 25 cm; may be excessively saline or very acidic; water table either less than 25 cm or below 250 cm in the dry season; low organic content, fertility, and water retention.

Class VII soil less than 25 cm deep; may be stratified in compact layers or have gravel throughout the profile; impermeable or rapidly permeable; greater than 32% slope; sharply undulating, broken, or cliff relief; degraded or weak blocky structure; severe erosion with A horizon usually removed through severe gullies; very poorly drained internally, external drainage destructive; may have hardpan below 25 cm; may be very saline or very acidic; water table may be superficial or absent for eight months of the year; fertility retention very low; water retention very low or excessively high; very low organic content.

Class VIII soil very shallow; impermeable or rapidly permeable; slope greater than 32%; sharply undulating, broken, or cliff relief; very severe erosion with the A horizon removed through very severe gullies with frequent torrents and landslides.

The populations of the sites in each square were estimated as a function of the site area and the density of ceramic sherds on the surface. The types of sites were defined according to surface area covered, and maximum and minimum population estimates have been averaged for each type of site except for large nucleated settlements, which have been calculated individually. These averages were then used in calculating the population of each zone for each time phase. The types of sites and the minimum and maximum population estimates for each are briefly described as follows:

1. TRACE OCCUPATION individual residence of 5 to 10 people

2. HAMLET small site of less than 4.5 ha in extent and light–moderate to moderate sherd density with a population of 20 to 50

3. SMALL DISPERSED VILLAGE covers 4.5–15 ha with a very light to light surface distribution of ceramics, has no civic–ceremonial architecture, estimated to have a population of 50 to 100

4. LARGE DISPERSED VILLAGE covers more than 15 ha with a very light to light surface scatter of ceramics, has no civic–ceremonial architecture, population estimated between 150 and 300

5. SMALL NUCLEATED VILLAGE covers 4.5–15 ha with a light to moderate distribution of surface ceramics, may have civic–ceremonial architecture, estimated to have a population of 100 to 200

6. LARGE NUCLEATED VILLAGE covers more than 15 ha with a light–moderate to moderate density of surface ceramics, estimated population of 500 to 1,000

7. REGIONAL CENTER large nucleated community usually covering from 15 to 30 ha with major civic–ceremonial–elite architecture and a moderate–heavy to heavy concentration of surface ceramics, may have a population of 1,000 to 10,000 (the one example calculated in the three test squares, Pinos (43–10–088), is estimated to have a population of 1,100 to 2,200)

8. PROVINCIAL CENTER large regional center covering more than 30 ha with major civic–ceremonial–elite architecture and a variable moderate–heavy to heavy distribution of surface ceramics (the one example calculated in the test squares, Guacamaya (33–40–355), is estimated to have a population of 1,000 to 2,000).

SQUARE 43

Square 43 is the westernmost and highest of the test squares considered in this study (Figure 2). Topographically, it is dominated by two basic features, the Cerro El Rejón in the southwest corner with its peak at 2,525 m and the Río Chitzirín–Chinimaya, which flows from the southeast to the north-central part of the zone. The slopes of Cerro El Rejón are covered primarily with evergreen forest and are uninhabited above 2,200 m. The modern population is chiefly concentrated in the two large nucleated villages of Santa María Cauque and Santiago Sacatepéquez as well as in two small dispersed villages and about two dozen small farms. The best farmland is located in the southeast corner of the square and in a strip running north by northwest along the river from Santa María Cauque (Figure 4a).

A total of 30 archaeological sites have been recorded in this square. Settlement of this square is first detected during the Early Formative as two isolated

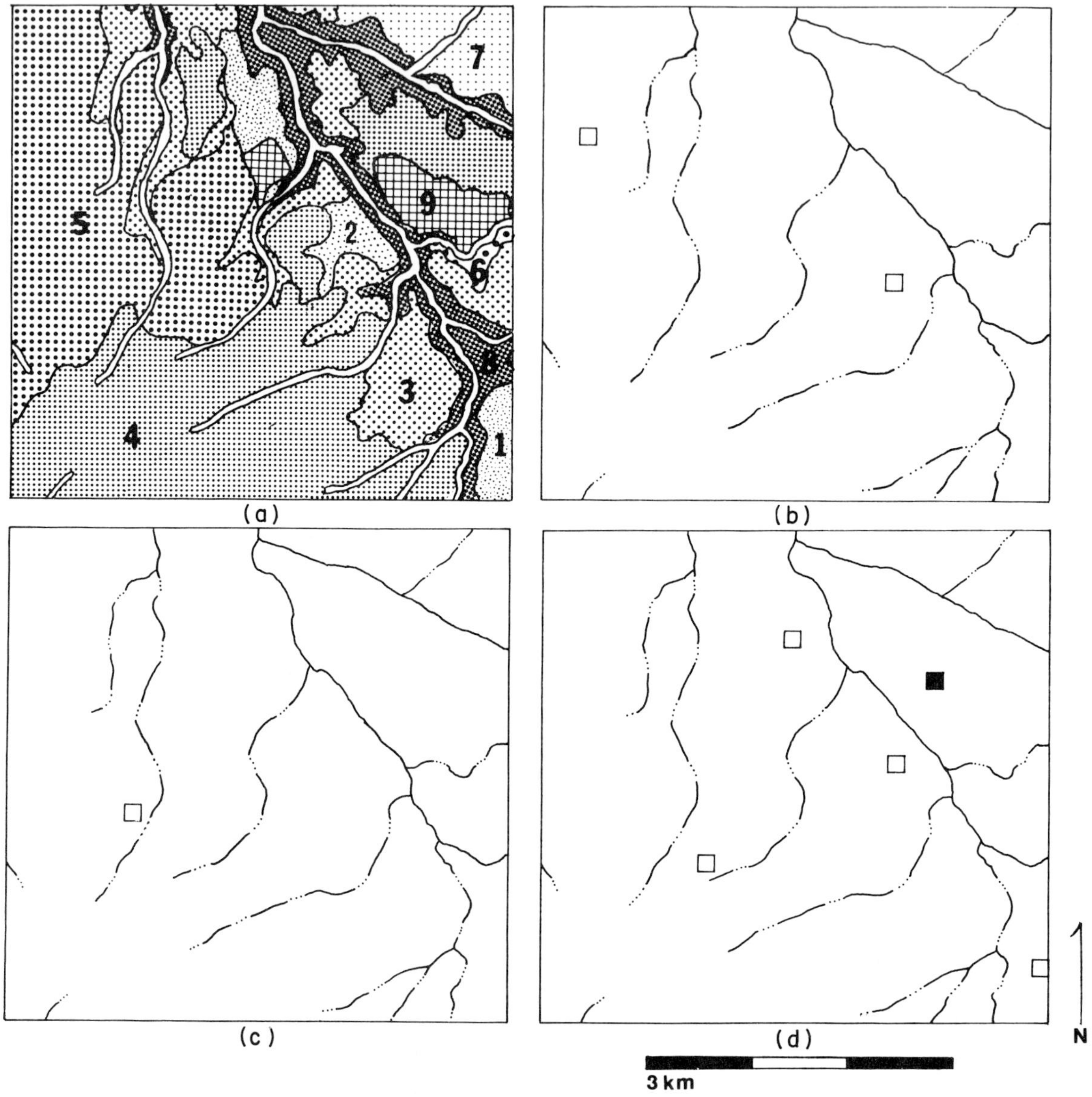

FIGURE 4. *Square 43 (a) Land-use capability classification: Class I (1), Class II (2), Class III (3), Class IV (4), Class V (5), Class VI (6), Class VII (7), Class VIII (8), and urban (9); and (b) Early Formative, (c) Middle Formative, and (d) Late Formative settlements (trace occupation, □; hamlet, ■).*

residences or small hamlets (Figure 4b). Only one such site has been detected for the Middle Formative (Figure 4c). Population density during these periods was about 1/km^2. During the Late Formative, at least one hamlet, at Santiago Sacatepéquez, and four additional trace occupations, most of which are located on the better farmlands along the Río Chinimaya were established (Figure 4d). These sites are estimated to have had a total of 35 to 75 inhabitants. The population remained at this level during the Terminal Formative A phase (Figure 5a) with over half the population living within easy access of Class II land near the river. In the Terminal Formative B phase, the population increased substantially to 330 to 670, living in one to three small hamlets and three small nucleated villages (Figure 5b). Two of these villages, Santa María Cauque (43–12–030) and Chachaya (43–23–286), each have two rectangular-plan earth-filled mounds (Figures 6a-b). Those of Chachaya are somewhat larger, and the larger of the two at Chachaya had a large irregular stela associated with it. Chachaya and the village immediately to the south of it on the same ridge are within easy access of an area of Class II land just to the north, while Santa María Cauque is located on an area of Class I land.

The population continued to increase during the Early Classic to 400 to 850, living in 3 small nucleated villages and 12 small hamlets (Figure 7a). While the villages continue to be oriented to the better farmlands along the river, the hamlets appear to concentrate more on the lower northern slopes of Cerro El

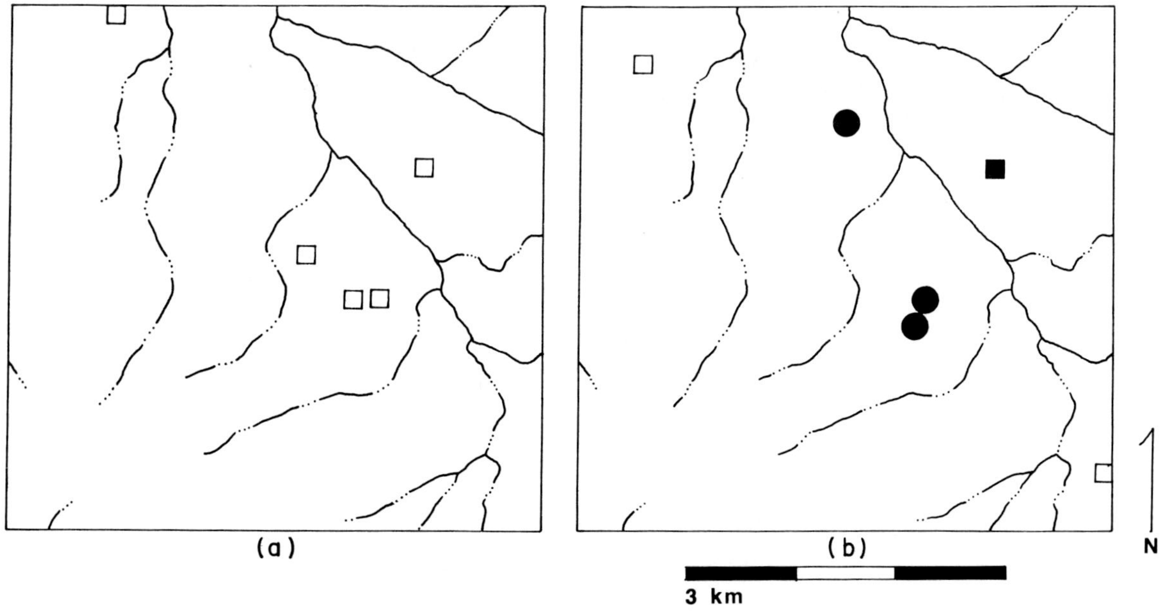

FIGURE 5. *Square 43 (a) Terminal Formative A and (b) Terminal Formative B settlements (trace occupation, □; hamlet, ■; small nucleated village, ●).*

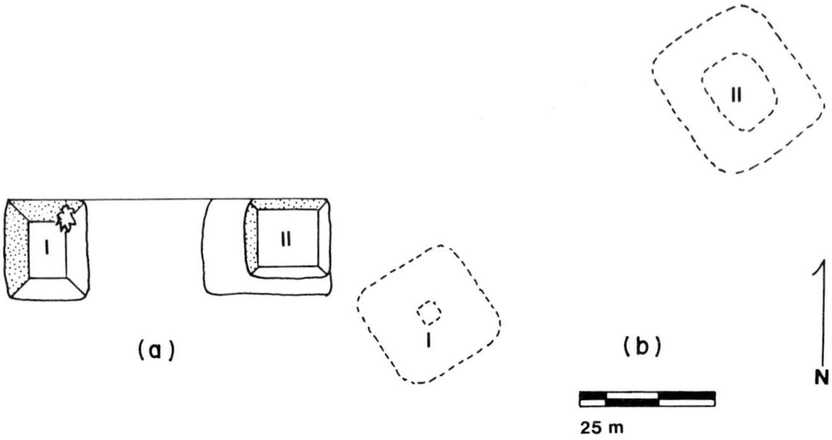

FIGURE 6. *Rectangular-plan earth-filled mounds at (a) Santa María Cauque (43-12-030) and (b) Chachaya (43-23-286).*

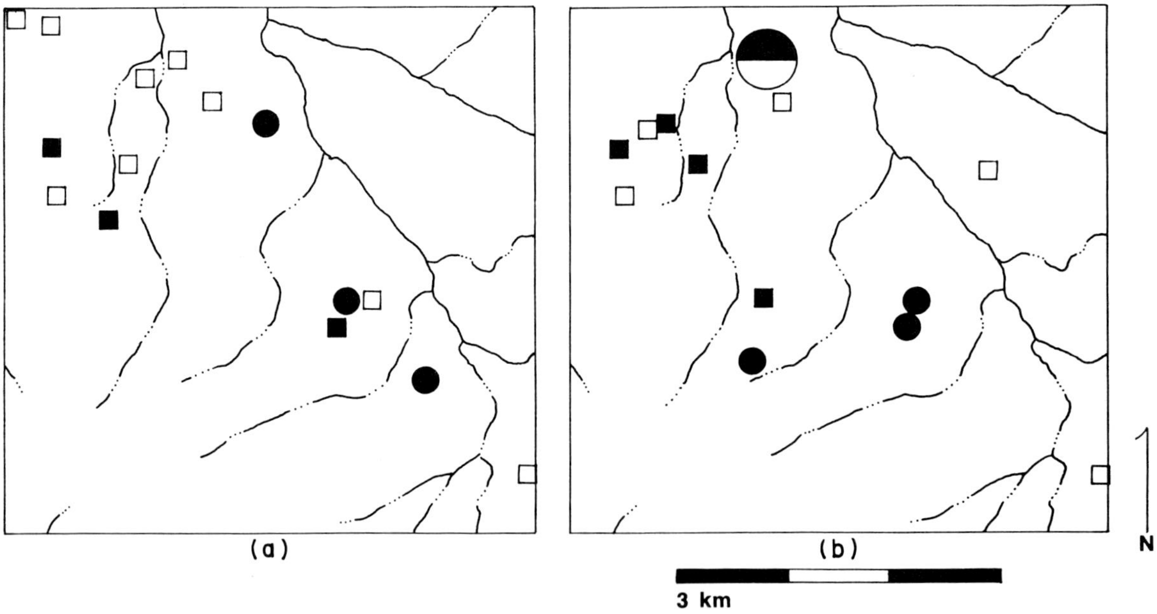

FIGURE 7. *Square 43 (a) Early Classic and (b) Middle Classic settlements (trace occupation, □; hamlet, ■; small nucleated village, ●; large dispersed village, ◓).*

Rejón. Those which appear as trace occupations may represent activities other than agriculture. In the Middle Classic, the population increased to 550 to 1,100, living in 1 large dispersed village, 3 small nucleated villages, and 9 small hamlets. The bulk of the population, as represented by the large dispersed village and 2 of the small nucleated villages as well as 2 hamlets, was located within easy access of the best Class I and II farmlands along the river (Figure 7b). During this period, a mound and an enclosed plaza were built at 43–33–003, the small nucleated village on the ridge just south of Chachaya (Figure 8).

During the Late Classic A period, the population of the zone reached its peak, more than doubling to 2,100 to 4,450. Most notable is the growth of Los Pinos (43–10–088) into a regional center with a sizeable rural surrounding population, living in a small nucleated village, a small dispersed village, and a number of small hamlets on the north slopes of Cerro El Rejón (Figure 9). It appears that at least the large southern mound complex at Los Pinos (Figure 10) was built at this time. The rest of the population, with the exception of the small nucleated village at Santiago Sacatepéquez, lived in a large nucleated village, a large dispersed village, a small nucleated village, and 3 hamlets, all of which are located on or near the better farmlands along the river. In the Late Classic B phase, the population declined dramatically to Middle Classic levels (450–900), living in a large dispersed Village on Class I land to the north of Santa María Cauque, 4 small dispersed villages, three of which are located on the north slopes of Cerro El Rejón, and 10 hamlets scattered throughout the square (Figure 11a).

The Early Postclassic witnessed a resurgence of population to a possible maximum of 1,650, with a much more concentrated settlement, 1 large nucleated village at Los Pinos, 2 small nucleated villages, 1 small dispersed village, and 5 small hamlets (Figure 11b). During the Late Postclassic, this population declined by about 75%, to 200 to 400, living in a small nucleated village on the north slope of Cerro El Rejón, a small dispersed village on Class II land near the river and 7 small hamlets scattered throughout the square (Figure 11c).

SQUARE 58

Square 58 is located on the western escarpment of the Valley of Guatemala (Figure 2). The western half of the square is essentially a series of natural terraces that descend abruptly to the valley floor in the eastern half. As a whole, the square is badly dissected by barrancas. Erosion has been especially severe in the western half where *talpetate* exposures are now common; most of this land is Class VI. In the eastern half, there are extensive stretches of relatively flat Class III land (Figure 12a), although, here too, the Río Mansilla and its tributaries have cut steep gorges into the plain. The present-day population is essentially rural in character, living in 2 small dispersed villages, El Aguacate and Campanero, and about a half dozen small farms. Most of the hilly land is now in cattle pasture or scrub oak forest and the flatter terraces are either in pasture or planted in maize.

The prehistoric settlement of this square has been previously discussed by

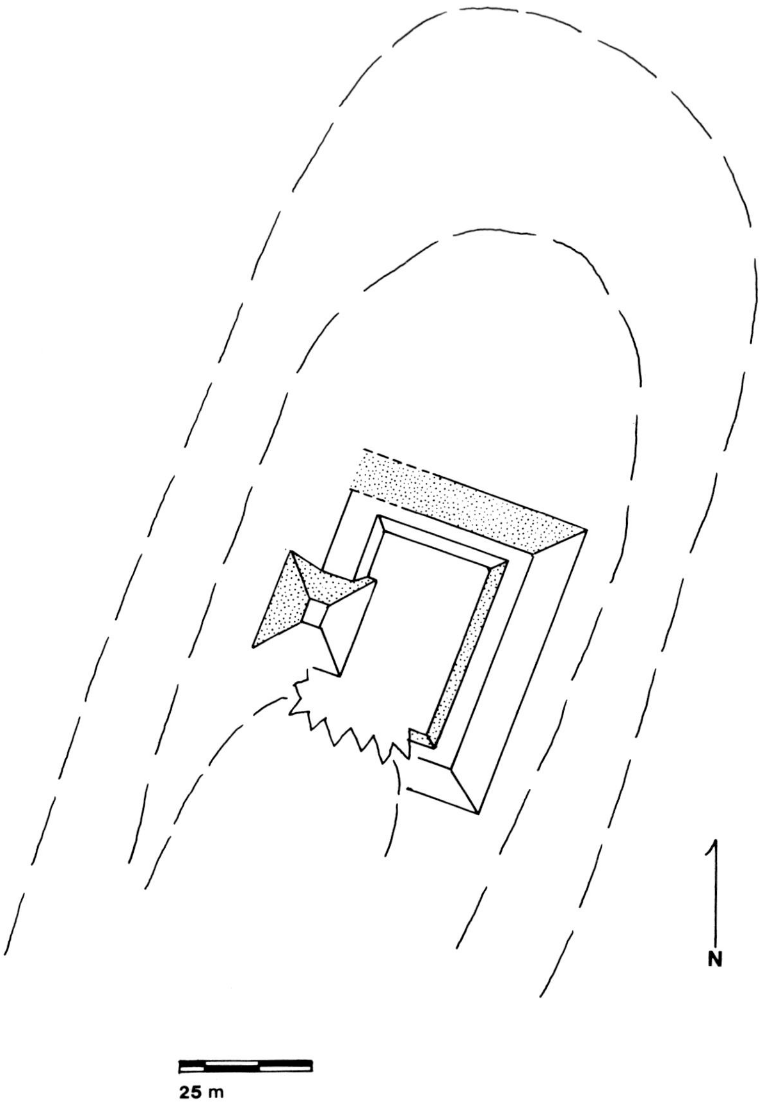

FIGURE 8. *Mound and enclosed plaza built at 43-33-003, the small nucleated village on the ridge just south of Chachaya.*

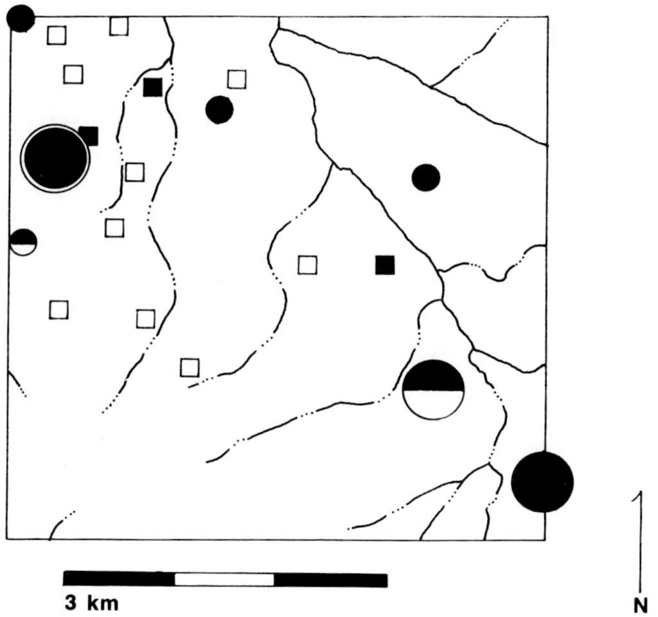

FIGURE 9. *Late Classic A settlements (trace occupation, □; hamlet, ■; small nucleated village, ●; small dispersed village, ◓; large nucleated village, ●; large dispersed village, ◓; regional center, ⊙).*

Michels, who has also published the dates for the various archaeological sites (1979:77–84). The present analysis is based, in part, on his data. During the Early and Middle Formative periods, there is evidence of 2 settlements (Figure 12b, c) for population totals of 10 to 20 in each phase. Both Early Formative settlements are located on Class VI land, and it is possible that they represent a hunting and gathering, rather than farming, economy. The 2 Middle Formative sites are located on Class IV and Class III land, the latter being the best agricultural land in this square. In the Late Formative, the population increased to 70 to 150, living in 11 small hamlets. With 2 exceptions, all of these sites are located on Class III land, only 1 site being located on the Class VI land in the northwestern quarter of the square (Figure 12d). During the Terminal Formative A phase, the population increased to 180 to 380 living in 1 small nucleated village and 10 hamlets, again principally located on Class III land (Figure 13a). In the Terminal Formative B phase, the population increased to 250 to 550 living in 1 small dispersed village and 16 hamlets, with over 90% of the population living on Class III land (Figure 13b).

During the Early Classic, the population doubled to 350 to 1,000, living in 1 large dispersed village, 2 small nucleated villages, and 20 hamlets (Figure 13c). More than 85% of the population lived on Class III land, and the Class VI land appears to have been abandoned for residence. In the Middle Classic, the population remained stable, living in 1 small nucleated village, 2 small dispersed villages, and 28 hamlets (Figure 13d). Again, most of the population lived on the Class III land of the valley floor, although one of the villages recolonized the

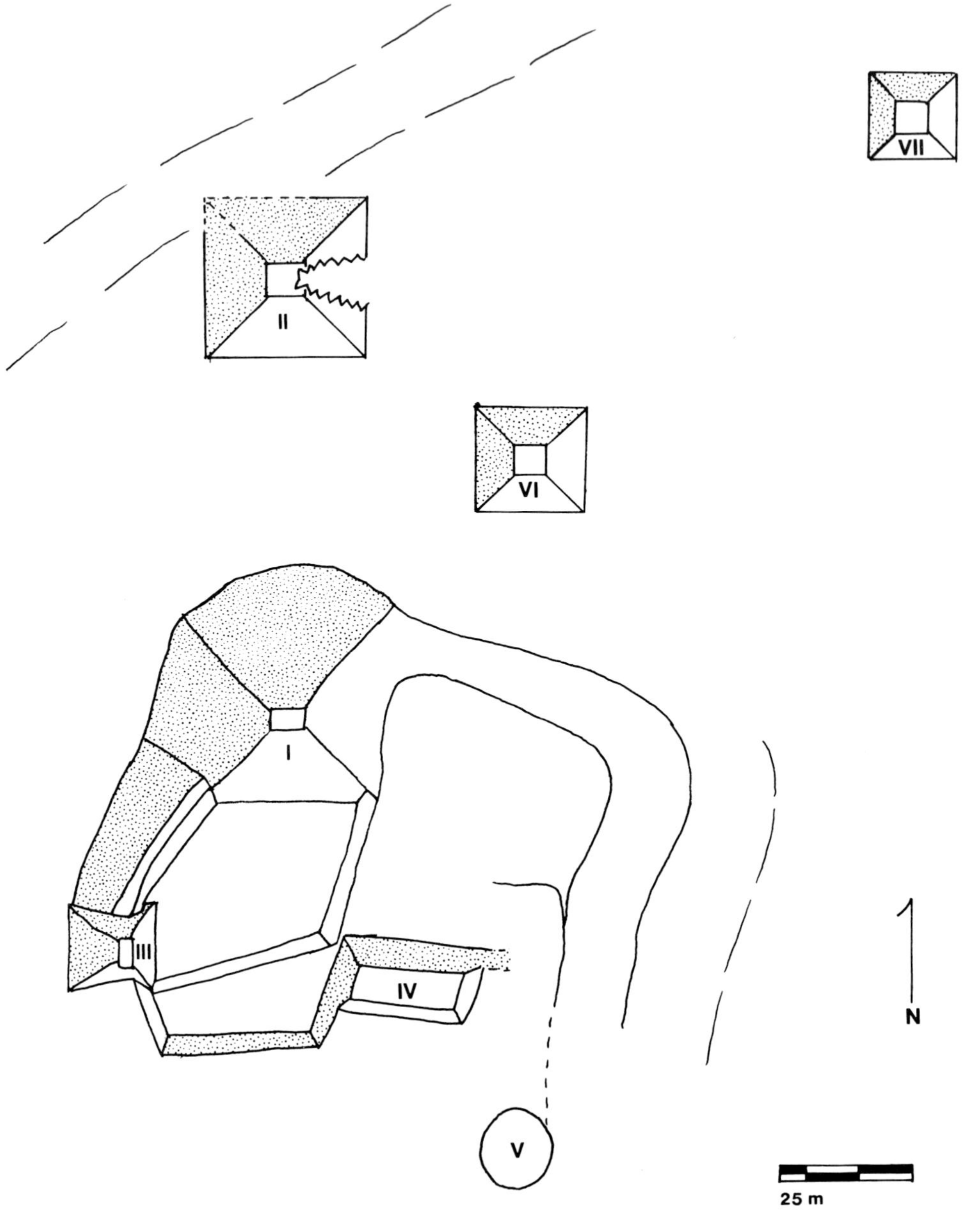

FIGURE 10. *Architecture at Los Pinos (43-10-088).*

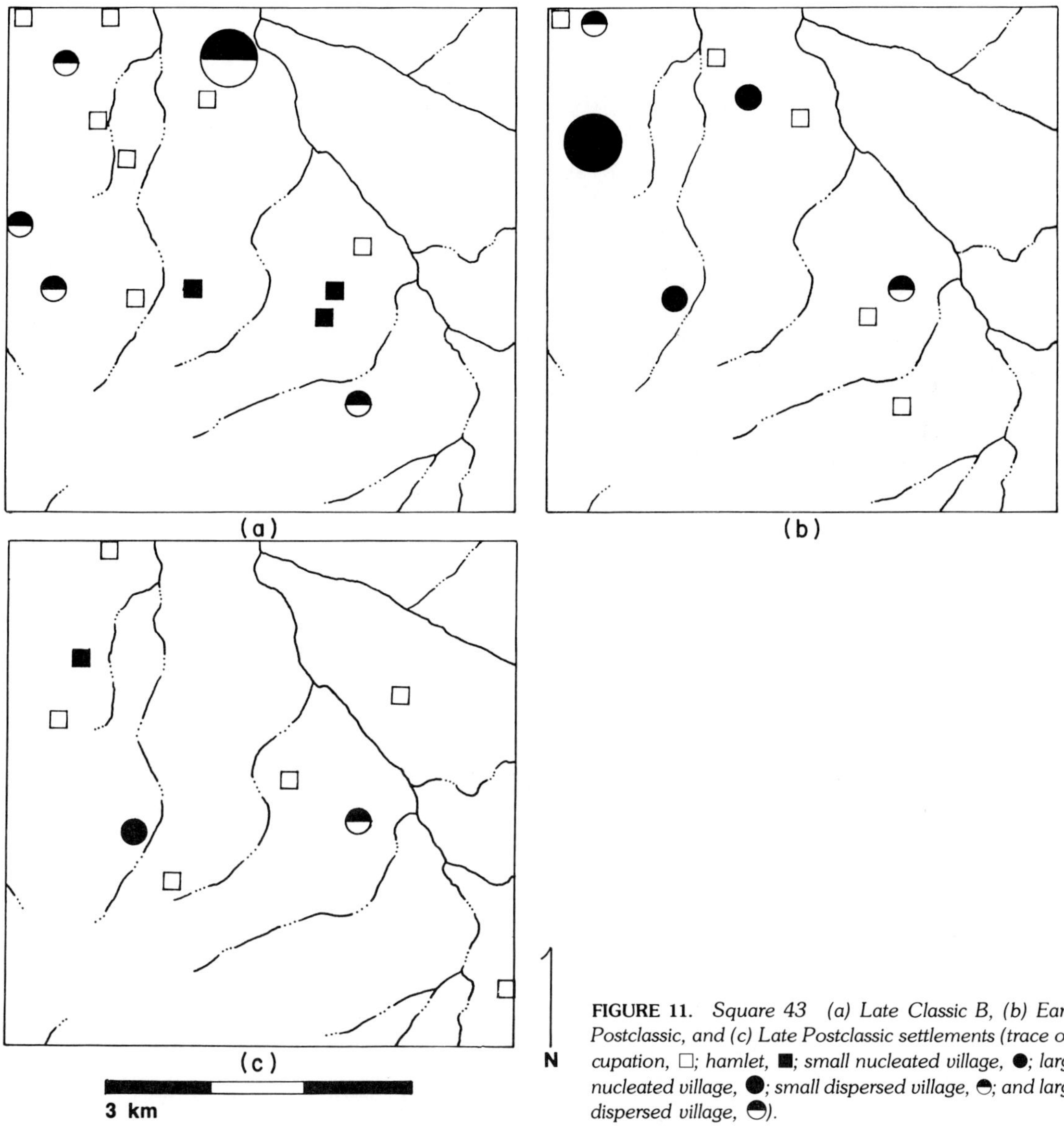

FIGURE 11. *Square 43 (a) Late Classic B, (b) Early Postclassic, and (c) Late Postclassic settlements (trace occupation, □; hamlet, ■; small nucleated village, ●; large nucleated village, ●; small dispersed village, ◓; and large dispersed village, ◓).*

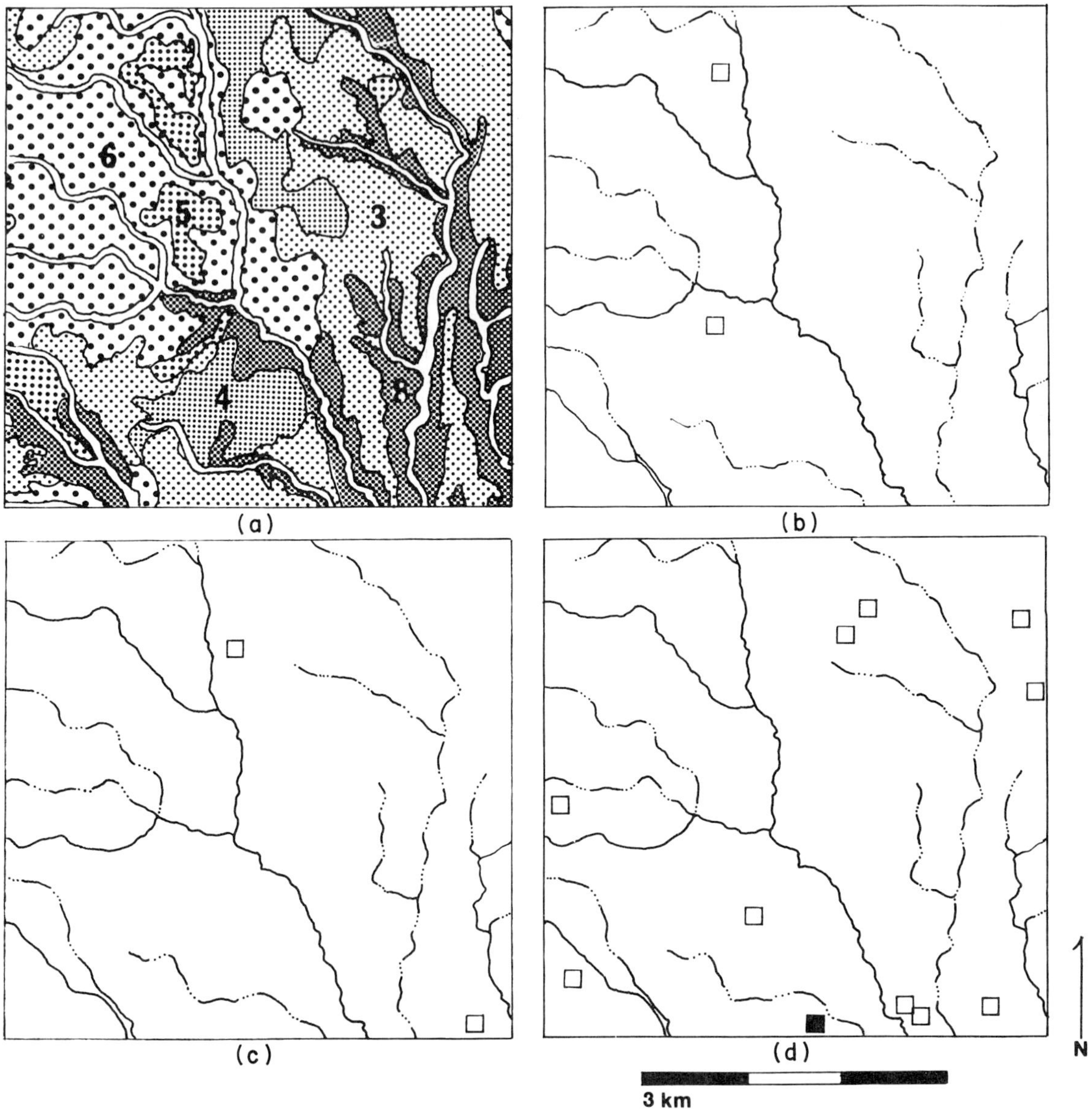

FIGURE 12. *Square 58 (a) land-use capability classification: Class III (3), Class IV (4), Class V (5), Class VI (6), and Class VIII (8); and (b) Early Formative, (c) Middle Formative, and (d) Late Formative settlements (trace occupation, □; hamlet, ■).*

Class VI land in the western portion of the square. This population more than doubled during the Late Classic A phase to 950 to 2,000, living in 1 large dispersed village, 3 small nucleated villages, 2 small dispersed villages, and 29 hamlets (Figure 14a). Settlements and population were generally distributed on all classes of agricultural land. This high population declined only slightly in the Late Classic B. Settlement distribution is essentially the same as in the Late Classic A phase except that a large proportion of the population was now concentrated in 2 large dispersed villages (Figure 14b). The El Calvario area in the southwest corner of the square was particularly densely settled.

During the Early Postclassic, the population was drastically reduced to 125 to 260, occupying 1 small dispersed village and 12 hamlets quite evenly distributed with regard to the land-use classification (Figure 14c). This population again declined in the Late Postclassic and was dispersed in small hamlets across the landscape (Figure 14d).

SQUARE 33

Square 33 lies on the plain in the central northernmost part of what can still be called the Valley of Guatemala (Figure 2). The south-central part of this square is dominated by the Cerro Naranjo, which was once apparently covered with oak forest but is now devoted to a few orchards, some pasture, and rapidly expanding real estate development. Apparently, the remainder of the square was once a relatively flat plain but is now badly dissected by northeastward-flowing intermittent streams that have cut steep gorges, in some cases more than 100 m deep, into the terrain. These gorges have practically isolated remnants of the valley plain, which continually lose ground to the gorges through frequent landslides caused by heavy rains and earthquakes (Figure 15a). The flatland that remains is rapidly being colonized by suburban development, especially since the 1976 earthquake, which was severely felt in more rural areas.

Prehistorically, this square began to be settled in the Early Formative (Figure 15b), having a population of 25 to 50 living in five settlements. The population and settlement pattern remained essentially the same during the Middle Formative (Figure 15c) except that the population began to shift to the southeastern quarter of the square. In the Late Formative, the population increased slightly to 45 to 90, still living in small hamlets (Figure 15d). During the Terminal Formative A phase, the population continued to increase to 175 to 370, living in a small nucleated village in the north-central portion of the square as well as in nine hamlets. As previously, the population appears to have been adapting primarily to the Class III land of the valley plain (Figure 17a). In the Terminal Formative B phase, the population again increased substantially to 340 to 720, and ceremonial architecture was erected at the site of Naranjo (33–33–299). Although this site is about the size of a small nucleated village, it is here designated as a ceremonial center because of the magnitude of the architecture and stela field (Figure 16). Shook (1952, 1943) has hypothesized that this site may have functioned as an astronomical observatory for the surrounding population,

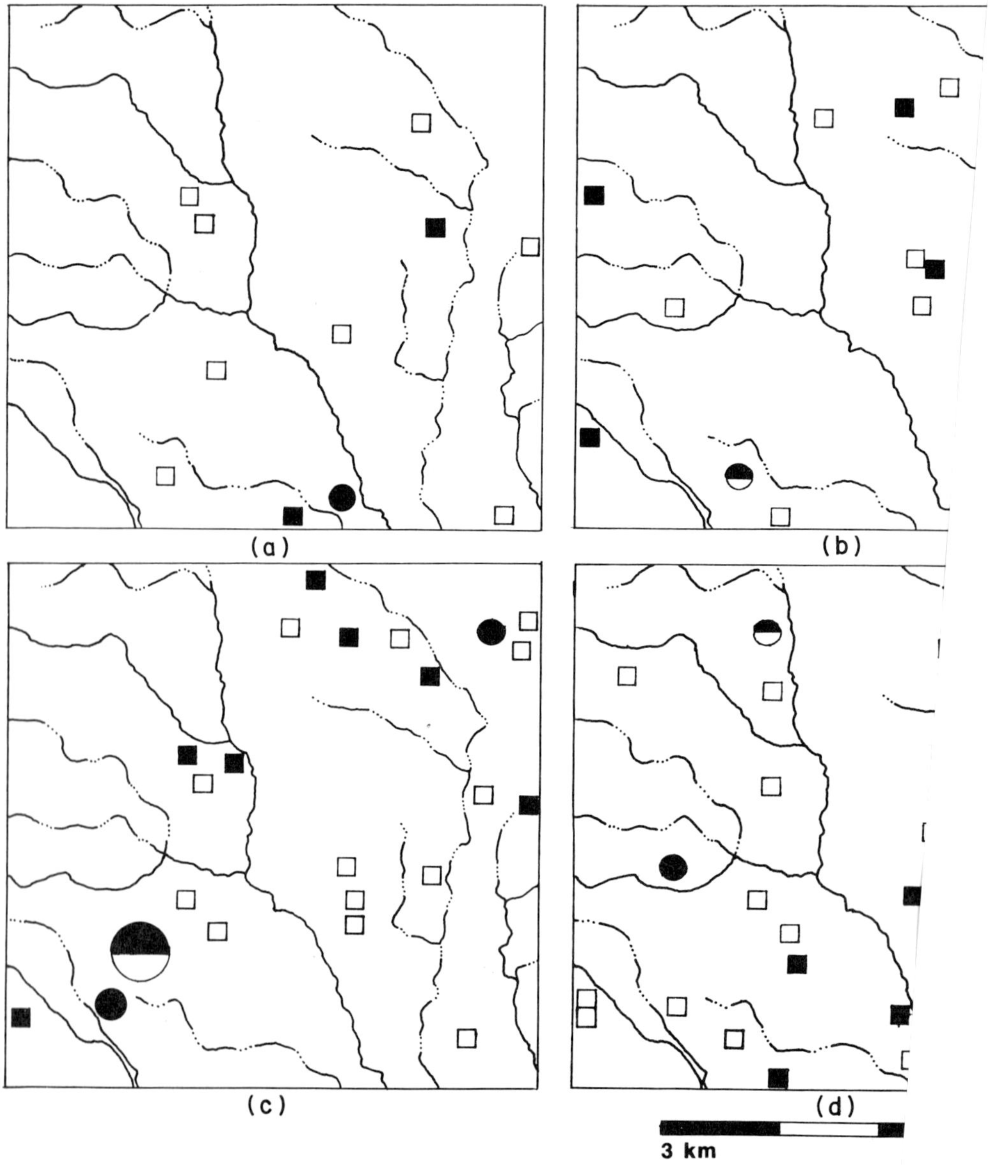

FIGURE 13. *Square 58 (a) Terminal Formative A, (b) Terminal Formative B, (c) Early Classic and (d) Middle Classic settlements (trace occupation, □; hamlet, ■; small nucleated village, ●; smal dispersed village, ◓; large dispersed village, ◓).*

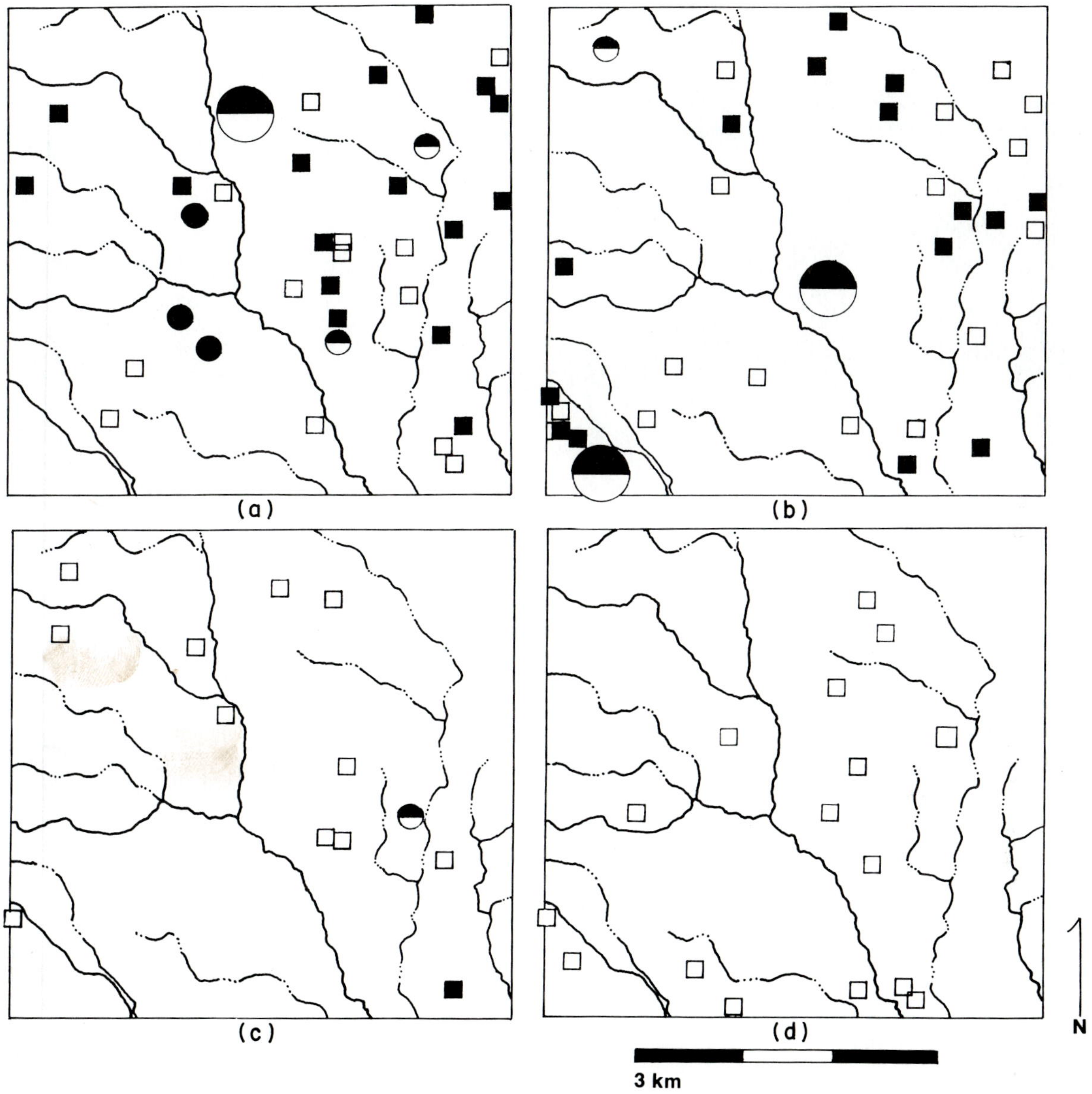

FIGURE 14. *Square 58 (a) Late Classic A, (b) Late Classic B, (c) Early Postclassic, and (d) Late Postclassic settlements (trace occupation, □; hamlet, ■; small nucleated village, ●; small dispersed village, ◓; large dispersed village, ◓).*

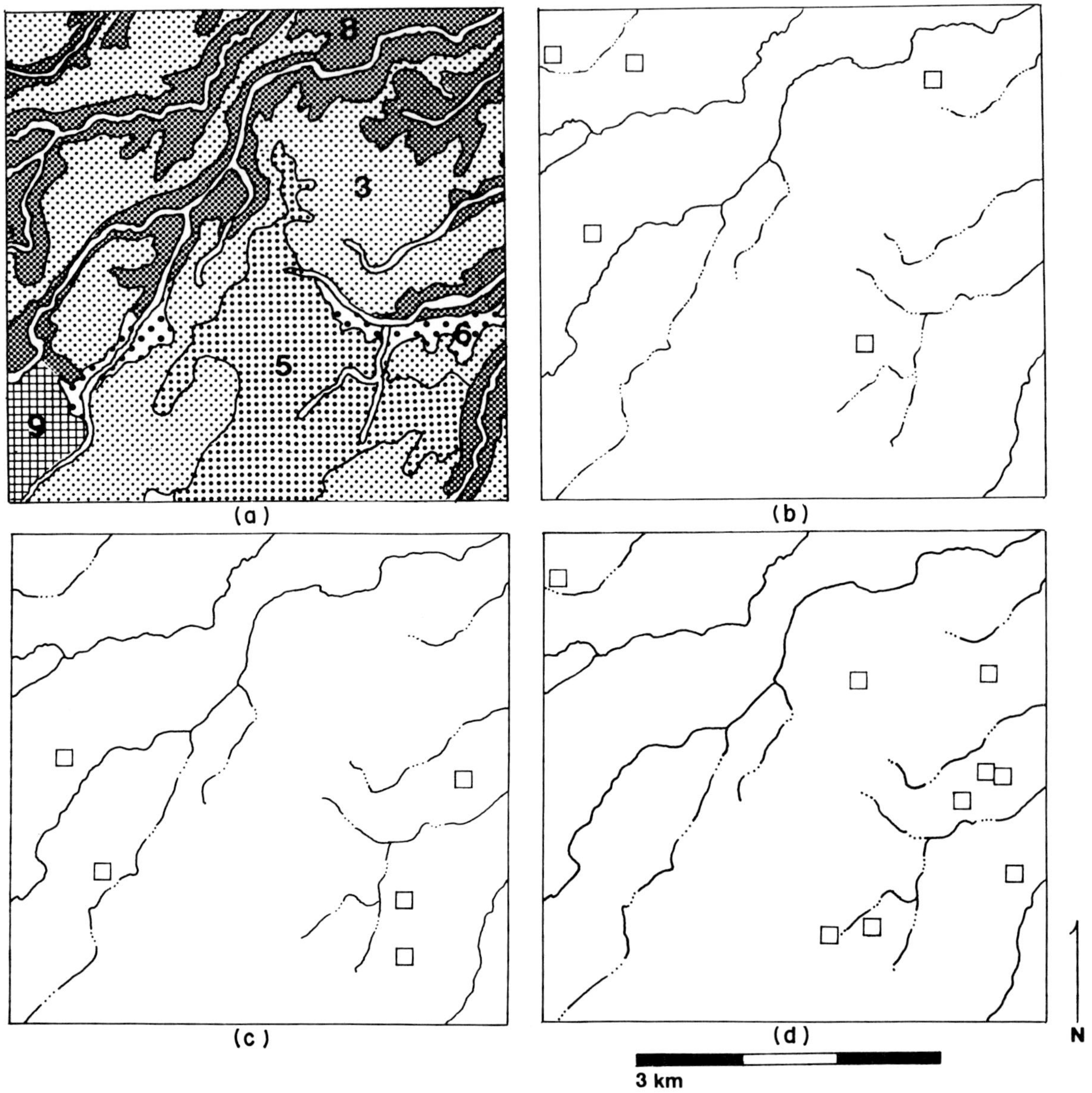

FIGURE 15. *Square 33 (a) land-use capability classification: Class III (3), Class V (5), Class VI (6), Class VIII (8), and urban (9); and (b) Early Formative, (c) Middle Formative, and (d) Late Formative settlements (trace occupation, □).*

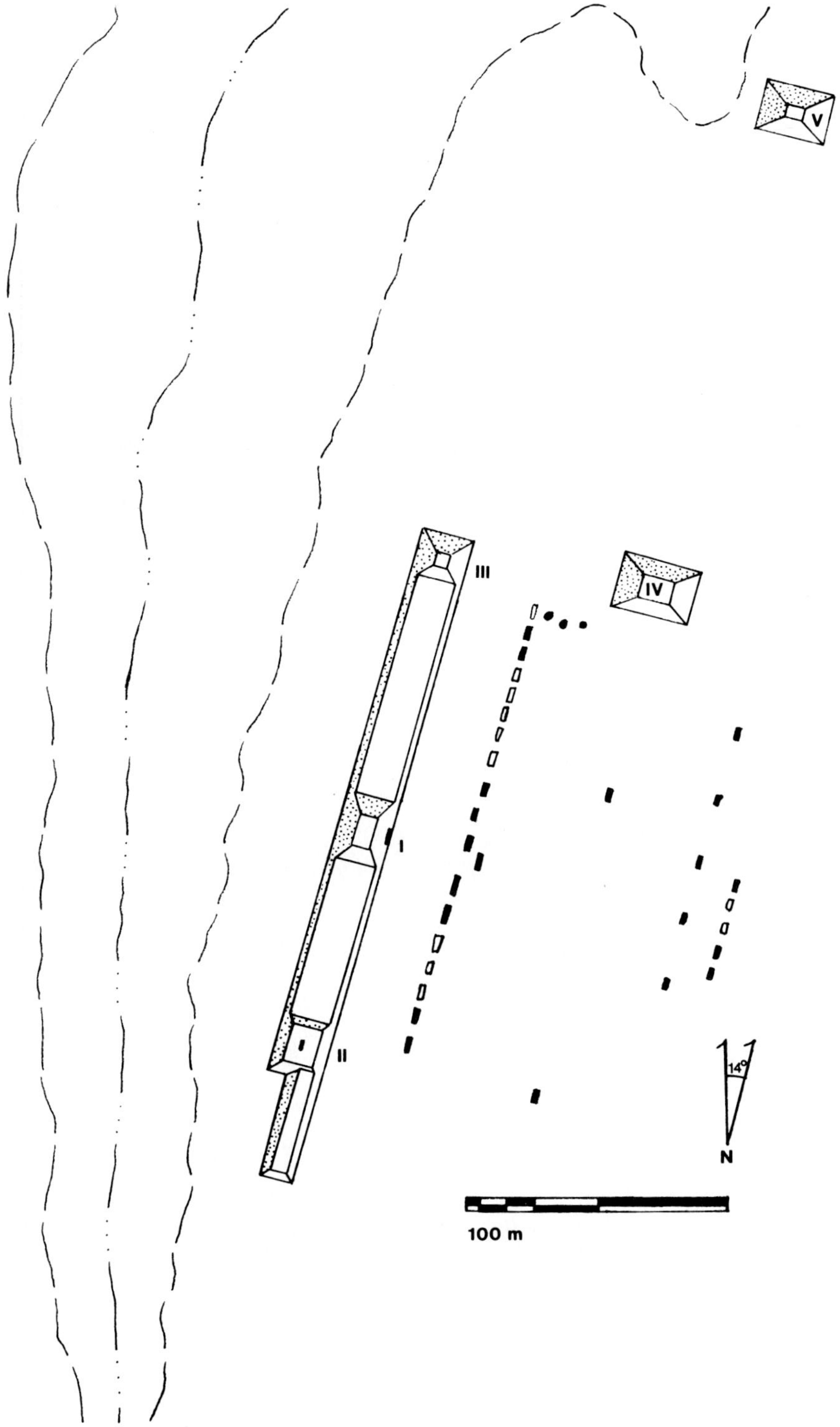

FIGURE 16. *Naranjo (33-33-299). (Redrawn after Shook, 1943.)*

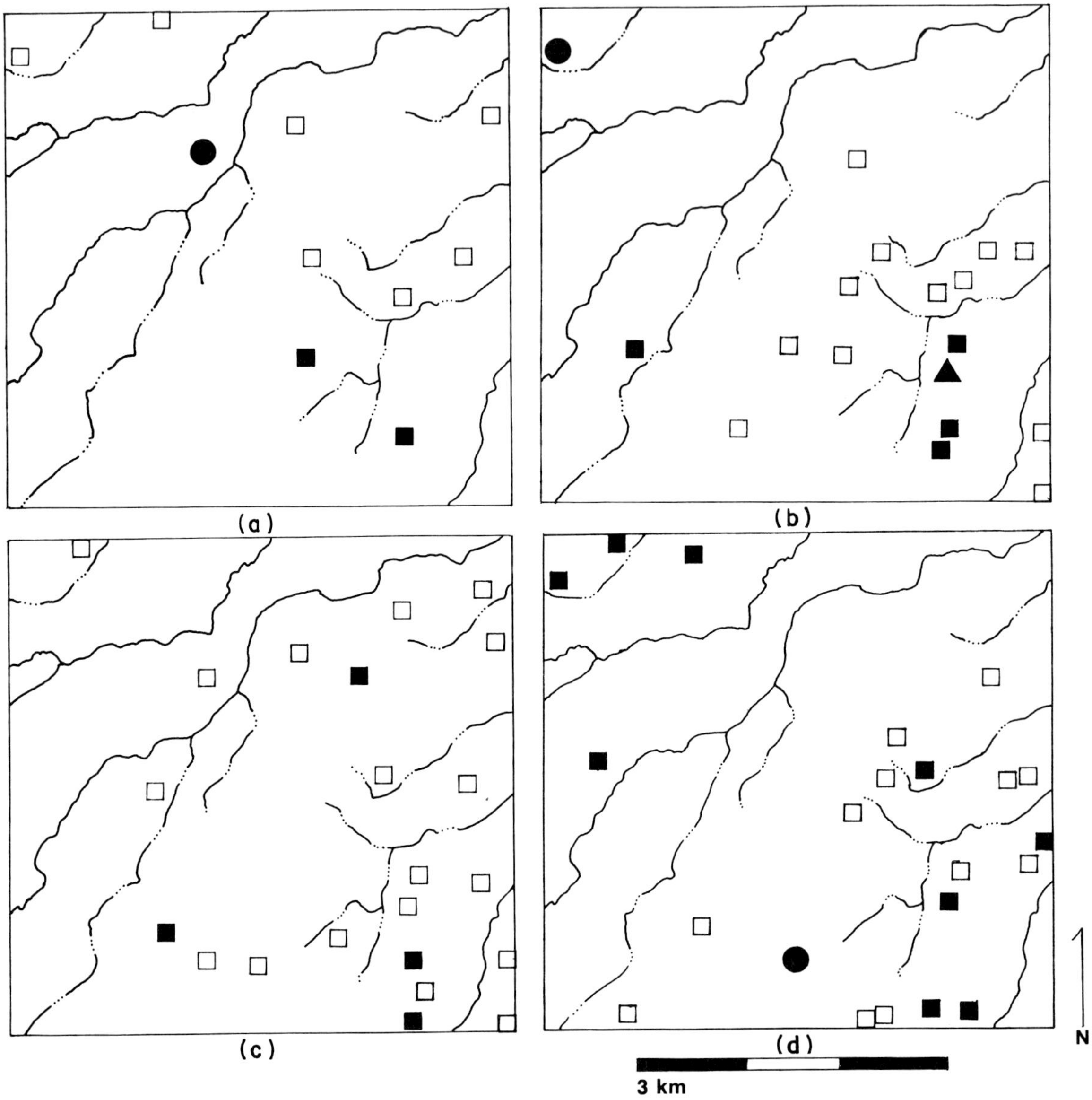

FIGURE 17. *Square 33 (a) Terminal Formative A, (b) Terminal Formative B, (c) Early Classic, and (d) Middle Classic settlements (trace occupation, □; hamlet, ■; small nucleated village, ●; ceremonial center, ▲).*

which generally appears to have been concentrated in the southeastern quarter of the square (Figure 17b).

During the Early Classic period, the population decreased to 170 to 380, probably due to migration into Kaminaljuyú, and was generally distributed in small hamlets throughout the square (Figure 17c). In the Middle Classic, the population increased to 340 to 770, and a small nucleated village was established on the slopes of Cerro Naranjo (Figure 17d).

In Late Classic A, the first really dramatic increase in the population of this square occurred, almost quadrupling to 1,420 to 2,810. Most of this growth can probably be attributed to in-migration from Kaminaljuyú, which began to disperse at this time. Almost a third of this population appears to have concentrated in the now-destroyed provincial center of Guacamaya (Shook 1952, 1949), which had two mound groups and a ball court and covered more than 40 ha. The rest of the population seems to have concentrated in two small nucleated villages and a number of hamlets in the southeastern quarter of the square (Figure 19a). Toward the end of this period, there arose a new type of small site with ceremonial architecture at Pelikan (33–43–139). Although these sites are about the size of hamlets, they each have two or three low rectangular mounds and a ball court (Figure 18). They probably represent elite residential compounds, occupied by a lineage head, his family, and his retainers.

During the succeeding Late Classic B phase, the population declined sharply to 440 to 1,000, living almost exclusively in hamlets scattered throughout the square (Figure 19b). Elite residential compounds continued to be occupied as Cristina (Figure 20a) and Guacamaya II (Figure 20b), and a small nucleated village was founded in the northwesternmost corner of the square (Figure 19b).

In the Early Postclassic, the population further declined to 300 to 720, living in hamlets scattered throughout the square (Figure 21a). During the Late Postclassic, there was a slight resurgence of population to 420 to 880, living in 2

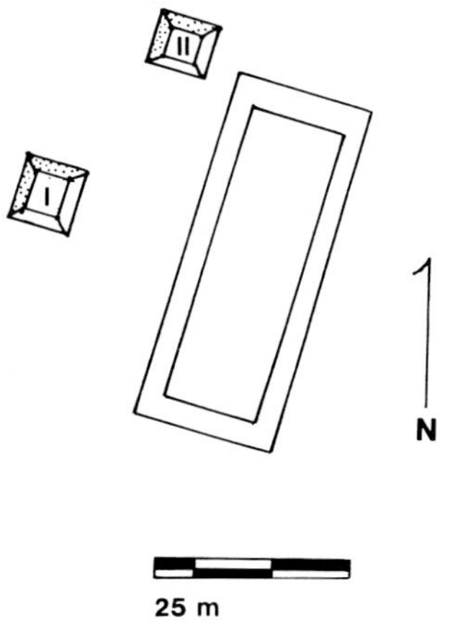

FIGURE 18. *Low rectangular mounds and a ball court at Pelikan (33-43-139).*

small nucleated villages and 17 hamlets, dispersed in a settlement pattern essentially the same as that of the preceding period (Figure 21b). The most notable site of this period is the Dale site (Figure 22), which includes a long ditch and parapet, which probably served as the advance fortification of the Lehnsen site further to the east along the ridge in square 34.

Settlement and Population History of the Valley of Guatemala

The general reconstruction of the history of settlement of the Valley of Guatemala offered here is based on a number of assumptions and assessments of our data at this stage of research.

1. While we have a number of reservations about the conclusions as to the demographic, political, and economic reconstruction of the history of Kaminaljuyú offered by Joseph Michels in his 1979 study, we will tentatively accept much of this in this chapter.

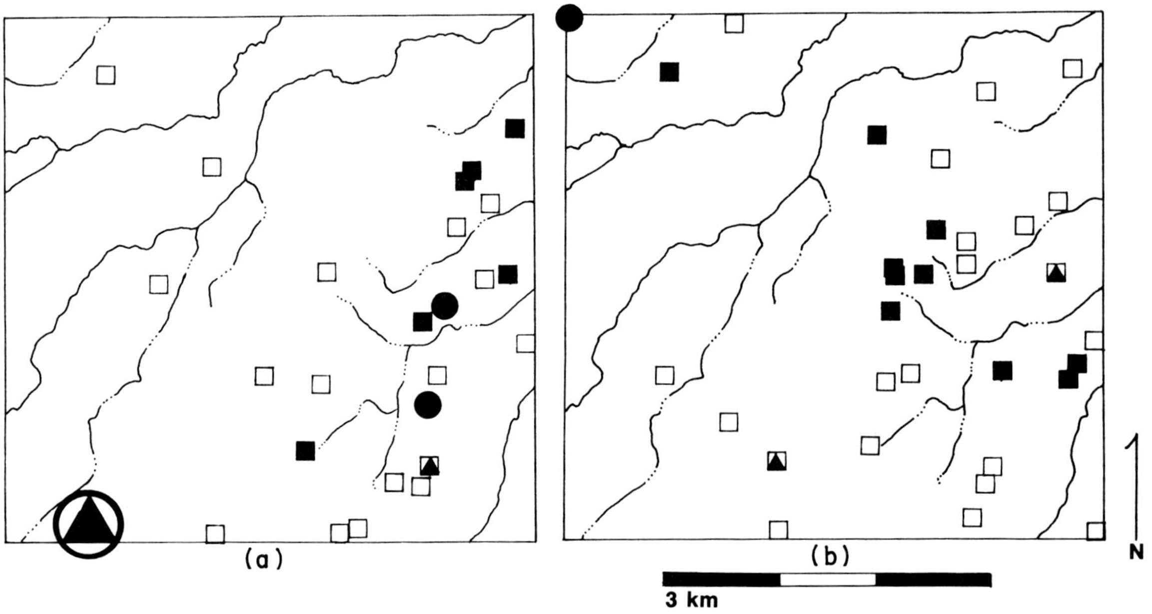

FIGURE 19. *Square 33 (a) Late Classic A and (b) Late Classic B settlements (trace occupation, □; hamlet, ■; small nucleated village, ●; elite residential compound, ▲; provincial center, ▲).*

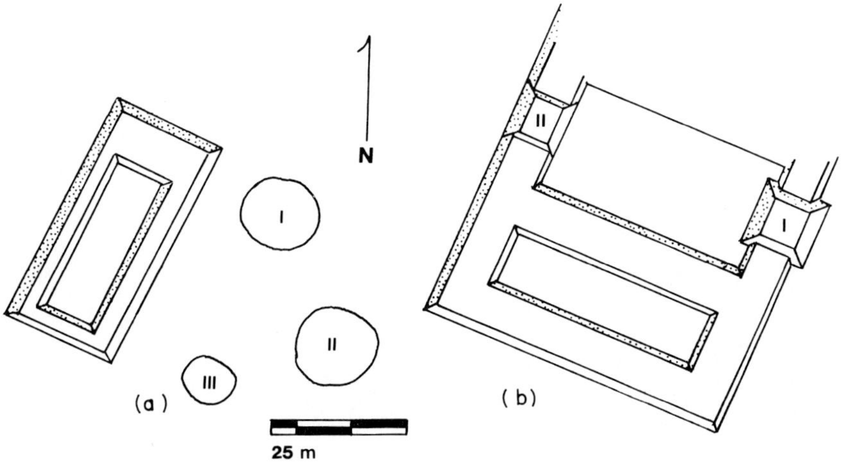

FIGURE 20. *Elite residential compounds at (a) Cristina and (b) Guacamaya II.*

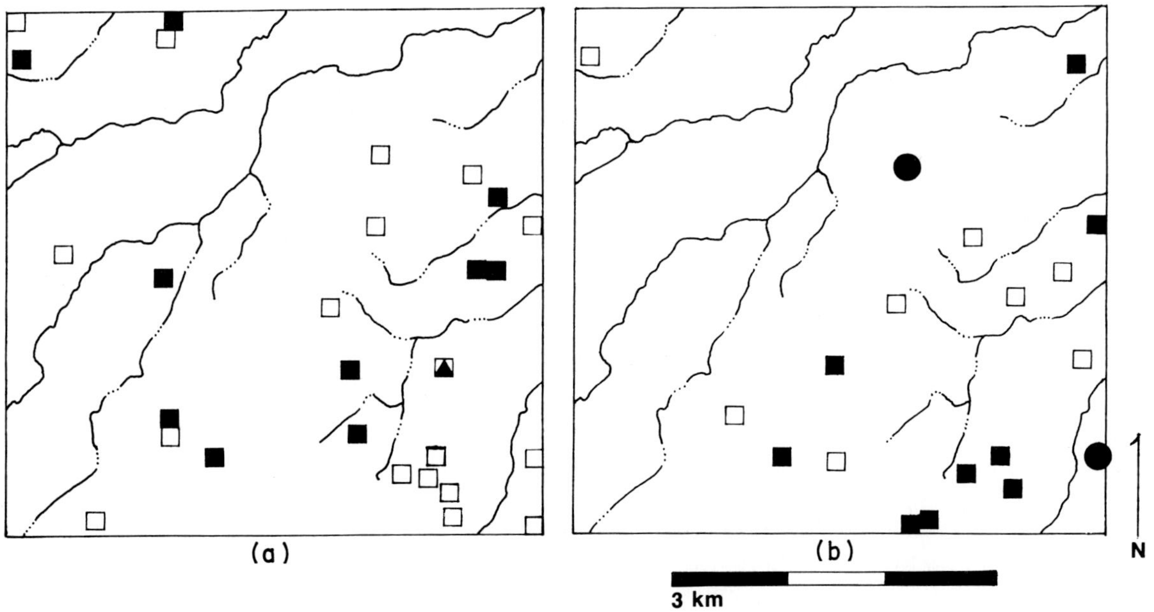

FIGURE 21. *Square 33 (a) Early Postclassic and (b) Late Postclassic settlements (trace occupation, □; hamlet, ■; small nucleated village, ●; elite residential compound, ▲).*

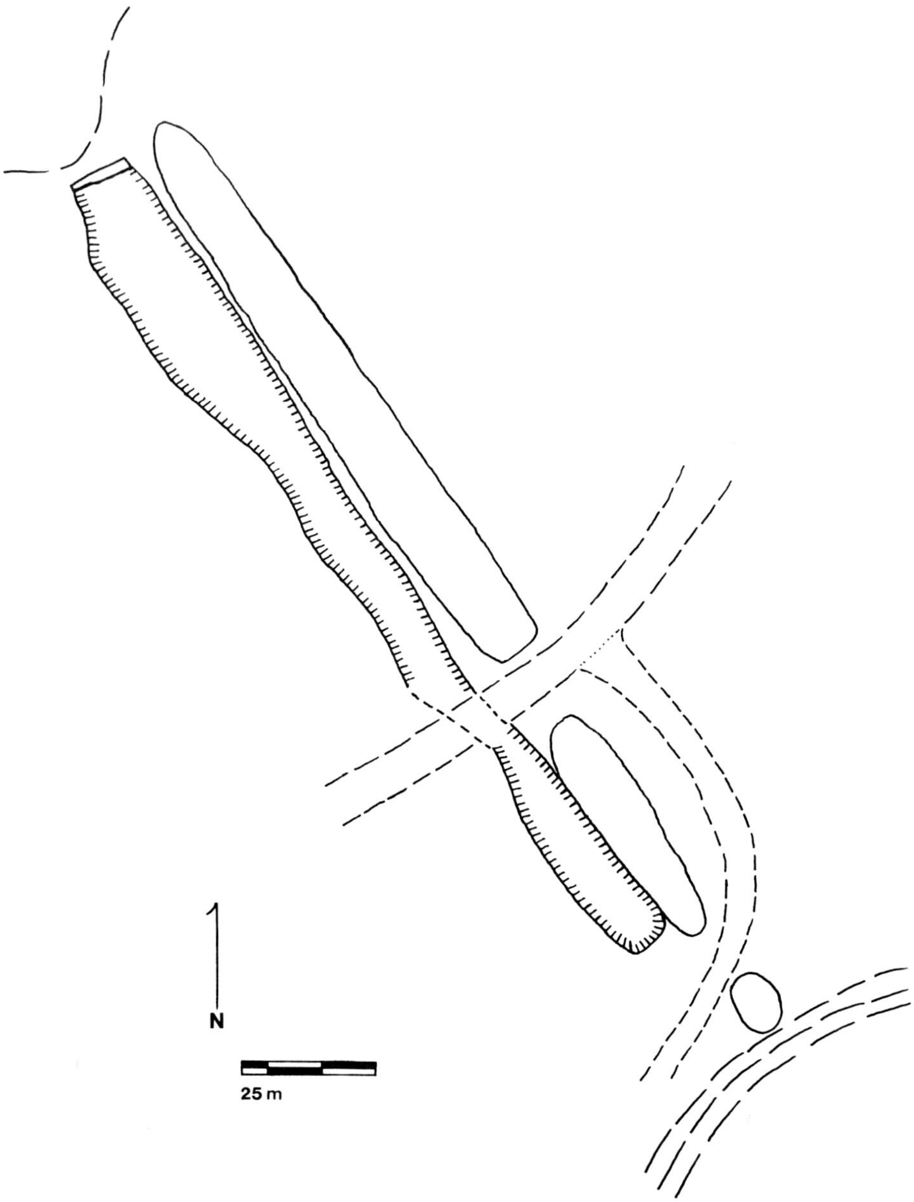

FIGURE 22. *Long ditch and parapet at the Dale site (33-24-175).*

2. We will assume that the demographic history of the 3 test areas is representative not only of the 12 intensively surveyed sectors, but of the entire 600-km^2 area we defined as the Kaminaljuyú sustaining area. Obviously, when the detailed data from all 12 test areas have been analyzed, this assumption of representation will be much more defensible.

3. We assume that our preliminary notions as to the chronology of major events in the balance of the survey area (400 km^2) that is not controlled by intensive survey is sufficiently well understood to arrive at a general picture of the cultural history of the valley.

4. We assume that our assessment technique of the population sizes of settlements and nature of individual settlements is relatively accurate (see Table 3). Bearing these points in mind, the following general summary may be made.

The earliest agricultural settlement for which we have evidence is that characterized by Arévalo and Las Charcas ceramics, which are equivalent to the overall Mesoamerican Early and Middle Formative phases. All sites consist of hamlets with estimated populations of less than 100 and a mean probably somewhere in the neighborhood of 50. The test data would suggest a maximum population of 1,200 in the area and a density of 1.2/km^2. Neither survey nor excavation revealed ceremonial architecture or evidence of ranking within or between settlements. Sites are rather evenly scattered throughout the various ecological zones of the valley, both on the sloping terrain and on the flatter plateau surfaces. Along with the lack of evidence of hierarchical differentiation, we find very little evidence of economic specialization.

During the succeeding Late Formative period, the population increased to perhaps 2,000–4,050. Neither the type nor the location of residential sites

Table 3
Population History of the Valley of Guatemala

Phase	Square 43	Square 58	Square 33	Average	Total 1,000-km^2 area	Density
Early Formative	10–20	10–20	25–50	15–30	600–1,200	.6–1.2
Middle Formative	5–10	10–20	25–50	13–27	520–1,080	.5–1.1
Late Formative	35–75	70–150	45–90	50–105	2,000–4,050	2–4
Terminal Formative A	25–50	180–380	175–370	127–270	5,080–10,800	5–11
Terminal Formative B	330–670	25–550	340–720	307–647	12,280–25,880	12–26
Early Classic	400–850	350–1,000	170–380	307–743	12,280–29,600	12–30
Middle Classic	550–1,100	450–1,000	340–770	447–957	17,880–38,280	18–38
Late Classic A	2,100–4,450	950–2,000	1,420–2,810	1,490–3,087	59,600–120,348	60–120
Late Classic B	450–920	750–1,600	440–1,000	547–1,173	21,880–46,920	22–47
Early Postclassic	825–1,650	125–200	300–720	417–857	16,680–34,280	17–34
Late Postclassic	200–400	80–160	420–880	233–480	9,320–19,200	9–19

change, but a new kind of site does emerge, the funerary mound ceremonial center, which consists of elongated plazas defined by burial mounds that apparently served as tombs for prominent lineages, with associated earth platforms of unknown functions. A number of the burial mounds at Kaminaljuyú are of considerable size (up to 9 m in height) and all consist of earth fill. There were five such complexes defined at the site of Kaminaljuyú, three in the main valley, and four on the Canchón plateau. In a previous publication, Sanders (1974) suggested that Kaminaljuyú was the center of a relatively large chiefdom and that the additional complexes represented centers of independent smaller ones. The archaeological evidence indicates the definite likelihood of ranking in the social system, accompanied by some degree of political centralization. The ceremonial precincts seem not to have been foci of population concentration, but rather functioned for chiefly interments and, presumably, commemorative funerary rituals as well. Studies of the ceramics from this phase would suggest some occupational specialization in pottery making, at least in the manufacture of funerary ceramics (Rice 1978).

Major changes are evident in the archaeological record for the Terminal Formative period. By the end of the period, the population increased to approximately 26,000, with an overall density of 26/km^2. Kaminaljuyú emerged as a major new focus of population with 3,000 to 4,000 people, or 10%–12% of the total population of the valley (Michels 1979). The funerary plazas of the Late Formative were replaced by a new type of ceremonial complex consisting of a temple pyramid (although the function of this is still primarily that of a funerary monument for the chiefly lineage) and associated platforms, the latter being substructures for residential buildings of the chiefly family. Civic centers of this type varied from 3 to 11 mounds each in the 10 or so such precincts at Kaminaljuyú during this period (Michels 1979). Each of these precincts has an attached residential ward, and each such population cluster around the civic center is separated from the others by empty zones of variable size, with the total complex distributed over an area of 5 km^2. Variations in the sizes of civic plazas at Kaminaljuyú and in the survey area would suggest that the chiefly lineages were ranked. Data from excavations within the ceremonial precincts suggest also that the population living in and around each of the precincts was internally ranked as well. A major social contrast would be between the precinct at Kaminaljuyú and the population living in the surrounding dependent settlements. Besides the 10 civic complexes at Kaminaljuyú, there are 7 additional ones scattered throughout the plain, within a few kilometers of Kaminaljuyú, and 7 more in the rest of the valley.

The basic rural settlement type continues to be the hamlet. One change of pattern from preceding periods is that very few Terminal Formative settlements and no ceremonial precincts were found on the Canchón plateau, a focus of Late Formative settlement. Within the rest of the area, hamlets are widely and rather evenly distributed on both flat and sloping terrain. The relatively small size of the outlying ceremonial precincts, in comparison with those at Kaminaljuyú, suggests that the valley was politically centralized at this time. There is also convincing evidence of specialization, not only in ceramics, but most particularly in the obsidian industry (Michels 1979).

During the Early Classic period, the population of Kaminaljuyú itself reached 5,000 and increased to its peak of 6,500 by Early Late Classic times (Michels 1979). By the end of the Middle Classic, the total population of the survey area had increased to a maximum of 30,000 and a density of 30/km^2. The Terminal Formative pattern of population distribution persisted, with perhaps ½ of the total population concentrated at (or within a few kilometers of) Kaminaljuyú, and the rest well distributed throughout most of the remainder of the valley, with the exception of the Canchón plateau, where settlement remained sparse.

Civic precincts at Middle Classic Kaminaljuyú were of two major types: a massive integrated complex of buildings, which we have designated the central acropolis, and a series of small ceremonial precincts, each with a ball court attached to and sharing a common platform with, a residential compound. The latter portion of this dual complex includes a small pyramid temple, which was probably funerary in function and served the chiefly lineage resident at the compound. This type of site also occurs widely dispersed throughout the surrounding countryside.

During the initial centuries of the Late Classic, the population of the valley doubled to a total maximal figure of 120,000 people or 120/km^2. A major political event in the Late Classic is the apparent decline of Kaminaljuyú as the major center for the valley and the growth of a number of new centers (7 in all), 2 of which were as large as Kaminaljuyú when it was at its peak. All of these centers had civic precincts comparable in form and function to those described for the Middle Classic and were supported by substantial permanent populations. At least 40 additional small ceremonial–residential complexes of the ball court–chiefly compound type were dispersed through the settlement areas, concentrating largely on the valley floor, particularly around Kaminaljuyú and El Frutal, one of the noted other large centers. That several of these, associated with a series of hamlets, occur on the Canchón plateau indicates substantial reoccupation of this region, which had been abandoned by the end of the Late Formative. While approximately 60% of the total population of the survey area still resided in the hamlet settlement type, a major change occurred in the distribution of this type of site, now largely limited to areas of relatively flat terrain; much of the moderate to steeply sloping areas settled during the Formative and early portion of the Classic period were abandoned for residence.

Starting with the final centuries of the Classic and continuing through the Postclassic period there occurred a steady population decline in the survey area. Except for occasional ceremonial uses, Kaminaljuyú was completely abandoned during this period. A new center emerged at Chinautla, located in the hilly, rugged terrain on the north edge of the great plateau around Kaminaljuyú; The situation of the center suggests defense as the determinant of location; the presence of moats and fortification walls supports this interpretation. Despite the distinctiveness of its setting, Chinautla, like Kaminaljuyú, was composed of a series of discrete civic centers, each including pyramids, temples, and elite residences, all of which were comparable in their functional characteristics to the civic precincts known in the region from the Terminal Formative to the Late Classic. As in the earlier periods, each is associated with a small, densely settled residential area. Because of the requirement for defense and the character of the topography at Chinautla, these have lost their discreteness and appear as a single physical settlement; even if analyzed as such, the total population concentrated at Chinautla did not number more than a few thousand.

Including the population of Chinautla, several small centers located in the rest of the survey area, and a great number of hamlets, the total population probably did not exceed 19,000, which was approximately the size of the Terminal Formative occupation. Even with this reduced population level, however, the distribution of hamlets more closely resembles that of the Late Classic period, occurring primarily on the plateau surface of the plain of Kaminaljuyú and only secondarily on the Canchón Plateau. This observation would suggest that the flat plain areas were favored for agriculture. Although the site of Chinautla itself is situated in hilly broken terrain, the ridges on which the site is built are sufficiently closely juxtaposed to the prime agricultural land of the north edge of the flat plain around Kaminaljuyú to assure regular and easy access from the center.

Agricultural History of the Valley of Guatemala

The demographic history of the region reveals a process of continuous population growth from about 1200 B.C. to approximately A.D. 800, doubling, on the average, every 250–300 years (a rate common among preindustrial farming societies). In the Late Classic B Phase and the Postclassic period, from A.D. 800 to A.D. 1524, there was a rapid population decline to a level $\frac{1}{5}$ that of the peak, or a decline roughly comparable to the rate of increase.

We have very little direct botanical data on the history of crop utilization. Only during the final year of the project did we become aware of new developments in flotation techniques to retrieve such remains. One of the graduate students on the project, Nancy Stenholm, then collected soil samples for analysis, but the results of this study are, as yet, available only in very preliminary form (Stenholm 1979). Her excavation was confined to an Early–Middle Classic house, with, as expected, maize and beans as definite cultigens. Tsukada and Deevey's (1967) pollen cores from Lake Amatitlán indicate maize as the staple food source throughout the prehistoric sequence. Tools and techniques of cultivation can be reconstructed on the basis of several direct and indirect lines of evidence.

Because the numbers and densities of population closely reflect the behavior, particularly the economic behavior, of that population, one strong indirect source of data is settlement types and distribution. The pattern can be summarized in terms of four major stages of occupation. During stage 1 (the Early, Middle, and Late Formative periods), all of the population resided in hamlets rather evenly dispersed throughout the survey area. Although in stage 2 (Terminal Formative and Early and Middle Classic) the hamlet was still the most common type of settlement, at least 40% of the population resided in a number of large settlements with populations in the hundreds or even thousands. Settlement as a whole was widely distributed throughout the various ecological zones, with the exception of the almost abandoned Canchón plateau, but with a definite tendency to increasingly uneven population distribution. The concentration of settlement on the central (intermediate elevation) terrace areas around Kaminaljuyú and El Frutal is notable. During stage 3 (the Late Classic A period), a phase of heavy focus of settlement in relatively flat terrain, approximately half the population resided in large settlements and about half in the hamlets; the relatively level surfaces of the Canchón plateau, abandoned by the end of the Late Formative period, were in part recolonized. The fourth phase, the Late Classic B phase and the Postclassic period, represents a broad continuation of the Late Classic A settlement distribution, but with a progressive reduction of population.

Excavations at Kaminaljuyú yielded evidence of massive deposition of soil on the flat plain in and around the site, presumably the product of extensive erosion of the surrounding slopes during the Formative and the Early and Middle Classic periods. There is a strong possibility that the deforestation of the sloping areas of the valley, and of the plain below, provoked a process of severe erosion that ultimately destroyed the sloping areas as a potential agricultural resource for a substantial period of time. Even in the absence of direct evidence, we believe that the extensive network of deep, wide barrancas on the plain itself is probably the product of this same process.

Our intensive survey of approximately 600 km^2 of the survey area revealed little direct evidence of features that would suggest intensive agricultural practices, such as terracing, even in areas where present-day evidence would suggest that erosion was a significant problem. Furthermore, from excavations at Kaminaljuyú and from our large number of survey samples from rural sites, we found no evidence of stone or shell hoes that would suggest the use of earth turning tools. Because of the possibility that such tools were manufactured entirely of wood (as were the Aztec *huictli* of the Conquest period), this negative evidence is not conclusive. We did find artifacts that may enhance the probability that more intensive agriculture was practiced: doughnut-shaped objects of stone very similar to comparable artifacts found in contemporary highland New Guinea, where they are used as digging stick weights. In New Guinea, digging sticks are used to turn over soils in areas where short fallow or permanent cropping techniques are used. Interestingly, these weights are found definitely associated primarily with our Middle and Late Classic sites, the period of maximum population of the survey areas. Another possible function of these artifacts is that they were used as clod breakers, a use which also suggests intensive land use.

Although the evidence is scattered, derives from a number of distinct lines of reasoning, is indirect, and is frequently inconclusive, we suggest the following reconstruction of the agricultural history of the survey area: The overall low population density, small size, and valley-wide distribution of Early and Middle Formative settlements imply the kind of rapid population growth, fissioning of settlement, and lateral expansion of population that is characteristic of a pioneering farming population with (following Boserup's model of the process of agricultural development) an extensive approach to land use. During the subsequent Late Formative, further fissioning and other population movements filled in previously vacant areas, but without significant change in land-use patterns. The larger population centers of the Terminal Formative and Early and Middle Classic phases suggest some intensification of land use, on at least a localized basis, concentrated in areas of Guatemala soils where soil fertility, friability, and relatively low risk of erosion produced nearly ideal agricultural conditions. It should be pointed out that even in such areas, however, population levels did not significantly exceed those capable of maintenance by relatively extensive land use (say a land-use factor of three or four). An exception—the most convincing case for a process of agricultural intensification—would be on the plain immediately around Kaminaljuyú.

During the early part of the Late Classic period, the phase of maximum population, much of the sloping terrain of the valley was so severely eroded that portions of these areas were abandoned; a process of contraction to the Guatemala soil area was initiated. This was accompanied by a process of increasing nucleation of the population into large settlements, combined with intensification of land use in the plain. Even the overall population density of $120/km^2$ for the 1,000-km^2 survey area exceeds the potential for swidden agriculture, but when one realizes that only approximately $\frac{1}{2}$ of the area was actually used, the effective density was at least double this figure, and, in some areas, must have exceeded 300 people. This is also the period when we have more direct evidence of intensive agriculture in the form of digging stick weights. Finally, formerly abandoned areas of level land in the Canchón Plateau were reoccupied, a colonization consonant in its timing with other indications of land pressure.

With respect to the subsequent continuous decline of population during the final centuries of the Late Classic, the Early Postclassic, and Late Postclassic phases, this process was probably related to a steady deterioration of the agricultural land resource, characterized by (1) the removal of virtually all sloping land from cultivation and (2) extensive barranca cutting in the plain. This latter process reduced the surface area available for cultivation by a substantial amount. Approximately 13% of the total surface area today (30% of the Guatemala soil area), consists of barranca beds and walls. The Late Postclassic was also a phase of intense military competition, as the location of the central town, Chinautla, with its mesa top position and its wall and moat complex, suggests.

Conclusions

Our final remarks are in part an update of the conclusions offered by the senior author in a previous publication (Sanders 1974) as to the interaction between environmental adaptation and cultural evolution in the Valley of Guatemala, but with some significant changes.

Essentially the conclusions offered in the earlier paper were as follows:

1. The demographic profile consists of a sustained and steady rise of population to reach a peak in Late Classic times, followed by a precipitous decline in the Postclassic period.
2. The population history was correlated with a process of political evolution from egalitarian to ranked to stratified social systems.
3. Both political and demographic processes were closely correlated with a process of agricultural intensification, which resulted in extensive damage to the environment in the form of sheet and gulley erosion on the slopes and barranca cutting in the plains.

This interesting set of interrelationships suggested that social evolution was the product of a gradual per capita reduction of the agricultural land resource, and, therefore, the product of intense competition over a basic resource.

Our new study not only substantiates most of these conclusions but, because of our higher population estimates, reinforces them. A major modification in this respect lies in our remodeling of the final 900 years of the demographic profile. In the new version, the peak of the population was reached by A.D. 800, and the population at the time of the Spanish Conquest was considerably higher than our earlier estimates (about 2½ times). The decline was, therefore, much less precipitous than that suggested in our first analysis and fits our model of environmental deterioration much more closely. To elucidate further, even accepting the notion that many of the slope areas were lost to cultivation, the Late Postclassic population that was estimated in our initial study was still much smaller than the remaining land resources would permit. Our new estimate would bring the number more in line with the carrying capacity of the deteriorated landscape.

Another conclusion, which can be drawn from this restudy, is that some factors apparently acted to produce social fissioning when political groupings reached the size of 20,000 to 30,000 people. This was approximately the population of the valley during the Terminal Formative period when Kaminaljuyú was the center of a valleywide chiefdom; by Late Classic times, when the population had reached several times this size, instead of a larger polity forming, a series of polities roughly comparable in size to the Terminal Formative chiefdom were present. This process of social fissioning and the lack of evolution of larger systems suggests a rather weak administrative structure, and throws doubt on our original assumption that the period from the Terminal Formative to the Late Classic witnessed a shift from a chiefdom or ranked society to a stratified and state society. We are of the opinion, in this study, that chiefdom organization probably characterized the Valley of Guatemala throughout the archaeological sequence. What factors acted to prevent the formation of large sociopolitical groupings and more complex organization is not clear presently, but it probably has to do with the nature of the agricultural system.

We believe that the most important implications of our studies, in a broad theoretical sense, lie in the question of how traditional farmers adapt to their environment. Our central conclusion is that most of what anthropologists describe as agricultural technology and techniques represents an effort to insure the success of a specific crop for a specific year, i.e., the resolution of short-term goals. We disavow a sacred cow in cultural anthropology: that traditional farmers are conservationists, that they have a kind of ecological wisdom that expresses itself in ideological notions and rituals that effectively regulate environmental conditions over the long term. For example, we see no evidence of population regulation in the history of the area. Secondly, a recent study by Donkin (1979) of agricultural terracing in Latin America shows a striking correlation between extensive, well-dated terraces and dry upland environments. There is a strong possibility that the function of terracing was not so much erosion control but runoff control, i.e., the farmer's purpose was to reduce runoff and, hence, the risk variable in cropping such lands. What makes this hypothesis particularly attractive is that the behavior is a response to immediate short-term goals. The long-range effects of this response to short-term problems would in this case be highly adaptive, and there is a significant difference in the ecological process of occupation of subhumid versus humid environments. Erosion does, of course, occur in arid lands, but it is the product of population decline (i.e., well-managed terrace systems are abandoned as in the case of the central plateau of Mexico during the sixteenth century), not the cause of it. One may, therefore, legitimately raise the question as to whether terracing was ever done as an erosion control technique. While we admit that we are overstating Donkin's position, we conclude that traditional farmers do not, in fact, consciously practice erosion control. Its virtual absence in the Valley of Guatemala (except in cases where terraces are closely associated with houses), combined with evidence of dense population and environmental degradation, is in strong support of our position.

The process we have described in this small area perhaps provides, in microcosm, a clue to what might have happened in the Maya Lowlands, keeping in mind, of course, the difference between the two areas in scale and degree as well as certain other differences produced by contrasting features of the two natural environments.

With respect to scale, as far as we can tell the Valley of Guatemala was unique in the Guatemala Highlands in terms of the density of its population and the consequent environmental effects. It is probable that even in the other volcanic valleys, significant agricultural occupation was not achieved until Late Formative times, and in the northern limestone ranges, population was very light until the Classic period. Many areas, particularly the latter, did not reach maximum levels until the time of the Spanish Conquest. Overall, the highlands probably reached its maximum population level at the time of the Spanish Conquest. Our extrapolation from the sixteenth-century tax data for the period of the Conquest is a population of 500,000–1,000,000 with an average density of only 10–20/km^2. In contrast, recent data from the Maya Lowlands suggests that an area of about 80,000 km^2 in the heart of the Yucatán Peninsula had a continuously dense population by A.D. 800 that was at least comparable to that of the Late Classic A Phase in the Valley of Guatemala, by A.D. 800. Even if we accepted this relatively conservative average of 100 people per km^2, the population would then be approximately 8 million, and some Mayanists would provide even higher figures. The most generous allowance for the population of this core area of the Maya Lowlands at the time of the Spanish Conquest would be 100,000 people. The Postclassic decline, therefore, was much more drastic than in the Valley of Guatemala, apparently occurring over a period of 300 years, as contrasted to 700 years in the highland valley. Another interesting contrast lies in the growth rate; in the Maya Lowlands, the best guess is a doubling rate of every 400 years, contrasting to the 250- to 300-year doubling rate in the Valley of Guatemala. In summary, the population grew more slowly in the lowland region, higher densities were achieved over much larger areas, and the decline was much more rapid.

The basic similarity of a sustained growth followed by a rapid decline we believe is related to the effects of agricultural intensification on a humid, topographically uneven landscape. The differences in the histories of the two areas relate to a complex combination of factors. Although we do have some settlement in the Valley of Guatemala as early as Arévalo times, settlements were small and widely dispersed and may not have been fully agricultural communities. We do not really have effective agricultural colonization until well into the Middle Formative. The valley was probably colonized from the nearby Pacific Piedmont Coastal province, where populations are substantially older. In contrast, parts of the Maya Lowlands were settled as early as 2500 B.C. by a sedentary agricultural population. The achievement of a dense population over a much larger area, even with the slower growth rate, is probably the result of this earlier colonization. The slower growth rate most probably relates to differential mortality produced by the greater amount of disease pressure in this tropical habitat.

The more rapid decline may possibly relate to the combination of a more stressful biological environment with the process of deterioration of the physical environment common to both areas. A very interesting question is, why did the population level off at a considerably higher level in the highland valley? We believe this relates to significant differences in the two natural environments. First, the soil layer in the highlands rests on a deep bed of volcanic ash rather than on limestone bedrock, as in the case of the Yucatán Peninsula. Its removal was less serious, and its effect on the agricultural potential of the area would have been more short-term. Second, and more importantly, the best agricultural land in the highlands is on the floors of the valleys (i.e., the lower areas that were much less affected by the erosional process, or perhaps in part even benefited from it). In the Maya Lowlands, the best agricultural land consisted of well-drained slopes, while the intervening bajos, or low areas, were characterized by heavy, infertile, poorly drained clays. The erosional process in the highlands, then, reduced the amount of agricultural land but preserved its most productive sector; the erosional process in the Maya heartland, on the other hand, destroyed the prime agricultural resource.

References

Bryan, K.
1945 Soils and climatic chronology in Guatemala. *Carnegie Institution of Washington Yearbook* 44:168–170.
Donkin, R. A.
1979 *Agricultural Terracing in the Aboriginal New World.* Tuscon, Univ. of Arizona Press.
Hurtado de Mendoza, L. A.
1977 Obsidian studies and the archaeology of the Valley of Guatemala. Unpublished Ph.D. dissertation, Department of Anthropology, Pennsylvania State Univ.
Klingebiel, A. A., and P. H. Montgomery
1961 *Land Capability Classification.* Agriculture Handbook No. 210. U. S. Department of Agriculture Soil Conservation Survey. U. S. Government Printing Office, Washington, D. C.
Koch, A. J., and H. McLean
1975 Pleistocene tephra and ash-flow deposits in the volcanic highlands of Guatemala. *Geological Society of America Bulletin* 86:529–541.
Michels, J. W.
1973 Radiocarbon and obsidian dating: A chronometric framework for Kaminaljuyú. In *The Pennsylvania State University Kaminaljuyú Project—1969–1970 Seasons: Part I—Mound Excavations,* edited by J. W. Michels and W. T. Sanders, pp. 21–65. Department of Anthropology, Occasional Papers in Anthropology No. 9, University Park.
1979 *The Kaminaljuyú Chiefdom.* Monograph Series on Kaminaljuyú. University Park, Pennsylvania State Univ. Press.
Michels, J. W., and C. A. Bebrich
1971 Obsidian dating. In *Dating Techniques for the Archaeologist,* edited by H. N. Michael and E. K. Ralph, pp. 164–221. Cambridge, Massachusetts, MIT Press.
Michels, J. W., and R. K. Wetherington
1979 The Kaminaljuyú test trenches: Component assemblage definition and sharing. In *Settlement Pattern Excavations at Kaminaljuyú, Guatemala,* edited by J. W. Michels, pp. 619–720, University Park, Pennsylvania State Univ. Press.
Rice, P. M.
1978 Ceramic continuity and change in the Valley of Guatemala. In *The Ceramics of Kaminaljuyú,* edited by R. K. Wetherington, pp. 401–510. University Park, Pennsylvania State Univ. Press.
Sanders, W. T.
1974 Chiefdom to state: Political evolution at Kaminaljuyú, Guatemala. In *Reconstructing Complex Societies,* edited by C. Moore. Cambridge, Massachusetts, MIT Press.
Shook, E. M.
1943 Unpublished sketch map, Field notes 1943, on file, Antigua, Guatemala.
1952 Lugares arqueológicos del altiplano meridional central de Guatemala. *Antropología e Historia de Guatemala* 4(2):3–40.

Simmons, C. S., J. M. Tarano, and J. H. Pinto
1959 *Clasificación de Reconocimiento de los Suelos de la República de Guatemala.* Ministerio de Agricultura, Instituto Agro-Pecuaria, Guatemala.
Smith, G. D.
1977 A preliminary proposal for reclassification of Andepts and some Andic subgroups. *Advances in Agronomy* 29:229–261.
Soil Survey Staff
1975 *Soil Taxonomy.* U. S. Government Printing Office, Washington, D. C.
Stenholm, Nancy A.
1979 Identification of house structures in Mayan archaeology: A case study at Kaminaljuyú. In *Settlement Pattern Excavations at Kaminaljuyú, Guatemala,* edited by J. W. Michels, pp. 31–182, University Park, Pennsylvania State Univ. Press.
Tsukada, M., and E. S. Deevey
1967 Pollen analysis from four lakes in the southern Maya area of Guatemala and El Salvador. In *Quaternary Paleoecology,* edited by E. J. Cushing and H. E. Wright. New Haven, Yale Univ. Press.
Wetherington, R. K.
1978 *The Ceramics of Kaminaljuyú, Guatemala.* Monograph Series on Kaminaljuyú. University Park, Pennsylvania State Univ. Press.
Williams, H.
1960 Volcanic history of the Guatemala Highlands. *University of California Publications in Geological Sciences* 38:1–72.

2

An Ecological Model of the Early Maya of the Central Lowlands

Barbara Voorhies

Introduction

THE proposed model[1] represents significant relationships that linked the early Maya of the central lowlands to their biophysical and greater social environments. By the central lowlands, I am referring to the Department of the Petén, Guatemala and the adjacent lowland regions (Figure 1). This is the area in which some of the Classic period traits (such as carved stone monuments) first appear in significant numbers, and later develop into their most quintessential forms. Accordingly, geographic centrality, and the precociousness and preeminence of Classic period art and architecture combine in making this a key region in Maya prehistory.

At the present time, the central lowlands consist of gently rolling hills covered with mature but disturbed tropical rain forest. This upland forest is interrupted in places by patches of savanna and by *bajos*, closed basins that support varieties of swamp forest (Turner 1978a). Perennial surface water is critically absent, except for several lakes that are located in the southern part of the area. In the literature on the prehistory of this area, the environment has been characterized frequently as being resource depauperate (e.g., Rathje 1971; Tourtellot and Sabloff 1972; Rathje *et al.* 1978; Parsons and Price 1971); yet perplexingly, it was precisely this region that witnessed the transition from a relatively simple to a complex society. This conundrum has yet to be explained adequately.

The model that I am proposing stresses the richness of the tropical forest environment and its resource potential for forming widespread exchange

[1]In this context I am using the term model to indicate a scaled-down, idealized representation of reality.

ISBN 0-12-259780-X

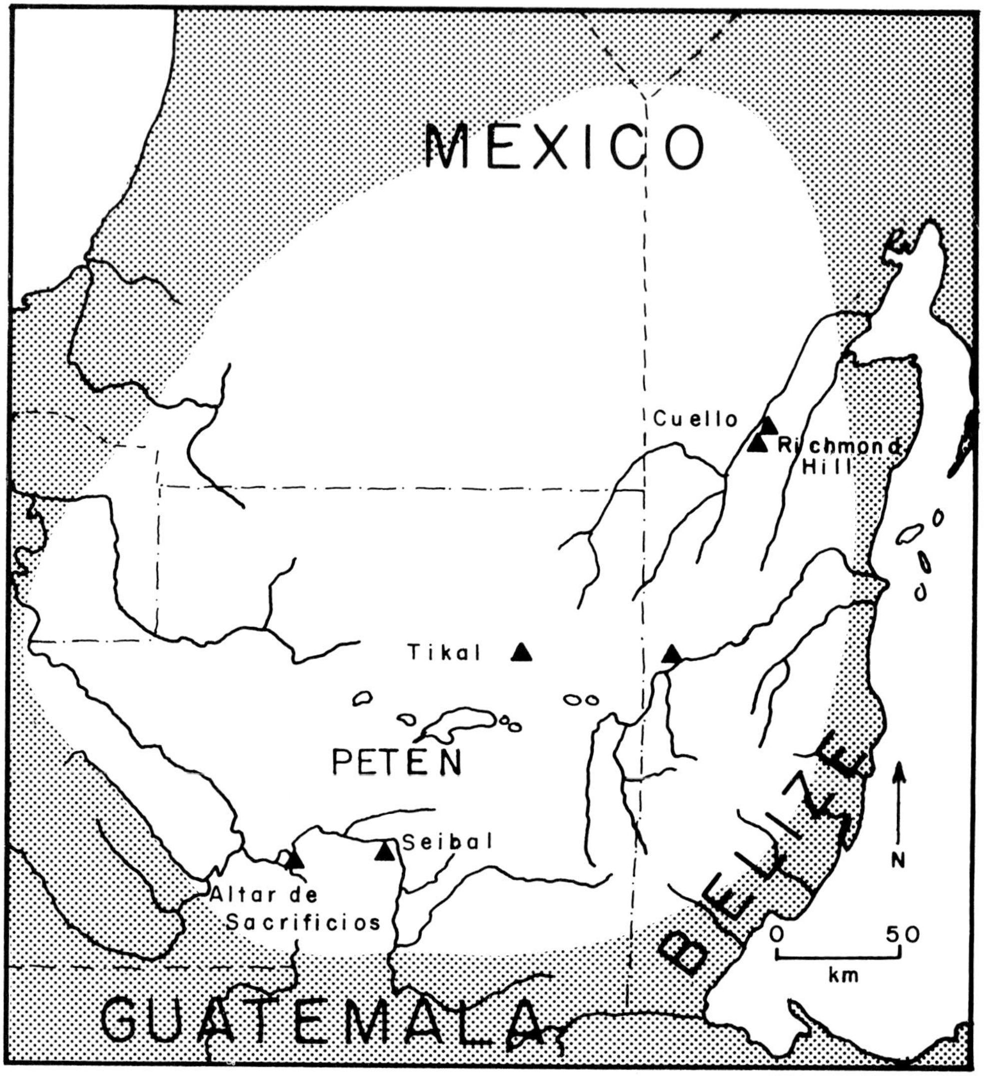

FIGURE 1. *The Central Maya Lowlands with sites mentioned in text (after Turner 1978a).*

networks. Although this potential has been recognized in the past (e.g., Thompson 1970; Dillon 1975), it has never been systematically tested nor have the implications been fully realized as they pertain to the Preclassic period.

Pioneer Maya and the Tropical Forest Habitat

The early Maya evidently migrated into a high tropical forest habitat when they first entered the central lowlands. Apparently this habitat was approximately similar to that found today in the same region. The reconstruction of a primeval forest is based on studies of pollen deposited in stratified and datable lake sediments (e.g. Deevey *et al.* 1978). No known archaeological data are available to document the initial penetration of the central lowlands by pioneer Maya; in fact, the initial glimpse of the early migrants comes only from the record of floral, faunal, and nutrient fluctuations recorded in stratified lake deposits (Covich 1978 in passim; Cowgill and Hutchinson 1963a, 1963b, 1966; Deevey *et al.* 1978; Rice 1976; Wiseman 1975). These disturbances have been dated to approximately 3000 B.C. (Deevey *et al.* 1978; cf. Wiseman 1975). Among the environmental disturbances are carbonized flecks of vegetation, which have led palynologists to conclude that beginning at about this date, periodic burnings occurred in the catchment areas of the lake basins. The burn indicators suggest that the environmental disturbances recorded in lake sediments were due to the presence of swidden farmers in the region.[2] Swidden farming is a simple agricultural system that involves burning the natural vegetation as a means of clearing fields prior to planting. It is well suited to the tropical forest habitat as has been demonstrated by Harris (1972a; 1972b). As swidden systems generally produce high yields per amount of human energy expenditure, they are often utilized in situations where farmers are blessed with unlimited tracts of virgin land. Accordingly, a swidden system would have been an appropriate form of farming for Maya pioneers.

Although there is insufficient archaeological evidence to permit us to pattern the migration of the earliest Maya into the central lowlands, we can model this process on a similar ethnographic situation. A comparable situation is that of the Iban of Sarawak who, like the early Maya, practiced swidden agriculture and penetrated a rain forest environment (Vayda 1969). The Iban population first settled in riverine locations and then subsequently expanded into the hinterland. Vayda, the ethnographer who described this process, explains that this particular pattern is the result of solutions to competing push–pull factors experienced by the Iban. Both the attraction of the forest for the production of wild products and

[2]Turner (1978b:15) has emphasized that the paleoecological data can be interpreted in ways other than as support of the swidden hypothesis, but he appears to favor a model of agricultural intensification increasing through time with the initial system being a swidden one (Turner and Harrison 1978:357–358).

the squeeze of population growth attract new settlers into the hinterland. Counteracting these tendencies are the relative ease with which secondary (as contrasted with primary) forest can be cleared and the preference for riverine locations, which provide ready sources of food, water, and transportation.

The model of early Maya migration into the lowlands specifies that swidden farmers would have settled first near rivers and then subsequently moved away from them. This particular pattern has been proposed specifically for the Maya (Puleston and Puleston 1971); however, I posit an earlier occurrence than was proposed first by the Pulestons.

The earliest archaeological evidence[3] currently available has been recovered from a small number of widely separated sites, all of which became major centers in the later Classic period (A.D. 200–900). This evidence (referred to as the Xe, Jenney Creek, Swasey, Real, and Eb complexes) has been recovered from Altar de Sacrificios, Barton Ramie, Cuello, Seibal, and Tikal (Figure 1). Rather than documenting the initial pioneer stage, as the Pulestons had supposed in 1971, the earliest archaeological evidence instead may record the beginnings of significant concentrations of people and permanent architecture associated with the growth of centers functioning as nodes in the economic system. Although there is no unanimity among Mayanists concerning the importance of these centers as economic nodes during the Classic period, the importance of the economic factor has been stressed recently (e.g. Sidrys 1977; Moholy-Nagy 1976). I propose that economic factors were in effect also at the time of the initial foundation of these same centers. The specific economic factors that I am about to describe certainly would not have been the only factors responsible for the establishment of early villages, but these are the ones that I wish to consider here.

The actual locations of early centers, and the incentive for their growth in architecture and population, are tied to the development of an external demand for rain forest commodities. The demand arose on the part of the organizationally more advanced peoples living in the adjacent highland environments.[4] These people developed a taste for exotic items that were obtainable only in rain

[3]There are some tantalizing bits of evidence for occupations predating the earliest farming occupation described in the text. Shook (1951) for example, reports a cut sloth bone from the Pasión drainage and Puleston (1975; see also Miller 1976) reports a large site in Belize (Richmond Hill) with heavily patinated artifacts. Interpretation problems are associated with each of these finds. The sloth bone could have been transported from the highlands and secondarily deposited in the lowlands, since it was not found in stratified deposits that could be interpreted as primary. The Richmond Hill site, despite intriguing comparisons with paleo-Indian assemblages (Puleston 1975:531; MacNeish 1978:181) has not been dated and may even be a late aceramic manifestation (Hammond *et al.* 1979:99).

In addition, Wiseman (1975) has analyzed sediments from Lake Quexil and interpreted an early pollen pulse, at approximately 4000 B.C., as an indication of human disturbance. As Rice (1976:304) has discussed, this pulse is neither confirmed nor refuted by other core data, the early date can be questioned, and other factors might be responsible for such low-level frequencies.

[4]Hughes (1973) has presented a clear analysis of the relative economic motivations for highland—lowland exchange in New Guinea:

forest environments. The lowland resources that were especially appreciated by highland peoples were not essential items necessary for food or tool manufacture, but rather were diverse, nonessential items. Before discussing these items and the spatial expectations of the modeled system, I shall first discuss the data on which the reconstruction of a long-distance trading system has been based.

There is indisputable evidence that the Preclassic period Lowland Maya had access to highland resources. This evidence is based on the presence of artifacts at lowland sites that have been manufactured from obsidian, a raw material available only in the igneous regions in the middle and high elevations of southern Mesoamerica. Although the quantities of obsidian found in Preclassic period deposits are small, this material has been recovered from Preclassic period deposits at various sites (summaries available in Nelson *et al.* 1977:220; Nelson *et al.* 1978; Rovner 1976) and increases in frequency from early Preclassic period deposits to late. Logically, the lowland people could have obtained this highland resource in one of only two possible ways: either they procured it directly, or it was a commodity in an exchange system by which goods were moved between contrasting highland and lowland environments.[5] Sourcing studies have indicated that the bulk of obsidian in early deposits was obtained from source areas in the vicinity of the Valley of Guatemala. This source region was also supplying people in Campeche (Nelson *et al.* 1977) and the upper Grijalva Basin (Clark 1979) during the Late Preclassic period. But it is significant that small amounts of obsidian found at central lowland sites originated at several additional and widely separated sources throughout the highlands.

In my opinion, exchange, rather than direct procurement, is the best model for the movement of obsidian from the highlands to lowlands. This is in part because of the apparent high cost of direct procurement, which would necessarily involve long distances, primitive transportation, and considerable investment in time and energy. In addition, the motivation for incurring such expenditures is not readily apparent since the Maya Lowlanders may have had locally and

---

> One tends to assume that the people of the highlands fringe and lowlands had a greater economic need than did the highlanders and for that reason they could be expected to show more initiative in trade. . . . I do not believe this is so. The thousands of highlanders had needs which, though they could have been met from local products, could better be met with fibres and woods from the lowlands. Those living on the outer limits of highlands settlements wanted the luxury of lowlands fruits, in particular oil pandanus, as well as vegetable oil. MORE IMPORTANTLY, THEY HAD UNSATISFIED AND GROWING WANTS FOR ORNAMENTS AND VALUABLES, FEATHERS AND SKINS OF LOWLAND BIRDS AND ANIMALS, THE LIVE CREATURES THEMSELVES, AND IN PARTICULAR SEA-SHELLS (Hughes 1973:109; [my emphasis]).

Hughes continues his discussion with a demonstration that the people who can be considered the initiators of an exchange system are not necessarily the ones who actually travel the greatest distance for purposes of exchange. This is an important lesson for archaeologists to keep firmly in mind.

[5]At this stage of analysis I am concerned only with explaining the movement of items from their source areas. As Plog (1977) has emphasized, the complete description of an exchange network necessitates many other considerations.

perhaps widely available chert deposits that could be and were exploited to produce cutting tools (cf. Culbert 1973:10). This view that raw material for cutting tools was locally available to the central Lowland Maya is contrary to that of Rathje (1971) who has championed a very different model. It is important to keep in mind that, at present, we know very little about the actual distribution of economic resources in the central lowlands (Adams and Culbert 1977:17–18). Better resource characterization of the mineral deposits in the Maya Lowlands is a pressing research goal. At the present time, however, exchange, rather than direct procurement, provides the simplest model for the movement of highland obsidian to lowland sites, and this is the view generally held by Mayanists.

If such an exchange system were in operation during the Preclassic period, then we must consider in detail the nature of this system. First, it is important to identify all commodities that were being moved and, if possible, the relative volumes of each item. Highland exports were definitely not restricted to obsidian but entailed other items, some of which were also mineralogical in origin. This is significant because minerals are durable and survive well in archaeological deposits. Rather than itemizing the array of probable highland exports, this chapter focuses on the more perplexing problem of identifying possible lowland exports.

The problem of identifying lowland exports is perplexing because almost no lowland resources are found in highland sites. One interpretation for this situation is that highland resources were obtained directly by lowlanders, but for reasons that I have already discussed, this model is not attractive. An alternative model is that the lowlanders exported local resources, but that they are archaeologically invisible. The likelihood that this second model is the more valid one is enhanced by an objective consideration of the nature of economically esteemed resources present in tropical forest environments.

Potential Exports of the Central Lowlands

In this section, I evaluate the natural resources of the central lowlands in terms of their potential roles as commodities in long-distance exchange systems. In such an exercise it is imperative to document that each resource (1) has an economic value, (2) can be verified to occur within the target region, and (3) could have figured logically as a commodity in a primitive system of long-distance exchange. Ideally, for each item considered, the geologic record should be used to verify past local occurrence, and the archaeological record should be used to verify past economic utilization. There is insufficient paleoenvironmental and paleoeconomic data to permit this inductive approach at the present time. Moreover, such an approach could be very misleading in the hot, humid tropics where many economic resources are organic, and organic remains have scant chance of being preserved in archaeological deposits. In order to compensate for the difficulties inherent in the inductive method, I have utilized an approach based on deduction. These two approaches are not to be viewed as competing methods but as necessarily complementary.

The procedure that I have followed here is to establish that an item has economic value by referring to relevant literature pertaining to people living in the same, or nearly the same, habitat as the Preclassic Maya of the central lowlands. For example, I consulted Roys's (1931) work on Maya ethnobotany, which is a *materia medica* based on several sources written in the early postcontact period. There is, of course, no guarantee that an item identified as having economic value in the sixteenth century would have been so recognized as early as the third millennium B.C. However, a chance exists that it might have been, so it is justified to list the item as a POTENTIAL resource. In speaking only of floral resources, Lundell (1937:11) has speculated that the Maya may have utilized nearly all of the native flora in their area. The number of plant species that I have considered in generating Table 1 is considerably smaller than the total number of species in the area, so in this respect, any possible error minimizes, rather than inflates, the number of potential resources.

Verification that a known economic item occurs within the central lowlands was accomplished by referring to the literature on the present-day environment. Again this method is clearly not the most desirable one, since my objective is to determine the availability of resources during the Preclassic period, rather than in the twentieth century. Mineralogical resources are probably not greatly affected by this gap in time, but organic resources may have changed considerably over the maximum 5,000 year period of human interference with the natural ecosystem of the central lowlands. Despite the well-recognized problems inherent in this approach, lack of paleobotanical and paleozoological data for the central lowlands makes it the only approach possible at the present time.

The requirement that an item has potential for long-distance exchange has been met by imposing a set of arbitrarily determined, but logically warranted, criteria. These criteria are the following:

1. TRANSPORTABILITY I am considering here only economic items (determined from ethnographic information) that are comparatively compact and lightweight. Heavy and bulky economic items, such as timbers or lime for construction purposes, are arbitrarily excluded from the list. For this same reason, I have excluded agricultural products, which if they were used for food (rather than as seeds for planting) would have had to have been moved in large volume. By exclusion of such heavy and bulky items, I do not mean to imply that they could not have been exported from the lowlands. This possibility requires examination and, of course, cannot be predetermined. I am overlooking the possibility in the present analysis in order to demonstrate the diversity and attractiveness of other available resources.

2. IMPERISHABILITY Economic items that are highly perishable, for example, fruits, are arbitrarily omitted from my roster. My reasoning is simply that products that spoil quickly in the tropics logically would not be moved over long distances because of the slowness of human powered transportation. Of course, it is entirely possible that dried or conserved fruit, seeds or seedlings were regularly

Table 1
Roster of Selected Economic Plants in the Central Lowlands

Name	Product	Use	Habitat	Reference
Acacia angustissima Kuntze.	Roots, plant	Medicine	Solitary in savanna	Roys 1931:294
				Lundell 1937:62
Acacia farnesiana Willd.	Heartwood, root	Medicine	Not specified	Lundell 1937
	Flowers	Perfume, sachet		Roys 1931
	Pods	Ink		O'Gorman 1961
				Lundell 1938:55
				(see Gates 1939:126)
Acalypha unibracteata Muell.	Leaves	Medicine	Secondary upland forest	Roys 1931:236
	Branches	Bird cages		Lundell 1937:65
Achras zapota L.	Fruit	Edible	Climax forest	Roys 1931:297
	Gum	Chewed[a]		Lundell 1937:72
	Wood	Lintels, timber		Lundell 1938:48
Adiantum tricholepis Fée	Juice	Medicine	Limestone outcrops and ruins where common	Roys 1931:285
				Lundell 1937:49
Agave sisalana	Leaf fiber	Cordage	Swamp forest[a]	Lundell 1938:51
				Lundell 1937:55
				Roys 1931:234
Alvaradoa amorphoides Liebm.	Leaves[a]	Medicine	Quite common in secondary upland forest	Roys 1931:217
				Lundell 1937:64
Anacardium occidentale L.	Seed (roasted), fruit	Food	Not specified	Lundell 1938:44
Annona reticulata L.	Leaves (dried)	Medicine	Upland forest, also cultivated	Roys 1931:271–272
	Fruit	Edible		Lundell 1937:41, 60–61
Annona squamosa L.	Leaves	Medicine	Cultivated + other	Roys 1931:313–314
	Fruit	Edible		Lundell 1937:61
Argemone mexicana L.	Not specified	Medicine	Common in clearings	Roys 1931:214
				Lundell 1937:61
Arthrostylidium pittieri Hack.	Stems	Fish spearshafts	Not specified	Lundell 1938:55
A. spinosum Swallen	Stems	Fish spearshafts	Not specified	Lundell 1938:55
Asclepias curassavica L.	Not specified	Medicine	Common in clearings	Roys 1931:215
				Lundell 1937:74
Asclepias longicornu Benth.	Not specified	Medicine	Occasional in grasslands	Roys 1931:220
				Lundell 1937:74
Asplenium pumilum Sw.	Infusion	Medicine	Common on limestone in climax forest and ruins	Roys 1931:310
				Lundell 1937:49
Bactris spp.	Nuts	Food	Not specified	Lundell 1938:46
Bauhinia divaricata L.	Plant[a], roots, flowers	Medicine	Common in secondary and upland forest	Roys 1931:315
				Lundell 1937:62
Bixa orellana L.	Seeds, leaves (can be dried[a]), fruits	Food additive, medicine, dye	Secondary vegetation	Roys 1931:260
				Lundell 1938:52

				Gates 1939:140
Blechum pyramidatum Urban.	Not specified	Medicine	Swamp forests and common in clearings	Roys 1931:214, 260 Lundell 1937:77
Bombax ellipticum H.B.K.	Bark, root	Medicine	Occasional in climax forest	Roys 1931:229–230 Lundell 1937:68 O'Gorman 1961:14
Brosimum alicastrum Swartz.	Pits Fruits Sap	Diviner's rattle Edible Medicine	Widely distributed through upland forest, especially near ruins	Roys 1931:272 Lundell 1937:58
Bromelia karatas L.	Fruits Infusion	Edible Medicine	Savanna[a]	Lundell 1937:54 Roys 1931:229
Bursera simaruba Sarg.	Resin Leaves, fruits, shoots, bark	Mastic Incense, medicine	Climax and secondary upland forests	Roys 1931:227–228 Lundell 1937:65 Lundell 1938:55
Byrsonima crassifolia DC.	Fruits Plant[a]	Edible Medicine	Savanna	Roys 1931:306 Lundell 1937:65
Calea urticifolia DC.	Fruit juice, leaves	Medicine	Common in scrub forest[a]	Roys 1931:295 Lundell 1937:79
Calocarpum mammosum Pierre	Fruit Fruit, seeds, oil Oil	Edible Medicine Paint fixative	Wet forests, associated with ruins	Roys 1931:228 Lundell 1937:72 Lundell 1938:42 Standley 1924:1121
Carica papaya L. (wild)	Sap	Medicine	Not specified	Roys 1931:236
Cassia anisopetala Donn. Sm.	Root	Medicine	Not specified	Roys 1931:250 Lundell 1937:62
Cassia emarginata	Vapor[a]	Medicine	Marginal forest, young, secondary upland forest	Lundell 1937:195 Roys 1931:287
Cassia laevigata	Bark	Medicine	Not specified	O'Gorman 1961:50
Cassia occidentalis L.	Not specified Seeds	Medicine Beverage	Inhabited clearings in savanna near *aguadas*	Roys 1931:216 Lundell 1937:169 (see Gates 1939:124)
Castilla elastica Cerv.	Gum Leaves	Medicine and balls Medicine	Upland forest	Roys 1931:255 Lundell 1937:58 Lundell 1938:55 Gates 1939:128
Cecropia obtusa Trec.	Not specified	Medicine	Low forest	Roys 1931:256 Leopold 1950:514
Cedrela mexicana Roem.	Wood Young leaves, roasted leaves, gum	Timber and boats Medicine	Widely distributed in climax forest, common in some areas	Roys 1931:258 Lundell 1937:64
Cedrela odorata L.	Leaves (roasted), gum	Medicine	Not specified	Roys 1931:258 Leopold 1950:514

(*Continued*)

Table 1 *(Continued)*

Name	Product	Use	Habitat	Reference
Ceiba aesculifolia H.B.K.	Root, leaves	Medicine	Widely distributed in climax forest	Roys 1931:238, 276
	Fiber	Cloth, stuffing		Lundell 1938:52
Ceiba pentandra	Fiber	Cloth, stuffing for pillows	Widely distributed in climax forest	Roys 1931:298 Lundell 1938:52 Baker 1965
Celosia nitida Vahl.	Plant	Medicine	Common in clearings	Roys 1931:302
	Leaves	Medicine		Lundell 1937:60
Chamaedorea graminifolia Wendl.	Not specified	Medicine	Not specified	Roys 1931:298 Lundell 1937:53
Chenopodium ambrosiodes L.	Not specified	Medicine, spice	Planted, secondary successions	Roys 1931:262 Lundell 1937:60 Benítez 1974:75
Chiococca alba Hitchc.	Not specified, root	Medicine	Common in secondary upland forest	Roys 1931:223 Lundell 1937:78
Chlorophora tinctoria Gaud.	Wood (fustic)	Dye (yellow-brown, green)	Planted (may not be native)	Lundell 1938:52
Clematis dioica L.	Root	Medicine	Secondary upland forest	Roys 1931:265 Lundell 1937:60
Clerodendron ligustrinum	Not specified	Spice	Common on swampy banks	Roys 1931:248
	Leaves	Medicine		Lundell 1937:75
Clusia flava Jacq.	Not specified	Medicine	Marginal forest	Roys 1931:240 Lundell 1937:69
Cocoloba schiedeana Lundau.	Leaves	Wrappers for chile	River banks	Roys 1931:217 Lundell 1937:59
Commelina elegans H.B.K.	Root	Medicine	Common in clearings, occasional in climax forests	Roys 1931:273 Lundell 1937:54
Cissampelas pareira L. (*C. tomentosa*)	Leaves	Medicine	Common in recently abandoned clearings	Roys 1931:275 Lundell 1937:60, 167
Cissus rhombifolia Vahl.	Shoots, roots	Medicine	Marginal forest of central Petén savanna	Roys 1931:281
Cissus trifoliata L.	Leaves, root	Medicine	Not specified	Roys 1931:218
Crataeva tapia	Not specified, leaf	Medicine	"Forests"	Roys 1931:257
Crescentia cujete L.	Fruit	"Gourd vessels"	Not specified	Lundell 1938:54
	Fruit juice	Medicine		Roys 1931:262
Croton glabellus L.	Bark	Spice"	Not specified	Roys 1931:275
	Root, leaves	Medicine		Lundell 1937:65
Curatella americana L.	Leaves (dried ?)	Sandpaper	Not specified	Lundell 1938:55
	Bark	Tanning		

Cydista aequinoctialis	Vine	Lashing thatch and pack loads	Not specified	Roys 1931:228
Cymbopetalum penduliflorum Baill	Dried petals	Spice	Climax forest	Lundell 1938:47 (used by Aztecs) CIW[b] 1940:15–17
Cynodon dactylon (L.) Pers.	Stems, roots	Medicine	Common in clearings	Roys 1931:223 Lundell 1937:51
Dalbergia glabra Standl.	Bark	Cordage	Climax forest	Roys 1931:320, 260 Lundell 1937:62
Desmodium purpurem	Herb (dried[a])	Medicine	Northern Yucatán forest (only?)	Roys 1931:255
Desomoncus spp.	Stems	Baskets	Not specified	Lundell 1938:51
Dipholis salicifolia DC.	Wood	Utensils	Occasional in climax forests, and in savannas	Roys 1931:290 Lundell 1937:73
Diphysa cathaginensis Jacq.	Young leaves, leaves	Medicine	Brush and forest, near lakeshore	Roys 1931:316 Lundell 1937:62
Dorstenia contrajerva L.	Root, plant	Medicine	Common in climax forest, secondary upland forest and clearings	Roys 1931:222 Lundell 1937:58 (cf. Gates 1939:130)
Eupatorium albicaule Schultz.	Not specified	Medicine	Occasional in low secondary bush	Roys 1931:307 Lundell 1937:80
Euphorbia hirta L.	Juice, sap or gum, plant, leaves	Medicine	Clearings	Roys 1931:294–295, 243 Lundell 1937:66
Euphorbia pulcherrima	Leaves (dried[a]) Sap	Medicine Depilatory	Clearings, central Petén savanna	O'Gorman 1961:58 Lundell 1937:108
Ficus cotinifolia H.B.K.	Sap	Medicine	Not specified	Thompson 1970:156 Roys 1931:226 (cf. Gates 1939:122, 137: *F. nymphaefolia L.* and *F. petiolaris*)
Gossypium spp.	Shoots, seeds, leaves, juice, flowers Floss	Medicine Cloth	Not specified	Roys 1931:282 Lundell 1938:51
Guaiacum sanctum	Wood	Vessels, medicine	Not specified	Roys 1931:311
Guazuma ulmifolia Lam.	Stems Wood Plant[a] + shoots	Rope Boat ribs[a] Medicine	Common in secondary upland forest and clearings	Roys 1931:276 Lundell 1937:69 Lundell 1938:52
Haematoxylum campechianum L.	Heartwood	Dye, medicine	Very common in swamp forest	Roys 1931:240 Lundell 1937:63, 90, 170 Lundell 1938:52
Hamelia erecta Jacq.	Not specified, leaves	Medicine	Clearings	Roys 1931:250 Lundell 1937:78

(*Continued*)

Table 1 (*Continued*)

Name	Product	Use	Habitat	Reference
Hippocratea grisebachi Loes	Leaves	Medicine	Not specified	Roys 1931:284 Lundell 1937:67
Ichyomethia communis	Leaves (dried")	Medicine	"Forests"	Roys 1931:242
Imperata contracta Hitchc.	Grass leaves	Packing material, thatching, medicine"	Common in savannas	Lundell 1937:51 Lundell 1938:50 (cf. Roys 1931:213)
Indigofera anil L. (*I. suffruticosa* Mill.)	Plant Leaves	Dye Medicine	Secondary growth, common in recently abandoned clearings	Roys 1931:238 Lundell 1938:53 Lundell 1937:47
Jacobinia spicigera	Not specified Plant	Blue dye Medicine	Occasional in secondary bush	Roys 1931:290 Lundell 1937:77
Jacquinia aurantiaca Ait.	Bark Fruit	Medicine Fish poison	Climax forest, stream banks	Roys 1931:267 Lundell 1937:72
Krugiodendron ferreum	Wood Leaves, root, bark	Construction Medicine	Occasional in climax forest	Roys 1931:237 Lundell 1937:68
Lagenaria siceraria Standl.	Fruit shells	Containers	Cultivated (only?) (may not be native)	Roys 1931:261 Lundell 1937:79 Lundell 1938:54
Laportea mexicana Mig.	Leaves, sap	Medicine	Occasional in open hill forest on limestone slopes	Roys 1931:261 Lundell 1937:59
Lepidium virginicum L.	Seeds, leaves	Medicine	Common in inhabited clearings	Roys 1931:280 Lundell 1937:61
Leucaena glauca Benth.	Shoots, leaves (dried")	Medicine	Secondary bush	Roys 1931:291
Lonchocarpus longistylus Pittier.	Root, leaves (dried") Bark or root	Medicine Beverage	Not specified	Roys 1931:216 Lundell 1938:47
L. rugosus Benth.	Leaves (dried)	Medicine	Not specified	Roys 1931:250
Lycopersicum esculentum Mill.	Leaves	Medicine	Cultivated (only?)	Roys 1931:272 Lundell 1937:76
Lysiloma bahamensis Benth.	Wood Leaves	Boats Medicine	Climax forests, common on lake banks	Roys 1931:290 Lundell 1937:63
Malvaviscus arboreus Cav.	Leaves	Medicine	Occasional in low secondary bush	Roys 1931:282 Lundell 1937:68
Marsdenia coulteri Hemls.	Sap or gum	Medicine	Occasional in climax forest	Roys 1931:241 Lundell 1937:74
Metopium browei Urban.	Plant"	Medicine	Common in upland forests and swampy habitats	Roys 1931:219–220 Lundell 1937:67
Morinda yucatanensis Greenm.	Root	Red dye	Common in secondary	Roys 1931:245

			upland, occasional in swamp forests	Lundell 1937:78
Nicotiana tabacum L.	Leaves	Medicine	Cultivated (only?)	Roys 1931:259 Lundell 1937:76 Lundell 1938:55 (cf. Gates 1939:135)
Ocimum micranthum Willd.	Leaves	Spice[a]	Climax forest in clearings	Roys 1931:221–222 Lundell 1937:75
Orbignya cohune Dahl.	Kernels Leaves	Oil Thatching	Moist valleys and stream banks	Lundell 1937:53 Lundell 1938:50
Pachira aquatica Abl.	Nuts	Food	Not specified	Lundell 1938:46
Parmentiera edulis DC.	Not specified, flowers, leaves, fruit	Medicine	Occasional in climax forest	Roys 1931:223 Lundell 1937:77
Passiflora coriacea Juss.	Root	Medicine	Occasional in climax and secondary forests	Roys 1931:295 Lundell 1937:70
Paullinia fuscescens H.B.K.	Vine	Binding	Occasional in swamp forests	Roys 1931:254 Lundell 1937:67
Pedilanthus itzeus Millsp.	Gum or sap	Medicine	Not specified	Roys 1931:299 Lundell 1937:66
Peperomia sp.[a]	Leaves + other unspecified	Medicine	In climax forest or swamp forest	Roys 1931:263 Lundell 1937:56
Persea americana Mill.	Fruit Seeds, young leaves	Edible Medicine	Upland forest[a] cultivated	Roys 1931:271 Lundell 1937:61
Petiveria alliacea L.	Leaves, root	Medicine	Wastelands	Roys: 1931:274 Lundell 1937:60
Phyllanthus conami Swartz.	Plant	Medicine	Common in secondary upland forest	Roys 1931:274 Lundell 1937:66
Phyllanthus nobilis Muell.	Gum	Medicine[a]	Common in secondary upland forest	Roys 1931:268 Lundell 1937:66
Pimenta officinalis Lindl.	Dried fruits Wood	Spice Timber	Common in climax forest	Lundell 1938:48 Lundell 1937:71
Piper auritum H.B.K.	Leaves (roasted) Leaves	Medicine Food, spice	"Damp places"	Roys 1931:263 Lundell 1938:48
Piper medium Jacq.	Leaves (dried[a])	Medicine	Not specified	Roys 1931:275
Pisonia aculeata L.	Not specified	Medicine	Not specified	Roys 1931:217
Pithecolobium albicans Benth.	Fruit Bark Wood	Dye Tanning Timber	"High forest"	Roys 1931:239 Lundell 1938:56, 48
Pithecolobium unguis-cacti Mart.	Root, bark	Medicine	Bush and forests	Roys 1931:315
Pluchea odorata L.	Leaves,sap Leaves	Medicine Spice	Clearings	Roys 1931:233 Lundell 1937:80

(*Continued*)

Table 1 (*Continued*)

Name	Product	Use	Habitat	Reference
Plumeria rubra L.	Flowers, sap	Medicine	Planted + other unspecified	Roys 1931:231, 270 Lundell 1937:73
Portulaca oleracea L.	Plant	Medicine	Clearings	Roys 1931:296 Lundell 1937:60
Protium copal Engl.	Resin	Incense, medicine	Occasional in climax forest	Roys 1931:277–278 Lundell 1938:55 Lundell 1937:65
Psidium guajava L.	Leaves, fruits Fruits	Medicine Edible	Upland forests, common in inhabited clearings	Roys 1931:276 Lundell 1937:71
Psittacanthus calyculatus	Not specified	Medicine	Marginal forests of central Petén	O'Gorman 1961:122 Lundell 1937:141
Quaribea fieldii Millsp.	Flowers Branches	Spice (for cacao) Cacao frothers	Occasional in climax forest	Roys 1931:263 Lundell 1937:69 Lundell 1938:56
Rhoeo discolor L.	Plant crushed or boiled	Medicine	Ruins	Roys 1931:233 Lundell 1937:55
Ricinus communis L.	Oil, leaves, seeds, pith, fruit	Medicine	Clearings	Roys 1931:255 Lundell 1937:66
Rivina humilis L.	Juice of berry Juice, leaves	Dye Medicine	Clearings	Roys 1931:260 Lundell 1937:60
Ruellia tuberosa L.	Leaves (dried), plant	Medicine	"Open country"	CIW[b] 1940:175 Roys 1931:221
Sabal mexicana Mart.	Leaves Heartwood, root	Thatching, mats, hats Medicine	Cultivated (Lundell [1937:53] has never seen wild)	Lundell 1937:53 Lundell 1938:51
Salvia coccinea Juss.	Root, stalk, leaves	Medicine	Clearings	Roys 1931:232 Lundell 1937:75
Sapindus saponaria L.	Fruit Seeds	Soap Adornment	Occasional in climax forest	Roys 1931:309 Lundell 1937:67 Lundell 1938:56 (cf. Gates 1939:122)
Sapranthus campechianus Standl.	Not specified	Medicine	Not specified	Roys 1931:270 Lundell 1937:61
Scheelea lundellii Bart.	Nuts, leaves	Food, thatching	Not specified	Lundell 1938:46, 50
Sebastiana adenophora Pax and Hoff	Root, plant	Medicine	Occasional in secondary upland, climax forest	Roys 1931:251 Lundell 1937:66
Serjania adiantoides Radlk.	Not specified	Medicine	Swamp forest	Roys 1931:219
Serjania atrolineata	Leaves, vine[a]	Medicine, fish poison	Not specified	Roys 1931:219 Lundell 1938:56

Sida acuta Burm.	Leaves	Medicine	Common in clearings	Roys 1931:236 Lundell 1937:68
Smilax mexicana Griseb.	Root, plant, spines	Medicine	Tikal	Roys 1931:215, 225–226 Lundell 1937:55
Solanum nigrum L.	Plant	Medicine	Common in clearings	Roys 1931:248 Lundell 1937:76
Spondias purpurea L.	Root	Medicine	Not specified	Roys 1931:213 Lundell 1937:67
Stachytarpheta jamaicensis Vahl.	Not specified	Medicine	Common in inhabited clearings	Roys 1931:247 Lundell 1937:75
Swietenia macrophylla King	Wood Gum	Timber, boats Medicine	Occasional" in climax forest	Lundell 1937:64 Roys 1931:280
Syngonium podophyllum Schott.	Leaves	Medicine	Common in open climax forest	Roys 1931:271 Lundell 1937:54
Tabebuia chrysantha Niche	Not specified, root	Medicine	Climax forest	CIW 1940 Roys 1931:214
Tabebuia pentaphylla Hemsl.	Leaves, roots	Medicine	Occasional in climax forest	Roys 1931:244 Lundell 1937:77
Theobroma cacao L.	Seeds	Edible, medicine, dye	Cultivated, climax forest"	Roys 1931:222 Lundell 1938:46–47 Gates 1939:140 Lundell 1937:69
Theobroma bicolor Hamb. and Bonpl.	Seeds Roots, flowers	Edible Medicine	Not specified	Roys 1931:216 Lundell 1938:47 cf. Gates 1939:129
Trixis radialis Kuntze	Leaves, gum	Medicine	Common in low secondary bush	Roys 1931:286 Lundell 1937:80
Typha angustifolia L.	Stems and leaves Fluff	Mats Pillow stuffing	Common in shallow water	Roys 1931:279 Lundell 1937:50 Lundell 1938:51
Urera baccifera Gaud.	Fruit Not specified	Edible Medicine	On steep limestone slopes in open hill forest	Roys 1931:261 Lundell 1937:59
Vanilla planifolia Andrews (*Vanilla fragrans* Ames.)	Pods	Spice	Not common, although widely distributed in climax forest	Roys 1931:310 Lundell 1937:56 Lundell 1938:47 cf. Gates 1939:104 Correll 1953
Vitex gaumeri Greenm.	Leaves	Medicine	Common in climax and secondary upland forests	Roys 1931:300 Lundell 1937:75

(*Continued*)

Table 1 (*Continued*)

Name	Product	Use	Habitat	Reference
Waltheria americana L.	Stalk, root	Medicine[a]	Swamp forest	Roys 1931:305 Lundell 1937:69
Zamia furfuracea L.	Roots	Rat poison and "criminal purposes" cooked and eaten	"Forest"	Lundell 1938:55
Zanthoxylum caribaeum Lam.	Shoots, leaves (fresh?)	Medicine	Occasional in climax forest	Roys 1931:309 Lundell 1937:64
Zanthoxylum fagara Sarg.	Root, bark	Medicine	Coastal forest (only?)	Roys 1931:283

[a] Uncertain identification.
[b] CIW, Carnegie Institute of Washington.

exchanged, but I am overlooking this possibility for the same reason that agricultural products are not being considered.

3. EFFICACY Economic items that must be utilized directly after procurement in order to be effective are also eliminated from further consideration. I am reasoning that commodities will not be exchanged over long distances unless their valued properties retain their efficacy over prolonged periods.

Using the general methods outlined above, I have compiled two lists of resources that might have been exported from the central lowlands to highland locations. For convenience, one list treats floral resources only (Table 1), whereas the other list (Table 2) identifies faunal and mineralogical resources.

In the case of Table 1, species were not recorded unless they met all of the specifications that I have imposed. For example, *Spondias mombin* L. is both economically significant and occurs within the central lowlands. However, this species was not tabulated because the only economic use that I found reported for it was for its fruit, which is eaten and used as a poultice (Roys 1931:235). My reasoning, resulting in the omission of the item, is that the fruit, being highly perishable, would not survive long-distance trade. In contrast, in cases where several uses are reported for a single species, I have recorded all of them whenever a single one meets the requirements that I have imposed. This was done simply for the sake of completeness. An example of this decision is *Achras zapota* L., which has been listed because of the possibility that its gum may have been a trade commodity, rather than because of the well-esteemed fruit which this tree produces.

Efficacy was the most difficult criterion to assess. Usually it was not possible to determine from the consulted sources whether or not a plant product when dried, retained its efficacy. In the few instances where this seemed unlikely, I have not tabulated the species. In most cases where freshness is not specified, I have tabulated the species.

It can be seen (Table 1) that there is a significant number of plant species that could have figured in a long-distance exchange system. Most of these potential commodities can be considered as nonessential items rather than as critical items necessary for the survival of their users. Potential commodities include dyes, herbal medicines, spices, perfumes, incense, oils, fibers, and sundry other items. Far fewer items of zoological and mineralogical origin have been listed (Table 2). Zoological items include medicines, pelts and plumage. These items also are nonessential rather than utilitarian in nature. A single mineralogical item, chert, has been recorded. This raw material could be considered utilitarian but the prevalence of obsidian (an equivalent or superior raw material) in the highlands could also mean that if this item were imported to high elevation populations, it was for status demarcating, rather than for pragmatic and utilitarian functions.

If the items that I have listed are actually representative of the suite of items possibly exported from the lowlands, then it can be argued that the commodities generally were raw materials, highly diverse, and nonutilitarian in social function;

Table 2
Roster of Selected Animals and Minerals of Economic Value in the Central Lowlands

Name	Product	Use	Habitat	Reference
Aratinga spp.	Green feathers	Adornment	Flocks in rain forests and elsewhere	Alvarez del Toro 1971:81–82
Ara macao	Red feathers	Adornment	Solitary in rain forest	P. Haemig (personal communication)
	Wing	Medicine		Davis 1972:52
				Alvarez del Toro 1971:81
				Roys 1931:208
Cardinalis cardinalis yucatanicus Ridgeway, *Richmondena cardinalis*	Red feathers	Medicine		Roys 1931:62 Davis 1972:218 Smithe 1959:7
Ceophloeus scapularis Vigors.	Beak	As scalpel		Roys 1931:185
Coccus axin	Wood lice	Oil for medicine, *jícaras,* wood crafts	Host is *Acacia angustissima* in savannas	Roys 1931:294 Lundell 1937:62 (host)
Cotinga amabilis	Blue feathers (body and flight feathers)	Adornment	Rain forest	Alvarez del Toro 1971:144 Davis 1972:124 Haemig (personal communication)
Cyanerpes cyaneus L.	Blue feathers (body plummage)	Adornment	Probably in rain forests or open woods	Haemig (personal communication) Van Tyne 1935:43 Davis 1972:207
Dasyprocta punctata	Claws, blood	Medicine	Tropical forests, nocturnal predominately, usually singly	Roys 1931:62 Leopold 1959:391–392
Didelphis marsupialis	Tail	Medicine	Including tropical forests, usually nocturnal and singly	Roys 1931:195–196
	Fur	Adornment		Leopold 1959:326–328
	Flesh	Food		
Felis concolor	Pelt	Adornment	Including rain forests, generally nocturnal and solitary	Roys 1931:330, 70
	Fat	Medicine		Leopold 1959:476–482
Felis onca	Pelt	Adornment	Tropical forests,	Roys 1931:70

	Fat	Medicine	nocturnal and usually solitary	Leopold 1959:464–470
Felis pardalis and *F. Wiedii*	Pelts[a]	Adornment	Rain forest (fairly common at Uaxactún)	Alvarez del Toro 1971:217 Davis 1972:186 Smithe 1959:7 Van Tyne 1935:45
Habia gutturalis	Red feathers	Adornment	Rain forest	Alvarez del Toro 1971:232 Davis 1972:214
Heloderma horridum	Animal's ashes	Medicine	Often in houses	Roys 1931:114, 333
Heterogeomys torridus Merriam	Excrement	Medicine	Widespread, subterranean	Roys 1931:138
Hystrix mexicanum Kerr. L., *H. prehensilis* Schreb.	Spines, tail	Medicine	Not specified	Roys 1931:198
Iguana iguana	Gall, whole animal's ashes	Medicine	Mainly arboreal in tropical forests near water, solitary	Roys 1931:167, 186–187 Alvarez del Toro 1972:59–62
Mazama gouazouibra	Bladder, blood, dung	Medicine	Rain forests, singly or perhaps in pairs	Roys 1931:342 Leopold 1959:513—518
Melipondae	Honey Wax	Sweetener, medicine Mastic, medicine	Rain forests, in swarms	Roys 1931:64 Swartz 1945, 1948
Myotis californicus Aud. and Bach.[a]	Wing tip, blood	Medicine		Roys 1931:343
Odocoileus virginianus	Antlers, bezoar stones, tail, hair, dung	Medicine	Secondary growth	Roys 1931:329, 70, 206 Leopold 1959:507—513
Tamandua tetradactyla mexicana Saussure.	Toes, claws	Medicine	Rain forest, arboreal possibly solitary	Roys 1931:93 Leopold 1959:337–338
Tangavius aeneus	Whole bird	Medicine		Roys 1931:64 Davis 1972:188
Chert or flint	Raw material	Tools	In nodules throughout limestone bedrock	Culbert 1973:1

and probably did not involve volumes of any one item.[6] In their general characteristics these items are analogous to the commodities of Oriental and African origins of paramount importance in early medieval Mediterranean trade, and significant importance in the commercial life of the late Middle Ages (López and Raymond 1955:108).

The resources that have been identified as possible export commodities of Lowland Maya origin are derived for the most part from species that occur in the tropical forest and/or in successional stages of that forest. Since a basic premise of my model is that these products gained special significance because they figured in an early exchange system, it is necessary to consider their distribution patterns in time and space. Such patterns would have had significant effects on the organization of their human procurers (e.g., see Flannery 1968). The distributional characteristics of the potential commodities are reported, if known, in Tables 1 and 2. Although the distributional data are spotty, a characteristic pattern can be detected. Moreover, this pattern is more generally typical of rain forest ecosystems, and for this reason, I contend that it exerted a causal effect on the organizational characteristics of the early Maya.

Organizational Characteristics of Tropical Forests and Their Procurement Systems

The organizational characteristics of tropical rain forest ecosystems have been described by ecologists, beginning significantly with the work of Richards (1952). It is helpful to conceptualize the tropical forest ecosystem as a three-dimensional structure through which energy is cycling. The major structural characteristics of this system include (1) high species diversity, (2) relatively large amounts of total biomass perched high above ground level at the canopy layers, and (3) low density of individuals of a single species, with uniform spacing of conspecifics. The major functional characteristics of energy flow within the ecosystemic structure are (1) high rates of primary productivity, (2) high complexity of flow channel networks expressed by feeding relationships and low volumes of energy within each channel, and (3) the absence of sharp energy flow periodicities, other than those of the diurnal cycle. I have summarized some salient characteristics in the following.

1. Structural characteristics
   a. Species diversity
      exceptionally high (Jensen 1975:46; Longman and Jeník 1974; Greig-Smith *et al.* 1967; Odum 1959:413)

[6] This interpretation may vastly underestimate the trade potential of the resources I am discussing. For example, in the sixteenth century, the two tribute-paying Aztec provinces within the rain forest zone moved a total of over 30,000 handfuls of bird feathers on a yearly basis. Even though this exchange system is later and more complex than the one I am describing, the quantity of feathers is staggering.

human implication: wide diversity of potentially available resources

b. Vertical organization

plant and animal biomass concentrated in upper canopy layers (Odum 1959:371)

great diversity of arboreal species, such as birds (Amadon 1973:276)

human implication: many resources are difficult or impossible to obtain because of their arboreal nature

c. Horizontal organization

plant conspecifics are widely spaced (e.g., Fedorov 1966:9; Jensen 1975:46; Greig-Smith *et al.* 1967:483; Richards 1952; Cain and Castro 1959)

many animal conspecifics are also widely spaced

human implication: procurement of these resources requires wide spacing

2. Functional characteristics

a. Primary production

exceptionally high (Kormandy 1969:Tables 2–5)

human implication: potentially a large amount of energy available in the system

b. Channelization of energy flow

complex web of feeding relationships with relatively small amounts of energy flowing within each channel

human implications: diversification, rather than specialization, is a more appropriate response to unaltered system

c. Periodicities

seasonal variations are not pronounced; diurnal cycles are pronounced

reproductive periodicities tuned to temperature or inherent controls (Odum 1959:413; see also Boulière 1973:288–290) and not closely synchronized

human implications: present scheduling problems (Fedorov 1966:9).

Humans who participate as organisms within the natural ecosystem of a rain forest environment necessarily would be constrained by its characteristic organizational features. What this would mean for human procurers of wild resources is that many resources of potential economic value may be locally present, but each of these is available only in small amounts, and individuals of the same species are widely separated from each other. In addition, periodic events of economic significance, such as fruiting or annual ruts, occur sporadically, rather than being seasonally controlled and easy to predict. The tendencies toward uniformities in spatial distribution and temporal frequency mean that despite the abundance of natural resources within the rain forest environment, the procurement costs of these resources would be relatively high. The time and energy costs of procurement could be minimized if the procurers lived close to the resources, and in relatively small settlements that were widely separated from one another. In a classic paper by Murphy and Steward (1956) a similar close relationship between widely dispersed wild resources, procurement strategies, and settlement patterns has been formulated for specific high-latitude and low-latitude environments.

If the procurement strategies of wild forest products produced tendencies for the Maya population to distribute itself more or less uniformly over the landscape and to maintain low population densities in this initial period, these tendencies were compatible with the agricultural system that they practiced. As has been described by Harris (1972a), the characteristics of the swidden system make it the most land-extensive and least disruptive of natural ecosystems of all the known major forms of agriculture. This is not to say that the ecosystem remains unaffected in regions of swidden farming, but only that the impact is less devastating than is the case with other more intensive agricultural systems.

Accordingly, the procurement systems for both food and wild products for local and nonlocal utilization would produce centrifugal effects in population dispersion and would be compatible with slow rates of population increase. However, if wild resources became commodities in a system of exchange, rather than being utilized only locally, then it is possible that the human organization best suited for procurement would require further modification.

Organizational Characteristics of the Maya Export System

A basic question to answer in modeling an exchange system for the Preclassic Maya is, to what extent was the system centralized? According to Plog (1977:129), a highly centralized exchange system is one in which the flow of commodities converges on a single geographic locus. If the economic system of the Preclassic Maya of the central lowlands involved only transactions between individual trading partners, virtually no centralization would have occurred. In such a system there would be many traders, each of whom would export commodities to neighbors who were recognized trading partners. No professional traders or merchants would have existed, and no major ceremonial exchanges by leaders would have occurred.

The archaeological evidence that would be indicative of the hypothetical system just described would be a lowland regional settlement pattern in which all sites are equivalent in scale and virtually no hierarchical differences are apparent. Moreover, artifacts with highland origins would occur with the same frequencies at all lowland sites.

If, instead of the simple system just discussed, exchange took place either by ceremonial prestations exclusively or by such transactions in addition to barter transactions, then a greater degree of centralization of goods would be present. Within each region, local resources would be moved from their widely dispersed points of origin, to a single locus where bulking would have occurred. Theoretically, these loci would occur at the geographic centers of each of the procurement territories, as long as effort minimization principles were in effect. Other factors, such as the location of transportation routes, would also affect the specific locations of centers.

The empirical evidence necessary to validate the hypothesis that some economic centralization was in effect would be a regional settlement pattern consisting of sites that can be ranked into only a few hierarchical levels. The highest hierarchical level would have only one member, and this site would be located approximately central to the region. Since archaeologists are often unable to determine economic regions on the basis of the distribution of artifacts, this last criterion may be more idealistic than realistic. In addition, the artifacts suspected as having been commodities in ancient exchange systems would manifest distinctly higher frequencies at highest order settlements than at lower order settlements, thus demonstrating the highest order site's nodal positions in the exchange network.

On a macroregional scale, that is, from the perspective of the entire central lowlands, the exchange system I am describing must be considered decentralized because each central place was economically independent and politically autonomous. Validation of this hypothesis would be the iteration of the pattern just described over the entire geographical area and the absence of additional higher order settlements indicative of a greater degree of economic and/or political integration.

I am speculating that the exchange system of the early Maya, perhaps from its inception, involved some form of centralization at the regional level. In no way does this view preclude the possibility that transactions were also made between large numbers of trading partners, but only that this latter mechanism was not the only one operating.

According to my model, each of the central places would have been the point of convergence for both exports and imports. The flow of commodities at each center would have been controlled by central persons, i.e., people "upon whom the exchange of goods and of information focuses" (Renfrew 1975:24). Presumably, the central places, central persons, and economic territories would coincide respectively with administrative centers, political leaders, and political territories; that is, the same sites, persons, and regions would have had similar functional roles in the economic and political systems.

If the impetus for the growth of centers were ultimately tied to an external demand for local resources, then it follows that the earliest centers would have developed near the exterior margins of the forest and along transportation routes. Gradually, similar centers would have arisen in the interior. The current archaeological evidence (Puleston and Puleston 1971; Adams and Culbert 1977) fits the expected pattern, but the data are much too limited to be compelling.

The exchange network expanded over the central lowlands by adding on new units, that is, the process was agglomerative. These economic cum political units were allied by some form of ceremonial exchange. Dalton (1977) has discussed the salient characteristics of this type of economic system. The economic system functioned precisely because of the size of the network, which included not only tropical forest populations, but also populations living in different habitats. I think it is unnecessary to postulate that the highland people directly controlled the exchange system either by means of emissary traders or by an extractive colonial system. A simpler system consisting of a network of dyadic exchanges, but extending over a wide territory, would have sufficed. Such a system would be similar to that described by Hughes (1973, 1977) for New Guinea in which the exchange network encompasses varying physiographical, ecological, and cultural divisions. This network was formed by the interlocking exchange networks of individuals, and the "network itself far exceded the trade area of the most widely distributed goods (Hughes 1973:121)."[7]

Evaluation of the Tropical Forest Export Model

The proposed model specifies that Maya inhabitants were integrated into a viable long-distance exchange system during the earliest occupation that is currently documented archaeologically for the central lowlands. This system involved the two-way flow of commodities between the highlands and the lowlands of southern Mesoamerica. Highland commodities reaching the lowland populations included durable items of mineralogical origin. Of these, it appears that obsidian was moved in the greatest volume, and at present it is the best documented of the known highland exports. Commodities flowing from the lowlands to the highlands were primarily raw materials of organic nature that have not been identified frequently in the archaeological record. The invisibility of these lowland exports in the archaeological record of highland sites is not surprising because organic materials deteriorate rapidly in the humid tropics. Consequently, we cannot expect to directly verify the model by identifying the presence of diverse lowland exports at highland sites. However, I think that it is reasonable to expect that greater care in recovery methods as well as a research focus designed to test the model may eventually result in the recovery of some supporting evidence.

Future research can be designed to maximize the chances of identifying imports of rain forest origin in archaeologic deposits at highland sites. One approach is to employ the use of analogy in order to identify which lowland

[7]Charlton (1978) has previously used the New Guinea case described by Hughes as a model for trade in Preclassic Mesoamerica. He has pointed out that greater sociocultural complexity was present in the Basin of Mexico during the Early Preclassic compared with the New Guinea case, and links this development to an ultimate exchange connection with Olmec centers. He summarizes arguments in favor of considering key sites as gateway sites, that is, loci where for geographical and social reasons, most external exchanges were channeled. I do not expect to find similar gateway centers in the Maya Lowlands because of the absence of necessary geographical constraints.

commodities may leave archaeological traces. I have been pursuing this approach recently by examining the Aztec tribute lists pertaining to the provinces that occurred within the rain forest habitat. The justification of this approach is that the manner of preparing and packaging lowland items for transport to the highlands may have been the same in Aztec times as during the Preclassic period. This operational assumption permits the generation of a list of test implications that would have to be met generally in order to support the proposed model. Failure to meet a few of the test implications would not necessitate the rejection of the model since the tests are not absolute. However, the model can only be considered supported if many of the test implications are met. The research would be best designed so that the largest possible number of specific test implications would be formulated, presumably by means of reference to the largest possible number of relevant analogs.

It is important to emphasize that the basis for formulating a particular analogy should be ecological equivalency rather than historical continuity. This is the primary reason for scrutinizing the documented commodities that flowed from rain forest environments to the Valley of Mexico during the fifteenth century. Also, the proposed analogies should be limited only to the formulation of test implications for the documentation of specific commodities and should not be uncritically extended to other aspects of the exchange system since there is every reason to suspect the evolution of this system over time.

An example of the type of test implication that can be formulated by this approach concerns the movement of spotted cat pelts from the rain forest environment to highland sites. According to the artistic depictions in the *Matrícula de Tributos* (Castillo Farreras 1974), pelts of spotted cats retained head, tail, and paw bones, but the remainder of the skelton was removed. Hence the archaeological test implication of the hypothesis that spotted cat skins were moved from the rain forest to upland communities would be the recovery in highland archaeological sediments of *Felis* spp. head, tail, and foot bones but, significantly, not other skeletal parts.

This example is illuminating because a particularly promising method of testing the model may rely on faunal analysis. Test implications can often be generated that stipulate the presence of some bones but the absence of others from the same rain forest animal. Roys (1931:208), for example, reports that at the time of contact, macaw wings had recognized medicinal value. This observation permits the test implication that if this item figured as a commodity, macaw wings, rather than whole skeletons, will be found in upland archaeological deposits. It is encouraging to note that macaw wing bones have been reported from Early Preclassic period deposits in the Valley of Oaxaca (Flannery and Winter 1976:39), thus providing a small piece of support for the general model. Many more bits of confirming evidence must be assembled before the model can be considered validated.

In addition to a careful and systematic search for evidence of lowland imports at highland sites, it may be possible to generate testable hypotheses based on other considerations. Lathrap (1973) offers a provocative example of such an approach. In an article in which he discusses the problem of archaeologically invisible commodities in the rain forest of South America, Lathrap suggests that the production of flour and bread from bitter manioc enabled the development of long trading expeditions. These foods are compact, transportable, and suitable for long-term storage and are documented ethnographically as being used as provisions in long-term military and trading expeditions. Since the processing of bitter manioc can be deduced reliably from artifactual remains (e.g., by the presence of *budares),* Lathrap contends that the earliest presence of these remains signals the beginnings of extensive trade expeditions in Amazonia. Although I cannot generate an equally plausible and persuasive argument for the tropical forest region in Mesoamerica, this type of approach may prove productive in the future.

Summary

It has been my purpose in this chapter to describe a hypothetical model of Preclassic society in the central lowlands. The fundamental base of the model is that rain forest environments generally yield a variety of commodities that are highly valued for their intrinsic properties. The oils, spices, dyes, feathers, fibers, pelts, and medicines of the rain forest of the world have elicited vigorous interest on the part of non–rain forest peoples throughout recorded history. The proposed model specifies a comparable interest among the upland neighbors of the rain-forest-dwelling Preclassic period Maya. According to the model, the procurement and centralization of forest items led to a specific form of social organization that can be viewed as a compromise between centripetal and centrifugal demographic tendencies. The initial manifestation of this system was the foundation for the Classic period system that eventually emerged. I have not attempted to explain the changes that occurred as the initial system evolved through time. Instead, I have focused on describing a model of the initial system. This model is based on very little empirical evidence, and its validity has yet to be established.

Acknowledgments

I am grateful for the contributions of Linda Hail and the late Linda Eng Jolly in researching some aspects of the floral resources in the central lowlands. Thomas Charlton was kind enough to share some of his ideas on Preclassic trade and also referred me to the useful article by Hughes (1973).

References

Adams, Richard E. W., and T. Patrick Culbert
1977 The origins of civilization in the Maya Lowlands. In *The Origins of Maya Civilization,* edited by Richard E. W. Adams, pp. 3–24. Albuquerque, Univ. of New Mexico Press.

Alvarez del Toro, Miguel
1971 *Las aves de Chiapas.* Tuxtla Gutiérrez, Mexico, Estado de Chiapas.
1972 *Los reptiles de Chiapas.* Tuxtla Gutiérrez, Mexico, Estado de Chiapas.
Amadon, Dean
1973 Birds of the Congo and Amazon forests: A comparison. In *Tropical Forest Ecosystems in Africa and South Africa: A Comparative Review,* edited by Betty J. Meggers, Edward S. Ayensu, and W. Donald Duckworth, pp. 267–277. Washington, D. C., Smithsonian Press.
Baker, Herbert G.
1965 The evolution of the cultivated kapok tree: A probable West African product. In *Ecology and Economic Development in Tropical Africa,* edited by David Brokensha, pp. 185–216. Research Series No. 9, Institute of International Studies, Univ. of California, Berkeley.
de Benítez, Ana M.
1974 *Pre-Hispanic Cooking.* Mexico, Euroamericanas Klaus Thiele.
Bourlière, François
1973 The comparative ecology of rain forest mammals in Africa and tropical America: Some introductory remarks. In *Tropical Forest Ecosystems in Africa and South America: A Comparative Review,* edited by Betty J. Meggers, Edward S. Ayensu, and W. Donald Duckworth, pp. 279–292. Washington, D. C., Smithsonian Institution Press.
Cain, Stanley A., and G. M. de Oliveira Castro
1959 *Manual of vegetation analysis.* New York, Harper.
Carnegie Institute of Washington
1940 Botany of the Maya area: Miscellaneous papers XIV–XXI. *Carnegie Institute of Washington, Publication* 522, Washington, D.C.
Castillo Farreras, Victor M.
1974 Matrícula de tributos: comentarios, paleografia y versión. In *Historia de México,* Fasciculos 27–30, pp. 231–296. México, D.F., Salvat Editores de Mexico.
Charlton, Thomas H.
1978 Formative trade and cultural transformations in the Basin of Mexico. In *Codex Wauchope: A Tribute Roll,* edited by Marco Giardino, Barbara Edmonson, and Winifred Creamer. Human Mosaic No. 12:121–129 Tulane Univ.
Clark, John E.
1979 Lithic assemblage of La Libertad, Chiapas, Mexico. Paper presented at the International Congress of Americanists, Vancouver, B. C.
Correll, Donovan S.
1953 *Vanilla*—Its botany, history, cultivation and economic import. *Economic Botany* 7:291–358.
Covich, Alan P.
1978 A reassessment of ecological stability in the Maya area: Evidence from lake studies of early agricultural impacts on biotic communities. In *Pre-Hispanic Maya Agriculture,* edited by Peter D. Harrison and B. L. Turner II, pp. 145–156. Albuquerque, Univ. of New Mexico Press.
Cowgill, Ursula M., and G. Evelyn Hutchinson
1963a Ecological and geochemical archaeology in the Southern Maya Lowlands. *Southwestern Journal of Anthropology* 19:267–286.
1963b El Bajo de Santa Fe. *Transactions of the American Philosophical Society* 53 (Part 7):1–51.
1966 The chemical history of Laguna de Petenxil. *Memoirs of the Connecticut Academy of Arts and Sciences* 17:121–126.
Culbert, T. Patrick
1973 Introduction: A prologue to Classic Maya culture and the problem of its collapse. In *The Classic Maya Collapse,* edited by T. Patrick Culbert, pp. 3–19. Albuquerque, Univ. of New Mexico Press.

Dalton, George
1977 Aboriginal economies in stateless societies. In *Exchange Systems in Prehistory,* edited by Timothy K. Earle and Jonathon E. Ericson, pp. 191–212. New York, Academic Press.
Davis, L. Irby
1972 *A Field Guide to the Birds of Mexico and Central America.* Austin, Univ. of Texas Press.
Deevey, Edward S., Jr., Don S. Rice, Mark Brenner, and M. J. Flannery
1978 Classic Maya impact on a lacustrine environment. Paper presented at the Society for American Archaeology Meetings, Tucson, Arizona.
Dillon, Brian D.
1975 Notes on trade in ancient Mesoamerica. In *Contributions of the University of California Archaeological Research Facility, No. 24: Three Papers on Mesoamerican Archaeology,* pp. 80–135. Berkeley, Univ. of California Press.
Fedorov, A. A.
1966 The structure of the tropical rain forest and speciation in the humid tropics. *Journal of Ecology* 54(1):1–11.
Flannery, Kent V.
1968 Archaeological systems theory and early Mesoamerica. In *Anthropological Archaeology in the Americas,* edited by Betty J. Meggers, pp. 67–86. Washington, D.C., Anthropological Society.
Flannery, Kent V., and Marcus Winter
1976 Analyzing household activities. In *The Early Mesoamerican Village,* edited by Kent V. Flannery, pp. 34–47. New York, Academic Press.
Gates, William (translator)
1939 *The de la Cruz-Badiano Aztec Herbal of 1552.* Baltimore, The Maya Society.
Greig-Smith, P., M. P. Austin, and T. C. Whitmore
1967 The application of quantitative methods to vegetation survey: Part I, association analysis and principal component ordination of rain forest. *Journal of Ecology* 55(2):483–503.
Hammond, Norman *et al.*
1979 The earliest Lowland Maya: Definition of the Swasey Phase. *American Antiquity* 44(1):92–110.
Harris, David R.
1972a Swidden systems and settlement. In *Man, Settlement and Urbanism,* edited by Peter J. Ucko, Ruth Tringham, and G. W. Dimbleby, pp. 245–262. London, Duckworth.
1972b The origins of agriculture in the Tropics. *American Scientist* 60:180–193.
Hughes, Ian
1973 Stone-age trade in the New Guinea inland: Historical geography without history. In *The Pacific in Transition: Geographical Perspectives on Adaptation and Change,* edited by Harold Brookfield, pp. 97–126. New York, St. Martin's Press.
1977 New Guinea Stone Age trade. *Terra Australis* 3, Department of Prehistory, Research School of Pacific Studies, The Australian National Univ.
Jensen, Daniel H.
1975 *Ecology of plants in the tropics.* The Institute of Biology's Studies in Biology No. 58. London, Edward Arnold.
Kormandy, Edward J.
1969 *Concepts of ecology.* Englewood Cliffs, New Jersey, Prentice-Hall.
Lathrap, Donald W.
1973 The antiquity and importance of long-distance trade relationships in the moist tropics of Pre-Columbian South America. *World Archaeology* 5(2):170–186.
Leopold, A. Starker
1950 Vegetation zones of Mexico. *Ecology* 31:507–520.
1959 *Wildlife of Mexico: The Game Birds and Mammals.* Berkeley, Univ. of California Press.
Longman, K. A., and J. Jeník
1974 *Tropical Forest and Its Environment.* London, Longman Group.

López, Robert S., and Irving W. Raymond
1955 *Medieval Trade in the Mediterranean World.* New York, Columbia Univ. Press.
Lundell, Cyrus L.
1937 The vegetation of Petén. *Carnegie Institution of Washington Publication* 478, Washington, D. C.
1938 Plants probably utilized by the Old Empire Maya of Petén and adjacent lowlands. *Papers of the Michigan Academy of Science,* Part I:37–56. Ann Arbor, Michigan.
MacNeish, Richard S.
1978 *The science of archaeology?* North Scituate, Massachusetts, Duxbury Press.
Miller, Arlene V.
1976 Arti-fact or fiction?: The lithic objects from Richmond Hill, Belize. In *Maya Lithic Studies: Papers From the 1976 Belize Field Symposium,* edited by Thomas R. Hester and Norman Hammond, pp. 119–135. Special Report No. 4, Center for Archaeological Research. Univ. of Texas, San Antonio.
Moholy-Nagy, Hattula
1976 Spatial distribution of flint and obsidian artifacts at Tikal, Guatemala. In *Maya Lithic Studies: Papers from the 1976 Belize Field Symposium,* edited by Thomas R. Hester and Norman Hammond, pp. 91–108. Special Report No. 4, Center for Archaeological Research. Univ. of Texas at San Antonio.
Murphy, Robert F., and Julian H. Steward
1956 Tappers and trappers: Parallel process in acculturation. *Economic Development and Cultural Change* IV:335–355.
Nelson, Fred W., Kirk K. Nielson, Nolan F. Mangelson, Max W. Hill, and Ray T. Matheny
1977 Preliminary studies of the trace element composition of obsidian artifacts from Northern Campeche, Mexico. *American Antiquity* 42(2):209–225.
Nelson, Fred W., Raymond V. Sidrys, and Richard D. Holmes
1978 Trace element analysis by x-ray fluorescence of obsidian artifacts from Guatemala and Belize. In Excavations at Seibal, Department of Petén, Guatemala. *Memoirs of the Peabody Museum of Archaeology and Ethnology,* Harvard University, Vol. 14, Nos. 1, 2, and 3:153–161.
Odum, Eugene P.
1959 *Fundamentals of ecology.* Philadelphia and London, Saunders.
O'Gorman, Helen
1961 *Mexican Flowering Trees and Plants.* Mexico City, Ammex Associados.
Parsons, Lee A., and Barbara J. Price
1971 Mesoamerican trade and its role in the emergence of civilization. In Observations on the Emergence of Civilizations in Mesoamerica, edited by Robert F. Heizer and John A. Graham, pp. 169–195. *Contributions of the University of California Archaeological Research Facility, No.* 11.
Plog, Fred
1977 Modeling economic exchange. In *Exchange Systems in Prehistory,* edited by Timothy K. Earle and Jonathan E. Ericson, pp. 127–140. New York, Academic Press.
Puleston, D. E.
1975 Richmond Hill: A probable early man site in the Maya Lowlands. *Actas del 41 Congreso Internacional de Americanistas* :522–33. Mexico.
Puleston, Dennis E., and Olga Stavrakis Puleston
1971 An ecological approach to the origins of Maya civilization. *Archaeology* 24(4):330–337.
Rathje, William L.
1971 The origin and development of Lowland Classic Maya civilization. *American Antiquity* 36(3):275–285.
Rathje, William L., David A. Gregory, and Frederick M. Wiseman
1978 Trade models and archaeological problems: Classic Maya examples. In Mesoamerican Communication Routes and Cultural Contacts, edited by Thomas A. Lee, Jr., and Carlos

Navarrete, pp. 147–175. *Papers of the New World Archaeological Foundation, Number* 40, Brigham Young University, Provo, Utah.

Renfrew, Colin
1975 Trade as action at a distance: Questions of integration and communication. In *Ancient Civilization and Trade,* edited by Jeremy A. Sabloff and C. C. Lamberg-Karlovsky, pp. 3–59. Albuquerque, Univ. of New Mexico Press.

Rice, Don Stephen
1976 *The historical ecology of Lakes Yaxhá and Sacnab, El Petén, Guatemala.* Unpublished Ph.D. dissertation, Department of Anthropology, Pennsylvania State Univ. Univ. Microfilms, Ann Arbor, Michigan.

Richards, P. W.
1952 *The Tropical Rain Forest: An Ecological Study.* Cambridge, England, Univ. Press.

Rovner, Irwin
1976 Pre-Columbian Maya development of utilitarian lithic industries: The broad perspective from Yucatán. In *Maya Lithic Studies: Papers from the 1976 Belize Field Symposium,* edited by Thomas R. Hester and Norman Hammond, pp. 41–53. Special Report No. 4, Center for Archaeological Research, Univ. of Texas at San Antonio.

Roys, Ralph L.
1931 *The Ethno-Botany of the Maya.* The Tulane University of Louisiana Middle America Research Series Publication No. 2. New Orleans, Louisiana ISHI Reprints on Latin America and the Caribbean, Institute for the Study of Human Issues, Philadelphia, Pennsylvania.

Shook, Edwin M.
1951 The present status of research on the Pre-Classic horizons in Guatemala. In *Civilizations of Ancient America,* edited by Sol Tax, pp. 93–100. Chicago, Aldine.

Sidrys, Raymond
1977 Mass-distance measures for the Maya obsidian trade. In *Exchange Systems in Prehistory,* edited by Timothy K. Earle and Jonathan E. Ericson, pp. 91–107. New York, Academic Press.

Smithe, Frank B.
1959 *Birds of Tikal.* 645 West 44 Street, New York 36, N. Y., private publication.

Standley, Paul C.
1924 *Trees and Shrubs of Mexico,* Vol. 23, Part 4. Washington, D. C., Smithsonian Institution.

Swartz, Herbert F.
1945 The wax of stingless bees (Meliponidae) and the uses to which it has been put. *Journal of the New York Entomological Society* 53:137–144.
1948 Stingless bees (Meliponidae) of the Western Hemisphere. *Bulletin of the American Museum of Natural History.* Vol. 90, New York.

Thompson, J. Eric S.
1970 Trade relations between Maya Highlands and Lowlands. In *Maya History and Religion,* pp. 124–158. Norman, Univ. of Oklahoma Press.

Tourtellot, Gair, and Jeremy A. Sabloff
1972 Exchange systems among the ancient Maya. *American Antiquity* 37(1):126–135.

Turner, B. L., II
1978a Ancient agricultural land use in the central Maya Lowlands. In *Pre-Hispanic Maya Agriculture,* edited by Peter D. Harrison and B. L. Turner II, pp. 163–183. Albuquerque, Univ. of New Mexico Press.
1978b The development and demise of the swidden thesis of Maya agriculture. In *Pre-Hispanic Maya Agriculture,* edited by Peter D. Harrison and B. L. Turner II, pp. 13–22. Albuquerque, Univ. of New Mexico Press.

Turner, B. L. II and Peter D. Harrison (editors)
1978 Implications from agriculture for Maya prehistory. In *Pre-Hispanic Maya Agriculture,* pp. 339–373. Albuquerque, Univ. of New Mexico Press.

Van Tyne, Josselyn
1935 The birds of northern Petén, Guatemala. *Miscellaneous Publications No.* 27, Museum of Zoology, Univ. of Michigan, Ann Arbor.
Vayda, Andrew
1969 Expansion and warfare among swidden agriculturalists. In *Environment and Cultural Behavior: Ecological Studies in Anthropology,* edited by Andrew P. Vayda, pp. 202–220. Garden City, New York, American Museum Source Books in Anthropology.
Wiseman, F.
1975 The earliest Maya. Paper presented at the 40th Annual Meeting of the Society for American Archaeology, Dallas, Texas.

II
Archaeological Investigations of Preclassic and Classic Maya Subsistence

3

Prehistoric Agricultural Systems in El Salvador

Payson D. Sheets

Introduction

ALTHOUGH the cultural historical framework of the past three millennia for El Salvador is fairly well known (cf. Sharer 1978), little is known about ancient agricultural features, practices, and cultigens. Research during the past few years in central and western El Salvador has recently contributed significant information, and there are indications that future research should yield extraordinarily detailed data. Two volcanic eruptions are now known to have preserved agricultural fields, and as archaeologists learn how to exploit the preservative nature of volcanic deposits, the nature of prehistoric agricultural knowledge should change from a condition of famine to one of feast.

In general, the relative scale of agricultural features directly affects their rate of recovery. Large-scale features, such as terraces, raised fields, canals, dams, and reservoirs, are becoming quite well known in the Maya Highlands and Lowlands. For example, Matheny and Gurr (1979) document a variety of large-scale water control features in semiarid Chiapas. These macrofeatures were constructed for multiyear use, tend to be extensive, and often preserve well. At the other end of the scale are the microfeatures, such as maize mounds, small ridges, beds, and pits, constructed for use only during a single growing season. Such deliberately evanescent microtopographic features are rarely preserved from prehistory in the Maya area or elsewhere because they are small and fragile and are usually destroyed during the following growing season. When they ARE preserved, it is because of unusual depositional conditions.

The purposes which traditional Mesoamerican agriculturalists had in constructing such microtopographic features include control of soil erosion, crop protection, water conservation and retention, and aeration (Wilken 1977). The

ISBN 0-12-259780-X

specific empirical effects of various slope management schemes remain controversial.

El Salvador (Figure 1, inset) lies within the latitudinal tropics, and its location on the Pacific drainage results in a tropical monsoon climate of alternating wet and dry seasons ('Aw' in the Köppen system). Fully 90% of the moisture falls during the May–October rainy season; mean annual precipitation for most of the country is between 1,500 and 2,000 mm. Rainfall from year to year is quite variable, causing problems for agriculturalists in crop growth and erosion. This variability is indicated by the 300-mm standard deviation in annual rainfall in San Salvador.

Most archaeologists refer to the El Salvador area as the "Southeast Maya Highlands," but its highland or lowland nature needs to be examined here. Virtually all Precolumbian settlements were located below 1,000 m, placing aboriginal habitation within *"tierra caliente."* Daugherty's reconstruction (1969) of the original flora matches the Petén much more closely than it does the highland forests of southern Guatemala–Chiapas. Tsukada and Deevey (1967) found much the same in their palynological study of the highlands and lowlands. In comparing Lakes Izabal at sea level, Güija at 426 m, Cuzcachapa at 650 m, and Amatitlán at 1186 m, they found Cuzcachapa in El Salvador to be much closer in flora to Izabal than to the highlands near Guatemala City. Güija was unusual because of dryness, and xerophytic species predominated there. The floor of the Zapotitán Valley, with its elevation of 400 to 450 m and 1,700 mm of precipitation, should be placed within the category of seasonal, humid *"tierra caliente."*

So—despite the hilly topography and the fact that it has been so often called the Southeast Maya Highlands—ecologically, the lower, inhabited areas of El Salvador have more in common with the Maya Lowlands. An implication of this includes the lessened adjustments, for example, of Classic period immigrants coming to El Salvador from the Petén–Belize area.

Cultural History and Agricultural Systems

The main section of this chapter examines the evidence for agricultural systems in Prehistoric El Salvador within a cultural historical framework. We begin at about 1200 B.C. with the first known sedentary agricultural settlement known in El Salvador. Almost nothing is known about early hunter–gatherer exploitation of wild resources in the Paleo-Indian period or in the agricultural transition period, known as the Archaic period (if there was one in El Salvador). The period names and dates are taken from Sharer (1978) unless otherwise noted.

EARLY PRECLASSIC PERIOD, 1200–900 B.C.

Chalchuapa apparently was colonized in about 1200 B.C. by expanding maize-based agriculturalists from the Chiapas–Guatemalan Pacific coastal plain.

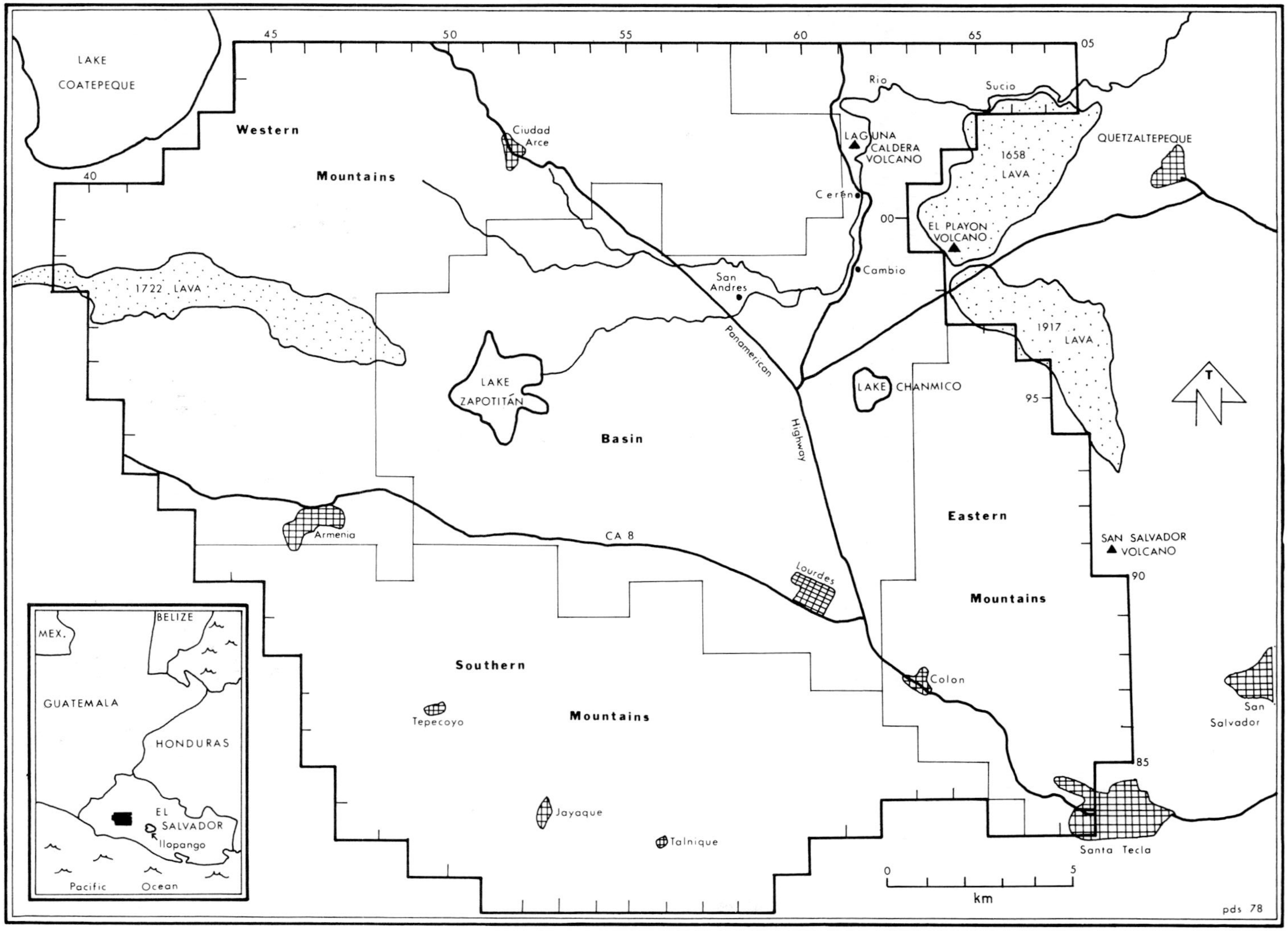

FIGURE 1. *Map of the Zapotitán Valley, El Salvador, with the 1978 Protoclassic Project research area outlined. Note the location of Cerén site and Laguna Caldera Volcano in northeastern corner.*

Indirect and admittedly weak evidence of a reliance on seed crops (probably maize as a staple) is provided by the recovery of an abundance of *manos* and *metates* that date to the earliest occupation. Both root crop and tree crop cultivation are possible at this time, but there is no evidence whatsoever of their actual cultivation. Chalchuapa probably was an egalitarian farming village producing its own food as well as provisioning for the traders dealing in Ixtepeque obsidian, hematite, jade, and other commodities.

MIDDLE PRECLASSIC PERIOD, 900–400 B.C.

It is during the Middle Preclassic period that Chalchuapa grew considerably, and probably crossed the threshold into a chiefdom. Numerous direct Olmec connections can be observed in ceramics, figurines, sculpture, and architecture. Structure E-3-1 reached 20 m in height, and was one of the earliest pyramids of that size anywhere in Mesoamerica. It may have been conical in form. It is likely that primary subsistence was still maize-based at this time, but the evidence for this is no better than that for Early Preclassic subsistence.

Toward the end of the period there is evidence of settlement in eastern El Salvador. Andrews (1976) dates Quelepa's earliest (Uapala) phase to ca. 500 B.C.–A.D. 150. He believes maize agriculture was practiced, as evidenced by the presence of *comales, manos,* and *metates.* He interprets the presence of dart points and deer bones as evidence of hunting.

LATE PRECLASSIC PERIOD 400 B.C.–A.D. 300

The Late Preclassic was a time of population growth, economic expansion, vitality, and rapid cultural change in the southern and southeastern Maya area. A number of large chiefdoms or small states occupied El Salvador, each serving as a primary regional center for goods and services.

For the first time in reviewing the cultural history, specific, direct evidence of agriculture can be cited. Maize agriculture is confirmed at Chalchuapa by the discovery of a carbonized corn cob in sealed structural fill. Three sites have preserved microtopographic features.

Two of the sites are roadcuts where small ridges are exposed. At km 35 along the Opico Highway (1 km southeast of the Cerén site), agricultural ridges are preserved under volcanic ash from the Ilopango eruption (Figure 2). At km 9 along the Panchimalco highway, similar small field ridges were buried by Ilopango ash and sectioned by a bulldozer (Figure 3). Probably, the fields were not irrigated, but rather were dryland farmed, relying on rainfall for moisture. Ridge size is the same as contemporary nonirrigated maize ridges made by traditional agriculturalists in the southern Maya area, and it is highly probable that these ancient ridges were used for maize as well. The volcanic ash dates both of them to the third century A.D.

Also preserved under the Ilopango ash is a ridged field that probably was irrigated. Earnest (1976) excavated 176 m^2 of ridges, each spaced about a meter apart. A thin zone of microsiltation and sorting in the swales, lacking in the

FIGURE 2. *(A) Late Preclassic agricultural field, (B) buried by Ilopango volcanic ash and (C) later Laguna Caldera eruption. The ridges probably were "maize rows" for nonirrigated corn cultivation. Location: Km 35 on Opico Highway, near the Cerén site.*

FIGURE 3. *Late Preclassic agricultural field buried by Ilopango volcanic ash at Km 9 on the Panchimalco Highway. Fieldworker Bill Loker points to contact between a field ridge and the Ilopango ash. These ridges probably were for corn and were not irrigated.*

roadcut sites, was found at Earnest's Río Grande site, indicating that these fields were irrigated. The ridges seem too large for maize, and I suggest the possibility that cotton was cultivated as a cash crop here.

The agent of agricultural preservation for the archaeologist at these sites was the agent of agricultural destruction for the aboriginal inhabitants: the explosive eruption of the Ilopango Volcano. The eruption, radiocarbon dated to A.D. 260 ± 114 (a composite of nine MASCA-corrected dates), probably blasted more than 40 km^3 of tephra (i.e. volcanic ash, pumice, etc., that is airborne) into the air, which fell in thick deposits close to the source. Deposits over 50 m thick have been measured close to the vent; it is 9 m thick at 15 km, and it is about 1 m thick as far as 75 km away. Most people within 10 to 20 km of the vent would have been killed, but most people beyond that, but within a radius of 100 km, probably survived the initial ash fall. Agricultural damage by the sterile ash layer would have exceeded their technological capacity to adjust, thus migration probably was chosen as the most common solution.

Is there any evidence of where the migrants may have gone? I believe there is because artifacts characteristic of the southeast Maya area prior to the eruption do show up as intrusive in the indigenous tradition at many Maya Lowland sites. A population increase in a circumscribed area is frequently known to promote agricultural intensification as well as centralization of authority and diversification of social ranking or class, and I believe that one effect of the eruption and migration was to accelerate these processes, which were ongoing prior to the eruption, among the Lowland Maya. The immigrants also may have introduced new cultigens or elements of agroeconomic technology to the lowlands, but there is, as yet, no direct evidence of this. A major direct effect apparently was economic, since Tikal seized control of the main long-distance trade route that traversed southern Guatemala to El Salvador in the Preclassic period and rerouted it, trans-Petén, through Tikál during the Classic period. Overall, then, I see the effects of the Ilopango eruption as being catalytic; that is, it accelerated trends that were already underway, rather than introducing fundamentally new artifacts or institutions into the lowlands.

CLASSIC PERIOD A.D. 300–900

In the decades following the Ilopango eruption, the rains began to erode the ash blanket as well as to weather it to form soil. Plant succession would have begun with lichens, followed by mosses, ferns, grasses, and finally, forests. Little is known about faunal recovery, but recent research has resulted in considerable information about human recovery.

Thompson (1970) has documented the Chortí Maya southward expansion from the southern Petén–Southern Belize areas through Copán and Quiriguá, and into northern El Salvador during the late fifth and sixth centuries A.D. Our data from the Zapotitán Valley (Figure 1) both extend Thompson's Chortí migration slightly farther south and substantiate his dating of the movement.

At the Cerén site (Figure 4), the Chortí had established housing and agricul-

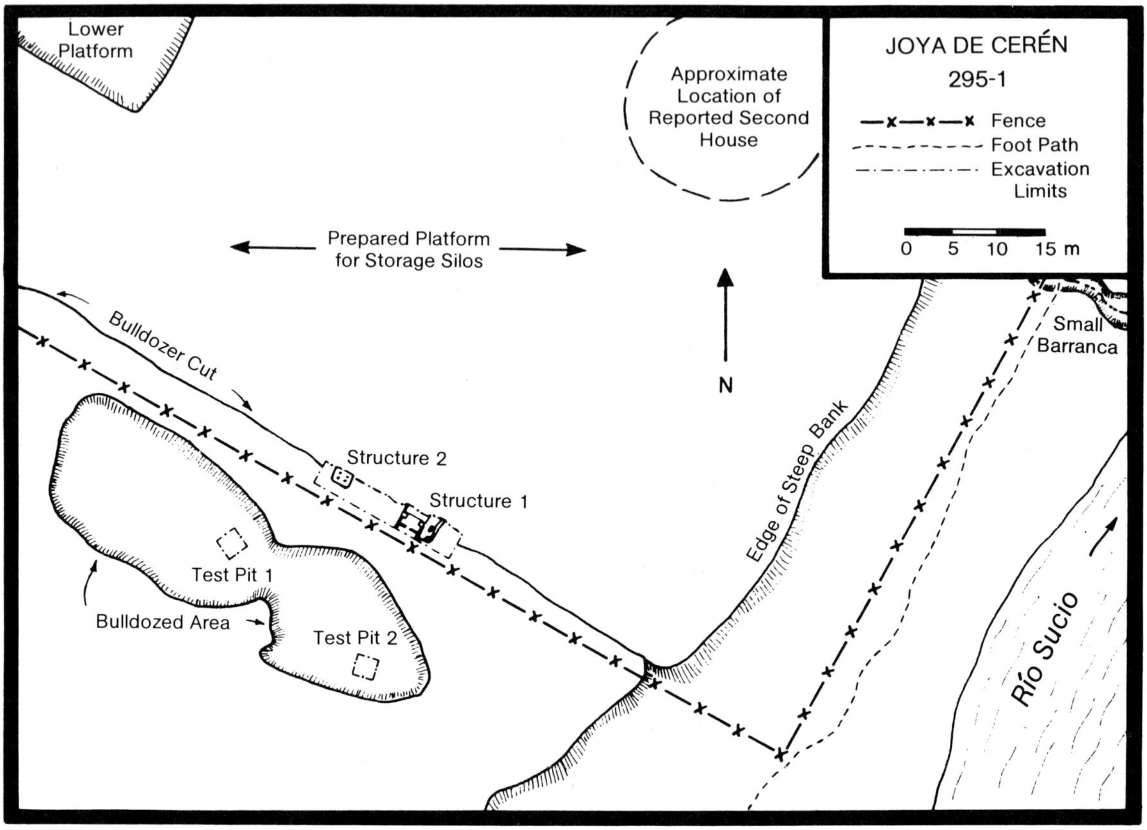

FIGURE 4. *Map of the Cerén site, with farmhouse and outbuilding (structures 1 and 2, respectively) and associated agricultural field (test pits 1 and 2) excavated in 1978. Geophysical survey (see Figure 10) located more houses to the west and southwest. Drawing by C. Zier.*

tural fields by the middle of the sixth century A.D. (Sheets 1979a). They had also established towns and villages of various sizes in other parts of the valley. The soil developing in the Ilopango tephra, in which they planted their cultigens, was a weak one for agriculture since it had yet to develop a high organic content or other needed nutriments. It was weak in a number of important elements for plant growth, including phosphorous, magnesium, potassium, calcium, and manganese. Nitrogen (NO_3 and NH_3) and iron were about average for tropical volcanic soils, and the soil pH was 7.1, so these latter factors did not inhibit plant growth (soils information from Gerald Olson, personal communication 1978). It is clear that, by the sixth century, the soils had not fully recovered from the Ilopango disaster.

The Cerén site consists of a farmhouse, an outbuilding, and an associated agricultural field. These were buried, and extraordinarily well preserved, by the eruption of Laguna Caldera volcano 1.5 km to the north of the site.

The Cerén farmhouse (Figure 5) was constructed by wet-laying clay floors and columns and firing them; then wattle-and-daub walls and a palm thatch roof were added. Preserved inside the house are activity areas such as the pantry with beans stored in pots, weaving areas, a pottery making area, and perhaps a young girl's room. The outbuilding is a fired clay platform, roofed with palm thatch, that was used for the male activities of obsidian tool manufacture and re-sharpening.

At the very end of the 1978 field season two test pits were excavated about 15 m southwest of the structures (Figure 6). At both pits agricultural fields on the slightly weathered Ilopango tephra, contemporary with the farmhouse and outbuilding, were encountered. One of the fields was in fallow, and the other was planted. The Laguna Caldera tephra preserved plants in both test pits as casts; the ash packed around the stalks and leaves had preserved even finer vein and even individual cellular features.

At test pit 1, 2.5 × 2.5 m, six NW–SE field ridges and two NE–SW field ridges were uncovered (Figure 7). The ridges, measuring from top to top, are spaced about 40 cm apart, and stand about 10 cm high. The overall slope of the ground surface is 2.5°. A lava bomb landed hot and exploded on the surface, leaving a deep indentation and destroying features at that location. The lava bombs and other tephra fell at temperatures hotter than 575°C according to progressive thermal demagnetization analysis (Hoblitt, personal communication 1979). The surface was littered with rust-orange plant casts of grasses and leaves, the majority of which were lying flat on the surface although some were still standing (Zier 1979). The field apparently was in fallow, which is not surprising in that the Classic ground surface appears to be an erosional landscape (Hoblitt, personal communication 1978); thus, the more weathered Ilopango ash appears to have been eroded away, likely by soil abuse by the earliest Chortí immigrants. The ridges are low and rounded, and probably date back to the previous rainy season. Vague footprints are preserved here.

Four parallel field ridges were encountered in test pit 2 (Figures 8 and 9). They are 65–70 cm apart, with crests 15–20 cm above the swales. The average slope is 1.5°, draining to the southwest. Fifteen casts of maize stalks and leaves were encountered, spaced an average of 48 cm apart (Zier 1979). Each ridge is slightly enlarged around each maize plant, giving a slight "maize mounding" appearance to the field.

Was the Cerén field irrigated? Two lines of reasoning indicate that it was not. The most direct evidence is a lack of the fine microsorting and siltation that takes place at the bottom of each swale of an irrigated field. The minimal sorting I observed in the Cerén swales appears more likely to be due to ponds formed by rainfall and runoff than to irrigation. The other line of reasoning involves hydrography and topography. There is a notable lack of water sources in the Cerén area that could have been channeled directly into the field. If the Río Sucio were used as a water source, the canal would have had to have begun at least 4 km upstream. There is no evidence of irrigation canals in the valley during the

FIGURE 5. *The Cerén farmhouse and strata. The fertile Preclassic soil is visible at the bottom of the cut, overlain by the white volcanic ash from Ilopango. The ash weathered into a soil, and people recolonized the area, constructing a house at this location. The house was destroyed and preserved by the Laguna Caldera eruption.*

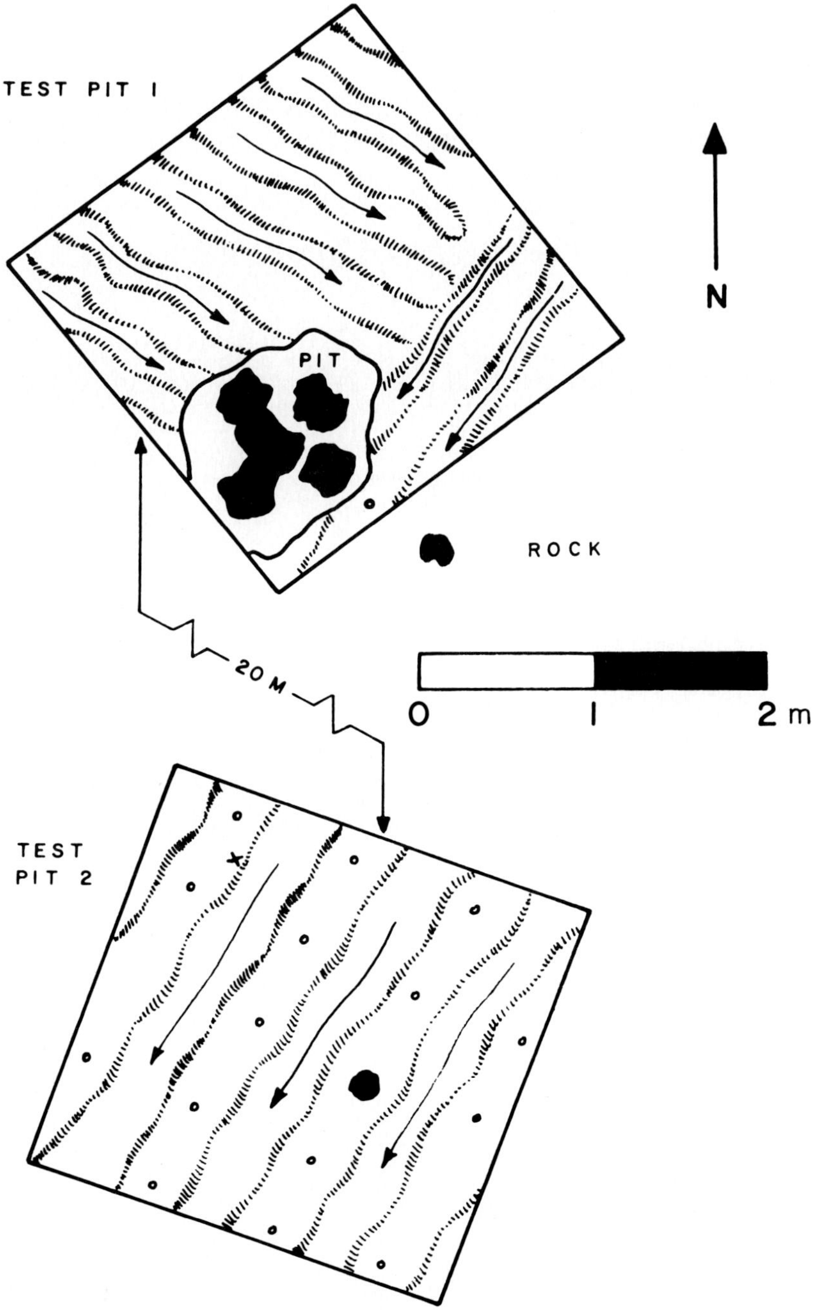

FIGURE 6. *Agricultural field associated with the Cerén house. Test pit 1 contains a ridged field, apparently in fallow. Test pit 2 contains ridges, with corn plants spaced approximately ½ m apart. Because the field apparently was not irrigated and the plants had recently germinated, the Laguna Caldera eruption probably occurred in late May or early June. Hachures delineate cultivation rows; arrows in troughs indicate direction of drainage.* **o**, *Cast of young cultivated plant;* ×, *cast of broad leaf plant (possibly a weed). Drawing by C. Zier.*

FIGURE 7. *Test pit 1, the field apparently was being fallowed when it was buried by the Laguna Caldera tephra. Arrow is 25 cm long. Photograph by C. Zier.*

FIGURE 8. *Test pit 2, the field had been recently planted with corn on the top of the ridges (small flags mark plant locations) when it was buried by the Laguna Caldera tephra. Photograph by C. Zier.*

FIGURE 9. *Closeup of test pit 2. Ridges probably were constructed to retard soil erosion and maximize water retention. The coarse tephra layer above the ridges fell at 575°C.*

Classic period. If the Cerén field was NOT irrigated, and relied on rainfall for moisture, the fact that the plants were only 10–15 cm high indicates that the Laguna Caldera eruption occurred very early in the growing season. Thus, it is an archaeological irony that we know the month of the eruption, late May or early June, but we can only estimate the year.

Soil ridging for maize rows is explained by contemporary Maya traditional agriculturalists as being done for a number of reasons, including moisture retention, drainage of excess moisture, root aeration, and erosion control. While field ridging of lowland swampy tropical soils may be directed toward aeration, I believe aeration was an unlikely objective at Cerén because the soil there was developed by minimal weathering of the very porous tephra of the Ilopango eruption. Moisture retention and erosion control are the most likely objectives.

Moisture retention is indicated by the blocking rows of test pit 1. Drainage to the southeast is blocked by perpendicular ridges, allowing more "effective moisture" to sink into the soil.

The Cerén field may be considered a "high-performance *milpa*" (Wilken 1971:442). The term milpa in the Maya Lowlands implies swidden agriculture, but in the Highlands a cornfield or 'milpa' may need little or no fallowing, and it may undergo considerable interplanting. Numerous indigenous farmers in the Maya Highlands continue to ridge their milpas and to plant in the tops of the ridges using hoes and digging sticks formally analogous to prehistoric implements. An example is provided by the hand-hoed terraces at San Miguel Milpas Altas, near Antigua, Guatemala (Wilken 1971:434). Maize is planted on the ridges, and the depressions serve as small water reservoirs for rain runoff.

The maize ridges at Cerén are a form of Wilken's (1976) traditional "slope management," and would be classified toward the simpler end of the spectrum he describes. Cerén agriculturalists did not change the overall gradient, which was about 2°. Rather, the ridges are microtopographic features to increase yield. Such careful surface modification of agricultural lands characterizes Mesoamerican traditional farming (Wilken 1977:1). By way of comparison, the broad "*camellones*" ridges (1.5 m wide and 30 cm high) of the western Guatemalan Highlands conserve water, retarding drainage and thus, erosion. The plant density of 41,667 plants per hectare, a figure common in Highland Guatemala, is almost twice the plant density of test pit 2. Plant density in test pit 2, if extrapolated to a hectare for comparative purposes, would be 28,800 plants, and the Cerén density would have to be further decreased if test pit 1 does indeed indicate fallowing during the growing season. The western Guatemalan figure is based on an average of five plants per digging stick hole; yet only one plant germinated and grew per digging stick hole at Cerén. Placing only one seed per hole probably was a response to low soil fertility at Cerén, in part owing to erosion of topsoil and in part because of the minimal weathering of the volcanic ash.

The labor input of Cerén field ridging can be estimated. If the average ridge is 20 cm high, and they are spaced about 60 cm apart, a hectare of prepared field involves moving and shaping approximately 250 m^3 of soil. If a farmer, using traditional implements and human labor only, can move the shape about 8 m^3 of soil a day (Wilken 1976:Table 1), an estimated 31 man-days of work would have been needed to prepare a hectare at Cerén.

Field ridging, of course, is only a part of the entire labor input needed in production. Other activities include planting, weeding, intercropping other cultigens, harvesting, storing, processing, and finally, consuming. An indication of planting effort is available from Stadelman's descriptions (1940:102–103) at Todos Santos and other villages in western Highland Guatemala. At Todos Santos, a family of five needs about 1.2 ha for their annual maize production. Some surplus production is now needed to exchange for other goods, and some families cultivate up to 3 ha. Planting by digging stick involves placing five maize seeds about 8 cm deep, spacing the plantings about 50 cm to 1 m apart. One person can plant almost $\frac{1}{5}$ ha/day. Thus, I would estimate a hectare of the Cerén field represents about five man-days of planting time.

To the best of my knowledge, the Cerén field is the only prehistoric agricultural field yet found in the New World where both the microtopography and the cultivated crops are preserved, but there are other cases of prehistoric microtopographic agricultural features being preserved, such as the Late Preclassic examples from El Salvador mentioned previously. During the recent excavations at Kaminaljuyú, maize mounds (without maize plants) were encountered under Late Preclassic to Middle Classic structures (Reynolds and Cardenas 1973; Bebrich and Wynn 1973). Seele (1973) found a prehistoric highland milpa buried under volcanic ejecta in Puebla, Mexico. The ridge sizes there are very similar to those of Cerén, and they probably were used for maize cultivation. Kelley (1938) excavated a ridged agricultural field at the Macon Plateau site in Georgia, and asserted that it was a cornfield. The ridges were spaced about 40 cm apart and were about 20 cm high. The final comparison is with the ridged agricultural field Berlin *et al.* (1977) encountered in the A.D. 1065 Sunset Crater tephra near Flagstaff, Arizona. It was probably a cornfield and perhaps was intercropped with squash. They suggest a 3.66-m spacing of seed hills similar to that used by the Hopi today. Ridgetops are spaced 3.0–4.5 m apart. It should be noted, here, that the field evidently POSTDATES the tephra fall, and that the thin layer of cinders were used as a mulch.

Wider questions to be answered about the Cerén area are: what is the spacing of farmhouses? and how much agricultural field belonged to each house? Present data indicate that Cerén area farmhouses were spaced about 60 m apart. If we use this tentative figure for calculations, each household would have had only .34 ha surrounding the house for family production. Given the weakness of the Ilopango-derived soil and plant density (each family would have less than 10,000 maize plants), this is not enough area to support one family for a year. I suspect that swidden cultivation of nearby hillslopes or other subsistence alternatives were exploited in some form of an infield–outfield system.

Emplacement of the Cerén tephra from the ca. A.D. 590 ± 90 eruption of Laguna Caldera volcano preserved the farmhouse, outbuilding, agricultural field, and cultigens. The eruption occurred rapidly, with little or no warning, and deeply buried a relatively small area (about 20 km^2). Research is planned for the next few years in excavations of households, farmlands, possible swidden plots on hillslopes, and possibly, a village or town with a ceremonial center. Given our knowledge of Classic period settlement patterns in the area, a village or town probably is buried under the tephra, but no research has been undertaken as of yet to discover them. Recent geophysical research (Figure 10) has encountered anomalies in the field south of the previously excavated structures. Two of these anomalies have been confirmed, by core-drilling in January, 1980, as buried structures. The excavations planned for 1981 have been delayed indefinitely by political violence in El Salvador.

POSTCLASSIC PERIOD, A.D. 900–1532

Most of the archaeological research conducted in El Salvador has concentrated on the Preclassic and Classic periods. The Postclassic has been neglected, and such work as has been done with Postclassic sites has concentrated primarily

FIGURE 10. *Geophysical survey for additional buried Maya houses to the southeast of the 1978 test pits. The ox cart is transporting a ground-penetrating radar antenna (extreme right); inside the ox cart are a gas-powered electrical generator, a graphic recorder, an instrumentation tape recorder, and other instruments. Additional buried houses were discovered, and excavations are planned for the future.*

on architecture. Thus, little is known about Postclassic agriculture. However, ongoing research by a number of scholars (including William Fowler, Jane Kelley, Stanley Boggs, and Karen Bruhns) at the large Early Postclassic site of Cihuatán may alleviate this problem. Preliminary analysis of flotation debris has confirmed maize, squash, and beans as parts of the Postclassic diet, and analyses are continuing (Bruhns, personal communication 1979). Bruhns suspects cotton and cacao were grown extensively at Cihuatán, but there is, as yet, no direct evidence. Phytoliths that resemble manioc bark have been discovered on house floors, but it is unclear whether these are Postclassic or Historic because phytoliths can be transported downward considerable distances in porous soils by rainwater percolation or other agents of disturbance.

Historic agriculture is beyond the scope of this chapter, so I will make only a few general comments. Subsistence agriculturalists throughout the Historic period in El Salvador have focused on seed crops (maize and beans primarily) as primary cultigens, but a significant component of the diet has come from root crops (including manioc and jícama) and tree crops (including ramón, nance, cacao, avocados, and palms). Early Historic records note three plants used for export production; cacao, indigo, and balsam (Browning 1971), and these probably have a considerable time depth in prehistory.

Summary and Conclusions

The most notable characteristic of ethnohistoric and ethnographic descriptions of traditional agriculture in El Salvador is its diversity. Diversity is manifested by the wide variety of seed crops, root crops, and tree crops that were cultivated, as well as by the long list of wild species that were exploited. Hunting of numerous animal species, fishing, and shellfish collecting are known to have been important subsistence components until the past few decades. In the past few decades, most of the wild animals that were originally hunted and consumed have been eliminated from El Salvador. The diversity in species utilized in El Salvador almost matched the variety of specific subsistence technologies used there, with the range of farming techniques used in the Historic period being from very extensive to quite intensive. It is likely that such a diversity in species and in technologies has a considerable antiquity in El Salvador. Presently, only the barest framework of prehistoric El Salvadorean agriculture is known, but research in a number of sites in the country is beginning to fill in that outline with some very detailed knowledge.

Acknowledgments

The assistance of three geologists in reconstructing past volcanic events in El Salvador is gratefully acknowledged: Dr. Virginia Steen-McIntyre of Colorado State University, Dr. Richard

Hoblitt of the U.S. Geological Survey in Denver, and Bill Hart, a graduate student in Geology at Rutgers. Dr. Gerry Olson, of the Agronomy Department at Cornell, has contributed essential fertility analyses of soils of the present and of various periods in the past and his analyses have determined that full soil recovery from the Ilopango disaster has yet to occur. I appreciate Dr. Karen Bruhns' prompt response to my request for recent information about research into agriculture and habitation at the Postclassic site of Cihuatán. The assistance of hardworking field crews, under less than ideal conditions, is gratefully acknowledged. I particularly wish to acknowledge the influence Denny Puleston's fervent interests in paleoagroeconomic matters had on me during my years as a graduate student at the University of Pennsylvania.

References

Andrews V, E. W.
1976 The archaeology of Quelepa, El Salvador. *Middle American Research Institute, Tulane Univ., Publication* 42.
Bebrich, C., and J. Wynn
1973 Mound B-V-6: A Late Formative ceremonial structure. In *Occasional Papers in Anthropology No.* 9 edited by J. Michels, University Park, Pennsylvania State Univ. Press.
Berlin, G., J. Ambler, R. Hevly, and G. Schaber
1977 Identification of a Sinagua agricultural field by aerial thermography, soil chemistry, pollen/plant analysis, and archeology. *American Antiquity* 42:588–600.
Browning, David
1971 *El Salvador: Landscape and Society.* Oxford, England, Clarendon Press.
Daugherty, H. E.
1969 *Man-induced ecologic change in El Salvador.* Unpublished Ph.D. dissertation, Department of Geography, Univ. of California, Los Angeles.
Earnest, H., Jr.
1976 Investigaciones efectuadas por el Proyecto No. 1, Programa de rescate arqueológico Cerrón Grande, en la Hacienda Sta. Barbara, Dpto. de Chalatenango. *Annals of the National Museum* D. Guzmán, 49:57–73.
Jashemski, W.
1973 Large vineyard discovered in ancient Pompeii. *Science* 180:821–830.
Kelley, A. R.
1938 A preliminary report on archeological explorations at Macon, Georgia. *Bureau of American Ethnology Bulletin* 119, Washington, D.C.
Matheny, R., and D. Gurr
1979 Ancient hydraulic techniques in the Chiapas highlands. *American Scientist* 67:441–449.
Reynolds, J., and D. Cardenas
1973 Mound B-V-4: A Late Formative ceremonial structure and middle class residence complex. In *Occasional Papers in Anthropology* No. 9, edited by J. Michels and W. Sanders, University Park, Pennsylvania State Univ. Press.
Seele, E.
1973 Restos de milpas y poblaciones Pre-hispánicas cerca de San Buenaventura Nealticán, Puebla. In *Comunicaciones* No. 7, edited by W. Laner and E. Garmsen. Puebla, Mexico.
Sharer, R. J. (general editor)
1978 *The Prehistory of Chalchuapa, El Salvador.* Vols. 1–3. Philadelphia, Univ. of Pennsylvania Press.
Sheets, P. D.
1979a Environmental and cultural effects of the Ilopango eruption in Central America. In *Volcanic Activity and Human Ecology,* edited by P. Sheets and D. Grayson, pp. 525–564. New York, Academic Press.

1979b Maya recovery from volcanic disasters: Ilopango and Cerén. *Archaeology* 32(3):32–42.

Spencer, J., and G. Hale

1961 The origin, nature, and distribution of agricultural terracing. *Pacific Viewpoint* 2:1–40.

Stadelman, R.

1940 Maize cultivation in northwestern Guatemala. *Contributions to American Anthropology and History, Carnegie Institute Publication No.* 523:83–263.

Thompson, J. E. S.

1970 *Maya History and Religion.* Norman, Univ. of Oklahoma Press.

Tsukada, M., and E. Deevey

1967 Pollen analyses from four lakes in the southern Maya area of Guatemala and El Salvador. In *Quaternary Paleoecology,* edited by E. J. Cushing and H. E. Wright, pp. 303–331. New Haven, Yale Univ. Press.

Wilken, Gene C.

1971 Food producing systems available to the ancient Maya. *American Antiquity* 36:432–448.

1976 Traditional slope management: An analytical approach. Paper presented at a symposium on Hill Lands—Their Effective Use and the Future, Morgantown, West Virginia.

1977 Minor agricultural landforms in Middle America. Paper presented at the Annual Meeting of the Association of American Geographers, Salt Lake City.

Zier, C.

1980 *A Classic-period Maya agricultural field in western El Salvador. Journal of Field Archaeology* 7:65–74.

4

Subsistence and Society in Eastern Yucatán

Peter D. Harrison

Introduction

THIS chapter deals with two separate study areas and, therefore, is presented in two parts. Part I summarizes some results of a settlement survey made in the southern half of Quintana Roo, Mexico in 1972 through 1974 under the auspices of the Royal Ontario Museum. This survey centered on that large zone of Quintana Roo in which few sites appear on distribution maps for the Lowland Maya. The survey provided some concrete conclusions about the ancient demography of this portion of the Yucatán Peninsula. It also resulted in some theoretical conclusions concerning ancient subsistence in this area. Part II deals with a subsequent field study that was addressed directly to the subsistence question. Some of the problems which were raised by the original survey in Quintana Roo have been answered by this newer, more recent fieldwork, but others remain.

The Quintana Roo survey, called the Uaymil Survey, has been partially reported in a variety of papers (Harrison 1972 a, 1972 b, 1974, 1975, 1977, 1978, 1979), but some points which have already been published bear reviewing here as a background for the more recent subsistence study.

For both programs, the original survey in Quintana Roo and the subsequent study in Belize, ceramic testing and analyses were conducted by Robert E. Fry of Purdue University. Similarly, the basic chronological frameworks were established by Dr. Fry's active participation, and the ceramically based dates that are quoted in this paper are the result of his work (Fry 1972).

ISBN 0-12-259780-X

Part I

Of the 110 sites which were recorded in the Uaymil Survey, only 5 are considered to have status as "major centers." Of course, ascription of such status is based on the self-contained comparison of the local "universe," so that these major centers are not on the massive scale of recognized "capitals" in the Petén and elsewhere (Figure 1). Large sites in southern Quintana Roo have a noncentralist scattered distribution, a pattern which seems to be characteristic of Río Bec–Chenes or central Yucatecan sites (Adams 1981). One possible difference in Quintana Roo is that these major centers consist of one large ceremonial center and usually two smaller associated but separate centers. Thus, each major center is part of a nucleated cluster.

For the majority of sites, lack of architectural preservation made it difficult to distinguish between the characteristics of the Río Bec features, as opposed to those of Chenes. Also, elements which are common to both styles are found at the same sites as far north as Chunhuhub and as far east as Lake Bacalar.

At this point, it is necessary to discuss a side issue that is important to the question of architectural affiliations as well as to the relationship of site distributions to the natural depressions known as *bajos.* One result of the survey is recognition of a northern extension of the Petén style of architecture into this part of the Yucatán Peninsula—a culturo-geographic feature that I have referred to elsewhere as the "Petén Corridor." This corridor winds through the southern half of Quintana Roo from the sites of Kohunlich and Tzibanche in the south to near the modern community of Felipe Carrillo Puerto in the north. The significance of this corridor is linked to the distribution of sites around two complexes of bajos. It has been noted previously that nearly all sites in southern Quintana Roo are located within a maximum distance of 1 km from the littorals or edges of these bajos. The Petén Corridor includes the southern complex and all of the sites in association with its borders, excepting the western limits of Bajo Morocoy. Close to the western edge of this bajo is the modern town (and the ancient site of the same name) of Nicolás Bravo, where Río Bec traits dominate in the architecture.

To the north, the corridor curves eastward, avoiding the northern complex of bajos. Surrounding the northerly series of bajos, all sites, from which evidence was retrieved, exhibit only architectural traits of the Central Yucatecan variety, to the exclusion of the Petén style. The survey data terminate somewhat south of Felipe Carrillo Puerto, but it seems quite probable that this culturally intrusive corridor may continue to the northeast to include the site of Muyil (Chunyaxche) near the coast and ultimately reach Coba, where it must surely terminate. These two northern sites, Muyil and Coba, have been noted for the presence of Petén-style traits of architecture during the Classic period. The occurrence of such traits so far to the north has seemed isolated and suggestive of a distant colonization. In light of the corridor in at least the southern portion of Quintana Roo, the connection to the north is not as distant. Of course, an explanation of the

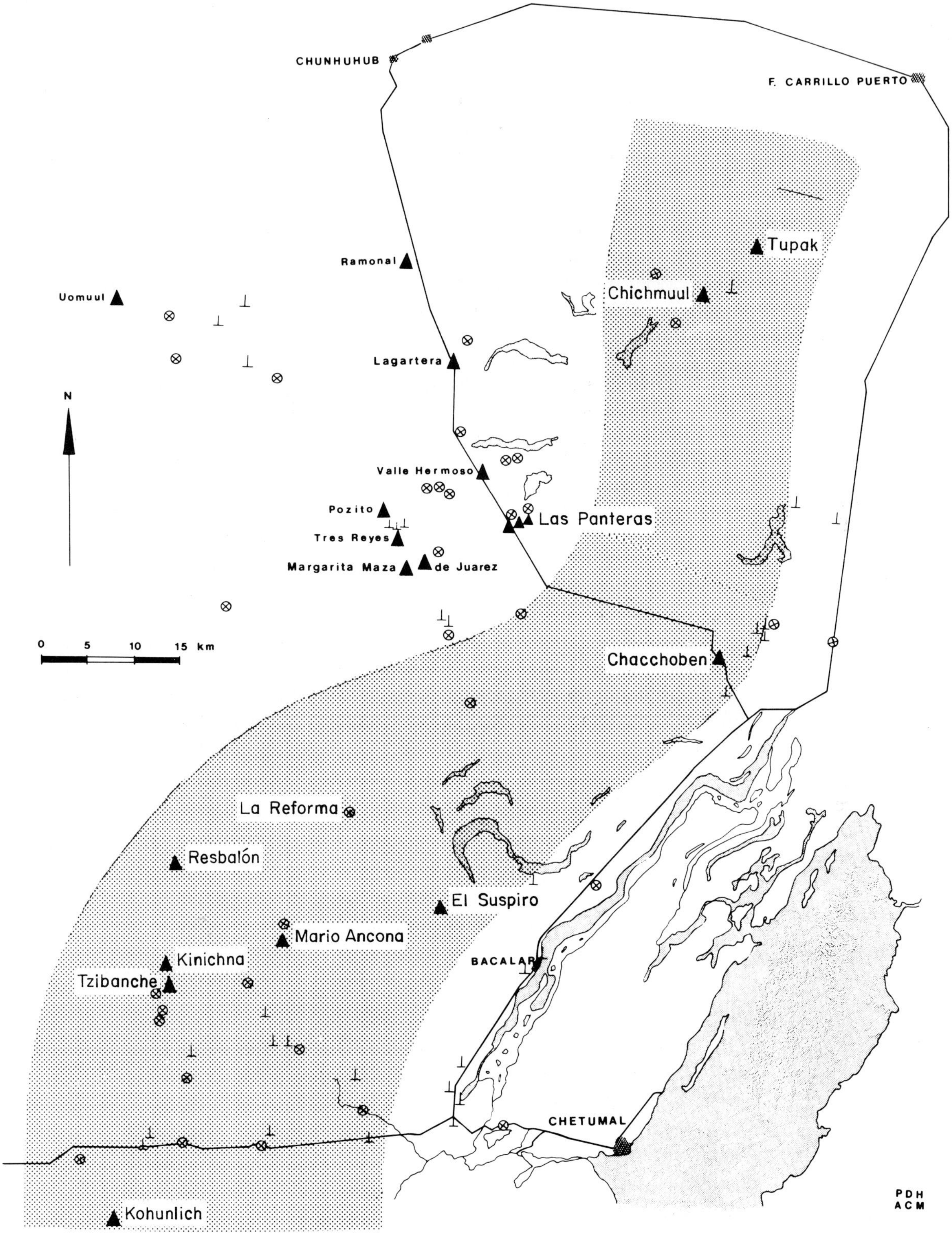

FIGURE 1. *Site distribution in southern Quintana Roo, showing the limits of the "Petén Corridor." (Site designations: ⊥, small; ⊗, medium; and ▲, large.)*

corridor itself—how it came to exist and how it persisted despite the change that was occurring around it—is still lacking.

Petén-related ceramics crosscut the corridor in the sense that they are present throughout southern Quintana Roo and not limited to the narrow architecturally defined zone. The Petén-type ceramics have chronological, rather than geographical, parameters. The influence of such ceramics, whether an import product or one which was locally produced, is visible in the ceramic assemblages up to a point in the Late Classic (approximately early Tepeu 2 in the Uaxactún chronology). Petén types are then supplanted by a stronger influence from the north, since slatewares predominate during the later part of the Late Classic and Early Postclassic.

As I have already stated, site distribution in this area is characterized by a clustering of sites around the edges of bajos, and this observation involves a number of controversial concepts. The first problem is: what constitutes a natural depression deserving of the term bajo? This term has been applied to a variety of environmental conditions that are as varied in their specific qualities as are all those stones that are collectively and generically referred to with the term "jade." A certain range of soil types and of plant species, in the presence of a specific kind of hydrology, are indicators used to define bajos. However, each of the indicators is variable. As more attention becomes focussed on the role of bajos in the life of the ancient Maya, we will require more precise definitions in order to ensure that different researchers are discussing the same phenomenon.

A second and even more controversial problem concerning the role of bajos in site distribution is their use in ancient times as settings for intensive agriculture. Aerial photographs of the Bajos Morocoy and Acatuch in the southern complex described previously display an impressive extent of quadrilinear patterning of foliage, which I have interpreted as evidence of the presence of ancient raised fields (Harrison 1978, 1979). I have also argued that the clustering of the sites around the bajos reflects an early economic exploitation of the depressions. However, as I have stated elsewhere, "the urgent need for ground verification is obvious" (Harrison 1978:253). It should also be noted here that my interpretations have been hotly disputed, although not disproved (Sanders 1979).

As a final topic in this summary of the results of the Quintana Roo settlement survey, I will discuss some chronological information that may be noted from the ceramic collections. The periods represented range from Middle Preclassic to Late Postclassic. Peaks or spurts of population were estimated from variable quantities of sherds recovered in test excavations. The times of these peaks show some geographic variation, which is interesting in light of the architectural traits discussed earlier. The first detectable increase in population occurred in the Late Preclassic, and the evidence for this increase is fairly general throughout the survey area. The absolute quantity of ceramic material increases for the later time periods; therefore, it is likely that the population similarly increased. The second noticeable spurt, however, occurred in the Middle Classic, but this peak was centered only around the southern bajo complex, that is, in the Petén Corridor. The next peak was geographically exclusive of the previous one, and occurred in the late Late Classic around the northern bajo complex. This peak, incidentally, coincides, or agrees chronologically, with the surge of Puuc development in the north. Finally, a very late Postclassic occupation is evidenced over the whole of southern Quintana Roo, but this ultimate peaking of population was on a lesser scale and definitely followed the major abandonment and collapse of Classic culture.

Extending from these data and interpretations from southern Quintana Roo, I have previously concluded that the majority of Classic Maya populations were supported by a variety of forms of intensive agriculture. The most prominent form of food production in this area, it was argued, was the use of chinampa-like raised fields in the extensive bajo systems that are found there (Harrison 1977, 1978). My argument proposed that such forms of intensive agriculture came into prevalent use at the time of the hiatus (Middle Classic), and that their use continued throughout the Late Classic, coming to an end at differential times according to the local date of collapse—the earliest being in the Petén, and the latest in northern Yucatán, notably in the Puuc zone. This argument was largely theoretical, based upon indirect or interpretive evidence.

The remainder of this chapter deals with a more recent program of ground verification.

Part II

Since the time of the original survey, no new direct evidence has been recovered to establish either the validity or the extent of raised fields in the bajos of southern Quintana Roo. There is serious question today whether such verification will ever be possible from the southern complex, where the visual evidence was the strongest. This zone has become the site of a government-sponsored program of agricultural development and population resettlement. Bajo Morocoy and parts of Bajo Acatuch, which comprise most of the southern complex, are being leveled by chains drawn between tractors and bulldozers to prepare the land for modern agricultural use. It is a pity that the evidence for ancient use could not have been recovered first, since little evidence can survive such intense mechanical disturbance.

Further, the project which was designed to perform the urgently needed ground verification in Quintana Roo was stymied by new tax laws imposed by Mexico's Instituto Nacional de Antropología e Historia. As a result, it was necessary to locate a similar or comparable situation outside of the borders of Mexico. In order that a minimum number of variables would be altered, we thought it would be helpful if the new locus of investigation was as physically close to the southern bajo complex in Quintana Roo as possible.

A depression fulfilling these requirements was chosen in northern Belize. This depression, called Pulltrouser Swamp, is located near Orange Walk Town in

Orange Walk District. Sighting of quadrilinear patterning in this bajo was first reported by A. H. Siemens (1977, 1978), who had personally observed the patterning from the air during reconnaissance flights in northern Belize.

The new project for the study of ancient raised fields was supported by a grant from the National Science Foundation received by B. L. Turner II of the Department of Geography, University of Oklahoma, with myself as Co-Principal Investigator.

Pulltrouser Swamp differs from the southern bajo complex in Quintana Roo not only in that it is much smaller in size, but also in that it has a longer cycle of water retention. The swamp is contiguous at its southern tip with the New River. The presence of the river may have made, and still makes, some contribution to the water levels in the depression. This relationship has yet to be established. A functional relationship may exist between the agricultural use of certain depressions and the presence of either ancient or current river drainage in or near them. Such a relationship between river drainage and agriculture is likely in the larger depressions of the southern Quintana Roo complex. The headwaters and collection basin of X'Kan Río originate in a large depression west of Bajo Morocoy. This drainage passes south of the peninsula of high ground on which is located the large site of Tzibanche, and continues on through Bajo Morocoy and Acatuch. The name of the drainage changes to Ucum ('river' in Yucatec Maya) when it crosses the Escárcega Highway and joins the major drainage of the Río Hondo. If the two drainages of X'Kan Río and Ucum are in fact connected, as the topography suggests, then the hydrological regime of the Río Hondo would be extended as far west as Nicolás Bravo. Complex drainage patterns through bajos, such as these, may be the key to discovering whether some of them were used for agricultural purposes even though these drainages are not fully operative or apparent today.

The choice of Pulltrouser Swamp was based on the visual presence from aerial photos of the aforementioned quadrilinear pattern, and on its proximity to the southern Quintana Roo complex (an average distance of 45 km). In the first days of the study program, Turner and his crew were able to locate the features on the ground that had been visible in the aerial photographs (Figure 2). Subsequent study convinced us that these features were man-made and ancient. We feel that this verification justifies the use of such photographic evidence for the identification of the location of ancient agricultural fields. Ground verification was accomplished for the aerially visible evidence in Pulltrouser Swamp.

The depression edge is marked by a drop in ground level of between ½ to 1 m and by a marked transition in vegetation. In recent times, most of the "high ground" was cleared and ploughed (even close to the edge of the bajo in some places) for sugar cane planting. Just inside the lower elevation and presently ringing the depression is a dense growth of *escobal* approximately 10–15 m in height and varying in width. Beyond the trees, the center of the bajo is occupied by tall grasses (including saw grass) and areas of open standing water. The water recedes from the littorals around April or May, leaving a surface of cracking

FIGURE 2. *Artificially created raised fields separated by a canal in Pulltrouser Swamp, northern Belize.*

montmorillonitic soils, which raises the question of *gilgai* formation in the bajos (Puleston 1977, 1978). Our soil study left no question of the environmental unsuitability in this bajo for the formation of *gilgai.* The soils never dry to a depth greater than 10 cm; therefore their wet period in each annual cycle is too long and their dry period too short for the formation of *gilgai* to be possible.

The full results of the Pulltrouser study cannot be presented here for a number of reasons: laboratory analyses are not yet completed, the data are not all within my right to disclose, and space would not permit it. Investigation of the raised fields was under the supervision of Turner, and I will restrict this report on that portion of the project to a few general but salient observations. The fields occur in different physical forms due to differing methods of construction. Such differing forms may occur alongside one another. Today, the fields are visible, both from aerial photocoverage and on the ground, as clusters two or three ranks deep around the edges of the southern and eastern branches of the depression. The hydrologic situation in Pulltrouser West is somewhat different from the other two branches, and raised fields are accordingly less prevalent there. It is not certain whether the present visible distribution represents the total ancient presence of raised fields in the bajo. Water movement and increased erosion in the center of the bajo may simply have rendered their presence there more difficult to ascertain. Further study is required.

Lithic and ceramic artifacts were recovered from the fields themselves, in surprising quantity. Puleston reported recovery of such artifacts from within riverine fields at San Antonio, about 13 km west on the other side of the land ridge which separates the New and Hondo Rivers.

I conducted a settlement survey that concentrated on a community near the south end of the west edge of Pulltrouser South (Figure 3). This ancient community was named Kokeal, after consultation with Maya-speaking assistants, for the *Koke* vine, a spiny nuisance prevalent at the site. Habitation remains extend beyond the southern tip of the depression to a smaller swamp not connected to the Pulltrouser complex. The community is lineal, extending nearly 2 km, oriented roughly north–south, and having a maximum breadth of 750 m from the edge of the bajo. South of the depression limit, there is a series of "ditches" of unexplained origin oriented roughly north–south from the swamp, and forming the eastern limit of the site beyond the southern tip of the swamp. House platforms at Kokeal were constructed as close as 10 m from the swamp edge or from one of the bordering ditches at the south end. More commonly, they were situated 50 m from these eastern limitations. Approximately $\frac{1}{2}$ km west of the bajo is a benchline or terrace, rising $2\frac{1}{2}$–3 m above the flatland "plain" adjacent to the bajo. This terrace is oriented at an angle to the swamp, more closely paralleling the course of the New River. A series of complex house clusters follows the edge of the terrace, spaced about 60 m apart and extending northwards from two raised ceremonial plazas or small acropolises. There latter groups are located at the extreme southern tip of the site, as it has been defined, and are comprised of a number of structures. Four of these are tall (6–8 m) and pyramidal, suggesting the ceremonial function. The remains of a looter's pit also indicate that a tomb was extracted from one of these "pyramids."

To the west and north of the community, the surrounding terrain is high, dry, and arable, but nearly devoid of structural remains for a distance of at least 1 km. Although a few scattered mounds do occur to the north and northwest, the decline in density of occupation is dramatic outside the mapped confines of the site. The community does not extend outwards from its core in a rambling fashion over the landscape, but rather has definite limits, except to the south, where another site begins a few hundred meters away. This site extends more than 1 km further south, overlooks the New River, and has been given a separate designation.

Generally, the house platforms at Kokeal are large, measuring 10 × 6 m on

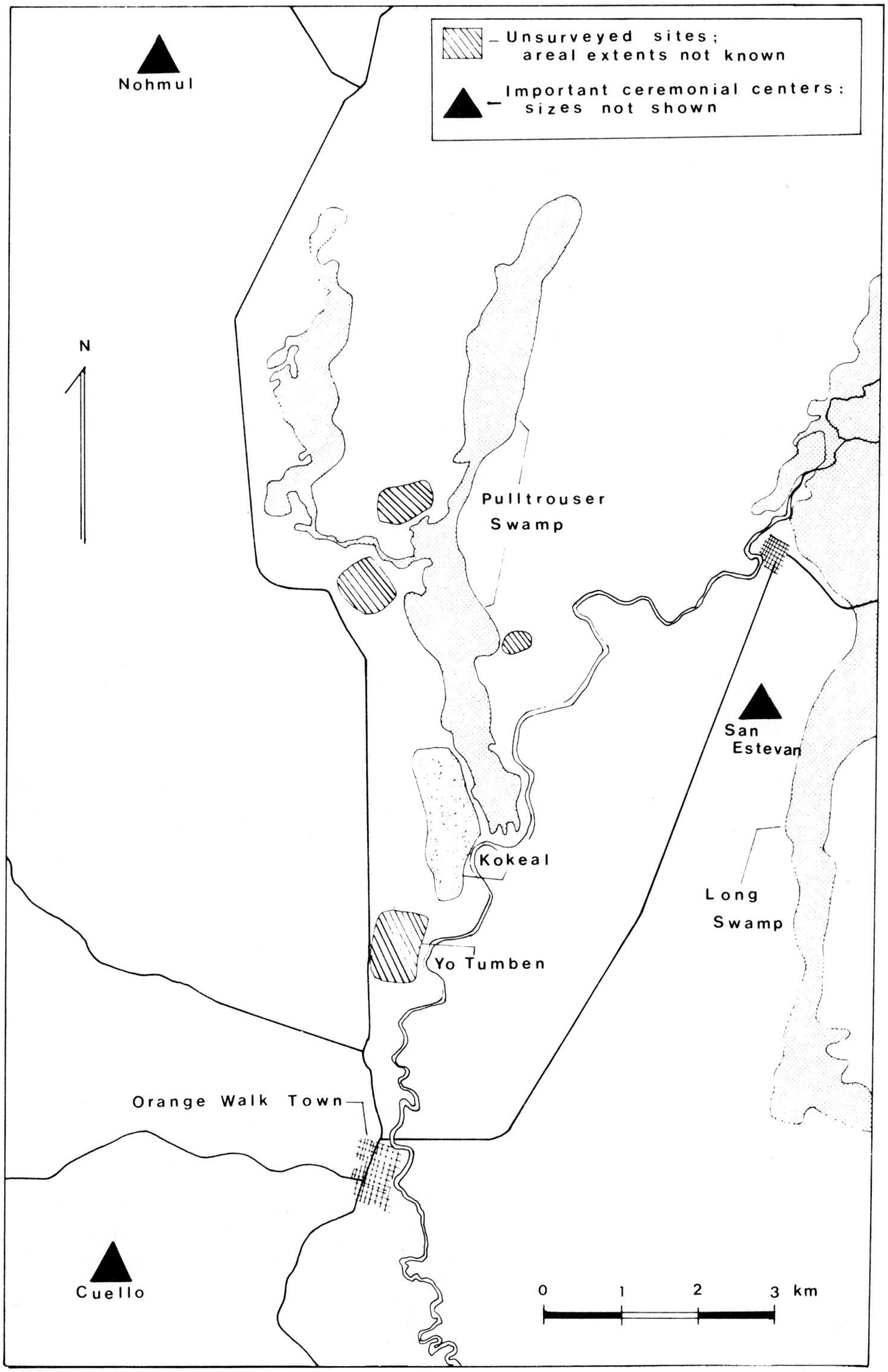

FIGURE 3. *Map of Pulltrouser Swamp, indicating the location of the site of Kokeal, three unnamed and uninvestigated sites, and three locally important sites.*

the average, and some are considerably larger. Associated middens and the contents of construction fill occasionally produced fine ceramic wares and polychromes, as well as fragments of religious or decorative paraphernalia. These items suggest a moderate degree of wealth, somewhat higher than would be expected from a purely rural, peasant community. However, despite this show of wealth in construction fill and middens, there is no trace of stone architecture above the level of the building platform. There are no room walls, foundations, or vaults of permanent masonry, even on the elite platforms and probable temples. Stone architecture was simply not utilized at any social level or for any function within the community. This is particularly curious considering that the ceremonial center of San Estévan, a mere $6\frac{1}{2}$ km away on the other side of the New River, did have such masonry during the Classic period. Of course, San Estévan was a larger and more important site. Ceramic sampling from test excavations throughout the community showed that a small population was present on the site as early as the Middle Classic. A startling burst of population occurred in the Late Preclassic. Of 191 excavation lots, 102 (53%) contained Late Preclassic ceramic material. Similarly, 21 of 46 surface lots (46%) contained ceramics of the same date. The quantities and distribution of Classic ceramics indicate continued but unexpansive occupation during the Early Classic, with a final surge of growth in the Late Classic. The bare trace of Postclassic material recovered is small enough to be considered accidental rather than indicative of any occupation in this period. The relative absence of Postclassic remains at the site is unexpected given the local setting, where Postclassic censer fragments and ceramics are a nearly ubiquitous feature of surface collections.

The final analysis of the Pulltrouser study will be a collaborative effort of nine researchers, in what may be the most comprehensive interdisciplinary study yet accomplished on a small scale. As noted earlier, the results of examination of C-14 samples, pollen, soils, mollusca, and hydrology are not yet available. However, it is appropriate to conclude with some impressions of the kinds of information that are expected to emerge from the Pulltrouser study and some questions that might be approached with these kinds of data in hand.

Conclusion

Briefly, I see the community of Kokeal as having served the role of a special purpose community, one of several such communities around the littorals of the three branches of the Pulltrouser complex. The direct association with the proven raised fields leads inevitably to the conclusion that the site arose in response to the personnel needs of the raised field industry—at least for their working and maintenance, if not for their construction. The dates of occupation for the community probably reflect the dates of construction of the fields, and hence the introduction of intensification of agriculture. These dates suggest a beginning in the Late Preclassic, with continued development of the system throughout the

Early Classic, followed by a final surge in the Late Classic after which their usage terminated. This represents an alteration of my earlier argument that the raised fields were introduced in the Middle Classic in southern Quintana Roo, but that argument was based on theory only.

There are a number of related issues of theoretical significance which are presented here in the form of questions we are still asking ourselves prior to the final analysis.

1. How did the population of this small community compare to the potential caloric production from the raised fields in Pulltrouser South? Was this production higher than could be consumed by a maximum population in the community of Kokeal?

2. There is a significant contrast in the discontinuity of settlement around the edges of the bajo, as opposed to the apparently continuous distribution of the raised fields in at least two branches of the swamp. If the food produced from the fields were for local consumption only, how do we explain this major difference in distribution?

3. What might be the relationship of the small sites located at the edges of the bajo itself to the larger sites distributed along the ridge of high ground between the New and Hondo Rivers? Could the small sites be "worker" or "supply" sites providing food to the larger centers?

4. What was the condition of Pulltrouser Swamp in Preclassic times? Was it the same as it is today, or has the hydrology altered? These two questions will be at least partially answered by the results of the ecological program, and such results should have a strong bearing on the nature and role played by other bajos or depressions such as those in southern Quintana Roo.

However, the results of one study cannot be inexorably applied to another zone, and we are painfully aware of this problem. In order to finally resolve the major question of the role of bajos in the economy of the ancient Maya, it may be necessary to conduct a study of the sort that is reported here in preliminary fashion for each and every bajo in the Maya Lowlands that is associated with habitation. Unfortunately, that amounts to every bajo on the landscape!

References

Adams, R. E. W.

1981 Settlement patterns of the central Yucatán and the southern Campeche regions. In *Lowland Maya Settlement Patterns,* edited by Wendy Ashmore, Albuquerque. Univ. of New Mexico Press.

Fry, R. E.

1972 The archaeology of southern Quintana Roo: Ceramics. In *Atti degli XL Congresso Internazionale degli Americanisti,* 1:487–493. Rome, International Congress of Americanists.

Harrison, Peter D.

1972a Precolumbian settlement distributions and external relationships in southern Quintana Roo,

Part 1: Architecture. In *Atti degli XL Congresso Internazionale degli Americanisti.* 1:479–486. Rome, International Congress of Americanists.

1972b The lintels of Tzibanche, Quintana Roo. In *Atti degli XL Congresso Internazionale degli Americanisti,* 1:495–501. Rome, International Congress of Americanists.

1974 Archaeology in southwestern Quintana Roo: Interim report of Uaymil Survey Project. Paper presented at the XLI Congresso Internacional de Americanistas, Mexico City, Mimeograph available from author.

1975 Intensive agriculture in southern Quintana Roo, Mexico: Some new lines of evidence and implications for Maya Prehistory. Paper presented at the Fortieth Annual Meeting of the Society for American Archaeology, Dallas. Mimeograph available from author.

1977 The rise of the bajos and the fall of the Maya. In *Social Process in Maya Prehistory: Studies in Memory of Sir Eric Thompson,* edited by Norman Hammond, pp. 469–508. London, Academic Press.

1978 Bajos revisited: Visual evidence for one system of agriculture. In *Pre-Hispanic Maya Agriculture,* edited by P. D. Harrison and B. L. Turner II, pp. 247–253. Albuquerque, Univ. of New Mexico Press.

1979 The Lobil Postclassic phase in the southern interior of the Yucatán Peninsula, in *Maya Archaeology and Ethnohistory,* edited by Norman Hammond and G. R. Willey, pp. 189–207. Austin, Univ. of Texas Press.

Puleston, D. E.

1977 Experiments in Prehistoric raised field agriculture: Learning from the past. In *BISRA, Journal of Belizean Affairs, Special Issue: The Río Hondo Project, an Investigation of the Maya of Northern Belize,* pp. 36–43. Belize City, Belice.

1978 Terracing, raised fields, and tree cropping in the Maya Lowlands: A new perspective on the geography of power. In *Pre-Hispanic Maya Agriculture,* edited by P. D. Harrison and B. L. Turner II, pp. 225–245. Albuquerque, Univ. of New Mexico Press.

Sanders, William T.

1979 The Jolly Green Giant in tenth century Yucatán, or fact and fancy in Classic Maya agriculture. In *Reviews in Anthropology* (Vol. 6, No. 4), edited by Michael H. Logan, pp. 493–506. Pleasantville, New York, Redgrave.

Siemens, A. H.

1977 Some patterns seen from the air. In BISRA, *Journal of Belizean Affairs, Special Issue: The Río Hondo Project, an Investigation of the Maya of Northern Belize,* pp. 5–21. Belize City, Belice.

1978 Karst and the Pre-Hispanic Maya in the southern Lowlands. In *Pre-Hispanic Maya Agriculture,* edited by Peter D. Harrison and B. L. Turner II, pp. 117–143. Albuquerque, Univ. of New Mexico Press.

5

Subsistence, Trade, and Development of the Coastal Maya

David A. Freidel and Vernon Scarborough

Introduction

> The meeting place of the two armies was cultivated land, cut by many ditches and deep streams, difficult to cross, among which our men became confused and disorganized . . . the foot went to the right, crossing ditches at every step (López de Gomara in Simpson 1966:46).

THE battle at Cintla ('corn' in *Nahuatl*) near the trading port of Potonchan in Tabasco began badly for the Spaniards. Somehow the natives managed to lead the would-be conquerors away from the town by way of several paths that converged on the area described above. Eventually, Cortez managed to maneuver his cavalry out of the fields and on to high ground, where they proceeded to rout the enemy. The legacy of this minor historical incident in the conquest of Mexico is a precise description of ridged- or raised-field agriculture in the vicinity of a Maya coastal port (Scholes and Roys 1968:58) at the time of contact.

There are several good reasons why the people of Potonchan engaged in highly productive intensive agriculture. If the name of the battle ground is any guide, and, indeed, food was being produced, then it can be noted that

> the internal trade of Tabasco centered mainly on maize, beans, chile, and squashes. Cacao-growing by other groups was so profitable that the producers were much inclined to buy their food staples from their neighbors or from the Zoque towns at the foot of the Sierra (Roys 1972:106).

A food surplus would have allowed this Tabascan community to (1) maintain subsistence autonomy and avoid having to trade exotics or precious agricultural products for food, (2) trade food for cacao, or (3) maintain a large work force committed to the labor intensive production of cacao.

ISBN 0-12-259780-X

The people of Potonchan were not the only ones to see the value of commercial agriculture and intensification. Itzamkanac, the capital of the Acalan merchants, is thought to have been located on the Río Candelaria (Scholes and Roys 1968:map 3) in precisely the region identified by Siemens and Puleston (1972) as containing the remains of intensive raised- or ridged-field agriculture. There is good reason to believe that these people also produced substantial food surplus:

> Cortés tells us that Acalan was 'very rich in food supplies and there was much honey'; and his statement is amply confirmed by the rapidity with which Bernal Díaz obtained a hundred canoe loads of grain and other food for the expedition (Scholes and Roys 1968:59).

Grain is not mentioned as a trade commodity. Cacao tops the list of Acalan agricultural products, yet evidently was not grown there for export (Scholes and Roys 1968). Hence, there is reason to suspect that food was being exchanged by the people of Acalan for cacao within the Tabasco network. The people of Itzamkanac diversified commercial production in several ways. In addition to the just mentioned honey, which may have been traded into Tabasco (Roys 1972:105), they also produced copal incense and cotton as trade commodities (Scholes and Roys 1968:59).

The correlation of commercial production with trade centers can be documented at other locations on the lowland coasts. Chetumal produced honey, wax, and cacao (Roys 1957), while Nito and Naco were in a rich cacao-producing district. Cozumel produced honey, wax, and fruit. Even the great trading center of Chauaca, located near the rich north-coast salt beds, diversified production into groves of trees bearing copal incense (Roys 1957).

Beyond Potonchan, the correlation of trade centers with agricultural intensification is more problematic, but is still promising. Contact period Cozumel and the east coast of Quintana Roo in general show an extraordinary investment in field-wall networks (Sabloff and Freidel 1975; Freidel 1976) and such walls are described by early observers of the coast (Wagner 1942). Regardless of how one interprets these strange features, they undoubtedly relate to intensified regulation of agricultural production. Identical field-wall networks are found at the massive Classic period community of Chunchucmil on the west coast (Vlcek *et al.* 1978). This site dominates the rich salt beds of the coast but, like Cozumel and the east coast, it is located in very marginal agricultural land. In these cases, commercial surplus of food is out of the question, and we are likely dealing with intensification aimed at avoiding or limiting the expensive importation of food. Whether or not any of the raised field systems found in Belize were still being used at the time of contact remains an open question. Data gathered by Puleston (1977a) and Siemens (1977) would suggest that they were not. On the other hand, raised fields have been identified in the vicinity of Lamanai (Hebda and

Pendergast, personal communication 1979) which was still an important community during the Postclassic era.

In brief, there is reason to believe that Contact period Maya trading communities were, in many instances, entrepôts (Vance 1970) involved in the gathering of local agricultural products for sale, as well as the local distribution and regional trans-shipment of exotic commodities. There is also reason to believe that trading centers in the more marginal agricultural areas generally attempted to avoid having to expend their precious capital resources on food, and thus intensified or regulated food production in order to maintain autonomy. In all cases, intensive labor investment in agricultural production had ultimately a pecuniary motive. There is no suggestion in the literature that such practices were aimed at avoiding want in the face of population pressure.

The situation found at the end of Maya civilization may be mirrored in its beginnings in the Late Preclassic period (300 B.C.–A.D. 100). In the case of at least one important Late Preclassic coastal trading community, Cerros (Freidel 1978, 1979), a complex water-management system relating to agricultural intensification has been found. The organization of this system suggests that the upgrading of food production in the community, and/or the producing of commercial crops, motivated its construction. This same organization refutes the alternative possibility that the community grew up around a locale inherently suitable for agricultural intensification. Moreover, the settlement-pattern evidence does not indicate that its construction was a response to population pressure at the local or areal levels. The system to which we now turn is discrete and community oriented.

Preclassic Canalization at Cerros, Northern Belize

The Late Preclassic Lowland Maya center of Cerros is situated on the northern leeward shore of Lowry's Bight, Northern Belize (lat. 18°12′ N., long. 88°21′10″ W.) (Figure 1). An intensive field excavation and survey program has recorded 178 mounded features within a 1.5-km^2 survey area (Figure 2). Fifty mounds have been tested or horizontally stripped. A clear Late Preclassic period date has been obtained for the major construction of approximately 90% of these features though an ephemeral Classic and Postclassic occupation is apparent.

Cerros has recently demonstrated the presence of a Late Preclassic canal-like feature circumscribing the most dense concentration of mounds at the site. The approximately 37 ha enclosed by the canal contain 95 mounded structures. The area is comparable to that enclosed by the Late Preclassic (Pakluum phase) ditch at Becan, Campeche(Ball and Andrews 1978; Webster 1976). In addition, at least 6 major feeder or lateral canals issue from the main canal. The terminus of one of the intensively investigated feeder canals (Figure 3) indicates the presence of 4 earthen platforms defined by narrower and shallower minor feeder canals.

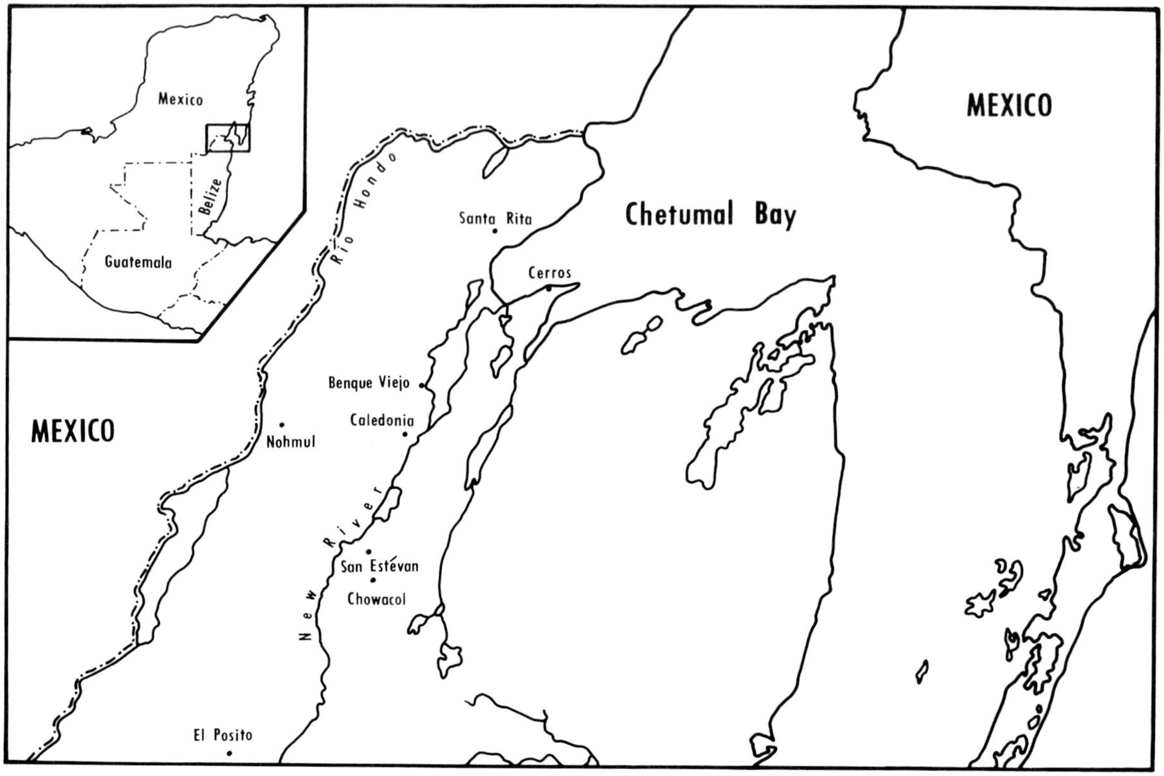

FIGURE 1. *Map of Cerros.*

Spatial Disposition of Features

Our survey program has revealed that the main canal extended over 1,200 m of the site, forming a great arc with its focus at the central precinct. Surface elevations indicate a gentle gradient of less than 1 m descending from west to east from within the infilled canal. Little consistent drop in elevation can be detected across the site along the banks of the canal or at other adjacent areas of high ground. The canal traverses three apparent microenvironments in its swing around the most dense concentration of mounded features at the site. Much of the canal passes through a depressed *bajo*-like setting characterized by *hulub* (*Bravaisia sp.*), entanglement, and poorly drained dark gumbo soils (Figure 4). This setting dominates the eastern and far-western portions of the main canal though most of the bajo-like settings lie outside the canal. The section of the canal to the south appears less depressed, being defined by thorn scrub savanna (Wiseman 1978) and thin clayey topsoils inside the area circumscribed by the canal, and a better drained high ground *monte alto* setting outside the canal. The canal is wider and less distinct in the bajo-like localities.

The canal was initially discovered as a result of its depressed appearance in spite of two millennia of infilling, and its relatively sparse cover of vegetation. The latter is thought to be a function of the impermeable clays which have infilled the canal as well as the depth of the present trough. These two factors are believed to have prolonged the annual period of ponding and prevented many species from adapting to the condition. However, the canal is dry during part of the dry season. Another factor affecting the canal's visibility is that the climax vegetation was removed recently though secondary and tertiary seres have rapidly moved in. Aerial photography has further verified the extent of the canalization at Cerros.

Damlike features were recorded, bridging the canal at various locations. Six of these features have been defined, measuring approximately 5 × 10 m though the present surface dimensions vary from feature to feature. These damlike features are best defined along the southern section of the canal, in areas of less depressed terrain, though this may be a consequence of preservation.

The major feeder canals issue from the main canal at five known locations and seem to diverge at any angle from the canal. The segments vary in length, the longest being over 100 m. These lateral canals appear to be wider and shallower than the main canal, at least when compared with the narrow southern section of the main canal. In two instances, the lateral canals flow into small elliptical depressions thought to be reservoirs or catchment basins. Within the survey area, numerous depressions or small seasonal reservoirs have been recorded. Though some of them may be *dolinen* 'sink holes' and attributable to natural processes (Sweeting 1973; Siemens 1978:136), many are associated with concentrations of mounded features.

At the north end of the major feeder canal (F122) issuing into the site area defined by the main canal are positioned a minimum of four earthen platforms, the dimensions of which range from 11 × 16 m to 19 × 34 m (Figure 3). They are oriented to the cardinal directions. Each platform is thought to be circumscribed by a narrow shallow channel though siltation of these minor feeder canals has somewhat obscured their definition. Although the vegetation is somewhat more sparse within the canals than on top of the earthen platforms, aerial photographs taken at approximately 1:1500 do not reveal these features. The surficial height of the platforms above the infilled canals is less than 30 cm, according to our spot check elevations and locations. (A transit contour map was made in the field of the ½-ha area most intensively investigated for hydraulic control works. The earthen platforms were simply pace-and-compass mapped.) The platforms at this location occupy a thornbush savanna microenvironment heavily invaded by *muk (Dalbergia sp.)* and *katsim (Acacia sp.)* and characterized by thin clayey topsoil, though the setting is better drained than the bajo-like locations.

Water management elsewhere in the settlement has been recorded. Seven earthen platforms defined by a shared system of channels have been pace-and-compass mapped at the margin of the New River's northeast terrace zone approximately 1,100 m southwest of the main canal. This setting is similar to that

FIGURE 2. *Structures, canals, ditches, and associated features at Cerros as of 1979.*

Sacbe
Sacbe
Canal
Raised Fields
Aguada
Aguada
MAPPED & ASSEMBLED BY VERNON SCARBOROUGH
ASSISTED BY SUSAN LEWENSTEIN
KAREN SMITH
FRED VALDEZ, Jr
JAMES WEBB

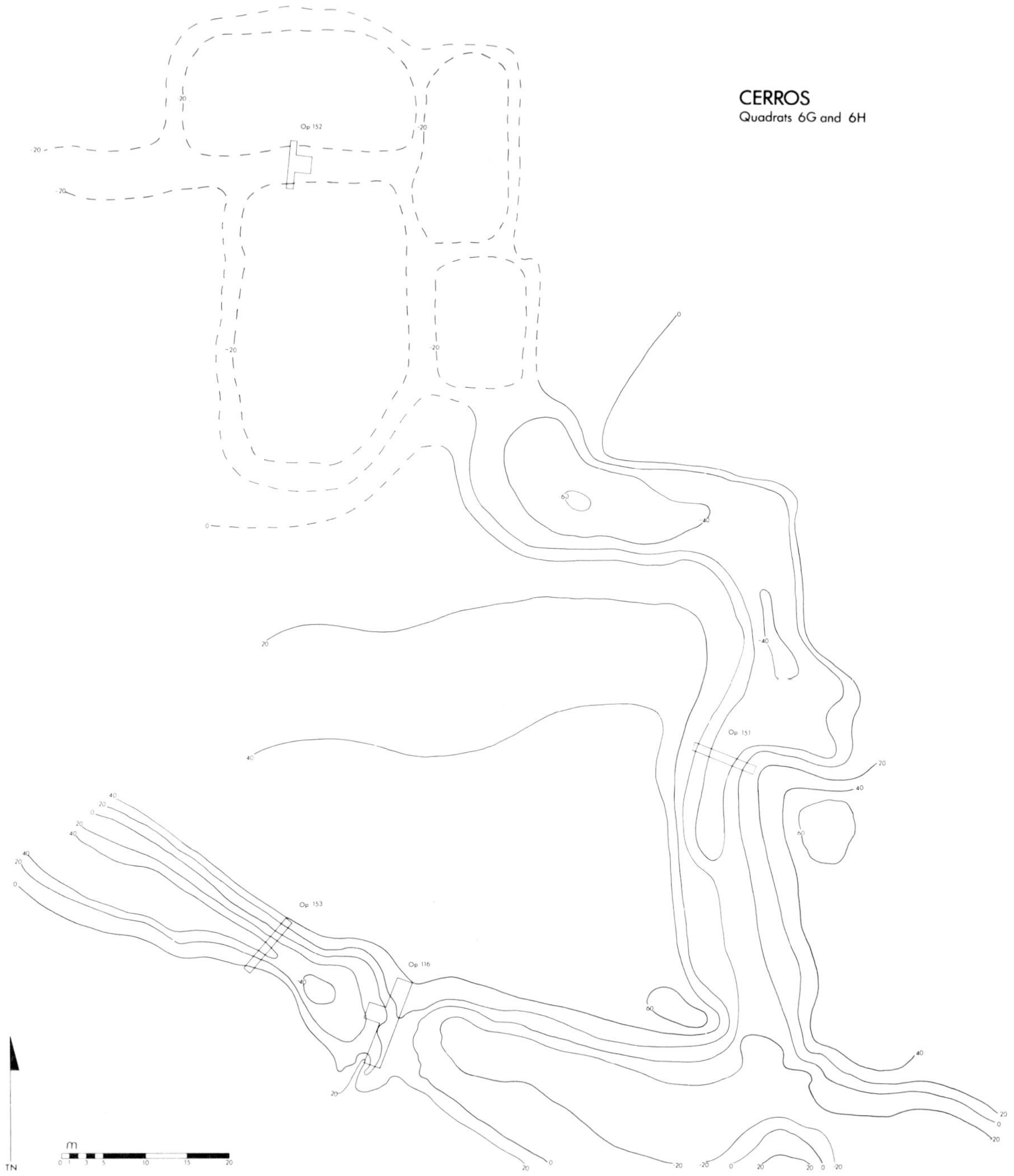

FIGURE 3. *Section of main canal, associated feeder canal and possible fields at Cerros. Test excavations as of 1979 are indicated by operation (Op) number. Transit mapped, ———; pace-and-compass mapped, – – –. Contours in centimeters. Prepared from 1:200 base map.*

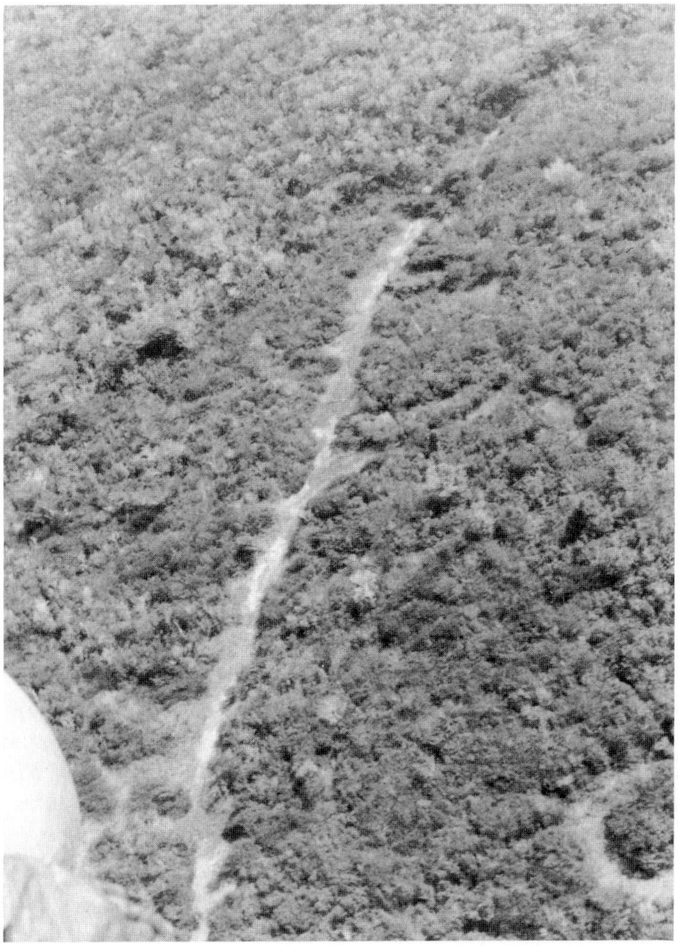

FIGURE 4. *Aerial view of Cerros, showing a portion of the main canal.*

defined by Siemens (see Chapter 8) for the majority of raised fields surveyed in Northern Belize. The platforms appear to be oriented perpendicular to the present shoreline (N 115° W), rather than to the cardinal directions as is the case with the platforms in the center. The platforms vary in dimensions but fall within the range of those described in the center, though they occupy a more bajo-like setting. House-mound density drops off significantly as one approaches this setting. No controlled excavations have been conducted in this location, but surface collections from the eroding shoreline suggest an Early Classic date.

Excavation of Features

Our excavation and recovery techniques involved the excavation and screening of naturally defined levels. Flotation samples were run from each stratum in the field, and microfossil examinations are currently underway. Pollen samples from 16 contexts are presently under study, as are chemical and physical soil tests. The latter are anticipated to aid in determining the origin and fertility of the sediments in question.

Excavation of the main canal has been carried out along the south-central portion of the feature (Figure 3). This location was selected because the canal relief contour was well defined and in proximity to the known earthen platforms. One of two trenches at this location was placed across the parallel to the long axis of one of the damlike features in an attempt to obtain a cross-sectional history of the infilling operation relative to the canal itself. This location was also selected to obtain an adequate sherd sample for dating the constructional episodes of the canal (after Puleston and Callender 1967:43). A second trench was placed 14 m west of the first in an attempt to reveal any local variability between the two sections. The cross sections appear to correlate between the two exposures. The initial canal was excavated through limestone caprock to a depth of 2 m and a width of 6 m.

Our initial trench across the damlike feature exposed 26 m^2 to a maximum depth of 2 m (Figure 5). The basal canal sediments were exposed in 1×2-m exposure only. The bottom of the canal was defined by a sterile white friable marl as well as the dry season water table. All canal sediments were moist. A 5-cm thick dark blocky loamy clay overlay the parent material though it feathered out near the center or bottom of the canal. The matrix was not viscous. Overlying and intruding into these matrices was a 20-cm layer of decomposing angular limestone gravel in the form of small cobbles overlain by pebble-size gravels. Again, the concentration of gravels was thickest on the southern side of the exposure and was found to pinch out toward the center or bottom of the canal.

The next stratigraphic level represented the bulk of the canal sediments. Most of the $1\frac{1}{2}$ m of friable blocky grey clays were removed from the entire horizontal exposure. These clays were found to grade from darker to lighter value as we ascended the profile though no boundary between the sediments was discernible. No microstratigraphic control of these sediments was possible since chemical recrystallization and the effect of burrowing snails have altered their appearance. The darker grey clays near the base of the exposure were more compact than those deposited later. A pure Late Preclassic sherd sample was taken from these grey clays. In addition, fragments of bone, charcoal flecks, and stone debitage were recovered.

Capping and intruding into the canal sediments at this location was an infilled lazy U-shaped deposit, 3 m in length and 80 cm in maximum depth, grading from a dark loamy clay at the top to a light grey clay near the bottom. The sediments were a loose blocky clay heavily intruded by limestone gravel ranging in size from pebbles to large cobbles. Though the texture, structure, and consistency of the fill seemed similar throughout the deposit, the upper 40 cm was of a darker value, being faintly segregated from the lower 40 cm by a

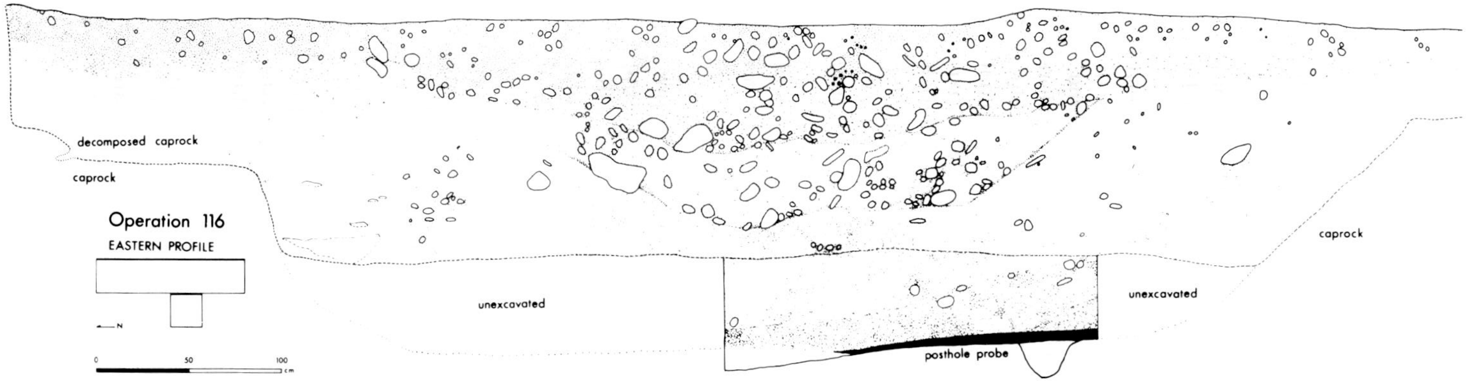

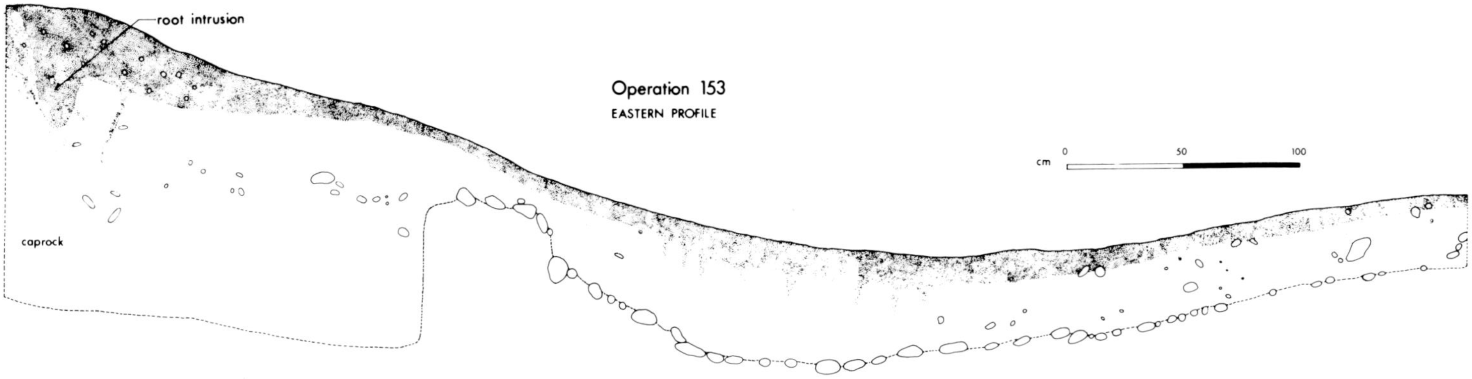

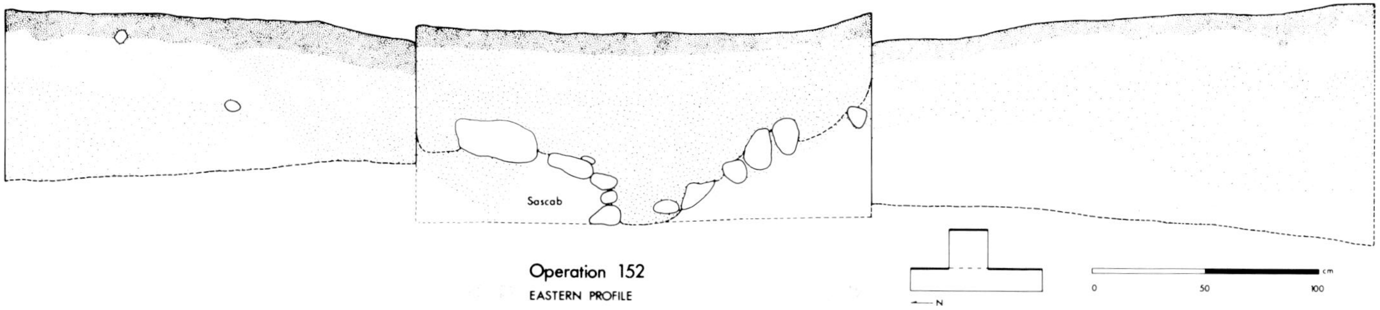

FIGURE 5. *Operation 116, profile of test trench through the main canal at Cerros showing two major episodes of excavation and the final construction of a rubble causeway or check dam across the canal at this location (see Figure 3).*

FIGURE 6. *Operation 153, profile of the eastern test trench across the main canal showing two major episodes of excavation. Second excavation of canal was followed by the construction of a stone lining.*

FIGURE 7. *Operation 152, composite profile of a test trench across a ditch between possible raised fields (see Figure 3) showing rock lining of the ditch walls.*

gradually smooth boundary. A somewhat similar deposit to that described for the lower 40 cm of light grey clay within the infilled U-shaped lens was found to intrude into the underlying grey clays near the northern margin of the canal profile. It was intruded by coarse pebble-size limestone gravel to a depth of 80 cm (see Figure 5). Early Classic ceramics were the most recent diagnostics taken from this infilling operation (R. Robertson, personal communication to Freidel).

Decomposing limestone and gravel were found on the immediate northern and southern margins of the canal sediments. Thin discontinuous lenses of granular friable yellow marl issued from the upper decomposing northern limestone caprock defining the vertical bank or sidewall of the canal. Excavation through 40 cm of the decomposing limestone caprock revealed the massive indurated caprock defining the lower reaches of the canal sidewalls. The original canal profile was U-shaped with a less steep southern slope forming an approximate 45° angle with the flat bottom. Overlying the decomposing upper caprock at the banks of the canal was a continuous 10-cm layer of mottled grey clays similar to those defined within the canal. These clays spill into the canal section. The complete excavation exposure was capped by a dark viscous blocky loamy clay intruded by pebble-to-small-cobble-size limestone gravels.

The second trench was placed across and perpendicular to the long axis of the main canal (Figures 3 and 6). Its precise location was selected to explain an apparent constriction in the width of the canal at this location. It was also anticipated that less energy and time would be expended to obtain an additional cross section, given the narrowness of the canal at this location. The excavations represented an 8-m^2 horizontal exposure to a maximum depth of 1.6 m. The same blocky friable light grey clays were found to comprise nearly all the fill in this exposure. Though we were unable to "bottom out" or define the basal sediments in the canal, we did identify the near-vertical northern canal sidewall. It was the same granular friable yellow decomposing limestone as defined in the first trench. The yellow limestone matrix was again found to spill into the grey clay canal sediments, producing thin discontinuous lensing. Below this lensing and within the grey clays was collected a pure, though obviously unsealed, Late Preclassic ceramic sample. A large chert blade was also recovered.

South of the northern exposure, we identified a shallow, single-course concentration of small cobble-size limestone gravel. These stones lined the remainder of our exposure, which extended approximately 6 m^2 to the south. These stones formed a lazy, asymmetrical U, having a steep northern sidewall in cross section. The sediments probed below this feature revealed the same light grey clays as located to the north of the stone lining. The sediments overlying the stone feature were a slightly darker grey clay of the same texture, structure, and consistency as those below. Overlying the entire deposit was a 10-cm layer of dark blocky viscous clay loam. Soil cracking was apparent at this level and chemical recrystallization and intrusive snails (principally *Pomacea*) were apparent throughout the light grey clays. An Early Classic date has been assigned to the debris taken from above the stone lining.

Forty-five meters northeast of the damlike feature, another trench was positioned across the width of a major feeder canal issuing from the main canal. This lateral canal lies at a right angle to the main canal and extends northward for over 70 m. At the northern end of the major feeder canal, the channel makes an abrupt dogleg west. At this location, the contour map indicates a small reservoir or catchment basin. This canal was selected for investigation due to its linkage with the defined earthen platforms. The specific location of the trench was chosen because of the well-defined eastern canal bank which would provide a convincing profile for the canal section. The construction of this feature was apparently not modified through time as the main canal was. The major feeder canal was much shallower and wider than the main canal, being approximately 90 cm deep and at least 8 m wide. This canal was defined by a shallow dish-shaped cross section cut into the limestone caprock, though our excavations did not extend far enough west to define the exact nature of the opposite bank. The flat bottom of the canal rose at a 45° angle in forming the eastern bank. Eight square meters of deposit were removed to a maximum depth of 90 cm. The fill was the same homogeneous blocky grey clay defined in the main canal section though it appeared to be of a slightly lighter value. The fill was not heavily intruded by limestone gravel though a few were removed. The sediments were recrystallized and affected by gastropod intrusions (*Pomacea*). No microstratigraphy was evident. Overlying the 80 cm of grey clays was a 10-cm cap of blocky dark clay loam topsoil. The boundary between these two layers was not abrupt, but graded from one to the other. The underlying parent material defining the canal was the same yellow limestone as that overlying the indurated caprock. The bottom of the canal was overlain by a decomposing limestone gravel, and the eastern bank was defined by the yellow decomposing limestone. Though the ceramic sample was a small, mixed one, the great majority of identifiable sherds date to the Late Preclassic period.

Four earthen platforms were located at the termination of the above lateral canal. Excavations carried out within and between the two platforms revealed (Figure 7) a narrow shallow channel (1 × 1 m) believed to circumscribe each platform. Our trench was positioned to expose both the matrices of the earthen platforms and the profile of a minor feeder canal. The exact position of the trench was chosen because of the relief found at this location. Nine horizontal square meters of deposit were removed to a maximum depth of 80 cm. The canal section was defined in part by a sterile off-white granular friable marl. Excavations into the flanking platforms suggest that this sterile sediment may have been intentionally mounded though the matrix was quite mottled. Lying above and intruding into the off-white clay were smooth, though pitted, cobble-to-small-boulder size limestone gravels positioned to form an ill-defined lazy, asymmetrical U-shaped cross section. Though the canal is thought to have been defined by these uncut stones, some of the stones have fallen from their original position. Overlying and settling between these stones were located dark blocky friable grey clays similar to those defined in the other canal sections. These sediments accounted for 80 cm of the canal fill, and in turn were capped by a 10-cm thick lens of dark blocky viscous organic-rich clay loam topsoil. Again, the sediments appear to be recrystallized and intruded by snails, though some lateral lensing was apparent. Ceramic debris taken from within the canal was badly mixed, spanning all periods of occupation represented at Cerros.

On either margin of the stone concentration, we exposed the adjacent platforms. Excavations were taken down to a depth comparable to that reached in exposing the flanking canal segment. Exposure of the northern edge of the southernmost platform revealed the off-white granular friable clay overlying the decomposing yellow limestone caprock. Though the off-white clay marl was severely mottled by the same postdepositional agents responsible for the condition of the canal sediments, the lens appeared to be thicker at the canal bank margin, contouring to the position of the overlying stone concentration. The southern end of the lens gradually sloped down out of the profile.

The sediments overlying this mounded deposit were a lighter blocky friable clay seemingly identical to those sediments within the canal, except for the value difference. The maximum 1-m-deep deposit was severely mottled and appears to have graded smoothly from the basal light clays to the surficial dark clays. The surface of the platform was covered by a 10-cm thick blocky viscous organic topsoil. Soil cracking was in part responsible for the mottled appearance of these sediments. The exposure on the northernmost platform was excavated down to a level 30 cm higher than the maximum depth elsewhere in the operation. However, it should be noted that the exposure was taken down to the level of the basal rubble lining the ditch, and not one stone was found in the fill of the southern platform. A few pebbles were removed from the northern platform. The 3 laboratory phosphate readings taken from the profile of the southern platform are significantly higher than the remaining 17 samples taken from other various contexts within the settlement. The ceramic sample from the fill of the two platforms, while small (less than 100 sherds), was exclusively Late Preclassic (R. Robertson, personal communication to Freidel). These sherds were large and unweathered; trash in the form of lithic debris and bone accompanied them. The ceramic sample from within the ditch defined by the rubble linings included both Late Preclassic and Early Classic diagnostics. These sherds were badly weathered (R. Robertson, personal communication to Freidel). Given that the platforms are artificial constructions containing exclusively Late Preclassic diagnostics, we infer that the fields were built during this period. The presence of Early Classic material in the ditch is not surprising because nearby mounds show evidence of ephemeral reoccupation during this period. The weathered quality of the sherds in the ditch proper suggests that the silting in was a slow process, and that the ditch was still open following the Late Preclassic abandonment of Cerros and well into the Early Classic period.

Interpretations

As has already been stated, the main canal had been excavated to a depth of 2 m and a width of 6 m through limestone caprock. It is unlikely that the canal was excavated by a natural river course that was later dredged of sediments since the width of the canal is much narrower than that of the nearby voluminous New River. In addition, the canal profiles reveal a steeply banked U-shaped cross section, rather than the lazy asymmetrical U-shaped cross section anticipated for a meander at this location (Blatt *et al.* 1972:136).

Moreover, although the fill was not thrown up to support a rampart or parapet of any consequence, it was apparently used in the construction of various mounded features within the settlement. At least six of the larger mounds flanking the edge of the canal appear to have been constructed from the canal fill, as does the 1-m-high plaza supporting the 10-m-high structure 29. In the case of structure 98, we have obtained a *terminus ante quem* for the canal by uncovering a Phase III Cabro Red: Cabro Variety vessel underlying 1 m of canal fill. A carbon sample was also collected from this context. Simple arithmetic calculations indicate that the fill necessary for constructing the small mounded features within the settlement could have easily been taken from the main canal excavation, though a quarry operation (possibly a *sascabero*) has been defined immediately southeast of the main plaza area.

The absence of a substantial rampart at Cerros does not deny the existence of a defensive function for the feature, but it does suggest that the fill from the canal was valued more for raised platform space than for protection from outside attack. Wooden palisades are reported during the Conquest in the Chan Maya province (Thompson 1977), and the use of thornbushes, such as the various species of *Acacia,* could have provided an adequate deterrent to most intruders. (Millon [1973:40] indicates a possible defensive function for the nopal cactus at Teotihuacán.)

This kind of multipurpose canalization is also suggested at Edzná in an examination of the main canal feeding the moat surrounding the "fortress" (Matheny 1976:Figure 3, 1978:Figures 10.7 and 10.8). These features relate to emic boundaries of the site—an undeniable barrier to outsiders questioning the perimeters of the site. The short-term benefits of the earthworks would be the obvious defensive advantage during attack. The long-term advantage would be the simple knowledge of its existence to those outside as well as inside.

Following the construction of the canal, the bottom accumulated a thin ephemeral lens of black sediment lying upon impermeable parent *sascab* (clean limestone marl). This sediment is thought to represent a humate horizon which eroded from the banks of the canal. It is argued that the adjacent fields were abandoned and left unmanaged, which resulted in the present inverted stratigraphy in the canal. The thick blocky deposit of grey clays are suggested to have been a raised-field platform matrix. Descending the stratigraphy, the grey clays grade from lighter to darker, with the expectably richer humate content occurring in the lower reaches of the profile. The stone and gravel found near the bottom of the canal is in part decomposing caprock, but it may also represent an ancient retaining feature supporting the earthen platforms that washed out of the suggested collapsed fields.

The argument that these sediments have eroded from the banks of the canal is supported by (1) the absence of microstratigraphy, possibly indicative of a rapid infilling episode following the abandonment of the site at the end of the Late Preclassic period, and (2) the slight bit of lateral lensing from the upper reaches of the canal, as well as the thinning lateral slope of the basal canal paleosol.

Following the partial infilling event of the canal, there appears to have been a period of restoration and reuse that culminated in the damlike feature in the easternmost exposure and the later stone-lined canal segment overlying the grey clays in the western trench. The damlike feature has provided a somewhat sealed context for dating the abandonment or disuse of the initial canal. From this easternmost trench, we have obtained sherds dating exclusively to the Chicanel ceramic sphere. In addition, we have collected a carbon sample from this context within the grey clays which should provide a *terminus post quem* for the abandonment of the initial canal construction. It should also be noted that numerous *Pomacea* shells were capped by the dam, suggesting the freshwater environment in which these grey clays were deposited.

The two trench exposures suggest contemporaneity in terms of complementary architectural form as well as in the appearance of basal flange bowl elements for the first time in the canal sediments. The latter occur in the stone fill of the damlike feature and above the stone-lined canal segment. It is argued that at this later moment in the prehistory of the canal, this segment between the two trenches functioned as a catchment basin for runoff from the deflated and collapsed field area. The absence of stone lining associated with the foot and the adjacent area of the damlike feature suggests that the narrow shallow lining defined in the western trench was designed as the constricted mouth of a small reservoir. The elevated position as well as the constricted mouth would trap a considerable amount of water during the dry season following the rains of May through October. The position of the feature suggests that the water filling the reservoir entered from the west. If these features are Early Classic in date, it is tempting to consider the ephemeral Early Classic component at Cerros as responsible for modifying the canal to utilize the previous drainage qualities of the hydraulic system. The absence of substantial amounts of the assumably redeposited raised-field grey clays above the exposed features would suggest little concern with intensive agricultural management at Cerros during these later periods—a thesis which is in keeping with the reduced populations suggested by the house-mound survey program. It is likely that the later residents of Cerros viewed the original canal as an impediment to traffic and a breeding ground for insect pests, rather than as a useful hydraulic system. The damlike feature may have been as important as a causeway as it was as any other function.

The major feeder canal is defined by a shallow dish-shaped cross section cut into the limestone. Our excavations of the main canal (as well as in other locations where we have contacted caprock) indicate that the upper 40 cm of limestone is quite friable as a result of ground-water percolation. It is suggested that once the main canal was established, quarrying activities for building stone were satisfied. Further energy expended in the acquisition of additional stone being unnecessary, it was easier to remove a wider section of canal than to excavate deeper to obtain the same water volume capacity for the major feeder canal.

The expected amount of light grey clays have infilled the major feeder canal. These sediments are identical to those defined in the main canal and are also attributed to the suggested raised-field platform erosional displacement. The absence of a redeposited paleosol at the bottom of the major feeder canal analogous to that described for the main canal is thought to be a function of the original drainage gradient. The higher elevation of this canal segment would tend to redeposit some sediments into the main canal until a gradient equilibrium could be established. It should be noted that the majority of identifiable sherds from this trench are dated to the Late Preclassic period.

At the north end of the major feeder canal are positioned four earthen platforms that have been interpreted as deflated raised-field platforms, though a residential function is also suggested. Each platform is flanked by a narrow system of minor feeder canals. The infilled matrix within each canal is identical to the grey clays found elsewhere and believed to have been eroded from the adjacent platforms. Of particular interest in our excavation is the presence of uncut fragments of boulder-size limestone resting in a manner that suggests their previous function as a stone retaining feature supporting the flanking platforms, as well as defining the width of the minor feeder canal. Though affected by leaching, the profile reveals what appears to be a shallow *sascab* bank that may have formed a diminutive levee into which the stone retaining feature would have been buttressed. Functionally, this would have prevented water from saturating the adjacent platform fields (due to the impermeable nature of the *sascab*) and inciting root rot as well as preventing water from dissipating into the fields in a premature, uncontrolled manner. The retaining feature would have aided in preventing the slumping of the fields into the canals, thereby reducing the amount of time and energy necessary for maintenance as well as securing spatial boundaries.

The cross section of the two adjacent fields was somewhat discouraging. Lateral slumping and erosion into the system coupled with leaching, wet/dry soil-cracking episodes, and snail (*Pomacea*) burrows have produced a mottled profile. The fields are believed to have been raised higher during the Late Preclassic period but never elevated by *sascab* platforms (Puleston 1977a, 1978). Although the soil tests are not complete, it is possible that the naturally low phosphate content of the soils on the peninsula (Wright *et al.* 1959) was increased by mixing beach sand with the naturally occurring clays. This would also produce a more fertile loam than that made available by the indigenous clays.

The ceramic sample obtained from this exposure has produced a collection of Sierra Red wares. The presence of large sherds, charcoal flecks, bone fragments, and high phosphate concentrations may suggest that kitchen compost was deposited to enrich the soils (see Wilken 1969:231). Our excavations at the margins of presumed house mounds at Cerros have not produced the midden debris reported from other sites (Haviland 1963; Fry 1969; Stoltman 1978). However, isolated post holing in depressed locations has frequently produced thin trash deposits or sheet midden. Though domestic trash may have been deliberately redeposited on the fields, its source is unknown. It is possible that the fields were maintained by households residing on the platforms, practicing a form of infield gardening (Wolf 1966; Netting 1974, 1977). Considering the absence of well-defined house-mound features inside the area defined by the main canal as well as the presence of a densely occupied, ground-level village on the coast during the initial phases of the site, it may have been that low earthen residential platforms were the rule at Cerros during the Late Preclassic period.

Speculation

Evidence supports the presence of drained fields at Cerros. The apparent system of reservoirs and canals may have permitted limited pot irrigation and potable water supplies through the dry season, given the presence of evaporation-retarding aquatic plants (Matheny 1978; Puleston 1977a) and other conservation measures. The possibility does exist, however, that the mouth of the New River has regressed up its channel, which formerly emptied into a low energy lagoon environment. The proximity of the river to the site and the rapid erosional rate recorded along the Corozal Bay shoreline (.25–.51 m/year [Belize Lands Department, personal communication]) may suggest that the main canal was excavated around the site and conveniently tapped into the New River. The absence of prograding deltaic conditions at the mouth of the New River and the shallow depth of the bay may further suggest a recent localized tectonic subsidence. The dense midden concentration associated with dark lacustrine clays and high frequencies of an associated shallow water, estuarine adapted snail (*Melongena melongena,* identified by Anthony Andrews) suggests that the environmental setting was considerably different from that shown today. Judging from the present proximity of the numerous lagoons and salt marshes along the New River and Freshwater Creek, it has been suggested that Corozal Bay was formerly a constricted mouth lagoon.

This latter scenario suggests that the New River may have been channeled via a man-made distributary into Cerros, providing year-round water supplies and irrigation to fields and house platforms. Our survey and excavation data suggest that this scheme was possible on formal grounds (see Figure 3). In fact, the position of the second or easternmost damlike feature, defining the southeastern intersection of the main canal and the just-examined major feeder canal, is ideally situated to function as a diversion dam with the current flowing from the west. This feature has not been excavated, and contemporaneity with the initial main canal cut has not been established. This type of hydraulic system is not unique to the Maya area; Matheny and Gurr (1979) have reported a similar diversion dam arrangement in the upper Grijalva River basin.

Within the site perimeter as defined by the canal, numerous depressions or small seasonal reservoirs have been recorded, usually in proximity to mounded features. Preliminary field data suggest that a system of interconnected depressions covered much of the site. This system of reservoirs may have allowed the community to cultivate infield gardens as well as to irrigate more extensive fields, to say nothing of the availability of adequate supplies of potable water. High ground, raised plaza and *sacbeob* would have connected most structures inside the canal. Such a network of low and high ground, undulating by as much as 2.5 m across the site, may have also provided an adequate means of defining spatial boundaries within the settlement.

Sanders (1976) mentions the manner in which floodwater irrigation is carried out in the alluvial plain of the Teotihuacán Valley today. The scope and magnitude of the example is more grand than that ever envisioned at Cerros, but the basic technique may have been employed 2,000 years ago in a drastically different environmental setting:

> A series of masonry dams with wooden gates have been constructed across the streams on the plain. When the gates are closed, the water is backed up into a large pond and immediately diverted by canals into the fields. When fields served by the canal have been irrigated, the gates are opened and the water is allowed to flow down to the next dam (Sanders 1976:104).

It should be made clear that the gradient of the canal at Cerros is probably less than 2 m along its entire 1,200-m length. Though Sanders is unclear as to the precise gradient of the barrancas involved in this floodwater system within the Teotihuacán Valley, a significant difference is implicit.

In addition, some of the feeder canals at Cerros, most notably those in the northeastern segment of the canal, may have been directed into the *aguada* system found throughout Lowry's Bight. This flow may have provided a water source during periods of drought. It should be noted that the largest *aguada* on the peninsula, lying approximately one km south–southeast of the canal, produced surface collection of Phase I Late Preclassic ceramics (Robertson, personal communication to Freidel), suggesting the premium placed on water and the distances traveled before relocating a village. A survey transect from the center to the *aguada* and quadrat survey units around the *aguada* have revealed no mounded features in the area.

Intensive agricultural technology has been reported for the interior of Belize as early as the Early Classic period (Belisle *et al.* 1977). In addition, on the grounds of a recent radiocarbon date (Puleston 1977a, 1978), portions of the Albion Island canal–field system are indicated to date before 1000 B.C. It is possible that with the modification of upstream watersheds and the more severe effects of deforestation as a result of intensive agricultural practices, rivers such as the New and the Hondo were made to carry and discharge considerable sediment loads (after Willey *et al.* 1965). If this were the case during the Late Preclassic period, the canal at Cerros would have required frequent dredging. An advantage to this seemingly difficult situation may have been the availability of rich humates which could be used to fertilize the rather poor soils at Cerros. (The soils on Lowry's Bight are quite adequate for arboriculture but are considered poor for maize cropping.) (Wright *et al.* 1959). Though our understanding of the kind and degree of intensive agriculture practiced upstream from Cerros is negligible, the siphoning of water from the New River would also have been of great interest to the Late Preclassic *Cerrosanos.*

Another function of the canal has been little touched upon. It treats the definition of social as well as political boundaries at Cerros. Whatever initiated the construction of the canal, it would appear that it delineated the limits of the site. Puleston (1974, 1977b) has treated this factor at Tikal, suggesting that the density of residential mounds inside the earthworks is considerably greater than that outside. This same pattern seems apparent from the limits of our survey and reconnaissance carried out, to date, at Cerros during the Late Preclassic period. Although the definition of space throughout the lowlands has been an elusive topic, given the apparent dispersed settlement pattern and the effects of jungle encroachment, boundary maintenance within, as well as between, sites would be expected in a stratified society.

In the highlands, canalization has been hypothesized as early as the Tzacualli phase (Terminal Preclassic) at Teotihuacán (Sanders 1976) and empirically demonstrated on a diminutive scale at Hierve el Agua in the valley of Oaxaca during Monte Albán I (Middle Preclassic) (Flannery *et al.* 1967). Chinampa agriculture as early as the Terminal Preclassic period is suggested near Tlaltenco in the valley of Mexico with the construction of a man-made island (Armillas 1971). Coe (1964) indicates a similar date. However, a canal as substantial as the one shown at Cerros has not yet been demonstrated elsewhere in Mesoamerica until the Palo Blanco and Venta Salada phases in the Valley of Tehuacán, Puebla (Classic and Postclassic) (Woodbury and Neely 1972) or at Santa Clara Xalostoc in the Basin of Mexico and assigned a pre-Coyotlatelco Phase (Classic) date (Sanders and Santley 1977). (However, it should be noted that well-developed canalization has been found at Snaketown in the American Southwest as early as the Pioneer period 300 B.C.–A.D. 400) [Haury 1975].) Although Late Preclassic canals are reported at Edzná, Campeche (Matheny 1976, 1978), the exact nature and extent of canalization during the Preclassic period is not known.

Conclusions

There is much work yet to be done on the canal and field systems at Cerros. More areas at the termination of feeder canals must be mapped. Limnological and sediment studies must be carried out on our samples. The abundant pollen samples in hand must be analyzed, and the radiocarbon dates run.[1] The soil chemistry data must be interpreted. Yet even at this preliminary stage in the research, certain salient points can be made. First, it is clear that the features are artificial and intentionally built. Second, strong associational data in the form of diagnostic ceramics indicates that these systems were built during the Late Preclassic florescence of Cerros and not by some later remnant population. Third, the system at Cerros was planned and designed around an existing community. This last observation is important. It is supported not only by the fact that the main canal forms a perimeter around the community, but also by the fact that the known fields associated with the canal are oriented to the cardinal directions, and not to the natural orientation of the river as they are elsewhere.

Regardless of how this water management system functioned, its association with fields strongly suggests that it was designed to intensify agricultural production, not on the peninsula of Lowry's Bight as a whole, but within the bounds of the complex community of Cerros. Such a highly localized system must have been constructed to meet the specific needs of the community. On the basis of ethnohistorical analogy presented at the outset of this report, the two likely motivations for the construction of such a system are the maintenance of subsistence autonomy and the commercial production of trade commodities.

At the present stage of research at Cerros, it is impossible to say which of these motivations may have been the stronger. The argument for subsistence autonomy is supported by the marginal quality of the agricultural land on Lowry's Bight (Wright, *et al.* 1959). The intensification of food production would have allowed a large resident population to live in the community without importing food. It would also have freed much of this population to pursue the nonsubsistence activities of a trading center. There are indications in our settlement research that the population at Cerros was larger than that reflected in the mounded features. As noted previously, sheet midden and evidence of ground-level occupation have been found within the community at a distance from the mounds. In the case of the fields examined to date, quantities of trash had washed into the ditch we excavated. These fields are at some distance from the nearest mounds. The general nature of this trash—including broken stone tools, large pieces of pottery, and animal bones—implies that it was not being moved

[1]One date has come back on carbonized material from deep sediments in the main canal, 2300 ± 150 B.P. (350 B.C.) (SMU 774 [5,568-year half-life]). Corrected to the 5,730-year half-life, this date would be 2370 B.P.; calibrated on the basis of tree-ring data, it would be 2372 ± 180 B.P. The confidence level is low due to small sample size, but even given a two sigma variation, the date falls in the Preclassic. The date is preliminary pending current calibration of the counter for efficiency and background.

very far. The possibility that people were living on the fields at ground level must be further investigated.

On the other hand, survey transects radiating out from Cerros onto Lowry's Bight indicate that the interior of the peninsula was sparsely occupied outside the community. Hence, much of this land could have been devoted to the agricultural production required to support the community. Moreover, excavation of several of the mounded groups within the perimeter has demonstrated that they are public facilities, despite their surface resemblance to household groups. Finally, extensive raised-field systems border the present mouth of the New River, which is less than 2 km away from the site center. These fields may postdate the major Late Preclassic occupation at Cerros, but at this point, we cannot be sure. In short, the possibility remains open that the community at Cerros could have maintained subsistence autonomy without resorting to intensification within its boundaries. Hence, the prospect that agricultural intensification at Cerros was aimed at the production of such commercial commodities as cacao, cotton, and copal must be considered. Hopefully, ongoing palynological and palaeobotanical studies at Cerros will shed light on this subject. In the meantime, the fact that the fields pervade the community proper supports the inference that crops grown on them were of particular value.

Finally, certain general points about agricultural intensification in the Maya Lowlands can be made on the basis of the data in hand at Cerros. Dennis Puleston persistently argued that intensification of agricultural production through water management was an early and pervasive development along the rivers of the Maya Lowlands (Puleston and Puleston 1971; Puleston 1977a, 1978). The data at Cerros support this contention. Not only can it be argued that agricultural production through water management was present in the lowlands by Late Preclassic times, but it also can be suggested with confidence that such intensification substantially predates the time of Christ. The system found at Cerros is anything but a tentative and experimental attempt. The planned design of this complex system of canals, drainage areas, and fields clearly indicates that it was the product of a fully developed and sophisticated technology—a technology that had moved beyond the needs of bare subsistence survival to meet those of a trading center.

Indeed, Puleston argued that meeting subsistence needs through agricultural production is only a potentially critical factor in Maya evolution if we confine our view of Maya agriculture to extensive swiddening with maize as the only major staple crop. The importance of arboriculture, suggested by Puleston as a source of staple food at Tikal (Puleston 1968; Puleston and Puleston 1971) is well attested in the historical literature (Roys 1972:40). Root crops, native to lowland environments, were well established in the Contact period (Roys 1972:38). In addition, as noted at the outset of this report, there is evidence that systems of intensive agriculture were still operative in the Contact period. While ethnohistorical information gave rise to the "swidden hypothesis," which for years blinded scholars to the agricultural potential and sophistication of Lowland Maya civilization, data from the Contact period may also open our eyes to the wide range of subsistence and commercial crops grown by these people even in their decline.

Evidence of land modification for purposes of agricultural intensification and regulation has generally kept pace over the past few years with the evidence for higher population densities than those previously imagined for the Lowland Maya. As interest in Maya agriculture grows, we strongly suspect that the former will eventually outstrip the latter, and it will become apparent that the Maya were at no time straining the productive capacity of their resources in terms of subsistence. On the basis of the available evidence, there is reason to believe that Maya interest in commercial agricultural production at the time of the Conquest was but a pale reflection of the former Classic glory. The Postclassic Yucatecan Maya, for example, were famous throughout Mesoamerica for their cotton textiles. A glance at the iconographic literature of the Classic era shows that these people were vastly more competent in this craft. The problem, of course, has always been in documenting the importance of such nonsubsistence crops in lowland environments. Palynological and paleobotanical studies may be able to gauge the presence of cotton, cacao, copal, and other commercial crops in the context of Maya settlements and agricultural lands. In the meantime, evidence such as that found at Cerros indicates that there was already an intimate association of agricultural and commercial interests at the beginning of Maya civilization.

References

Armillas, Pedro
1971 Gardens on swamps. *Science* 174:653–661.

Ball, J. W., and E. W. Andrews V
1978 Preclassic architecture at Becan, Campeche, Mexico. *Middle American Research Institute, Tulane University, Occasional Paper No.* 3. New Orleans, The Institute.

Belisle, Joseph, S. Musa, and A. Shoman (editors)
1977 Special issue: the Río Hondo Project; an investigation of the Maya of northern Belize. Journal of Belizean Affairs, No. 5.

Blatt, H., G. Middleton, and R. Murray
1972 *Origin of Sedimentary Rocks.* Englewood Cliffs, Prentice-Hall.

Coe, Michael D.
1964 The chinampas of Mexico. *Scientific American* 211(1):90–99.

Flannery, K. V., A. V. T. Kirkby, M. J. Kirkby, and A. W. Williams, Jr.
1967 Farming systems and political growth in ancient Oaxaca. *Science* 158:445–454.

Freidel, David A.
1976 *Pre-Columbian settlement patterns on Cozumel Island, Quintana Roo, Mexico.* Unpublished Ph.D. dissertation, Department of Anthropology, Harvard Univ.
1978 Maritime adaptation and the rise of Maya civilization: The view from Cerros, Belize. In *Prehistoric Coastal Adaptations,* edited by B. Stark and B. Voorhies. New York, Academic Press.
1979 Culture areas and interaction spheres: Contrasting approaches to Lowland Maya evolution in light of evidence from Cerros, northern Belize. *American Antiquity* 44(1):36–54.

Fry, Robert E.
1969 *Ceramics and settlement in the periphery of Tikal, Guatemala.* Unpublished Ph.D. dissertation, Department of Anthropology, Univ. of Arizona.

Haury, Emil W.

1976 *The Hohokam.* Tucson, Univ. of Arizona Press.

Haviland, William A.

1963 *Excavation of small structures in the northeast quadrant of Tikal, Guatemala.* Unpublished Ph.D. dissertation, Department of Anthropology, University of Pennsylvania.

Matheny, Ray T.

1976 Maya Lowland hydraulic systems. *Science* 193:639–646.

1978 Northern Maya Lowland water-control systems. In *Prehispanic Maya Agriculture,* edited by Peter D. Harrison and B. L. Turner II. Albuquerque, Univ. of New Mexico Press.

Matheny, R. T., and D. L. Gurr

1979 Ancient hydraulic techniques in the Chiapas highlands. *American Scientist* 67(4):441–449.

Millon, René

1973 *Urbanization at Teotihuacán, Mexico,* Vol. 1, *The Teotihuacán Map,* Part 1. Austin, Univ. of Texas Press.

Netting, Robert McC.

1974 Agrarian ecology. *Annual Review of Anthropology* 3:21–56.

1977 Maya subsistence: Mythologies, analogies, possibilities. In *The Origins of Maya Civilization,* edited by R. E. W. Adams. Albuquerque, Univ. of New Mexico Press (School of American Research Advanced Seminar Series).

Puleston, Dennis E.

1968 *Brosimum alicastrum as a subsistence alternative for the Classic Maya of the central southern lowlands.* Unpublished M.A. thesis, Department of Anthropology, Univ. of Pennsylvania

1974 Intersite areas in the vicinity of Tikal and Uaxactún. In *Mesoamerican Archaeology: New Approaches,* edited by Norman Hammond. Austin, Univ. of Texas Press.

1977a The art and archaeology of hydraulic agriculture in the Maya Lowlands. In *Social Process in Maya Prehistory,* edited by Norman Hammond. New York, Academic Press.

1977b Ancient Maya settlement patterns in the Petén. Preliminary version of a paper prepared for an advanced seminar titled Lowland Maya Settlement Patterns, at the School of American Research, Santa Fe, New Mexico.

1978 Terracing, raised fields, and tree cropping in the Maya Lowlands: A new perspective on the geography of power. In *Prehispanic Maya Agriculture,* edited by Peter D. Harrison and B. L. Turner, II, pp. 225–245. Albuquerque, University of New Mexico Press.

Puleston, Dennis E. and Donald W. Callender, Jr.

1967 Defensive earthworks at Tikal. *Expedition* 9:40–48.

Puleston, Dennis E. and O. S. Puleston

1971 An ecological approach to the origins of Maya civilization. *Archaeology* 24:330–37.

Roys, Ralph L.

1957 The Political Geography of the Yucatán Maya. *Publication* 613 *Carnegie Institution of Washington,* Washington, D.C.

1972 *The Indian Background of Colonial Yucatán.* Norman, Univ. of Oklahoma Press.

Sabloff, Jeremy A. and D. A. Freidel

1975 A model of a Pre-Columbian trading center. In *Ancient Civilization and Trade,* edited by J. A. Sabloff and C. C. Lamberg-Karlovsky. pp. 369–408. Albuquerque, Univ. of New Mexico Press, (School of American Research Advanced Seminar Series).

Sanders, William T.

1976 The agricultural history of the Basin of Mexico. In *The Valley of Mexico: Studies in Pre-Hispanic Ecology and Society,* edited by Eric Wolf. Albuquerque, Univ. of New Mexico Press, (School of American Research Advanced Seminar Series).

Sanders, William T., and Robert S. Santley

1977 A Prehispanic irrigation system near Santa Clara Xalostoc in the basin of Mexico. *American Antiquity* 42:582–587.

Scholes, France V. and R. L. Roys

1968 *The Maya Chontal Indians of Acalan-Tixchel.* (Reprint of the original, *Publication 560,*

Carnegie Institute of Washington.) Norman, Univ. of Oklahoma Press.
Siemens, A. H. and D. E. Puleston
1972 Ridged fields and associated features in southern Campeche: New perspectives on the Lowland Maya. *American Antiquity* 37:228–239.
Siemens, Alfred H.
1977 Special issue: The Río Hondo Project: An Investigation of the Maya of northern Belize. *Journal of Belizean Affairs. No. 5.* (Joseph Belisle, S. Musa, and A. Shoman editors).
1978 Karst and the pre-Hispanic Maya in the southern lowlands. In *Pre-Hispanic Maya Agriculture,* edited by Peter D. Harrison and B. L. Turner, II. Albuquerque, Univ. of New Mexico Press.
Simpson, L. B.
1966 *Cortés: The Life of the Conqueror by His Secretary Francisco López de Gomara,* translated and edited by L. B. Simpson. Berkeley, Univ. of California Press.
Stoltman, James B.
1978 Lithic Artifacts from two Complex societies. *Middle American Research Institute, Tulane University, Occasional Paper No. 2.* New Orleans, The Institute.
Sweeting, Marjorie M.
1973 *Karst Land Forms.* New York, Columbia Univ. Press.
Thompson, J. Eric S.
1977 A proposal for constituting a Maya subgroup, cultural and linguistic, in the Petén and adjacent regions. In *Anthropology and History in Yucatán,* edited by G. D. Jones. Austin, Univ. of Texas Press.
Vance, James E., Jr
1970 *The Merchant's World: The Geography of Wholesaling.* Foundations of Economic Geography Series. New Jersey, Prentice-Hall.
Vlcek, David T., S. Garza de Gónzalez, and E. B. Kurjack
1978 Contemporary farming and ancient Maya settlements: Some disconcerting evidence. In *Prehispanic Maya Agriculture,* edited by Peter D. Harrison and B. L. Turner, II, pp. 211–223. Albuquerque, Univ. of New Mexico Press.
Wagner, Henry R.
1942 *The Discovery of New Spain in 1518 by Juan de Grijalva,* translated by H. R. Wagner. Pasadena, California, The Cortes Society, Val Treiz Press.
Webster, David L.
1976 Defensive earthworks at Becan, Campeche, Mexico: Implications for Maya warfare. *Middle American Research Institute, Tulane University, Publication No. 41.* New Orleans, The Institute.
Wilken, G. C.
1969 Drained-field agriculture: An intensive farming system in Tlaxcala, Mexico. *Geographical Review* 59:215–241.
Willey, G. R., W. R. Bullard, Jr, J. B. Glass, and J. C. Gifford
1965 Prehistoric Maya Settlements in The Belize Valley. *Papers of the Peabody Museum of Archaeology and Ethnology, Harvard University,* Vol. 54.
Wiseman, Frederick M.
1978 Agricultural and historical ecology of the Maya Lowlands. In *Pre-Hispanic Maya Agriculture,* edited by Peter D. Harrison and B. L. Turner II. Albuquerque, Univ. of New Mexico Press.
Wolf, Eric
1966 *Peasants.* New York, Prentice-Hall.
Woodbury, Richard B. and James A. Neely
1972 Water control systems of the Tehuacán Valley. In *The Prehistory of the Tehuacán Valley,* Vol. 4, edited by F. Johnson. Austin, Univ of Texas Press.
Wright, A. C. S., D. H. Romney, R. H. Arbuckle, and V. E. Vial
1959 *Land in British Honduras: Report of the British Honduras Land Use Survey Team.* Colonial Research Publication 24. London, Her Majesty's Stationery Office.

6

Ancient Lowland and Highland Maya Water and Soil Conservation Strategies

Raymond T. Matheny

Introduction

THE focus of this paper is on two of the elements vital to man's survival—water and soil—and how the ancient Maya manipulated these in lowland and highland settings. Generally, in this paper, the greater emphasis is on water. The areas to be examined are the Yucatán Peninsula, Campeche–Tabasco coastlands, Petén forest, highland Chiapas, and Guatemala. Only parts of each area will be considered because there is great variability within these divisions. It is not yet possible to provide much understanding of ancient systems of water and soil conservation in the Maya area because our information base is still small and our experience is recent.

Lowland and Highland Watersheds

The coastal lowlands of Tabasco and Campeche, called the Tabasco Plain, are based in Quaternary sands, marls, coastal alluvia, and marine terraces. Limestone and karst formations are largely absent from the surface since they are covered by marine activated deposits. The area is broken only by the volcanic intrusion of the Tuxtla Mountains in the extreme west and by an occasional low hill on the coastal plain.

ISBN 0-12-259780-X

Adjacent to the Tabasco Plain, the Yucatán platform is made up of Tertiary limestone, sandy marls, marine clastics, and limestone that abuts older Mesozoic marine and continental sediments. Cretaceous and Jurassic limestones and Triassic shale are found in gradual upland environments.

The highlands are affected by Quaternary and Tertiary volcanics and various metasediments and intrusives such as Paleozoic to Cenozoic schists, gneisses, and granitelike formations.

Soils of the Tabasco Plain are hydromorphic, some of which are involved in the gleization process and others which consist of azonal alluvial soils found on floodplains, levees, and terraces. The Yucatán platform exhibits calcimorphic soils, which include brown forest and rendzina soils, and lithosols (resembling rendzina) that make up a large part of the Petén soils. The northern half of the Yucatán platform exhibits the *terra rosa* soils of forested, warm tropical regions. The gleization process is found in most developed valleys of the Petén in Guatemala and Campeche.

In the Chiapas highlands, there are spotty appearances of prairie soils, but mostly there are laterized, humid forest soils with their associated conifer growth. In highland Guatemala, young soils of volcanic origin and lithosols of a calcareous nature are widely distributed and dominated by conifers. Many subdivisions of soils have been made for all of the regions of the highlands and lowlands, and these can be found in Stevens (1964).

The Yucatán platform has an abundance of vegetation related to rainfall and to the soils of the fractured limestone surface. Rainfall increases from moderate amounts (500–1,000 mm) in the northwestern part of the platform to more than 1,000 mm in the Laguna de Términos area and the northern Petén. The 2,000-mm isobar undulates at the Tabasco–Campeche border through the northern Petén to about Belize City. This latter amount of rainfall continues to the mountains, where some areas receive in excess of 3,000 mm.

Drainage from the Chiapas and Guatemalan uplands trends northwestward on the Yucatán platform side. This creates the great river systems that reach the sea in the Gulf of Mexico lowlands. The Yucatán platform limestones become the aquifers of the peninsula and receive water, not only from the uplands, but directly through vegetal cover, karst formations, and numerous exposed, fractured surface areas. Sharp seasonal regimes of precipitation bring a long wet season (June–December) and an equally long dry season (January–May).

Too much surface water has been a perennial problem of some of the gulf coastlands, and too little water has been a problem of some of the interior of the Yucatán platform. Turner (1979:103) reminds us that in the northern ridge lands of Campeche and Quintana Roo, the water table is often over 100 m below the surface, and when 80% of annual rainfall occurs between mid-May and the end of November, a long dry period ensues. The last river on the Yucatán Peninsula is the Río Champotón marking the northern extent of the Tabasco Plain. From there, inland and northward, surface water is scarce. There are only a handful of lakes, small springs, *aguadas,* and open karsts and caverns where water may be obtained.

In December, 1973, I visited the headwaters of the Río Champotón, which is the last true river found above 19° north latitude on the Yucatán Peninsula. The exploration began at San Juan Carpizo, a village located about 100 km east of Campeche City. There are few ruins around this magnificent water source, which today, is rich in aquatic life and migratory birds.

The head of the river receives water from the Edzná Valley, 36 km north, and from other nearby valleys. The drainage to the head is mostly underground, where water has entered drainage crevices called *xuch* in Yucatec Maya. Water comes out in three large springs, the outflow of which joins the northern tributary of the Champotón. Stephens' (1963) map of the Yucatán Peninsula shows the headwaters of the Champotón as a large swampy area called *Lago de Los Lagartos.* No lake exists there today, but the swamp persists at the the springs. This is still a favorite place for hunting caimans, and their skeletal remains are commonly found on the river banks.

Large mollusks of an edible species abound in the headwaters and fish (catfish and *mojarra*) are abundant and are caught by children and adults almost daily. Despite the presence of a never-failing water source and all of the wildlife attracted to it, there are few known ancient settlements in the area. During an aerial reconnaissance over the upper reaches of the Río Champotón, a few hilltop Maya structures were noted, but no large settlements were found in this rich environment. The river is navigable by launch up from Champotón about 60 km, and then by canoe practically to the headwaters.

Cilvituc is a small site located at a natural lake south of the Champotón in central Campeche. The water is rich in aquatic life and attracts many forest animals and migratory fowl. Despite the rather obvious attractions of the headwaters of the Río Champotón and Cilvituc—two of the few places where water occurs naturally in significant abundance—no correspondingly large Maya settlements are to be found. Judging from these examples, it appears that the presence of water was not sufficient in and of itself to have enticed the Maya to settle.

There are many areas, particularly on the Yucatán Peninsula, where there are no permanent water sources of the sort discussed above, and yet these areas supported large populations in ancient times. Water dependency is obvious for any large population, and it is instructive to look at what the Maya did to satisfy this urgent need.

Lowland Hydraulic Techniques

Given the sparseness of surface water on the Yucatán Peninsula, Mercer (1975:43–44) commented in the nineteenth century:

> Whoever wants water must, generally speaking, go underground for it, whether by blasting a well through solid rock for his steam pump, or searching in subterranean passages, where water drips, flows, or rests in pools. . . . Much of the earliest archae-

> ology of the country seemed to depend upon the question of what the firstcomer did, before wells were dug and cities and cisterns built, to get water. As original immigrants, coming in the dry season, could not have found a satisfactory supply on the surface, it is certain that they must have discovered and ransacked the caves, and this fact gave the wet underground passages a new meaning. No matter how remote they were, no matter how difficult of access, they were natural and original sources of water supply at certain times. The firstcomer must have visited them or perished.

The Maya, and perhaps an earlier people, surely utilized the water available in the caves. It may have been, as Mercer has suggested, that the caverns were used seasonally by the earliest settlers, and later water collection devices were set up.

It is recorded ethnographically that the Maya have gone to extreme lengths to obtain water in caverns. Mercer (1975:92) recorded his observations at Rancho Chack, where eight ladders were used to descend about 30 m to the cavern floor (Figure 1). One then had to walk and crawl over a well-worn path, about 823 m horizontally, to reach a pool of water. Mercer found the remains of pots and bundles of twigs used for torches inside the cavern.

Stone receptacles up to 1 m in diameter used to catch dripping water were found at Actun Spukil "Cave of the Mice" near Oxkintok (Figure 2). Mercer notes 15 receptacles in the first part of the cave and a line of them in another part. These receptacles provided a visitor with a drink of water if he knew where to look. Explorations or hunting during the dry season in this part of Yucatán would have been very difficult without knowledge of the water available in caverns.

Stephens (1963), during his explorations in Yucatán in the 1840s, visited a number of caverns with water sources and describes descent into caverns as far as 137 m below the surface, as well as places where it was necessary to travel about 427 linear meters to reach water. It seems likely that the caverns were dependable sources of water throughout the Maya period of occupation.

Related to the caverns are open cenotes, an important source of water in ancient times. Morley (1956:16) reminds us "that there are many cenotes in Yucatán, and that in a country as devoid of surface water as northern Yucatán, cenotes were the principal factor in determining the location of the ancient centers of population. They were the most important single factor governing the distribution of the ancient population in northern Yucatán."

Cenotes are up to 61 m in diameter and are frequently open to a perennial and inexhaustible water supply, but many do not have large ruins around them. Water level in cenotes varies with locality and season from about 1 m below the surface to more than 30 m below the surface. Not all cenotes contain fresh water; some are saline, and others have stagnant levels of water. Some have small fish and shrimp in them (Tamayo 1964:99). About 99% of the pottery recovered from the famous cenote at Dzibilchaltún, Yucatán, dates to the Early Period II or Copo I phase, A.D. 600–830, (Andrews 1978). Pottery from

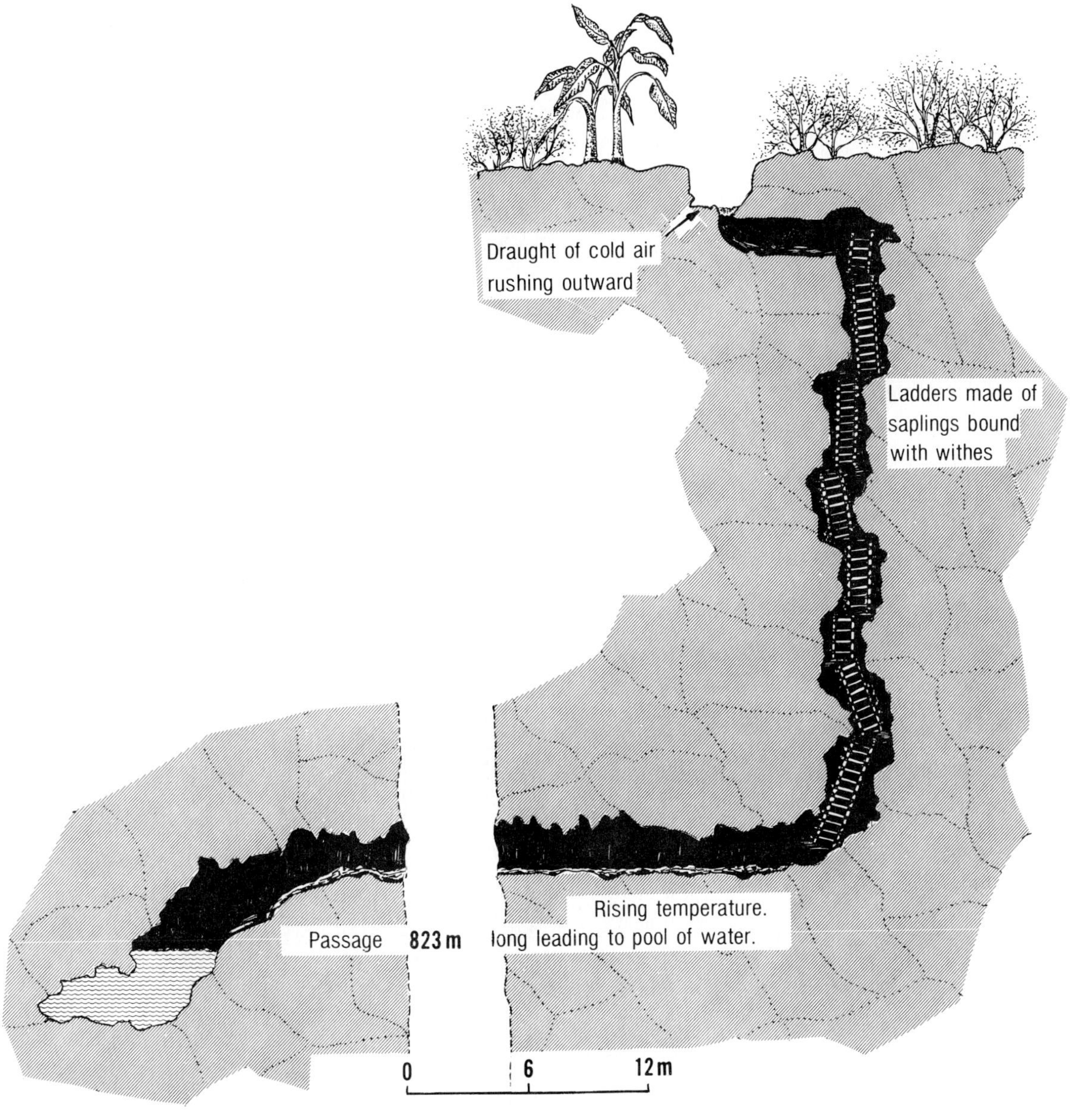

FIGURE 1. *Cavern at Rancho Chack, Yucatán, Mexico (redrawn from Mercer 1975).*

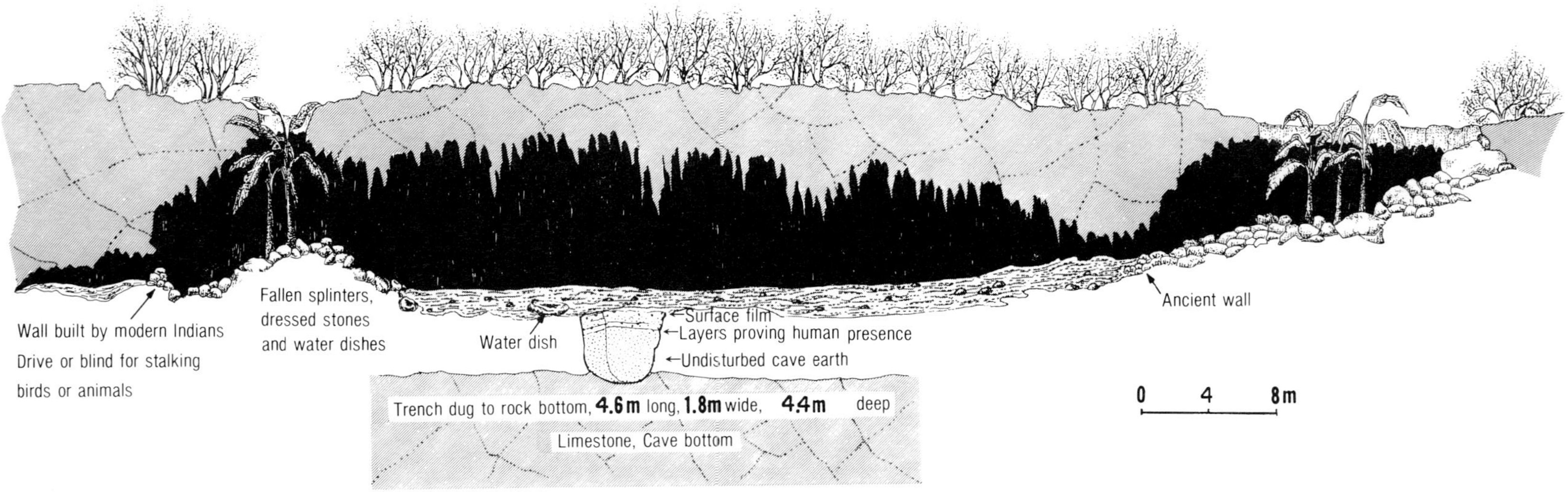

FIGURE 2. *Actun Spukil near Oxkintok, Yucatán, Mexico (redrawn from Mercer 1975).*

the Pure Florescent or Copo II phase, A.D. 830–1000, was also present. Most of the pottery recovered was the remains of water jars. This very reliable water source reduced dependency on other developments such as chultuns and reservoirs.

Evidence for manipulation of water sources at early times in the lowlands of the Tabasco Plain comes from the Olmec site of San Lorenzo. Coe (1968) reports drains up to 170 m long with 30 m of subsidiary lines, composed of U-shaped basalt sections totalling more than 30 tons. A great amount of effort went into procuring and transporting these pieces of basalt. This was an expensive public work that required the skill of an engineer and the backing of political power. The drains were connected to ponds that had been lined with bentonite to condition them to hold water, a practice that is still used by engineers today. Coe thinks the ponds may have been like the "pools of the temples and palaces of India and Ceylon, to which priests and the faithful repair for holy ablutions during festivals" (Coe 1968:87). He continues, "at any rate, whether ritual or not, we have here the first system of water control yet known for the New World." The water system at San Lorenzo probably had nothing to do with agriculture or with land used for gardening. The prime lands for farming were identified as river levees (Coe 1969). Other potential agricultural lands were identified by local informants for varying degrees of productivity and specialties for crops, but Coe was unable to show any land manipulation specifically used for food production. Huge quantities of soil were moved and used in platform construction for architectural purposes. The water constructions were made in soils and areas suitable for water collection, storage, and use.

In the Puuc hills of Yucatán, existing soil conditions do not generally allow for water collection and storage, hence the chultun served these purposes. The chultun was known in the Late Preclassic period at Dzibilnocac (Nelson 1973), but it is the dry-storage type with an offset chamber protected from rain drip by a low masonry partition. Other chultuns noted at Dzibilnocac were for water storage, but date from the Classic period.

Several Late Preclassic chultuns positively identified at Santa Rosa Xtampak (DeBloois 1970) were associated with Chicanel-like pottery. These chultuns were cut into solid limestone that was not badly fractured (Figure 3). Once the cavity was cut, crevices in the limestone were patched and sealed with lime cement. The entire interior was then coated with stucco to a smooth finish. Some chultuns showed several stucco layers of repair and other areas where major patching had occurred. Red pigment has been found on a few interior stucco surfaces which duplicated the red treatment of many exterior surfaces of buildings. Some of the chultuns at Santa Rosa Xtampak show evidence of having been built up around the rim to correspond to the level of the plaza in which they are found. The built-up area consists of small cut stones laid in mortar with a stucco finish contouring to the chultun mouth. Where preservation is good, the plaza floor shows a slope that provided good drainage to the chultun. Chultuns were located mostly in building complexes where there was a large catchment

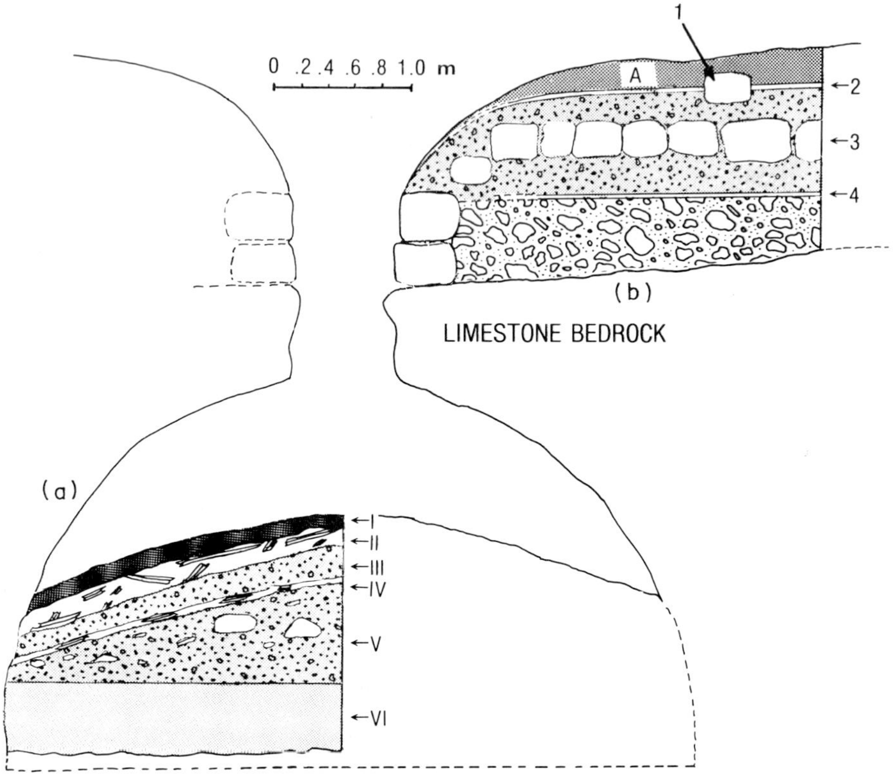

FIGURE 3. *Chultun number 1 at Santa Rosa Xtampak, Campeche, Mexico. Stratigraphy of (a) trench 1 (at the bottom of the chultun): organic fill (I), broken plaster from wall (II), dark fill with sherds (III), broken plaster (IV), dark fill with sherds (V), and sedimentary fill (VI). Stratigraphy of (b) trench A (at the neck of the chultun): east end of stone wall (1); pavement I, plaster, (2); pavement II, rock and plaster, (3); and pavement III, hard-packed earth, (4). (Redrawn from DeBloois 1970).*

area that included roofs, walls of buildings, and plazas. A plaza complex that was completely surfaced with stucco and kept clean could expect an excellent catchment of water.

There are 67 chultuns at Santa Rosa Xtampak that vary greatly in size, despite Morley's statement that chultuns consistently had a 28,500-liter capacity (Morley 1956:265). Twenty-eight chultuns at the site were measured, and their average capacity was estimated at about 35,500 liters of water. Capacities varied greatly for individual chultuns, from 7,000 to 86,000 liters. The potential water storage capacity at Santa Rosa Xtampak, if all chultuns were functioning at the same time, was about 2,400 m^3. The water collection areas for the chultuns were plazas, roofs, vertical walls of buildings, and slopes of pyramids. The "Cuartel" north of the central plaza has a collection area of about 2,196 m^2; if there were an annual rainfall of 1,300 mm, the potential accumulation of water would be about 2,855 m^3. This amount is more than the capacity of all the known chultuns at Santa Rosa Xtampak. It is calculated that a 35-mm rainstorm would cause the 2 chultuns located in the plaza of the Cuartel to overflow.

The chultuns at Labna, Yucatán, show stylistic differences but basically functioned in the same way as those described above (Thompson 1897). Collection areas at Labna were sometimes a 14- to 15-m circle of flat stones set in lime cement located between buildings and in plaza floors (Figure 4). Altogether, Thompson investigated 60 chultuns and excavated 33 at Labna between 1888 and 1891. The chultuns of Santa Rosa Xtampak, Xcalumkin and Labna differ significantly in construction.

I have excavated earthen chultuns on the Xicalango Peninsula at El Aguacatal (Matheny 1971). Here there are no limestone outcrops, and all surface land consists of alluvial and marine deposits. The land is only 1 m above sea level and is surrounded by water (the sea to the north and brackish lagoons to the south). The earthen chultun was constructed during the Late Classic period, but may have had an earlier history. In constructing the chultun, a pit 1.5–2 × 1–1.5 m was dug into the ground next to a house. The interior of the pit was

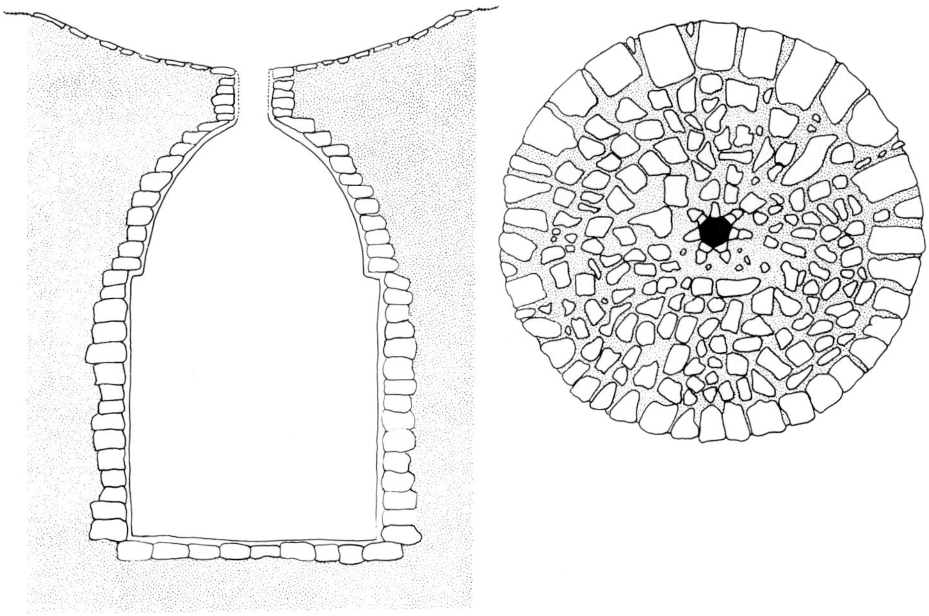

FIGURE 4. *Chultun and water collection pavement, Labna, Yucatán, Mexico (redrawn from Thompson 1897). Copyright 1897, by the Peabody Museum of Archaeology and Ethnology, Harvard University.*

plastered with clay similar to that used to make pottery. Then, a hardwood fire was built on the surface next to the chultun mouth and was pushed into it when sufficient coals had been produced. The burning mass in the chultun fired the clay inside, turning it into an impervious liner. The roof of the house was used as a water catchment area, and water was directed into the chultun. Informants in the area say that this type of chultun was still being constructed as recently as 50 years ago on some of the small islands found in the brackish lagoons of the Xicalango Peninsula.

WELLS

Wells were an important source of water in some parts of the Maya area. Nelson (1973:33–34) reports 19 wells at Dzibilnocac, Campeche, and he suggests that some wells could have been dug as early as the Middle Preclassic period. The best evidence, however, dates from the Late Classic period. The wells are not a dependable water source year round and dry up in February, or at least by March. The wells of Iturbide (near Dzibilnocac) were dry in February 1842, when Stephens passed through, and also in 1970, when Nelson was there.

The ancient wells at Dzibilnocac were dug in limestone and belong to the vertical shaft type, being about 1 m in diameter (Figure 5). A protective ring of stones without mortar was found around each well. This vertical extension probably served to keep small animals out of the well and provided a structure that could have been easily capped. Ancient wells at Dzibilnocac were dug down to at least 13.6 m below the surface. The wells may be deeper, but the danger of cave-ins prevented archaeological excavation below that point.

Shallow wells of the Xicalango Peninsula, dug into the sand and clay, and similar wells found at Punta de Cedro, on a low beach ridge at the mouth of the Río Balchaca, are two ethnographic examples of how water is traditionally obtained in an area where salt and brackish water predominate. These wells are hardly more than simple 1-m-diameter holes in the soil, dug down to where water seeps into them. Fresh water separates from the saline water and migrates to the surface where it can be scooped off. The water is foul tasting and dirty, but it is life sustaining.

During an exploration in the Xicalango area in 1971, Dennis Puleston, Alfred Siemens, and I discovered a walled town at Punta de Cedro. The site, to which I have assigned the same name, has 16 mounds in a row across the center and 3 large mounds to the side, all within the confines of three encircling walls that are each 750 m long. I have speculated elsewhere (Matheny 1976) that the walls were sea walls or tide walls to contain the sea during high tides in March and during northwest storms. It is likely that, in addition to that function, shallow wells could have been put into the walls to collect fresh water. Pottery from a looted burial located on the principal mound showed a span from the Post Classic to Historic periods.

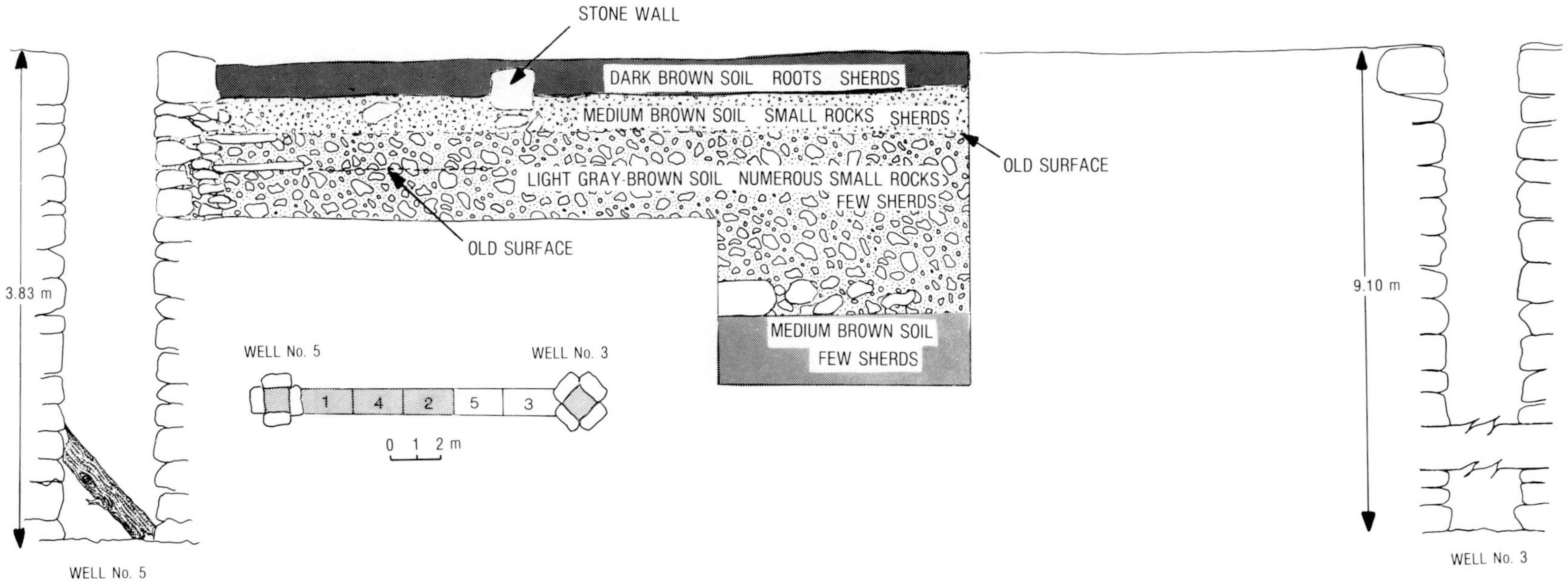

FIGURE 5. *Wells and pavements, trench A, at Dzibilnocac, Campeche, Mexico (redrawn from Nelson 1973).*

Andrews (1978) notes the finding of almost 100 "small natural or artificial wells" at Dzibilchaltún where annual precipitation is a scant 750 mm. These wells were used in addition to the cenote already mentioned.

AGUADAS, RESERVOIRS, AND CANALS

The ancient hydraulic system at Edzná is one of the most recently studied on the Yucatán Peninsula (Matheny 1976, 1978). The site is in central Campeche, situated in a shallow valley about 70 km from the coast. Its display of canals and reservoirs, with a storage capacity of more than 2 million m^3 of water is remarkable. This water storage system was part of a planned city that covers about 17 km^2. Most of the water system was built during the Late Preclassic period, and there are several mounds of this period built on top of the canal banks. These canals are huge constructions; one of them involved the removal of about 900,000 m^3 of soil. A moated fortress connected to that canal would have held about 186,000 m^3 of water. The fortress and main canal are Late Preclassic period constructions and can be considered among the great prehistoric public works of the early Maya. The 21 canals and 25 reservoirs at Edzná provided water in excess of culinary requirements, and it is possible that water was also used for pot-water irrigation. Along with the hydraulic system, there was much soil manipulation by banking, platform building, small-dam construction, causeway building, and channel excavating. In addition, canal mucks may have been worked into other soils much as the soils of Tlaxcala were treated (Wilken 1969).

RESERVOIRS

Uxmal, Yucatán, lacked a great cenote, and the ancient engineers turned their attention to the development of several large reservoirs which may have been interconnected. Brasseur de Bourborg (1865) described the ancient water system at Uxmal, which included bridges that provided foot traffic over a water course and chultuns, some of which were found in the bottom of a reservoir. He even noted a moated fortress, but I have not confirmed its presence.

In the Petén sites, such as Calakmul I, El Mirador, and Tikal, there was a dependency upon the reservoir system. Water-storage chultuns are also known in the area. At El Mirador, only six chultuns of the water-storage type have been found. The site has only been explored briefly and many more chultuns may be discovered, but we do know that they generally do not occur in the great plazas.

At Tikál (Puleston 1971), most of the chultuns investigated have been of the dry-storage type; only a few were designed to store water. The scarcity of the water-storage type of chultun in the Petén may be explained by the development of reservoir systems. Calakmul, Campeche, in the northern Petén forest, has three reservoirs located near the two 50-m-high pyramids; one of these reservoirs is very large and rectangular in form. At El Mirador, we have identified three good-sized reservoirs and expect to find others. The El Mirador reservoirs pick up water from adjacent building complexes and, in one case, from a partitioned *bajo.* It is likely that the reservoir system there was planned, and that the barrows for buildings and platforms were later made into reservoirs. Important to the success of the reservoirs was the strategic placement of building complexes that served as catchment areas. No dimensional figures are available for the El Mirador public building complexes or the reservoirs as yet, but the least that can be said about them is that they are large public works.

RAISED FIELDS AND TERRACES

Puleston's discovery of a post on the bank of a raised-field canal in Belize with a radiocarbon date of 1110 (±230) B.C. was a great surprise. Hammond (1978:33) has calibrated Puleston's date to 1400 B.C. and feels that the "raised-field econiche in the swamp margins could have been created early in the Formative."

Terracing will be considered here as a means of conserving water where no appreciable surface water is available. That many ancient terraces are found in the lowlands is well-recorded fact, and Turner (1978:168) states that for the Río Bec region alone, there are "hundreds of thousands of relic terraces and related stone works that cover an approximate contiguous area of 10,000 km^2. Harrison (1978:251) reports that 2,460 km^2 of patterns have been discerned on aerial photos taken in Quintana Roo. Harrison was unable to check ground truth of the patterns, and speculates that they may be raised fields and canals. The idea that 20,000 km^2 of land had been modified for agricultural production is staggering. Wiseman (1978:90) observed, "Terraces are good evidence for almost total land use, since all arable lowland would be under cultivation before the expense of terrace construction was undertaken."

We may have to revise much of our thinking about what the Maya did to the lowlands. Judging from the observations of Turner, Harrison, Wiseman, and others, it seems likely that the Maya may have had agricultural colonies for the purpose of subduing these difficult lands and supplying food to populations elsewhere. Vlcek *et al.* (1978:221) support the idea that food may have been imported to Chunchucmil, Yucatán. They report 12,000 inhabitants in 6 km^2, a figure that "equals the population that today occupies the 2,000 km^2 surrounding the site (Maxcanu and Celestun municipalities)." Soil is so poor that agricultural production is low, and the authors feel that "since Classic times, food was probably imported to sustain the large population indicated by the archaeological remains" (Vlcek *et al.* 1978:222).

We must be cautious in our use of data that, as yet, have not been substantiated by ground-truth investigation. Harrison (1978: Figure 13.1) defined vegetal patterning in bajo terrain near the road between Nicolás Bravo and Ucum, Quintana Roo. These patterns may represent relic raised fields over an area now estimated by Harrison (personal communication) to be 246.1 km^2. Harrison cautions that intensive ground-truth investigations are needed to determine the nature of the patterning.

The Maya Highlands

Strategies of land and water conservation used in the Maya Highlands differed considerably from those of the Lowlands, but many of the same principles applied. The highlands suffer from long dry periods as do the lowlands, and water must be conserved.

The highland areas that will be discussed here include the upper Grijalva Basin, the uplands to the east or Meseta Central de San Cristóbal, the Comitán Plain, and the Sierra Madre de Guatemala.

SPRINGS AND WELLS

Sites in the Meseta Central were most frequently located near springs which provided a dependable water source for drinking. Miller (1959) reports that at Huistán, Chiapas, a Tzotzil community of 227, the village water supplies are of four types: ponds (often in limestone sinks), streams, springs, and wells. The area is located at about 2,280 m above sea level in a white pine forest. The ponds collect rain water which is used for animals and for washing clothes. Women do most of the carrying of water to the house, but children help in this task. This pattern is repeated throughout the mountains from San Cristóbal de las Casas to Comitán. Sometimes the ponds are found outside villages, depending on where the limestone depressions occur. Wells are numerous, and some are patterned after ancient Classic period walk-in wells, such as those found at San Francisco. Several of these mountain walk-in wells are reported for the area (Thomas A. Lee, personal communication), but I have only visited one.

The well at San Francisco is about 8 m in diameter; it is made of cut stone set into concentric rows of diminishing diameters as the well descends. The entire well is stuccoed and painted. A staircase and an overflow drain are found facing northeast. A paved spillway blends into the soil downslope from the overflow. The inhabitants of San Francisco that we talked to had no idea how old the well was, or whether it was of ancient design. This well may be an ancient one revived by recent settlers, or it may have been patterned after a Classic period model. An ancient walk-in well is also found in one of the large plazas of Tenam Puente, located 15 km to the south of Comitán.

Some villages maintain several springs or water holes and find it necessary to shift to auxiliary sources as the dry season develops. The Zinacantecos have water-hole groups (Vogt 1969:145–148) which take their names from a prominent spring or water hole. Each water-hole group varies in size from 2 to 13 *snas* 'family units' in order to share a diminishing supply of water. The availability of water determines the size of the family units; in the winter, the groups are fewer and larger. Vogt provides an example with the hamlet ʔApas where "there are eight water-hole groups drawing water from eight water holes in the rainy season; in the dry season the same households regroup into four large water-hole groups drawing water from the four major water holes that normally contain water the year around."

Water holes are considered sacred by the Maya, and there are stories and myths developed for each of the important ones. Ceremonies and rituals are held at the water holes, and it is believed that the water-hole group's ancestral gods hold meetings there to review their descendants' affairs. "The *K'in Krus* ceremony for a water hole is performed by all the shamans living in the water-hole group. It follows the pattern of the ceremonies for the *snas* except that before the ceremony the men all clean out the water hole. . . . This ceremony appears to express the right which members of the water-hole group have to draw water from their water hole and their obligation to care for it properly. Because it includes rituals for the deities associated with the water hole, the ceremony links together the *snas* that compose the water-hole group and, hence, symbolizes its unity" (Vogt 1969). It seems likely that in the past, water holes, springs, wells, and other water sources were linked to specific social groups in the communities much as those in Zinacantán are today.

Walk-in wells in archaeological contexts are found in the upper Grijalva Basin at Pueblo Viejo de Mujica and Pueblo Viejo de los Limones (Matheny and Gurr 1979). I have taken photos from the air of other probable walk-in wells at sites in the area but lack ground-truth confirmation.

The principle of the walk-in well is that it is dug into deep soil down to the fracture zone of the rock. This means that a large upslope catchment area is required to direct drainage into the soil that is accumulated above a rock zone. The cases of Pueblo Viejo de Mujica and Pueblo Viejo de Los Limones are nearly identical; they are hilltop towns with public buildings (those of Mujica are larger), plazas, outside use areas nearly devoid of vegetation, and domiciles constituting a semi-paved catchment area from which rainwater drained into downslope deep soils where the wells are located. Wells were equipped with an overflow drain located on the downslope of a protective wall which surrounded the well (Figure 6).

Entry into the well was through the overflow drain, and descent was accommodated by the diminishing circles of cut stone. Wells at these sites are about 8 m in diameter, and water would have been accessible by walking into the wells at the level of the drain and continuing down to where the steps ended.

HILLSLOPE TERRACES

Another practical water conservation strategy of the Highland Maya was the construction of rock-wall terraces. The terraces are not haphazardly placed, but rather form a system of resource manipulation. In highland Chiapas, large areas of land were continuously terraced into what could be called MOUNTAIN GARDEN TOWNS. This would include sites such as Hunchavín near Comitán, Tenam Puente in the southwest range of the Comitán Plain, Tenam Rosario, south and below the escarpment, and a number of other sites known as Tenams 'fortresses' in the same general area which also fit into this classification. At Tenam Rosario, the main building site occupied the entire hilltop and terraces are found on the east, south, and west slopes down to the valley bottom. Little water and

FIGURE 6. *An ancient walk-in well at Pueblo Viejo de los Limones in the Upper Grijalva River Basin. A farmer dug this well free of debris and he claims that the lower stones are in their original configuration. This photograph was taken in May 1977.*

soil was allowed to escape in the system. Although the site is at about 18° north latitude, the north slope was ignored, suggesting seasonal use of the other slopes.

At Tenam Puente, an entire mountain valley and its surrounding hillslopes have been terraced (Figure 7). Even though this site was occupied in Late Classic times, there is still no appreciable erosion. All water, except that lost by evapotranspiration and internal drainage, is conserved. There are chultuns and a probable walk-in well but no other apparent water sources, although in the past, some springs may have been active. Tenam Puente, with its terraces, chultuns, well, and agricultural activity, must be considered as representative of a system of agroengineering. The site was built as a cooperative effort under a careful design. To sustain the population of a town of this size, a water system had to be conceived and constructed. The agricultural part of the system was designed to maximize retention of water and soil. It seems that the entire site and its surroundings were under careful political control that probably made it an efficient productive unit.

In highland Guatemala, there are a few valleys that may follow the mountain garden town theme, such as the Río Negro Valley at the upper Chixoy drainage, where Classic- and Postclassic-period irrigation canals have been reported (John Fox, personal communication), and the terraces at Totonicapan (Robert Carmack, personal communication); but I do not know the date of these constructions. Settlement generally occurred around springs, streams, and lakes. There seems to have been little development of wells and rock-banked terraces in ancient times. There are small towns on hilltops that exhibit rock-faced terraces, but these are primarily for structural purposes, and only secondarily used for gardening. These Guatemalan terraces are not generally similar to those in Chiapas. The earth-cut terraces seen today in Guatemala, called *tablones,* are described by McBryde (1945) as having been introduced since 1586 and are used to raise European vegetables.

DAMS AND CANALS

Dams and canals were used in the upper Grijalva River Basin as a technique to bring water close to habitation sites, as well as for flood-irrigation. An example is found at Lagartero, Chiapas where fossil dams are still visible. These dams pushed water to levels high enough to fill canals upstream which, in turn, directed water into several smaller fossil channels. There are many more dams and canals at the site that were a part of the complex hydraulic system (Susanna Ekholm, personal communication).

Perhaps the most ubiquitous conservation feature of the upper Grijalva Basin is the linear sloping, dry-field terrace. Aerial photographs show thousands of these stone alignments along the dry benches of the river valley (Figure 8). These terraces are not the soil-backed type found on steeper slopes, but are rows of stones set into the earth at irregular intervals. There was no effort to build

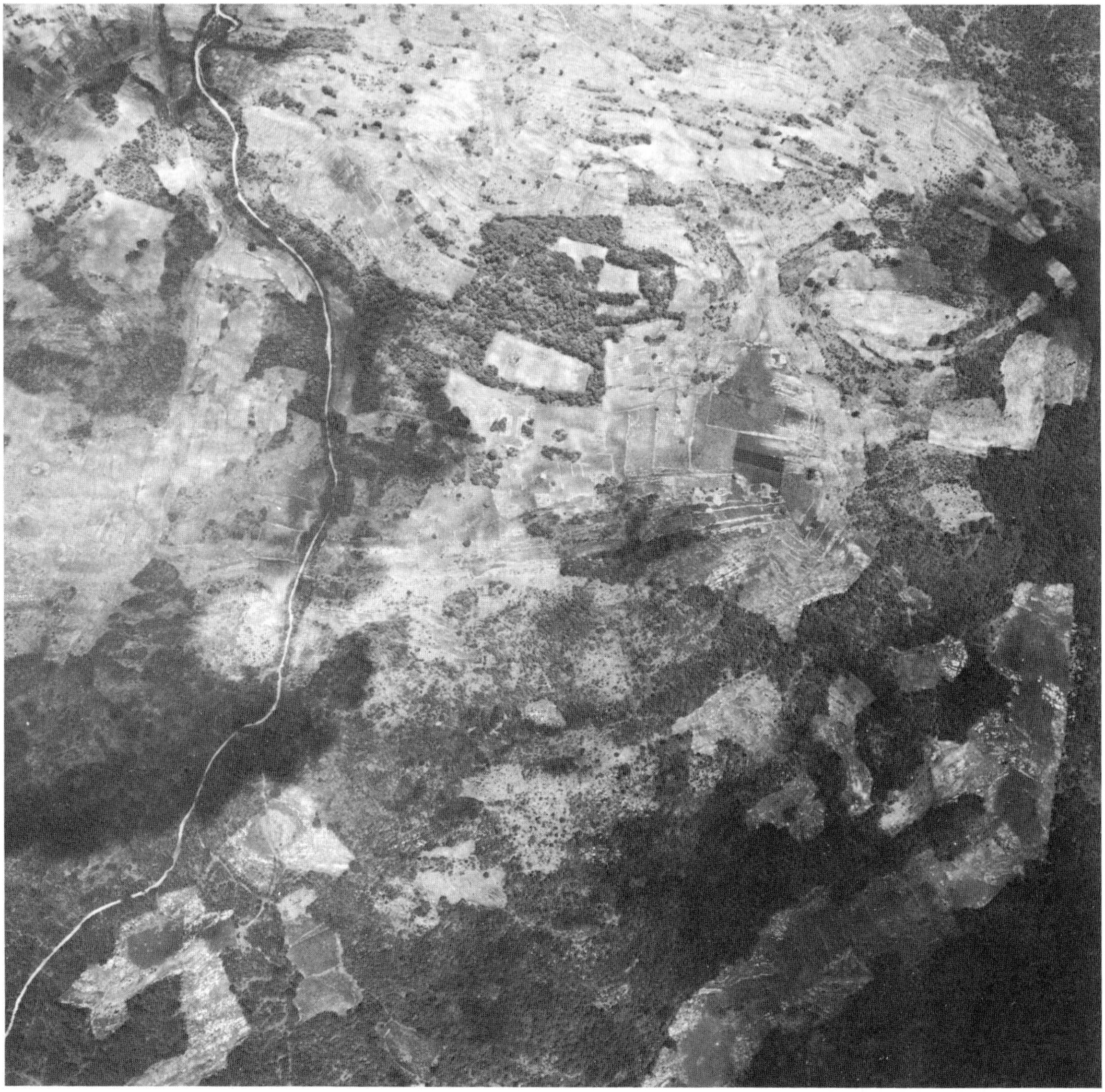

FIGURE 7. *An aerial view of Tenam Puente showing the many terraces that placed water and soil under careful control.*

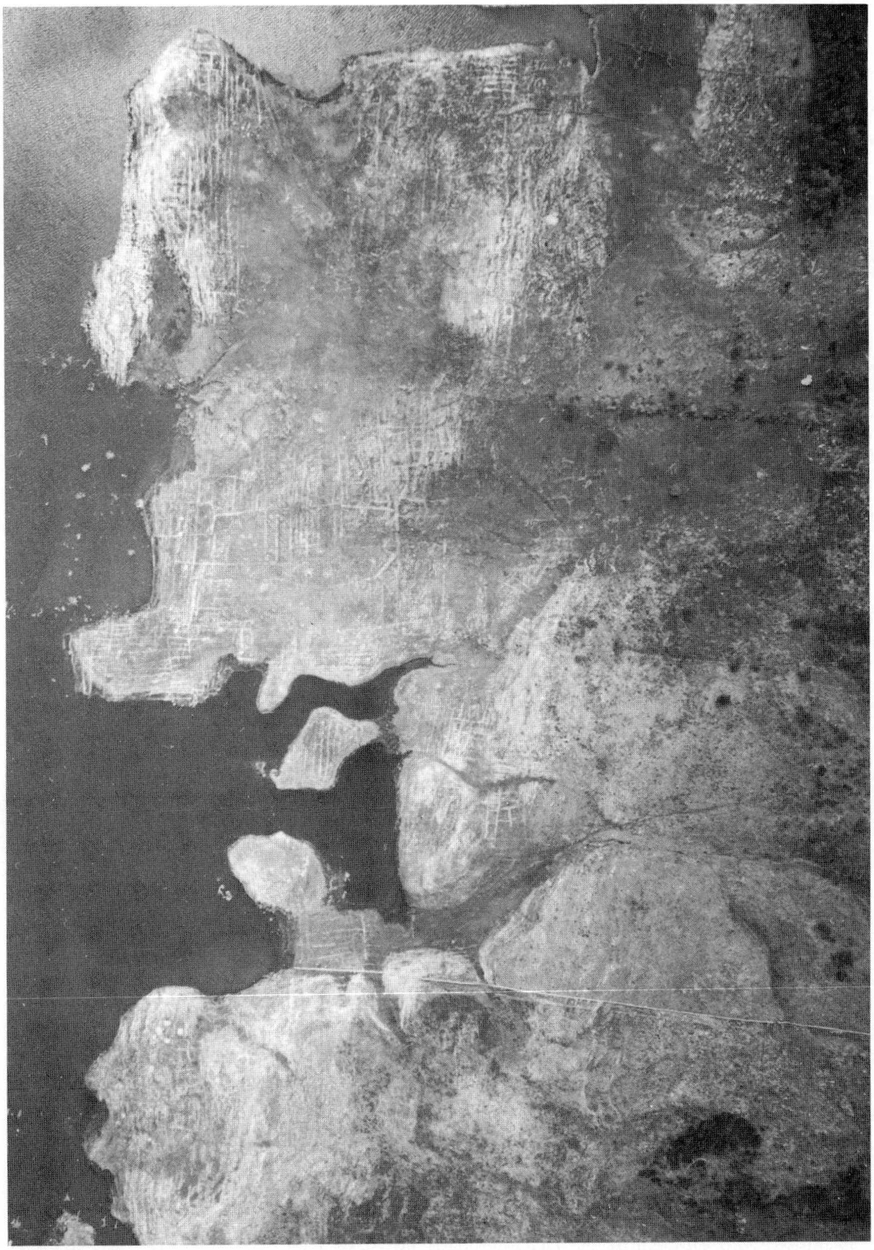

FIGURE 8. *An aerial view of linear-sloping, dry fields outlined by stones set into the ground. This site is located west of Pueblo Viejo de los Limones on the bank of the Angostura reservoir.*

a stepped slope, but sometimes a single row of stones served the purpose. Though there is no study of this type of terracing, Spencer and Hale (1961) suggest that water draining onto stone alignments may be more evenly distributed. The linear sloping, dry-field terrace put most of the dry basin soils and water under a minimal kind of control, and check dams are often found with them, which add to that control. This type of terrace provided some control with minimal effort. It is often found at small sites where a family group could have constructed it. At some large sites, there are large numbers of lineal dry-field terraces in surrounding areas.

Summary

It appears that the Lowland and Highland Maya left little to chance when it came to water and soil resources. Technologies for extracting, collecting, and retrieving water in both areas were highly developed. At large sites, this often involved the organization of a large number of laborers and the conceptualization of a complex plan. Edzná is an example of a site where the basic layout of the city was integrated with the plan of the water system. First, there was a conceptualization of what was possible for water collection; then a plan was made and executed, indicating a high degree of engineering skill. The Maya manipulated the upper Edzná Valley in the Late Preclassic period to satisfy their food production needs and to provide water for a population that built hundreds of constructions covering 17 km^2. The 180 km of canals along the Río Candelaria suggest an astonishing alteration of the natural drainage system by the Maya (Siemens and Puleston 1972). If the land terracing of the Río Bec area and the possible ridged fields of Quintana Roo are added as examples of land and water manipulation, then a picture of huge investment of time and resources by the Maya emerges.

At small- and medium-sized sites in the Lowlands and Highlands, a number of smaller scale manipulations of soil and water resources were carried out. In many cases, the Maya used a number of techniques at the same site to insure that there would be enough food and water to support their population. After the initial investment of building the systems of soil and water control, additional investment was required to maintain and preserve the systems. In the case of the larger sites, this may have proved burdensome and difficult to maintain, particularly during periods of decline or political instability.

As was mentioned at the beginning of this paper, our data base is still small concerning soil and water control practices of the ancient Maya. Much more work needs to be done before we can understand the intricate systems that existed in the past. However, present evidence leaves no doubt that the Maya devised and used a large number of techniques in both lowland and highland settings to give them control over soil and water.

References

Andrews, V. E. W.
1978 *Dzibilchaltún.* Instituto Nacional de Antropología e Historia, Mexico.

Coe, M. D.
1968 *America's First Civilization,* New York, American Heritage.
1969 Photogrammetry and the ecology of Olmec civilization. Paper presented at the Working Conference on Aerial Photography and Anthropology, Cambridge, Massachusetts.

Brasseur de Bourbourg, C. E.
1865 *Rapport sur les ruines de Mayapan et d'Uxmal au Yucatán (Mexique), adresse a Son Excellence M. Le Ministre de L'Instruction Publique,* Paris, Imp. Imperial.

DeBloois, I. E.
1970 Archaeological researches in northern Campeche, Mexico. Department of Sociology and Anthropology, Weber State College.

Hammond, N.
1978 The myth of the Milpa: Agricultural expansion in the Maya Lowlands. In *Pre-Hispanic Maya Agriculture,* edited by Peter D. Harrison and B. L. Turner II. Albuquerque, Univ. of New Mexico Press.

Harrison, Peter D.
1978 Bajos revisited: Visual evidence for one system of agriculture. In *Pre-Hispanic Maya Agriculture,* edited by Peter D. Harrison and B. L. Turner II. Albuquerque, Univ. of New Mexico Press.

Matheny, R. T.
1971 Modern Chultun Construction in Western Campeche, Mexico. *American Antiquity* 39(4):473–475.
1976 Maya Lowland hydraulic systems. *Science* 193:639–646.
1978 Northern Maya Lowland water-control systems. In *Pre-Hispanic Maya Agriculture,* edited by Peter D. Harrison and B. L. Turner II. Albuquerque, Univ. of New Mexico Press.

Matheny, R. T., and D. L. Gurr
1979 Ancient hydraulic techniques in the Chiapas highlands. *American Scientist* 67(4):441–449.

McBryde, F. W.
1945 Cultural and historical geography of southwest Guatemala. *Smithsonian Institution of Social Anthropology, Pub. No.* 4, Washington, D.C.

Mercer, H. C.
1975 *The Hill-Caves of Yucatán: A Search for Evidence of Man's Antiquity in the Caverns of Central America.* Norman, University of Oklahoma Press.

Miller, F. C.
1959 Ethnographic report on Huistán, Chiapas. In *Report on the Man-in-Nature Project of the Department of Anthropology, University of Chicago in the Tzeltal-Tzotzil Speaking Region.*

Morley, S. G., (revised by G. W. Brainerd)
1956 *The Ancient Maya.* Third edition. Stanford, Stanford Univ. Press.

Nelson, F. W.
1973 Archaeological investigations at Dzibilnocac, Campeche, Mexico. *Papers of the New World Archaeological Foundation, No.* 33. Provo, Brigham Young Univ. Press.

Puleston, D. E.
1971 An experimental approach to the function of Classic Maya chultuns. *American Antiquity* 36(3):322–335.

Siemens, A. H., and D. E. Puleston
1972 Ridged fields and associated features in southern Campeche: New perspectives on the Lowland Maya. *American Antiquity* 37:228–239.

Spencer, J., and G. Hale

1961 The origin, nature and distribution of agricultural terracing. *Pacific Viewpoint* 2:1–40.

Stephens, J. L.

1963 *Incidents of Travel in Yucatán,* 2 Vols. New York, Dover.

Stevens, R. L.

1964 The soils of Middle America and their relation to Indian peoples and cultures. In *Handbook of Middle American Indians,* Vol. 1, edited by R. Wauchope. Austin, Univ. of Texas Press.

Tamayo, J. L., in collaboration with R. C. West

1964 The hydrography of Middle America. In *Handbook of Middle American Indians,* Vol. 1, edited by R. Wauchope. Austin, Univ. of Texas Press.

Thompson, E. H.

1897 The chultuns of Labna, Yucatán. *Memoirs of the Peabody Museum of Archaeology and Ethnology, Harvard University, Vol.* 1, *No.* 3.

Turner, B. L. II.

1978 Ancient agricultural land use in the central Maya Lowlands. In *Pre-Hispanic Maya Agriculture,* edited by Peter D. Harrison and B. L. Turner II. Albuquerque, Univ. of New Mexico Press.

1979 Prehispanic terracing in the central Maya Lowlands: Problems of agricultural intensification. In *Maya Archaeology and Ethnohistory,* edited by Norman Hammond and G. R. Willey. Austin, Univ. of Texas Press.

Vlcek, D. T., S. Garza, and E. B. Kurjack

1978 Contemporary farming and ancient Maya settlements: Some disconcerting evidence. In *Pre-Hispanic Maya Agriculture,* edited by Peter D. Harrison and B. L. Turner II. Albuquerque, Univ. of New Mexico Press.

Vogt, E. Z.

1969 *Zinacantán: A Maya Community in the Highlands of Chiapas.* Cambridge, The Belknap Press of Harvard Univ. Press.

Wilken, G. C.

1969 Drained-field agriculture: An intensive farming system in Tlaxcala, Mexico. *Geographical Review* 59:215–241.

Wiseman, F. M.

1978 Agricultural and historical ecology of the Maya Lowlands. In *Pre-Hispanic Maya Agriculture,* edited by Peter D. Harrison and B. L. Turner II. Albuquerque, Univ. of New Mexico Press.

III

Contributions of Geography and Soil Science to an Understanding of Ancient Maya Subsistence

7

Hydraulic Agriculture in the American Tropics: Forms, Measures, and Recent Research

William M. Denevan

Introduction

IT is remarkable that until only a decade or so ago, the prevailing view of Indian agriculture, not only in the Maya Lowlands, but throughout tropical America was one of shifting cultivation. Because of this view, and the fact that shifting cultivation cannot support dense populations, evidence for large populations was ignored or explained away and the cultural implications of this evidence were consequently missed. Complex cultures were accounted for by some as intrusions from more favorable (i.e., nontropical) environments and were seen as doomed to failure because of environmental limitations in the tropics that made shifting cultivation and sparse populations inevitable.

However, there are no environmental limitations to the development of agriculture, only cultural limitations. "Agricultural potential" is a cultural phenomenon; it is not something inherent in nature that can be measured, that exists independent of culture. Today, with available technology, agriculture can be carried out anywhere on earth. Whether it is or not in any given habitat is dependent on whether the culture involved has the necessary technology, and whether or not there is a perceived need in relation to the costs involved (capital, material, labor). Today our technology permits us to control temperature, move water, and make soil. Nevertheless, we seldom farm in Siberia or in the Atacama

ISBN 0-12-259780-X

desert, not because we can not, but because it is too expensive in relation to output gained. The actual limits then are economic, not environmental. However, economic limits are not fixed; they change as perceived needs increase, particularly in relation to demographic pressure or markets, or when technology is made cheaper. We should think in terms of a "cost-comparison" model, rather than fixed carrying capacity (Glassow 1978). This principle applies not only to modern (neotechnic) production systems, but also to traditional (paleotechnic) systems, past or present. We are increasingly learning that aboriginal farmers, when they needed or wanted to, were (and still are) capable of irrigating dry lands, terracing steep slopes, draining swamps, and making infertile soils fertile, usually at the cost of high labor inputs, rather than with complex tools, fossil fuels, and chemicals. Appropriately, the simple Classic Maya swidden farmer of just a few years ago has now been replaced by a sophisticated Classic Maya farmer who utilized a wide variety of ecosystems by means of a correspondingly wide variety of agricultural methods (Harrison and Turner 1978).

But why have we come to such knowledge so late, not only for the Maya, but for many other tropical cultures? The evidence has always been available since many of the ancient fields have survived and archaeologists have surely seen them. Some of these agricultural relic landforms either were mentioned during the Colonial period, such as the raised fields in the Orinoco Llanos (Castellanos 1955:1:539), or were reported earlier in this century, as were the Belize and Río Bec Maya terraces (Ower 1927; Ruppert and Denison 1943:13,50); but no one seriously followed up these hints. For one thing, New World scholars had not been very interested in ancient agriculture in the tropics or anywhere else except for a few studies of irrigation canals. Most important, apparently, was a "mind set" that Maya and all early New World tropical agriculture had always been dominated by forms of swidden comparable to those of surviving Indians today (Turner 1978b; Mathewson 1977).[1] Evidence to the contrary was considered unique and minor and was, therefore, ignored. Accordingly, the Maya house-mound counts indicating densities that could not have been supported by swidden were dismissed by concluding that only a portion of house sites were occupied at a given time (see discussions by Culbert [1974:42–46], Turner [1976:77–79], and Sanders [1973:329–332]). A few voices (Palerm and Wolf 1957:28; Wolf 1959:77–78; Wilken 1971) cried out that our logic was wrong, that the Maya had to have had more permanent forms of agriculture, but they had little evidence in support. Similar arguments arose elsewhere. I remember a lecture by Carl Sauer (1981) in 1965 in Madison in which he said: "This is not slash-and-burn cultivation. I wish people would not talk about that stuff so much. In this part of the world, it is nonsense." He was referring to the *montones* (manioc mounds) of Hispaniola. Bartolomé de Las

[1]It is ironic that there seems to be no PHYSICAL evidence for Precolumbian swidden agriculture anywhere, although it must have been widespread, whereas the physical evidence for intensive agriculture is considerable.

Casas (Sturtevant 1961:73) reported hundreds of thousands of them, but none seem to have survived, and, of course, when it came to high numbers, Las Casas was "suspect."

Substantial physical evidence for intensive tropical agriculture came instead from lowland South America where raised fields were first discovered in Surinam in 1939 (Boomert 1976) and in eastern Bolivia in 1961 (Figure 1) (Denevan 1962).[2] These were originally thought unique; however, others were then found in Colombia, Ecuador, and Venezuela (Parsons and Denevan 1967). These discoveries led Alfred Siemens to recognize Maya raised fields in Campeche while on a bush plane flight in 1968 when he was studying modern colonization, not the Maya; these fields were then studied by Siemens with Dennis Puleston. Subsequently, Maya raised fields were discovered and described in Quintana Roo, Belize, and Veracruz. By 1973, it was clear from the work of Bill Turner (1974) that terracing was much more widespread in the Maya Lowlands than previously believed.

In this essay, I briefly examine aboriginal hydraulic agriculture in tropical America, including forms, some tentative measurements, and a summary of recent research on raised fields. This will serve to place Maya raised-field drainage in a broader perspective.

Forms of Hydraulic Agriculture and Minor Water-Management Techniques

The known indigenous alternatives to rain-fed swidden agriculture in tropical America are: orchards, house gardens, mounding, terracing, playa and levee cultivation, irrigation, ditching, and raised fields. I would categorize all of these as intensive in the sense that while fallowing may occur, fallow periods are usually of shorter duration than cropping periods.

"Hydraulic" agriculture, in the broadest sense, can refer to any intentional manipulation of water in order to improve growing conditions for cultivated crops. When hydraulic civilizations or societies are mentioned, we commonly think in terms of canal irrigation including paddy rice.[3] However, drainage agriculture certainly should also be considered hydraulic when it involves major manipulation of water by means of landscape engineering.

Actually, all of the forms of agriculture listed at the beginning of this section

[2]Sauer mentioned the general importance of ridging and mounding as early as 1952 in *Agricultural Origins and Dispersals* (p. 45).

[3]Wittfogel (1957:3) distinguished between "hydraulic societies," involving small scale irrigation, and "hydraulic civilizations," involving government managed irrigation. See Matheny (1978) for a discussion of both in regard to the Lowland Maya. Here, I prefer to discuss "hydraulic agriculture" without any socioeconomic connotation. Certainly large-scale hydraulic works as well as minor water-management techniques may be associated with either centrally managed states or less complex societies (Figures 2 and 3).

FIGURE 1. *Precolumbian raised fields in the Llanos de Mojos in northeastern Bolivia. The larger ridges are about 6 m wide. Dry season, July 1961. Photograph by Tony English. From Denevan (1966). Courtesy of The University of California Press.*

FIGURE 2. *Present-day raised fields of the Dugum Dani in the Baliem Valley in highland West New Guinea. The crop is sweet potatoes. About 1962. Photograph by Karl Heider. From Heider (1970). Courtesy of Karl Heider.*

involve water management to some extent, or at least in some circumstances. It is useful to differentiate between MINOR WATER-MANAGEMENT TECHNIQUES and HYDRAULIC AGRICULTURAL TECHNIQUES, such as canal irrigation and drained fields. The distinction, however, should be one of scale rather than technique.

House Gardens and Orchards are associated with most tropical farmers whose villages remain at one site for at least a few years. House gardens have been little studied for American Indian groups however (Denevan and Schwerin 1978; Covich and Nickerson 1966). Precolumbian evidence is meager, but the presence of rectangular stone walls in the Río Bec zone of Campeche–Quintana Roo suggests that house compounds may have had enclosed gardens (Turner 1978a:170–171). House gardens and orchards are not usually associated with irrigation agriculture; nevertheless, selected individual plants may be irrigated today via pots (containers), and it is likely that the same occurred in the past.

FIGURE 3. *Maintenance of raised fields by the Dugum Dani in New Guinea. Muck from the ditch is being scooped up by hand and placed on the ridge. Sweet potatoes have been planted on small mounds on top of the ridge. A similar scene can be visualized involving the Precolumbian raised-field farmers of the New World. Clearly, such labor intensive forms of agriculture are within the capabilities of egalitarian societies. Photograph by Michael Rockefeller (1961). From Gardner and Heider (1969). Courtesy of the Film Study Center, Peabody Museum, Harvard University.*

Mounds and Narrow Ridges (other than drained fields), usually small ones for either maize or manioc (or potatoes in the Andes), may serve to minimize upper-soil waterlogging. They also serve other functions, including soil aeration, weed control, and fertility addition (Denevan and Turner 1974). They do not survive well in the tropics, and we know little about them, but they probably were not swidden fields.

Terracing in tropical areas is mostly Precolumbian. While erosion control and slope modification are primary functions, some terraces were designed for water control by providing for subwall drainage, diversion walls, and drainage spouts, as in the Río Bec region (Turner 1979:111–112). While irrigation of terraces is common in dry lands, it seems to be rare in the tropics. Sloping and cross-channel terraces are found in Chiapas, Campeche, Quintana Roo, Belize, Petén, and Honduras (Turner 1974, 1979; Guzmán 1962). In South America, they occur in tropical montane regions in the eastern Andean foothills of Peru and Ecuador at an elevation as low as 800 m (Isbell 1968:114).

Playa and Levee Agriculture has also been virtually ignored; I know of no significant study of it. For brief accounts, see Higbee (1945), Meggers (1971:139–142), and Denevan and Schwerin (1978). Playa and levee agriculture occur throughout the large river floodplains in interior South America today (aboriginal, peasant, and commercial), and it undoubtedly was equally widespread in Precolumbian times, given archaeological and historical evidence of dense settlement (Denevan 1976). Playa cultivation involves annual cultivation of sand bars, shores, and islands exposed during low-water periods. Where exposure is long enough (about 3 months), annual cultivation of short growing season crops such as maize, beans, squash, and peanuts (and rice today) is possible. The alluvial soils are fertile, subsoil moisture is adequate for dry season crops, and the period of flooding serves to prevent or destroy weeds. Playa agriculture is not hydraulic in the sense that water is controlled, but it is hydraulic in the sense that cropping activity is carefully attuned to river behavior. Natural levee agriculture is common throughout the tropics today, and it undoubtedly is one of the earliest orientations of aboriginal agriculture. Coe and Diehl (1980 Volume 1:389) have suggested that it was a major form of Olmec agriculture in Tabasco. It must be emphasized that levee agriculture is not typical shifting cultivation. Present-day examples indicate that the cropping period is long and the fallow period (resulting from weed invasion, not fertility decline) is brief.[4]

Irrigation Agriculture in tropical America has also received little attention. It is practical where the dry season is long (about six months or more), at least for some crops, or it can make possible a second, dry season crop. It was reported

[4]Allen and Tizón (1973) did a study of Campa agriculture in the Alto Pachitea region of eastern Peru, and reported riverine cultivation averaging 1–3 years of fallow and 3–4 years of cropping for manioc and up to 20 years for bananas.

by the early Spaniards in Hispaniola (Sauer 1966:53) and in lowland Venezuela (Steward 1948:21, 481), but no canals have been found in either place. The recent discovery of a dam at Copán in Honduras may be indicative of irrigation (Turner and Johnson 1979:304). In the eastern Llanos of Venezuela today, Karinya Indians drain moriche palm swamps by ditching, but they also use the same ditches for irrigation during dry periods (Denevan and Bergman 1975). Maya canals and reservoirs at Edzná in Campeche may have been used for pot irrigation (Matheny 1976:643). More important is the irrigation associated with raised fields (Figure 4). A raised field and adjacent ditches can elevate crops and remove excess water during flooding. However, after floods recede the ditches will retain water into the dry season, and this may be available to crop root systems in the adjacent raised fields and, thereby, extend the growing season. If there is standing water in ditches, it can be made available to crops by splash irrigation, or by natural subirrigation through the sides of the ditches; both apply to the *chinampas* of Mexico. The raised fields of the Orinoco Llanos may have been seasonally irrigated (Zucchi and Denevan 1979:597). For some raised-field systems, ditches are at sharp angles to one another or are blocked off by the raised fields, and the intention may have been as much to inhibit drainage as to facilitate it. In any event, drainage can not be readily separated from irrigation.

Ditching Raised fields are not the only means of drainage for agriculture. In addition to the ditches and canals within all raised-field systems, I know of two examples in lowland South America of ditch systems that do not involve any significant building up of raised fields adjacent to the ditches. One is in the east-central Llanos de Mojos of Bolivia where thousands of ancient, narrow ditches occur, measuring .15–.30 m deep, about 120 m long, .60–1.20 m wide, and are spaced 1.50–7.50 m apart (Denevan 1966:88). The second is that of the present-day Karinya Indians in the Orinoco Llanos, mentioned previously, who channel water from field ditches into larger canals which carry excess water out of the swamps. The development of raised fields may have arisen out of a system of drainage which originally emphasized ditching, as suggested by Sanders *et al.* (1979:280) for the Mexican chinampas, and by Siemens (1982 present volume) for the Maya Lowlands. Also see Turner and Harrison (1981, 1982) on "channelized" fields in Belize.

Raised Fields By far, the most important form of Precolumbian hydraulic agriculture in tropical America was the large raised field in the form of a platform or ridge, with accompanying ditches and canals, whereby water and soil were carefully managed to improve crop growing conditions in otherwise marginal habitats (poor drainage, poor soils).

The Measurement of Raised Fields

From a comparative perspective, there are several themes regarding raised fields that might be examined. One of these is the raised-field ecosystem and

FIGURE 4. *Splash irrigation (using gourds) of a garlic crop on* tablones *at Aguacatán in highland Guatemala. The* tablones *are raised planting beds separated by ditches, which serve for both drainage and irrigation. Note the pile of crop residue in the foreground, which will be used for fertilizer. October 1974. Photograph by Kent Mathewson.*

Table 1
Raised-Field Measurement Comparisons

Location	Surface area of fields and ditches (ha)	Surface area of fields only (% of column 2)[a] (ha)	Total earth moved (column 3 × 1 m)[b] (m^3)	Total labor days (column 4 ÷ 2.6)[c] (labor days)	Population supported per cultivated ha	Total estimated population (column 3 × column 6) at 100% field usage[d]
Mojos, Bolivia	—	15,000 (Denevan 1966:90)	150 million	57.7 million	16 (manioc)[e]	240,000
San Jorge, Colombia	90,000 (Parsons, personal communication)	36,000 (40%) (Parsons, personal communication)	360 million	138.5 million	16 (manioc)	576,000
Guayas, Ecuador	50,000 (Denevan and Mathewson 1981)	10,000 (20%) (Denevan and Mathewson 1981)	100 million	38.5 million	16 (manioc)	160,000
Barinas, Venezuela	—	1,550 (Zucchi and Denevan 1979:26)	15.5 million	6 million	16 (manioc)	24,800
Southern Campeche, Mexico	150–200 (Siemens and Puleston 1972)	96 (40%) (Denevan)	0.7 million	0.27 million	19 (maize)[f]	1,300
Southern Quintana Roo, Mexico[g]	24,610 (Harrison, personal communication)	12,305 (50%) (Turner, personal communication)	123 million	47.3 million	19 (maize)	233,800
Northern Belize	3,200 (Siemens 1982b)	1,920 (60%) (Turner, personal communication)	19.2 million	7.4 million	19 (maize)	36,500
Lakes Texcoco, Chalco, and Xochimilco, Mexico	—	12,000 (Sanders *et al.* 1979: 390)	120 million	46 million	19 (maize)	228,000
Titicaca, Peru–Bolivia	82,056 (Smith *et al.* 1968)	37,746 (46%) (Stemper 1978)	377 million	145 million	5.7 (potato)[h]	215,000

[a] For most sites, the raised-field surface area is a percentage of the reported total area (column 2), which consists of raised fields, ditches, major canals, ponds, and other uncultivated land. These percentages were determined by measurement or estimates on the ground, from the air, or (usually) from air photos. Generally, the area of raised-field surface is underestimated because of vegetation cover, flooding, erosion, burial by sedimentation, or destruction by recent human activity.

[b] An average height of 1 m is used for all raised fields. Mathewson (1978) attempted a more precise estimate and obtained 1.8 m for the chinampas, 0.5 m for Mojos, 0.75 m for Barinas and Titicaca, and 1.0 m for the others. The range would seem to be from about 0.5 to 2.0 m. However, it is not always clear whether figures given in the literature refer to present or original heights, and, hence, it is best not to give comparative figures. (For calculating earth moved, heights should be measured from the original base of the raised field and not from adjacent ditch bottoms—original or present.) One meter is a convenient and probably conservative height that can be used as an overall figure until good measurements are available. For the calculation of total earth moved, it is assumed here that the field surfaces are flat, rather than cambered (ridged), which is true of most, but not all, raised fields.

[c] A figure of 2.6 m^3 of earth is used for the amount excavated per person in a work day of 5 hours. This is taken from Erasmus (1965) and is based on experiments with excavation using a digging stick. Puleston (1977b), for an experimental raised field in Belize, obtained data that can be converted into 2.7 m^3/person/day; but the work involved digging marl, which takes more time than digging earth (which is the way most raised fields are constructed), and it included short transport, whereas the earth for most raised fields is taken from the immediately adjacent ground. Also, Puleston's workers apparently used metal tools instead of digging sticks. Using Erasmus's 1:2.7 efficiency ratio for digging stick as compared to shovel, the material dug for the experimental field would be reduced to only 1.06 m^3/person/day. For the problems involved in estimating labor expenditures for raised fields, see Mathewson (1978) as well as Puleston (1977b). Note: The amount of earth (clayey soil) excavated and piled in a 6-hour day with metal tools in terrace construction in central Mexico was 2.5–3.75 and 3.5–5.5 m^3 according to Wilken (1979a:417–418).

[d] The populations calculated can be readily adjusted downward for estimates of less than 100% field usage at a given time.

[e] The estimate of 16 persons/ha for a manioc staple is an average for six Amazon groups, with a range from 9 to 25/ha (Cubeo, 12; Waika, 25; Aguaruna, 18; Yukpa, 9; Campa, 21; French Guiana tribes, 12). This assumes adequate animal protein; also, a higher proportion of total food comes from hunting and fishing than for Mesoamerican maize farmers. All 6 figures are derived from upland, rather than riverine, swiddens. Higher figures would be likely from raised-field systems.

[f] The estimate of 19 people/ha (.37 ha per family of 7 members) for a maize staple, with one crop a year, is from the calculations by Sanders *et al.* (1979:373, 380, 390) for the chinampas of Chalco–Xochimilco. They use an average of 3,000 kg of maize equivalent per ha per year of chinampa, and a maize equivalent of 160 kg consumption per person per year. Lacking better calculations for lowland raised fields with a maize staple, the same density of 19 persons/ha is used. However, in the lowlands two crops a year might have been possible, so that densities and total populations could have been as much as double those given here. Also, lowland varieties of maize were probably more productive. On the other hand, as Wiseman (1978:91) points out, corn losses to pests are probably greater in the lowlands than in the highlands; this might cancel out gains from a second lowland crop, which would be uncertain anyway given the irregularity of *bajo* and floodplain inundation.

[g] Harrison (1978:251) gives a figure of 2,460 km^2 of patterned ground in southwest Quintana Roo between Nicolás Bravo, Tzibanche, and Ucum (mainly Bajo Morocoy and Bajo Acatuch), in a block of land totalling 10,700 km^2. (Note: Most, but not all, of this block is shown in Harrison [1978: Figure 13.1, p. 248]). These figures are both errors, resulting from a misplaced decimal point. The area of the block is 1,070 km^2. As Harrison (1977:478) earlier indicated, 23% of the block (as measured on air photos) consists of patterned ground, which results in a corrected figure of 246.1 km^2 of patterned ground. (Note: The earlier figure given by Harrison, 1977:478, of 1,461 km^2 was meant to be 2,461 km^2 but correctly should also be 246.1 km^2.) The table figure of 50% (123.05 km^2 or 12,305 ha) for the proportion of patterned ground in raised-field surface is Turner's estimate (personal communication) based on air photo examination plus ground observations. Harrison (1977:478) indicates that considerable additional patterned ground exists north of the mapped block, and there is also some to the west and to the south; however, these are not included in either of his calculations.

The rectangular, patterned surfaces created by vegetation differences, originally reported by Harrison and by Turner from air photos, have recently been confirmed as ancient Maya fields by ground examination in Bajo Morocoy by Gleissman and Turner (1981). See the air photos in Harrison (1977:480, 481) and in Harrison and Turner (1978: 140, 250, 340, 341). Having observed from the air the patterns in Quintana Roo, I am certain that they are all the result of human activity of some sort.

[h] For the lake Titicaca raised fields (mostly in the Department of Puno, Peru), the density of 5.7 persons/ha for a potato staple is based on: (1) an average potato yield of 3,050 kg/ha/year (mostly peasant production of traditional varieties) in Puno between 1955 and 1964 (Christiansen 1967:82) (which is well below the Peruvian Sierra average of 5,340, and includes four drought years with yields below 2,000); (2) an average of 1,000 calories/kg for Peruvian potatoes (*papa amarilla,* 1,010 calories; and *papa blanca,* 990 calories [Collazos, 1957]); (3) 8,360 calories/ha/day ($1{,}000 \times 3{,}050 \div 365$); and (4) an average daily intake per person (men, women, and children of all ages) for the Quechua village of Nuñoa in the Department of Puno of 1,460 calories (obtained by averaging the figures for each age group given in Thomas 1976:385). The low productivity of potatoes compared to manioc and maize reflects the high elevation of the Titicaca Basin.

how it functions and is managed. How are (1) field and ditch size, height, and shape, (2) soil texture and fertility, (3) temperature, and (4) moisture all manipulated for the benefit of crops and other uses, and how does this relate to the maximization of production and the minimization of risk? We know little about these matters, although research in progress on chinampa ecosystems in Mexico is providing important insights; see, for example, the paper by Gene Wilken (1979) on the use of muck.[5] Also, attempts are being made at modeling in order to predict optimum conditions of field surface in relation to the ditch size necessary to provide adequate water and nutrients (Vandermeer and Gliessman 1980).

However, what I propose to do here instead is to compare different raised-field complexes in terms of basic measurements: field and ditch area, field surface area, field height, amount of earth moved, labor days required for construction, population supported per hectare of cultivated field surface, and total population supported by groups of raised fields.[6] This information is presented in Table 1 in tentative form for nine raised-field sites; seven of these are in the lowlands, and, for purposes of comparison, two are in highland areas (Titicaca and Texcoco-Chalco-Xochimilco). The reliability of information and the variables involved are such that a large margin of error exists for some items. Nevertheless, the effort seems worthwhile in order to provide some perspective on the magnitude of Precolumbian raised-field agriculture and, thus, its relative importance compared to other forms of subsistence, especially swidden cultivation. Certainly a basic question confronting the authors of this volume is whether raised fields, as well as other forms of intensive agriculture, were major or minor components of subsistence for the Maya as well as for other tropical cultures in the Americas.

A number of conclusions can be drawn from these preliminary attempts at measurement:

1. Overall, a very large amount of land was converted into raised fields and ditches, and an enormous amount of earth was moved to do this (ca. 770 km^2 of raised-field surface for the seven lowland sites examined here).
2. The magnitude for most areas, however, was relatively small, except for San Jorge and also Lake Titicaca in the highlands.
3. Regardless, even a small number of raised fields in a region is probably

[5]The cycling of organic matter from the aquatic system to the crop system or directly to humans is an essential component of raised-field agriculture. The vegetation biomass present in a marsh or swamp is about 2.5 times more than that present in a forest and 4–5 times higher than that in cultivated fields (Whittaker and Likens 1975). There is additional biomass present in the form of animal life, including fish. On the use of aquatic plants and animals gathered from drainage ditches in highland Mexico, see Wilken (1970).

[6]This attempt at measurement was motivated by unpublished preliminary studies by Kent Mathewson (1978) and David Stemper (1978). In most instances, however, my figures differ from theirs.

indicative of demographic pressure on the land and the likely existence of other forms of intensive agriculture.

4. The area of raised fields in most instances is probably greatly underestimated due to the lack of air photography, or because fields have been buried under sediment or recently destroyed.

5. The labor involved in raised-field construction may seem enormous, but this is deceptive. For San Jorge, for example, a work force of 100,000 men (out of an estimated population of 576,000) working 150 days/year could construct 35,000 ha of raised fields (360 million m^3 of earth) in under 10 years. Thus, it is not necessary to postulate a construction period over hundreds of years, although construction certainly could have been, and likely was, gradual.

6. A measurement of equal importance to field-construction labor time is that of field maintenance time; however, little information is available.

7. Populations supported by raised-field agriculture were substantial.

8. It might be argued that raised fields were not permanent fields, but that they were fallowed, and hence the population supported must be lowered. I doubt, however, that the labor involved in raised-field construction and maintenance would justify a significant length of fallowing, nor are similar fields today fallow for long. Undoubtedly, fields were not all farmed continuously; however, it seems unlikely that the fallow time was longer than the cultivation period.

9. For the Maya region, it is critically important that more ground research be carried out to confirm whether or not the extensive patterns seen on air photos are ancient Maya raised fields.

10. For all sites, many more accurate data are needed on raised-field distributions and measurements than are now available.

Recent Research on Precolumbian Raised-Field Agriculture in Latin America

Since the state of our knowledge regarding ancient New World raised fields was summarized in *Science* (Denevan 1970), there has been a considerable amount of new research and publication. The primary early studies were for northeastern Bolivia (Denevan 1966), the Río San Jorge area of northwestern Colombia (Parsons and Bowen 1966), the Río Guayas Basin of Ecuador (Parsons 1969), and the Lake Titicaca Basin of Peru and Bolivia (Smith, Denevan, and Hamilton 1968). Subsequent to 1970, large numbers of additional raised fields have been discovered in new areas, paleoecological studies have been initiated, and attempts have been made to reestablish this "lost" form of Indian agriculture. A large number of geographers, archaeologists, and ecologists are involved. This recent work is briefly summarized here.

Tropical South America Raised-field research was undertaken in 1975 by James Parsons and Roy Shlemon in the San Jorge region of northern Colombia

(Figure 5) and in the Guayaquil region of Ecuador with the objective of dating the fields (Parsons 1978; Parsons and Shlemon, in press). An argument that the main function of the San Jorge ditch–ridge system was for the raising of fish has been made by anthropologist Thomas Schorr (1973) of the University of Pittsburgh. Old raised fields have been observed by Warwick Bray and Robert Eidt in the Calima Valley northwest of Cali on the Pacific Coast of Colombia. The Guayaquil fields were more intensively studied from 1979 to 1980 by a University of Wisconsin project involving geographers and archaeologists (Denevan *et al.* 1981). The Surinam raised fields have received considerable study by Dutch geographers and archaeologists (Boomert 1976).

In 1972 and 1973 a small group of raised fields in southeastern Barinas in the Orinocos Llanos of Venezuela was studied and excavated by Venezuelan archaeologist Alberta Zucchi and University of Wisconsin geographers William Denevan and Marshall Chrostowski (Denevan and Zucchi 1978; Zucchi 1975a,

FIGURE 5. *Precolumbian raised fields in the Río San Jorge region of northeastern Colombia. June 1965. Photograph by James J. Parsons.*

1975b; Zucchi and Denevan 1979). These fields differ from those found elsewhere in that they consist of pairs of ridges separated by a ditch with large open areas between each pair of ridges.

The discovery of raised fields in the Llanos de Mojos (Figure 1) in 1961 received little attention within Bolivia until 1976. Since then there have been a number of preliminary archaeological projects in the areas of the fields and associated artificial mounds, including research by Victor Bustos (Bolivia), Bernardo Dougherty (Argentina), and Clark Erickson (University of Illinois). Only a few brief reports have thus far been written (Bustos 1976; Erickson 1980).

Raised fields have been reported in the swamps of the central Río Paraná region of northeastern Argentina, but they have not been confirmed.

Andean South America The lake plain on the west side of Lake Titicaca in Peru and Bolivia contains one of the largest concentrations of Precolumbian raised fields. The first archaeological study of these fields (area of Puno) was by Tom Lennon of the University of Colorado in 1977 (1979). Relic fields on the Bolivian slope of the lake will be studied by Alan Kolata of the Field Museum of National History. A small zone of still cultivated raised fields occurs in Bolivia near the town of Batallas (David Preston, University of Leeds, personal communication). Actual "floating gardens" consisting of potato fields grown on lake bottom muck placed on totora reed islands by the Uru Indians of Lake Titicaca were described in the sixteenth century (Maurtua 1906:1:295) and still exist (James Vreeland, personal communication). Raised fields have briefly been described in the Jauja area of the upper Mantaro Valley of Peru (Earle *et al.* 1980:11–13).

There is a small area of relic raised fields on the Peruvian coast in the lower valley of the Río Casma. These have been seen on air photos but have not yet been described on the ground.

Raised fields have been reported in some of the highland basins of northern Ecuador, including Cayambe (Batchelor 1980), Quito, San Pablo, and Ayora (Knapp 1981).

Additional relic ridged fields of the narrow lazy-bed type have been described for Quindío, Colombia by Bruhns (1981).

Yucatán The first discovery of raised fields in the Maya Lowlands was made in 1969 by Alfred Siemens and Dennis Puleston (1972) along the Río Candelaria in western Campeche, as well as at a few small sites in Chiapas. Subsequently, raised fields have been examined elsewhere in the Yucatán Peninsula and adjacent areas (see especially Harrison and Turner 1978). Recently, large areas (a minimum of 1,285 km^2) of additional apparent raised fields and canals have been identified in Petén and Belize on aerial radar imagery, including ground confirmation in several areas (Adams 1980; Adams *et al.* 1981). Previous observations from the air of rectilinear patterns in the vicinity of Tikal could not be confirmed on the ground (Dahlin 1979b). The largest concentrations of Maya raised fields may be in the *bajos* of Quintana Roo (see Table 1) (Turner 1974; Gliessman and Turner 1981; Harrison 1977, 1978). On the Gulf coast, raised fields have recently been described in Veracruz, north of the city of Veracruz, by the German archaeologist Peter Schmidt (1977), and others have been located by Siemens (1980, 1981). Relic fields have also been reported in Tabasco by Mexican archaeologist Lorenzo Ochoa, but these have not been confirmed.

Belize The most detailed and systematic research on raised fields to date, much of it currently in progress, has been in Belize, where there are large numbers of raised fields both in bajos and in the floodplains of the Río Hondo and the New River. This work was initiated with the interdisciplinary Río Hondo project under Siemens and Puleston starting in 1973 (Siemens 1977, 1982a, 1982b, [present volume]; Puleston 1977a, 1978; Puleston and Pohl, 1981; Dahlin 1977; Olson 1977; others in press or in progress). This project combined archaeology with ecology, soil science, paleoecology, and the construction of an experimental raised field. It will probably serve as a model for future raised-field team projects. In 1979, B. L. Turner II and Peter Harrison initiated a comparable interdisciplinary project focusing on raised fields in Pulltrouser Swamp (Turner and Harrison 1981, 1982). Bruce Dahlin who was with the Río Hondo Project, is continuing archaeological research in that area (Dahlin 1979a; 1980). Paleoecological studies of raised fields are under way at Lamanai along the New River by Richard Hebda (University of Waterloo) and by J. H. D. Lambert (1979) (Carleton University). Norman Hammond's Cuello archeological project is interested in associated raised fields, as is David Freidel's Cerros project (Scarborough 1980). An ethnohistorical examination of Maya raised fields is provided by Pohl (1981).

Highland Mesoamerica The chinampas or raised fields of Lakes Xochimilco and Chalco, and formerly in Lake Texcoco, all on the edge of Mexico City, are well known but have recently been subjected to more detailed archaeological (Armillas 1971), ethnohistorical (J. R. Parsons 1976), and ecological (Wilken 1979; also various Mexican scholars) study. Much of the latter is in response to the possibilities of expanding the chinampa system both in highland Mexico and in the tropical lowlands. Raised fields, in use and relic, are also found in the Mexican highlands in Tlaxcala, Puebla, and Oaxaca (Wilken 1969), and also in Hidalgo.

Raised fields currently in use, locally called *tablones* (Figure 2), have been described for highland Guatemala (Mathewson 1976).

Experimental Raised Fields in the Lowlands Finally, in the last few years the first attempts have been made to construct and cultivate experimental raised fields both as a means to interpret the form and functions of Precolumbian raised fields and as a means of reviving the raised-field system for present-day agricultural reclamation of poorly drained areas of the tropical lowlands. The first such experimental raised field was begun by Puleston (1977b) in Belize in 1974. Then experimental tropical chinampas, using chinamperos from Mexico City, were established from 1975 through 1977 by Arturo Gómez-Pompa (Instituto de Investigaciones Sobre Recursos Bióticos, Xalapa) at San Pedro Balancán in southern Tabasco and in the Lacandón rain forest of Chiapas (Gómez-Pompa and Venegas 1976; Gómez-Pompa 1978; Maier 1979). An experimental raised-field program has also been established by Stephen Gliessman (Colegio Superior de Agricultura Tropical, Cárdenas, Tabasco). In 1978, the governor of Tabasco began a system of large raised fields using dredges in the swamps near Villahermosa (Figure 6).

Summary

Interest in and research on raised fields have exploded since 1970. Numerous new discoveries have been made, and experimental fields have been

FIGURE 6. *Experimental "chinampas tropicales" near Villahermosa in Tabasco, Mexico. Visible crops include plantains, beans, and manioc. February 1979. Photograph by William Denevan.*

started. It is now clear that this form of Precolumbian agriculture was not unique, but rather was very common in both lowland and highland environments with poor drainage. Still surviving remains of these fields number in the millions. Only recently discovered, they constitute the most important form of hydraulic agriculture in the tropical New World, past or present. And for the Maya Lowlands, increasing evidence is suggesting that the Classic Maya may well have been a "hydraulic civilization." Significantly, the study of raised fields has moved from a period of basic mapping and description to one of rigorous analysis based on archaeology and ecology. Examples of past and present raised-field agriculture are also common in the Old World tropics (Figures 2 and 3) but are little studied (Denevan and Turner 1974). Their systematic analysis can also be anticipated in the future and should provide insights into the functioning of the ancient drained fields of Latin America.

References

Adams, Richard E. W.
1980 Swamps, canals, and the location of ancient Maya cities. *Antiquity* 54:206–214.

Adams, Richard E. W., Walter E. Brown, Jr., and T. Patrick Culbert
1981 Radar mapping, archaeology, and ancient Maya land use. *Science* 213:1457–1463.

Allen, William L., and Judy H. de Tizón
1973 Land use patterns among the Campa of the Alto Pachitea, Peru. In *Variation in Anthropology,* edited by D. L. Lathrap and J. Douglas, pp. 137–153. Urbana, Illinois Archaeological Survey.

Armillas, Pedro
1971 Gardens on swamps. *Science* 174:653–661.

Batchelor, Bruce E.
1980 Los camellones de Cayambe en la sierra de Ecuador. *América Indígena* 40:671–689.

Boomert, Aad
1976 Pre-Columbian raised fields in coastal Surinam. *Proceedings of the Sixth International Congress for the Study of Pre-Columbian Cultures of the Lesser Antilles,* pp. 134–144. Guadeloupe, Pointe a Pitre.

Bruhns, Karen
1981 Prehispanic ridged fields of central Colombia. *Journal of Field Archaeology* 8:1–8.

Bustos, Victor
1976 Investigaciones arqueológicas en Trinidad, Departmento del Beni. *Instituto Nacional de Arqueología, La Paz, Publicación No. 22.*

Castellanos, Juan de
1955 *Elegías de varones ilustres de Indias,* 4 vols. Bogotá, Editorial ABC.

Christiansen, Jorge
1967 *El cultivo de la papa en el Perú.* Lima, Perú.

Coe, Michael D., and Richard A. Diehl
1980 *In the Land of the Olmec,* 2 vols. Austin, Univ. of Texas Press.

Collazos, Carlos, *et al.*
1957 La composición de los alimentos peruanos. *Anales de la Facultad de Medicina, Lima* 40(1):232–266.

Covich, Alan P., and Norton H. Nickerson

1966 Studies of cultivated plants in Choco dwelling clearings, Darien, Panama. *Economic Botany* 20:285–301.

Culbert, T. Patrick

1974 *The Lost Civilization: The Story of the Classic Maya.* New York, Harper.

Dahlin, Bruce H.

1977 The initiation of the Albion Island settlement pattern survey. *Journal of Belizean Affairs* 5:44–51.

1979a Cropping cash in the Protoclassic: A cultural impact statement. In *Maya Archaeology and Ethnohistory,* edited by Norman Hammond and G. R. Willey, pp. 21–37. Austin, Univ. of Texas Press.

1979b Preliminary investigations of agronomic potentials in bajos adjacent to Tikal, Petén, Guatemala. In *Actes du XL11ᵉ Congrès International des Américanistes, Paris* 8:305–312.

1980 Ecological inference and ancient Maya agricultural systems. Ms. on file, Department of Anthropology, University of Colorado, Boulder.

Denevan, William M.

1962 Informe preliminar sobre la geografía de los Llanos de Mojos, noreste de Bolivia. *Boletín de la Sociedad Geográfica e Histórica Sucre* 47(446):91–113.

1966 *The Aboriginal Cultural Geography of the Llanos de Mojos of Bolivia. Ibero-Americana,* No. 48. Berkeley, Univ. of California Press.

1970 Aboriginal drained-field cultivation in the Americas. *Science* 169:647–654.

1976 The aboriginal population of Amazonia. In *The Native Population of the Americas in 1492,* edited by W. M. Denevan, pp. 205–233. Madison, Univ. of Wisconsin Press.

1980 Tipología de configuraciones agrícolas prehispánica. *América Indígena* 40:619–652.

Denevan, William M., and Roland W. Bergman

1975 Karinya Indian swamp cultivation in the Venezuelan Llanos. *Yearbook of the Association of Pacific Coast Geographers* 37:23–37.

Denevan, William M., Kent Mathewson, and Richard Whitten

1981 Mounding, mucking, and mangling: Recent research on the raised fields in the Guayas Basin, Ecuador. Paper presented at the Conference on Prehistoric Intensive Agriculture in the Tropics, Canberra, Australia.

Denevan, William M., and Karl H. Schwerin

1978 Adaptive strategies in Karinya subsistence, Venezuelan Llanos. *Antropológica,* Caracas 50:3–91.

Denevan, William M., and B. L. Turner II

1974 Forms, functions, and associations of raised fields in the Old World tropics. *The Journal of Tropical Geography* 39:24–33.

Denevan, William M., and Alberta Zucchi

1978 Ridged-field excavations in the central Orinoco Llanos, Venezuela. In *Advances in Andean Archaeology,* edited by D. L. Browman, pp. 235–245. The Hague, Mouton.

Earle, Timothy K., *et al.*

1980 Changing settlement patterns in the upper Mantaro Valley, Peru. *Journal of New World Archaeology* 4(1):1–49.

Erasmus, Charles J.

1965 Monument building: Some field experiments. *Southwestern Journal of Anthropology* 21(4):277–301.

Erickson, Clark L.

1980 Sistemas agrícolas prehispánicos en los Llanos de Mojos. *América Indígena* 40:731–755.

Gardner, Robert G., and Karl G. Heider

1969 *Gardens of War: Life and Death in the New Guinea Stone Age.* New York, Random House.

Glassow, Michael A.

1978 The concept of carrying capacity in the study of culture process. *Advances in Archaeological Method and Theory,* Vol. 1, pp. 31–48. New York, Academic Press.

Gliessman, Stephen R., and B. L. Turner II
1981 Raised fields at Bajo Morocoy, Quintana Roo. Ms. on file, Department of Environmental Studies, Univ. of California, Santa Cruz.
Gómez-Pompa, Arturo
1978 An old answer to the future. *Mazingira,* Oxford, 5.
Gómez-Pompa, Arturo, and Raúl Venegas
1976 La chinampa tropical. *INIREB Informa,* Xalapa, 5.
Guzmán, Louis E.
1962 Las terrazas de los antiguos Mayas Montaneses, Chiapas, México. *Revista Interamericana de Ciencias Sociales* 1:398–406.
Harrison, Peter D.
1977 The rise of the bajos and the fall of the Maya. In *Social Process in Maya Prehistory,* edited by N. Hammond, pp. 469–508. New York, Academic Press.
1978 Bajos revisited: Visual evidence for one system of agriculture. In *Pre-Hispanic Maya Agriculture,* edited by Peter D. Harrison and B. L. Turner II, pp. 247–253. Albuquerque, Univ. of New Mexico Press.
Harrison, Peter D., and B. L. Turner II (editors)
1978 *Pre-Hispanic Maya Agriculture.* Albuquerque, Univ. of New Mexico Press.
Heider, Karl G.
1970 *The Dugum Dani: A Papuan Culture in the Highlands of West New Guinea.* Chicago, Aldine.
Higbee, E. C.
1945 The river is the plow. *Scientific Monthly* 60:405–416.
Isbell, William H.
1968 New Discoveries in the Montaña of Southeastern Peru. *Archaeology* 21:108–115.
Knapp, Gregory
1981 El nicho ecológico llanura húmeda en la economía prehistórica de los Andes de altura: Evidencia etnohistórica, geográfica, y arqueológica. *Sarance* No. 8, Otavalo, Ecuador, in press.
Lambert, J. D. H.
1979 Raised field agriculture adjacent to the New River Lagoon, Lamanai, Belize. Paper presented at the XLIII International Congress of Americanists, Vancouver.
Lennon, Thomas J.
1979 An archaeological investigation of raised field patterns, Lake Titicaca, Peru. Paper presented at the XLIII International Congress of Americanists, Vancouver.
Maier, Elizabeth
1979 *Chinampa Tropical: Una Primera Evaluación.* México, Centro de Ecodesarrollo.
Maurtua, Victor M. (editor)
1906 *Juicio de Límites entre el Perú y Bolivia,* 12 vols. Madrid, Hijos de M. G. Hernández.
Matheny, Ray T.
1976 Maya Lowland hydraulic systems. *Science* 193:639–646.
1978 Northern Maya Lowland water-control systems. In *Pre-Hispanic Maya Agriculture,* edited by Peter D. Harrison and B. L. Turner II, pp. 185–210. Albuquerque, Univ. of New Mexico Press.
Mathewson, Kent
1976 *Specialized horticulture in the Guatemalan highlands: The tablón system of Panajachel.* Unpublished M.A. thesis, Department of Geography Univ. of Wisconsin, Madison.
1977 Maya urban genesis reconsidered: Trade and intensive agriculture as primary factors. *Journal of Historical Geography* 3:203–215.
1978 Estimating labor expenditures for raised-field complexes in the New World tropics. Ms. on file, Department of Geography, Univ. of Wisconsin, Madison.
Meggers, Betty J.

1971 *Amazonia: Man and Culture in a Counterfeit Paradise.* Chicago, Aldine.
Olson, Gerald W.
1977 Significance of physical and chemical characteristics of soils at the San Antonio archaeological site on the Río Hondo in Northern Belize. *Journal of Belizean Affairs* 5:22–25.
Ower, Leslie H.
1927 Features of British Honduras. *Geographical Journal* 70:373–386.
Palerm, Angel, and Eric R. Wolf
1957 Ecological potential and cultural development in Mesoamerica. *Social Science Monographs, III: Studies in Human Ecology.* pp. 1–37. Washington, D.C., Pan American Union.
Parsons, James J.
1969 Ridged fields in the Río Guayas Valley, Ecuador. *American Antiquity* 34:76–80.
1978 More on Pre-Columbian raised fields (camellones) in the Bajo San Jorge and Bajo Cauca, Colombia. In *The Role of Geographical Research in Latin America,* edited by W. M. Denevan, pp. 117–124. Conference of Latin Americanist Geographers, Publication No. 7, Muncie.
Parsons, James J., and William A. Bowen
1966 Ancient ridged fields of the San Jorge River floodplain, Colombia. *The Geographical Review* 56:317–343.
Parsons, James J., and William M. Denevan
1967 Pre-Columbian ridged fields. *Scientific American* 217:92–100.
Parsons, James J., and Roy Shlemon
1979 Mapping and dating the prehistoric raised fields of the Guayas Basin, Ecuador. *Miscelánea Antropológica,* Guayaquil, in press.
Parsons, Jeffrey R.
1976 The role of chinampa agriculture in the food supply of Aztec Tenochtitlán. In *Cultural Change and Continuity,* edited by C. E. Cleland, pp. 233–262. New York, Academic Press.
Pohl, Mary
1981 An ethnohistorical perspective on ancient Maya raised fields. In *The Economic Basis of Maya Civilization: An Interdisciplinary Approach to Maya Prehistory,* edited by Mary Pohl, manuscript.
Puleston, Dennis E.
1977a The art and archaeology of hydraulic agriculture in the Maya Lowlands. In *Social Process in Maya Prehistory,* edited by Norman Hammond, pp. 449–467. New York, Academic Press.
1977b Experiments in prehistoric raised field agriculture: Learning from the past. *Journal of Belizean Affairs* 5:36–43.
1978 Terracing, raised fields, and tree cropping in the Maya Lowlands: A new perspective on the geography of power. In *Pre-Hispanic Maya Agriculture,* edited by P. D. Harrison and B. L. Turner II, pp. 225–245. Albuquerque, Univ. of New Mexico Press.
Puleston, Dennis E., and Mary Pohl
1981 Excavations in Maya raised fields. In *The Economic Basis of Maya Civilization: An Interdisciplinary Approach to Maya Prehistory,* edited by Mary Pohl, manuscript.
Ruppert, Karl, and J. H. Denison
1943 *Archaeological Reconnaissance in Campeche, Quintana Roo, and Petén, Carnegie Institution of Washington, Publication No.* 543, Washington, D.C.
Sanders, William T.
1973 The cultural ecology of the Lowland Maya: A reevaluation. In *The Classic Maya Collapse,* edited by T. P. Culbert, pp. 325–365. Albuquerque, Univ. of New Mexico Press.
Sanders, William T., Jeffrey R. Parsons, and Robert S. Santley
1979 *The Basin of Mexico: Ecological Processes in the Evolution of a Civilization.* New York, Academic Press.
Sauer, Carl O.

1952 *Agricultural Origins and Dispersals.* New York, American Geographical Society.
1966 *The Early Spanish Main.* Berkeley, Univ. of California Press.
1981 Indian food production in the Caribbean. *The Geographical Review* 71:272–280.

Scarborough, Vernon L.
1980 *The Settlement System in a Late Preclassic Maya Community: Cerros, Northern Belize.* Unpublished Ph.D. dissertation, Department of Anthropology, Southern Methodist University, Dallas.

Schmidt, Peter J.
1977 Un sistema de cultivo intensivo en la cuenca del Río Nautla, Veracruz. *Antropología e Historia: Boletín del INAH,* México, 3(20):50–59.

Schorr, Thomas S.
1973 The structure, purpose and social organization of Pre-Columbian ridged-field systems. Paper presented at the 72nd Annual Meeting of the American Anthropological Association, New Orleans.

Siemens, Alfred H.
1977 Some patterns seen from the air. *Journal of Belizean Affairs* 5:5–21.
1980 Indications of the Pre-Hispanic agricultural use of wetlands in central Veracruz. *Biótica,* Xalapa, in press.
1981 Reconsidering the raised fields of Mexico's tropical lowlands. In *The Economic Basis of Maya Civilization: An Interdisciplinary Approach to Maya Prehistory,* edited by Mary Pohl, manuscript.
1982a Wetland agriculture in the lowlands of prehistoric Mesoamerica. *Annals of the Association of American Geographers,* Vol. 72, in press.
1982b Prehispanic agricultural use of the wetlands of Northern Belize. In *Maya Subsistence,* edited by Kent V. Flannery. New York, Academic Press.

Siemens, Alfred H. and Dennis E. Puleston
1972 Ridged fields and associated features in southern Campeche: New perspectives on the Lowland Maya. *American Antiquity* 37:228–239.

Smith, Clifford T., William M. Denevan, and Patrick Hamilton
1968 Ancient ridged fields in the region of Lake Titicaca. *The Geographical Journal* 134:353–367.

Stemper, David
1978 Raised fields and population densities: An analysis for South America. Ms. on file, Department of Geography, Univ. of Wisconsin, Madison.

Steward, Julian H. (editor)
1948 *Handbook of South American Indians,* Vol. 4. Bureau of American Ethnology Bulletin 143, Washington, D.C.

Sturtevant, William C.
1961 Taino agriculture. In J. Wilbert, editor, *The Evolution of Horticultural Systems in Native South America, Causes and Consequences: A Symposium,* edited by J. Wilbert, pp. 69–82. Caracas, Sociedad de Ciencias Naturales La Salle.

Thomas, R. Brooke
1976 Energy flow at high altitude. In *Man in the Andes,* edited by P. T. Baker and M. A. Little, pp. 379–404. New York, Dowden, Hutchinson, and Ross.

Turner II, B. L.
1974 Prehistoric intensive agriculture in the Mayan Lowlands. *Science* 185:118–124.
1976 Prehistoric population density in the Maya Lowlands: New evidence for old approaches. *The Geographical Review* 66:73–82.
1978a Ancient agricultural land use in the central Maya Lowlands. In *Pre-Hispanic Maya Agriculture,* edited by Peter D. Harrison and B. L. Turner II, pp. 163–183. Albuquerque, Univ. of New Mexico Press.
1978b The development and demise of the swidden thesis of Maya agriculture. In *Pre-Hispanic*

Maya Agriculture, edited by P. D. Harrison and B. L. Turner II, pp. 13–22 Albuquerque, Univ. of New Mexico Press.

1979 Prehispanic terracing in the central Maya Lowlands: Problems of agricultural intensification. In *Maya Archaeology and Ethnohistory,* edited by N. Hammond and G. R. Willey, pp. 103–115. Austin, Univ. of Texas Press.

Turner II, B. L., and Peter D. Harrison

1981 Prehistoric raised-field agriculture in the Maya Lowlands: Pulltrouser Swamp, Northern Belize. *Science* 213:399–405.

1982 *Pulltrouser Swamp: A Preliminary Study of Habitat, Land Use, and Settlement of the Prehistoric Maya,* Austin, Univ. of Texas Press.

Turner II, B. L., and William C. Johnson

1979 A Maya dam in the Copán Valley, Honduras. *American Antiquity* 44:299–305.

Vandermeer, John H., and Stephen Gliessman

1980 Agricultura sobre campos elevados en el trópico: Algunas consideraciones elementales de diseño. *Agricultura Tropical,* Cárdenas, Tabasco, México 2:33–40.

Whittaker, Otto, and G. E. Likens

1975 The biosphere and man. In *Primary Productivity of the Biosphere,* edited by H. Leith and R. H. Whittaker, pp. 305–325. New York, Springer-Verlag.

Wilken, Gene C.

1969 Drained-field agriculture: An intensive farming system in Tlaxcala, Mexico. *The Geographical Review* 59:215–241.

1970 The ecology of gathering in a Mexican farming region. *Economic Botany* 24:286–295.

1971 Food-producing systems available to the ancient Maya. *American Antiquity* 36:432–448.

1979a Traditional slope management: An analytical approach. In *Hill Lands: Proceedings of an International Symposium,* edited by J. Luchok, *et al.,* pp. 416–422. Morgantown, West Virginia Univ. Books.

1979b Mucks, mucking, and soils of the chinampas of Mexico. Paper presented at the XLIII International Congress of Americanists, Vancouver.

Wittfogel, Karl A.

1957 *Oriental Despotism: A Comparative Study of Total Power.* New Haven, Yale Univ. Press.

Wiseman, Frederick M.

1978 Agriculture and the historical ecology of the Lowland Maya. In *Pre-Hispanic Maya Agriculture,* edited by P. D. Harrison and B. L. Turner II, pp. 63–115. Albuquerque, Univ. of New Mexico Press.

Wolf, Eric R.

1959 *Sons of the Shaking Earth.* Chicago, University of Chicago Press.

Zucchi, Alberta

1975a Campos de cultivo prehispánicos vs. módulos de Apure. *Boletín Indigenista Venezolano* 16:37–52.

1975b La tecnología aborigen y el aprovechamiento agrícola de nuestras sabanas. *Lineas,* No. 219, Caracas.

Zucchi, Alberta, and William M. Denevan

1979 Campos elevados e historia cultural prehispánica en los llanos occidentales de Venezuela, *Montalban* 9:565–736.

8

Prehispanic Agricultural Use of the Wetlands of Northern Belize

Alfred H. Siemens

Introduction

DURING the 1973 and 1974 field seasons of the Río Hondo Project,[1] some 200 pace-and-compass mapping transects were carried out in the wetlands of northern Belize. Each was 50 or 75 m in width and anywhere from several hundred meters to a kilometer in length. Transects usually began on a riverbank and, where possible, ended in the forest on the terra firma beyond the floodplain. Whatever vegetation presented itself was penetrated in a rather determined fashion. This meant contending with webs of mangrove, the needles of the *jauacte* palm, the tangled low forest that succeeds a *milpa,* and the serrated edges of sawgrass. The objective was to clarify just what the rectilinear patterns detected from the air in many northern Belizean wetlands represented. It was apparent that they were complexes of raised fields, but much was still unclear about the environmental relationships of this agricultural system, to say nothing of its actual function and chronology.

Clearing and then surveying the terrain would have yielded more accurate

[1]The Río Hondo Project was an interdisciplinary investigation of northern Belize, directed jointly by the author and Dennis E. Puleston. It included two principal field seasons—1973 and 1974—as well as some follow-up work by various of the investigators. Parts of this essay represent material that was to have been coauthored with Dennis. He died before he was able to contribute any actual written material to a joint report, but his work was obviously basic to the investigation of Prehispanic wetland agriculture in the Maya Lowlands and has been acknowledged explicitly throughout the chapter. Furthermore, the author remains indebted to a colleague who was a stimulating field companion, an imaginative investigator, and a searching critic. Special acknowledgment and thanks are due The Canada Council, which supported the work on the wetlands at an early stage with several grants. Olav Slaymaker, Michael Church, John D. H. Lambert, Bruce H. Dahlin, William M. Denevan, and B. L. Turner II made valuable comments on earlier drafts of this essay.

ISBN 0-12-259780-X

large-scale maps, but it also would have yielded fewer of them by far, and would have involved the project in much greater expense as well as protracted right-of-way negotiations. Moreover, to disturb vegetation so drastically seemed basically inimical to an investigation that intended a close sensing of various physical elements of this landscape in relationship to one another.

The transects usually included the uncertain bottom of a good deal of swampy terrain. This meant breaching something of a barrier in field research within the Middle American tropics. There had already been extensive transecting from the center of Tikal out into its sustaining areas. Dennis Puleston, codirector of the Río Hondo project, had himself taken a leading role in this research and carried the conviction of its usefulness over into the northern Belizean work. Natural environmental information of various kinds was available, notably Lundell's topographic-vegetational profiles, and the maps and report of the 1952 survey, *Land in British Honduras* (Wright *et al.* 1959), as well as a scattering of useful material in other sources (Lundell 1937; Miranda 1958; Flores Mata *et al.* 1971; INIREB 1976). However, it is safe to say that there had not yet been a penetration of swampland to quite the extent undertaken in northern Belize. It represented not only a considerable expansion of the range of Maya subsistence studies, but also a setting aside of some deep-seated attitudes toward wetlands shared throughout the western world. The words in Germanic and Romance languages that designate them usually have highly unpleasant connotations. At best, the swamp is a blank on the collective mental map. It had been largely that in academic thought about Maya sustaining areas too. Now, it is to be considered as having been an agriculturally productive element of the landscape, and not just a useless and indeed malevolent interstice that needed to be drained before it could take on positive significance.

Wetlands of Northern Belize

The wetlands under discussion include floodplains, lake margins, and tenuously connected swampland surrounded by terra firma. They are similar to those examined by the principal investigators several years earlier along the Candelaria River of Campeche (Siemens and Puleston 1972). The New and Hondo Rivers emerge from largely karstic catchment basins, as does the Candelaria. The seasonal variations in their levels are dampened by the reservoir effect of such terrain (Siemens 1978). Maximum and minimum levels normally differ by only 1 or 2 m. Flooding is fairly regular and to moderate depths. The surrounding wetlands are occupied predominantly by herbaceous swamp vegetation designated by Wright *et al.* as a *rush–sedge* community. Palms and other marsh forest species are frequently found on hummocks within it. In general, it can be equated with the Maya term *chakan* or *sibal* (1959:298–99). The Motul dictionary indicates that the sixteenth-century meaning of these terms was "sabana o dehesa, vega o campollana o herbuage para pasto" (Martínez Hernández 1929:89, 411). Several current vernacular terms enhance these designations. *Estero* seems commonly applied to the wettest parts of such wetlands. Some open water remains within them all year, with little movement and little oxygen but abundant decomposition and deposition. More eloquent is the term *bañado,* which refers mainly to the seasonally submerged borders of the wetlands, which support vegetation like that just described (INIREB 1976:35–41). This is the environment of greatest interest to the investigation of raised fields. These lands had become useful in the sixteenth century for the pasturing of the newly introduced domestic animals, but apparently were not at that time, and are still not, generally associated with agriculture.

The *chakan* should be distinguished from *akalché,* which is defined by the Motul dictionary as "ciénaga o laguna entre montes e arboles." This is the typical *bajo* of the Petén, a characteristic feature of karstic topography. The bajos of the Petén have been surveyed quite extensively from the air for evidence of raised fields, particularly the wetter portions of them near the swallow holes, where the typical HIGH MARSH FOREST vegetation, Lundell's *tintal,* gives way to herbaceous communities (Wright *et al.* 1959:299; Lundell 1937). Very few indications of the raised-field system have been found in these locations; the extensive ground surveying carried out at Tikal and El Mirador has not reported any indication of raised-field systems either (Puleston 1978; Dahlin 1979). Some of the peculiarities of karstic hydrology may account for this (Siemens 1978).

Flores Mata *et al.* (1971) report vegetation in the bajos of southern Quintana Roo similar to that found in the Petén. However, the bajos are very extensively patterned by raised fields. The raised fields were identified during the air surveys that laid the basis for the Río Hondo Project and then were examined more closely by other investigators, but stratigraphic verification has not yet been feasible (Siemens 1977; Turner 1974; Harrison 1978a). The artificial origin of the patterning was questioned by Puleston; it seemed to him that it was attributable to the soil churning consequent on wetting and drying in montmorillonite clay soils of the kind found in bajos (Puleston 1978). If the patterning in the *bajos* of Quintana Roo is verified as artificial, the areal extent and hence the socioeconomic significance of the drained- or raised-field phenomenon in northern Belize increases massively (Denevan, see Chapter 7).

The wetlands investigated in northern Belize should also be distinguished from the extensive, labyrinthine wetlands around the lower courses of the various major rivers that cross the lowlands from western Campeche to southern Veracruz. These rivers vary a great deal seasonally; yearly differences between maximum and minimum levels are usually in the order of 10 m. Relict raised fields have been reported in one locality (Orozco-Segovia 1979; Gliessman 1979), but beyond that, the system has not been apparent in the lower basins of the large rivers during extensive air surveys by the author. Flood levels are probably excessive and too irregular over many areas that might otherwise have been used in this way. In addition, it is apparent from recent new field investigations in Tabasco and some air photo interpretation that traditional agriculture seems to migrate down the gentle slopes of swamp margins close behind receding floodwaters (Orozco-Segovia 1979; Gliessman 1979). Even the trough of the typical topographic profile occupied by aquatic vegetation such as the *Thalia geniculata,* commonly known as *popaleria,* can be planted to produce good dry season crops—one of the main and probably initial functions of the raised field.

Ground Verification of Wetland Patterning

Air photo analyses and light plane reconnaissance undertaken in June of 1972 had provided the evidence of intricate rectilinear patterning in the wetlands of northern Belize (Siemens 1977). This search, in turn, was an eastward projection of similar work done several years before along the Candelaria River in Campeche (Siemens and Puleston 1972). If the wetlands with a karstic hydrological regime had proved manageable for agriculture on the western side of the peninsula, then something similar might be expected in karstic wetlands on the eastern side. The program of transecting, referred to already, was to provide ground truth. More particularly, it was to yield information on the forms and magnitude of the phenomenon. The patterns seen from the air were expressed in vegetational color tones. What were the diagnostic species and topographic concomitants? Patterns were easily traced in nonforested parts of wetlands, but did they extend under the tree cover on land now somewhat drier than it once was?

It could not be expected that the configuration of the eroded vestiges of raised fields and canals would emerge from this method with any exactness. Before one could count paces, one needed to find a way through the vegetation, making allowances for deviations from the straight and narrow. Before it could all be recorded, one had to ward off the worst of the insects and keep a lookout for something that might be even worse. It was always difficult to match the strip maps that were drawn in the field with patterns of commensurate detail visible on the air-photo mosaic. The transectory technique itself precluded maps of entire raised-field complexes. Really satisfactory large-scale maps that do justice to topographic nuances measureable in centimeters rather than meters—under dense, often forested cover—must await the refinement of remote sensing techniques. One of the most promising of these is radar (Nielsen 1974).

The transects did verify a series of typical environmental relationships. They are shown on the accompanying schematic profile (Figure 1). This profile approximates the microrelief sensed through the bootsoles of the field crews and superimposes the associated vegetation. A typical transect would begin on the left and work through to, or at least toward, the terra firma on the right. Before going ashore, one might pluck some cocoplums from branches hanging out over the water, a last consolation for what lay ahead; then, it was up through a tangle

FIGURE 1. *Schematic profile across a river floodplain in northern Belize. Key to Vegetation and Landforms: (Local terms are followed by Spanish or Maya equivalents [where applicable] and the botanical designations [*Wright et al. *1959; Lundell 1957]). 1, variant of high marsh forest, diagnostic species—bribri* (guamo) Inga edulis *Mart., provision tree* (zapote bobo*)* Pachira aquatica *Aubl., bullet tree* (pucté*)* Bucida buceras *L., black poisonwood (chechem)* Metopium brownei *(*Jacq.*), botan palm* Sabal mauritiiformis *(Karst) Griseb & Wendl., and logwood (tinta)* Haemotoxylum campechianum *L.; 2, cocoplum* (icaco*)* Chrysobalanus icaco *L.; 3, characteristic palms on interior levee downslope, poknoboy (jauacte)* Bactris major *Jacq. and give-and-take palm (escoba)* Crysophilia argentia *Bartlett; 4, sawgrass,* Cladium jamaicense, *shorter sedges near water's edge; 5, Palmetto (tasiste)* Acoelorraphe wrightii *(Griseb); 6, water lily (naab)* Nymphaea ampla *L.; 7, similar array of species as in 1 and 3; 8, milpa; 9, terra firma; 10, vestiges of raised or drained fields; 11, hummocks resulting from natural progression of hydrosere; 12, natural relief, occasional raised fields; 13, levee.*

of roots, branches, and vines and on to the levee top for regroupment. The gradual descent would soon lead out of the forest proper into a zone of natural hummocks or relict raised fields.

A swamp, in the course of its own evolution, is typically filled in irregularly and very gradually, a process that has been called *Verlandung* (Richards 1966:283). Aquatic plants resist water movement and thus, hasten the deposition of sediments. Amphibious plants consolidate the sediments, change their texture, and add dead remains. A HYDROSERE is set in motion which culminates in forested, and, at least seasonally, dry land. Air and ground evidence indicated many rounded islets that seemed to exemplify this process. They were sometimes difficult to distinguish from the remains of raised fields around the lower margins of a complex.

Sawgrass tended to dominate most of the profile. "Islands" of palmetto would rise above this, separated by vaguely defined watercourses in which one might sink into a foot or two of soft sediments. Eventually the palmetto and sawgrass would give way to lower and sparser sedges and to water that might reach up to the waist. The ascent on the opposite side would probably go in reverse through a similar sequence, except that the vestiges of raised fields would be more frequent. The lower courses of the fields could never be very distinctly circumscribed, even though they were often visible on air photos, indicating that sediments may have buried a good deal. Often it was found that the fields extended slightly upslope under tree growth—a complication that had obvious consequences for air-photo interpretation: an additional hidden fraction would always have to be taken into consideration. More physical environmental data will be needed to interpret the fields under forest. Changing water levels may be indicated or simply the normal progress of a hydrosere.

Between the swamps and the fields of the shifting cultivator, one frequently finds a rather effective vegetational barrier to movement, which seems to add to the perceptual distance between the occupants of terra firma and the wetlands near them. Clearing does not usually go right to the swamp margin, leaving specimens of the forest to mature disproportionately in this boundary zone. The light that is given access through edaphic limitations on tree growth on the swamp side and clearing for agriculture on the other leads to a strip of vegetational tangle that is indeed a "jungle." One is tempted to think that such barriers, inadvertent or otherwise, may have served to insulate the crops on the raised fields from pest populations built up in neighbouring milpas, as Puleston (1980) has suggested. Experiments in the reactivation of traditional agricultural techniques being carried out in Tabasco include the maintenance of bands of forest vegetation around modules of intensive agriculture (Gliessman 1979). These are intended there as windbreaks, sources of natural predators and parasites for biological control, as well as for firewood and building materials. The barriers observed around the wetlands may have served, or indeed still serve, some of these functions too.

All these landscape elements can be identified in various combinations on oblique air photos. Figure 2 provides an introductory view over a swampy floodplain on the western, i.e., the Mexican, side of the Hondo River opposite Albion Island. Most of the schematic profile on Figure 1 is represented. There is a hint of raised fields on the downslope of the levee in the bottom right corner of the photo. *Verlandung* is apparent on the middle of the left margin. Raised fields line the landward margin of the floodplain; they are expressed by variations in the tone of herbaceous vegetation as well as by palmetto, the common indicator.

Figure 3 is a close-up of a raised field complex near San Antonio. The prehistoric canals show up as open water; sawgrass several meters in height prevails all around them. The lacerating leaves, poor footing, and serious danger

FIGURE 2. *Natural and artificial patterns on the Mexican side of the floodplain of the Hondo River, opposite Albion Island.*

FIGURE 3. *A complex of raised or drained fields near San Antonio.*

of poisonous snakes suggest that this terrain is seldom entered. Palmetto has colonized the highest vestiges of raised fields.

Figures 4 and 5 show some locational variations. Inside a curve of the Hondo River, the schematic profile has been occluded; the backslope of the levee has created a shallow basin that was usable entirely for raised fields. The characteristic location of raised fields is especially clear around Pulltrouser Swamp, which drains into the New River. The forms seem particularly rudimentary in this instance; the forest barrier between wetland and terra firma is well defined.

On the basis of vertical air-photo coverage, the oblique photographs obtained from our various air surveys, and the results of the transects, it was possible to prepare a map of prehistoric wetland use in northern Belize (Figure 6). The map shows, in the first instance, where raised fields were actually found or where they might be deduced to be. By actual measurement, these approach 3,200 ha, which is very much less than the 7,500 ha estimated earlier (Puleston

FIGURE 4. *Field vestiges within a curve of the Hondo River.*

1977a:454). The fields are arranged into many discrete complexes—in fact, much more than the inevitable generalization of a map of this scale would indicate. Contiguous zones often show morphological variations, and there is considerable range in the degree of rectilinearity. Little regularity in orientation is apparent, other than a frequent rough perpendicular alignment to the contours of the adjacent uplands.

Numerous longer canals, not directly related to the canals that separate raised fields, once crossed the floodplain and neighboring wetlands of the Candelaria River (Siemens and Puleston 1972). They are the most obtrusive vestiges of past human intervention in the region. Some may be detected in the wetlands of northern Belize as well. One such canal, on Albion Island, still had almost a

FIGURE 5. *Fields along the margin of Pulltrouser Swamp.*

meter of water in it near the end of an exceptionally long dry season in 1973 but was choked with fallen trees and weeds. A middle-aged informant remembered that there were canoes on the canal when he was young. Access from the river to terra firma, where most settlements and milpas are typically located, seems to have been the main point. Such waterways may also have been used for the exploitation of logwood (*Haemotoxylum campechianum*) or other forest products. As Thompson (1974) observed, the waterways may have been used before contact to facilitate fishing, and perhaps even a kind of pisciculture. They also would have been very useful to defenders in case of riverine invasion.

Figure 7 shows what seem to be the remains of larger canals on the eastern side and near the northern end of the New River Lagoon, somewhat to the south of the area mapped in Figure 6. These larger canals are drawn into the discussion

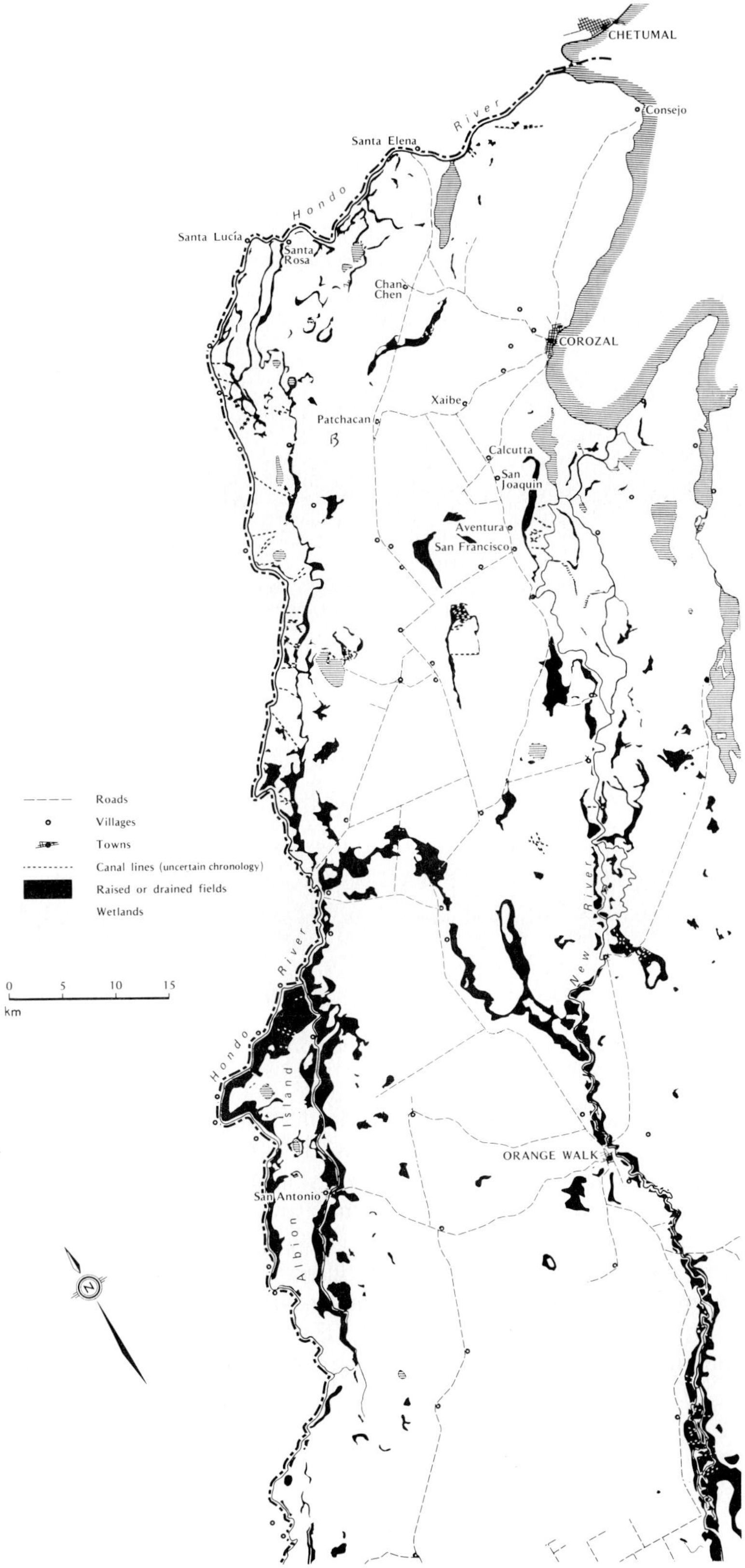

FIGURE 6. *Prehispanic agricultural uses of wetlands in northern Belize.*

FIGURE 7. *Vestiges of canals on the northeastern margin of New River Lagoon.*

here to indicate some of the potential in further analysis of early waterborne transportation through these lowlands. Together with other canals extending eastward from the lagoon and the river itself, they add substance to postulations about transport routes from the eastern Yucatán coast into the Petén. A prominent view on this is that movement into the interior was via the Belize River (Thompson 1970:129). A somewhat different route also seems likely, especially if waterways are as important for transportation into the interior as Thompson has suggested, and if it is true that "the Putun traders, who dominated the commerce of the peninsula, almost surely went by land only when they could not go by water" (Thompson 1970:134). It seems likely that canoes would have gone up the Belize to its "Big Bend," then up one of its tributaries, the Black Creek, and across the few remaining kilometers via canal or a short portage into the New River system. A route up this river and one or another of the complex waterways between the New and Hondo systems could conceivably have led up to the eastern ends of one or another of the large bajos of the Petén. If we then contemplate the possibility that the bajos were once negotiable by water more easily than they are now (Harrison 1977; Siemens 1978), the last part of a major waterway right into Tikal falls into place.

Figure 7 suggests port or passage facilities that would have been able to accommodate large seagoing canoes of the kind encountered by Columbus on his fourth voyage. These canals may also have served as prehistoric fisheries, a use that would be quite compatible with transportation.

Related Field Investigations

The Río Hondo Project went a good deal beyond air-photo analysis and the pace-and-compass mapping involved in transecting. A survey of Prehispanic settlement was carried out by Bruce Dahlin on an east–west transect 500 m in width across Albion Island. It was redrawn and has been included in a recent paper by Puleston and Pohl (1980). Two further transects were planned but could not be carried out. Dahlin's attempt cut through a sizeable community. It was subject to the usual doubts about the contemporaneity of occupancy, but its results were indicative of the possibility of a high population density in northern Belize. Some 700 people/km^2 were indicated, a figure comparable to that for the residential area of Tikal (Dahlin 1977:47).

From several studies of traditional subsistence activities persisting alongside agriculture in villages in northern Belize in the early 1970s, reminders emerge regarding the multiplicity of food-producing options available to the ancient Maya. Hunting in San Antonio, at the time of Mary Pohl's study there in 1973 and 1974, was still a source of some important nutrients (Pohl 1977). It had traditionally yielded a desirable item of exchange among relatives and brought the hunter small amounts of cash as well. Venison and other meats that came out of the forest were still highly desirable in the early 1970s, but had become scarce in the village. Hunting had become predominantly a commercial activity; game was being bought by relatively affluent outsiders and reserves were diminishing. The cash introduced by means of the expansion of sugar cane was at the root of this and many other changes in traditional livelihood patterns.

Abrams observed group fishing by the inhabitants of Xaibé, a predominantly Maya village some distance to the north of San Antonio (1977). It seems a strong echo out of the past uses of the natural open water stretches in the wetlands and the canals between the raised fields. From late February to May, when the water levels have dropped sufficiently in the floodplain wetlands and adjacent swamps to cut off the retreat of fish into the main streams, groups of kinsmen and friends go on fishing expeditions that are conducted virtually as competitive sporting events. Some of the men hold the net in the water, others drive fish toward it by striking the surface with sticks, coming in closer and closer. The net is closed and the thrashing fish are taken out by hand. All this evidently has had a long tradition in Xaibé.

Some experimentation with the reactivation of raised fields was first begun in 1970 along the Candelaria; a vestigial field in the oriented complex across from the village of El Tigre was cleared and planted in late May (Puleston 1977b). A basic lesson was learned from the seasonal floodwaters. This was obviously not a system to be used synchronously with the normal main wet-season shifting cultivation cycle unless field surfaces could be considerably raised. The planting was flooded in July, before any of the whole range of thriving experimental crops could mature. A dry-season planting on the vestiges would probably have yielded well. If the fields were originally maintained at levels a meter or more above the present eroded surfaces, they could have served the ancient Maya the year round.

In 1974, Dennis Puleston began his experimental reconstruction and management of a raised field near San Antonio in northern Belize. Relying on the stratigraphy of his nearby trenches as a guide, he built up an agricultural surface on what may have been a vestigial raised field using marl from neighboring outcrops and muck from reopened canals. This seemed to be promising research methodology that might have practical results as well. The use of raised fields to enhance current tropical agricultural development is under active consideration in various parts of the tropical lowland; their potential quickly occurs to anyone who sees the contrast between the current minimal uses of wetlands and the evidence for a more intensive Prehispanic use. To what extent such a labor-intensive system can be made attractive when reasonably well-remunerated wage labor is available, as it has been recently in northern Belize, remains very much an unresolved question.

After the raised surface was achieved, the persistent question of just what crops the fields could be made to produce, now as in the distant past, became particularly intriguing. Maize and cotton had already showed up in pollen samples (Puleston 1977a:454). Dahlin had argued that raised fields might well have supported groves of cacao, a valuable cash crop, or indeed other forms of arboriculture (Dahlin 1979:80). Puleston's own crop trials near the Candelaria had indicated a wide range of possibilities, and this was confirmed at San Antonio. It also became clear, however, that a good understanding of the rhythm of flooding was basic to such an operation. Moreover, birds, insects, and herbivores proved difficult to deal with. Much care and attention would have been required, especially if the fields had indeed been raised and were cropped continuously—a fact that should not be surprising to any horticulturalist, needless to say. Dahlin (1979:76) has pointed out how useful the canal itself would have been as a barrier to herbivores and terrestrial insects. Current experiments in the introduction of the *chinampa* system and other techniques of intensive production into the wetlands of Tabasco show how much of what seems to have been traditional wisdom regarding the control of diseases, pests, and weeds through advantageous juxtaposition needs to be relearned (Gliessman 1979). They also confirm the wide range of cropping possibilities.

The profiles drawn by Peter Stavrakis of the various trenches Dennis Puleston and his assistants dug, across what seemed fairly clearly to be several raised fields and canals at the village of San Antonio, remain to be fully analyzed and published. However, a report on soil analyses at various locations around San Antonio by Gerald Olson and preliminary information published by Puleston himself have allowed a beginning of the discussion of the stratigraphy of the fields (Olson 1974; Puleston 1977a, 1977b, 1978). The fields have been interpreted as constructions and periodic reconstructions out of marl (*sascab*) from nearby quarries, surfaced with sediments from the bottoms of the interstitial canals (Puleston 1977a, 1977b, 1978). Alteration of soil structure to enhance permeability as well as the addition of nutrients were also thought to have been objectives in all of this, rather than just the achievement of a certain elevation vis-á-vis maximum and minimum water level.

Some of the excavation Puleston has reported was extended considerably below the water table with the help of pumps. It yielded a sample of what may be expected from further application of this arduous technique. A "post, trimmed at one end with an axe or adze and driven into sediments on the edge of the canal, produced a date of 1110 ± 230 B.C. [1-7877A]" (Puleston 1977a:452). The cotton and maize pollen, referred to already, were identified in soil samples taken by coring near these trenches.

Reconsiderations

The amount of construction actually involved in "raising" the initial fields in northern Belize has been thrown into question by recent new excavations on and near the site of Puleston's experimental reconstruction of raised fields at San Antonio (Antoine *et al.*, see Chapter 9). What was interpreted as having been laboriously built up by human labor, now seems to have been naturally deposited during the aggradation in river floodplains consequent on the post-Pleistocene rise in sea levels. This interpretation is corroborated by Lambert and Arnason (1979) from recent excavations near Lamanai. Artificial canalization is still indicated by evidence from these two sources, and hence some limited build-up alongside will have been inevitable. Agricultural use of the "raised" (or perhaps one should again say "drained") fields is left as quite plausible; but in some areas at least, the system will have been more rudimentary than was hypothesized in the earlier investigations.

Both the Puleston argument and that of Antoine and his colleagues are based on a very limited sampling of the whole raised-field phenomenon in northern Belize. Neither relate specifically, for instance, to raised-field complexes clearly evident from the air, such as occur within several kilometers to the north and south of San Antonio. The corroboration from Lamanai broadens the base considerably. Evidence from the recent investigations by Turner and Harrison at Pulltrouser Swamp, between the New and the Hondo Rivers just north of Orange Walk, will undoubtedly broaden it further (Turner *et al.* 1980). Even so, a good deal more excavation and geomorphological as well as hydrological interpretation of wetland landscapes will be necessary before the range in the sophistication of this phenomenon and its environmental context is adequately understood. Unfortunately, the stratigraphy of the canals, from which most of the cultural evidence is to be expected, must also be expected to be very difficult to interpret. The poling of watercraft and the scooping up of the muck for fertilization will have mixed it all rather thoroughly.

Problems in Assessing the Significance of Maya Raised Fields

It is still very difficult to evaluate the past agricultural use of the wetlands with respect to some of its most tantalizing aspects: the labor required to construct and maintain the field systems and their carrying capacity. There are the uncertainties as to how much construction was involved as well as the resulting uncertainties over seasonal versus more intensive, all-year cultivation. Our understanding of the cropping of the fields is still a list of possibilities. Even the ratio of field to canal surface is not easily deduced in view of the smoothing of all surface profiles by erosion and the variation in the size and configuration of the fields. The experimental reconstruction carried out by Dennis Puleston on the premise that there had been considerable artificial build-up offered an opportunity to form some idea of the labor expended. However, man-hours proved an unsuitable concept for administration of the project, let alone the projection of labor requirements into prehistory (Puleston 1977b:41). In accord with traditional practice, each man was content to complete his assigned work quota (*tarea*) at his own pace. The *tarea* had to be quite arbitrarily defined since the work was strange to both workers and supervisor.

Denevan has made plausible assumptions in all of these respects and quantitatively compared the raised fields as they occur in various locations in the Americas (see Chapter 7). If used year-round and at otherwise comparable levels of sophistication for subsistence purposes, the 32-km^2 of fields postulated for northern Belize would have supported less than $\frac{1}{6}$ of the population supported by the chinampas of central Mexico. If the patterning in the bajos of southern Quintana Roo is drawn in, however, the carrying capacity of this system on the eastern flank of the Yucatán Peninsula becomes considerably larger than that of the chinampas. While these quantitative aspects await sharper resolution, it is reasonable to think of the significance of raised or drained fields in northern Belize along other lines: some of them at least seem to represent an early stage in the development of techniques for the agricultural use of wetlands in Middle America.

Summary and Conclusions

During the course of the Río Hondo project, it was possible to establish that there had indeed been extensive Prehispanic agricultural forays into the swampy terrain of northern Belize. Vestiges of raised or drained fields were found to be particularly frequent on the upper portions of the gentle inner slopes of the wetlands, over against terra firma, a zone with a well-defined annual rhythm of flooding and emergence.

In this context, one may envisage a relatively simple drained field, that is, a planting surface exposed each dry season and yielding during the leanest stretch of each year. This would admirably complement dry season milpas on the surrounding terra firma, hunting in the forest and milpas, gathering of fruits, fuel, and other material wherever possible, and exploiting the arboreal and other resources around the dwelling. A web of canals would speed the drying out of the surface on recession of the floodwaters. The configuration of the water table in the canal-separated fields would curve downward adjacent to the canals, which would themselves facilitate run-off, rather than move more slowly and evenly down as in an undisturbed area. These same canals would limit access to the fields by herbivores and terrestrial insects while they facilitated access by the agriculturalist. They would be a suitable medium for fish adapted to lentic as well as lotic conditions and would become a gigantic trap late in the dry season.

If the fields were also artifically raised above flood level, fertilized with muck out of the canals, and irrigated with scoops, they would have sustained continuous cropping. Under these circumstances, one might expect a rich and varied productivity approaching that of the central Mexican chinampas.

Seasonal use would certainly have complemented various other subsistence options and, thus, may be thought of as an intensification of overall resource exploitation; year-round use would qualify for the term "intensive agriculture," as it is commonly used (Harrison 1978b). In both versions, but particularly the first, this system would have to be thought of as an exploitation of the hydrological regime of the swamp more or less as it is. There is not much evidence yet for the facilities that would have been necessary for a sustained lowering of the groundwater level such as one would expect from a drainage project nor, indeed, for a sustained upkeep of water levels by various means as one sees it in the *zonas chinamperas* of central Mexico.

It is apparent that the raised field in the Maya area was initially a more rudimentary intervention than has been assumed in much of the discussion of its significance for the evolution of the culture. To what extent the use of these planting surfaces was intensified remains to be seen, but it is quite likely that instances of chinampa-like sophistication will be demonstrated. Something like a developmental sequence has long been apparent impressionistically. There is a range in the degree of rectilinearity among complexes of fields within the Maya area—from the barely quadrate, variously oriented, and seemingly uncoordinated groups typical for the wetlands near the Río Hondo, to the fairly strict parallelism traceable in some of the wetland west of Chetumal and at least one sizeable complex of fields near the Candelaria. The fields recently reported from central Veracruz (Siemens 1981) are more regular still, with frequent accordance in orientation (5° to 20° E of N) from complex to complex over many kilometers of separation. The chinampas of central Mexico, of course, epitomize the regularity—and show a similar orientation, i.e., 15°–17° E of N (Coe 1964:96). It is intended that these data will be elaborated on and tested by excavation at a range of sites, perhaps corroborating something like the model of development for individual regions and for Mesoamerican wetlands generally that the morphology suggests.

Postscript

Since this chapter was submitted to the editor, the investigation of the Precolumbian use of wetlands has advanced along several lines. The areal extent of the drained- or raised-field phenomenon in the Maya area has been immensely enlarged. Test excavations have confirmed that the patterning in the bajos of Quintana Roo is artificial (Gliessman, personal communication 1980). More dramatic evidence still has come from remote sensing. Side-looking airborne radar imagery from over northern Guatemala and Belize indicates numerous canals not previously noticed (Wilford 1980; Adams 1980). Many qualifications have had to be attached to these data, and much is still unclear. The scale of the original imagery (1:500,000) often allows the resolution of only major canal lines, not features like the many interstitial canals of raised-field systems. The impressive webs of canals that do show up could be of modern or historic as well as prehistoric origin; they might even be natural features. Nevertheless, there is the distinct probability that ancient modification of wetlands in the Maya Lowlands and elsewhere in Mesoamerica will be shown to have been much more extensive than imagined thus far.

Moreover, many specific aspects of this phenomenon have been pursued with good results in the Pulltrouser Swamp Project, codirected by B. L. Turner II and Peter D. Harrison, the voluminous field report of which has just recently come to hand (Turner *et al.* 1980). Many of the characteristic environmental concomitants searched out during the Río Hondo Project have been confirmed—with a good deal of additional nuance. The attractiveness to early Maya agriculturalists of wetlands with a limited fluctuation (in the order of 1 or 2 m) between high and low water has been emphasized. The Maya found these conditions in different geomorphological contexts. The floodplains of karstic rivers on the two flanks of the Yucatán Peninsula were used extensively for raised- or drained-field agriculture. The bajos of the Petén were not used in this way it seems; but at Pulltrouser Swamp, a feature that is considered by Turner and his colleagues to be a bajo as well, is patterned along its margins. Bajos in Quintana Roo have now been shown to be patterned end to end. Variation in elevation above sea level and the nature of sedimentation in particular contexts seem to have made the difference. The vegetation study of northern Belize by Wright and his colleagues, in particular the accompanying detailed and most intriguing map at 1:250,000, shows how depressions that might have taken on the character of *akalché* under other circumstances must be designated *sibal* instead—thus far, the prime raised-field environment. Vegetational and hydrological distinctions between wetlands remain critical.

The investigators have added very substantially to the understanding of the physical structure of the fields by clearly differentiating various types of construction and linking them to those found at San Antonio and Lamanai (Antoine *et al.,* see Chapter 9; Lambert 1979). Rudimentary fields, achieved by simple canalization, have been noted, as well as others requiring substantial build-up and considered not too different from central Mexican chinampas. A developmental sequence may be inferred; the chronology postulated for the Pulltrouser Swamp region certainly gives the phenomenon depth. The answer to the early question as to what was actually grown on the fields beyond corn, which has been confirmed, is still only a series of possibilities. The concomitants of such agriculture in settlement and society as well as its place in the culture history of the Maya must continue to be discussed in similar terms.

References

Abrams, Ira R.
1977 Group net fishing in northern Belize: Nutritional implications for the Maya Lowlands. *Journal of Belizean Affairs* 5:64–69.

Adams, R. E. W.
1980 Ancient land use and culture history in the Pasión River region. *Burg Wartenstein Symposium No.* 86(August):16–24. Wenner-Gren Foundation for Anthropological Research, New York.

Antoine, Pierre P., Richard L. Skarie, and Paul R. Bloom
1982 The origin of raised fields near San Antonio, Belize: An alternative hypothesis. In *Maya Subsistence* edited by Kent V. Flannery. New York: Academic Press.

Coe, Michael D.
1964 The chinampas of Mexico. *Scientific American* 211(1):90–98.

Dahlin, Bruce H.
1977 The initiation of the Albion Island settlement pattern survey. *Journal of Belizean Affairs* 15:44–51.
1979 Ecological inference and ancient Maya agriculture systems. Ms. on file, Department of Anthropology, Catholic University, Washington.

Denevan, William M.
1982 Hydraulic agriculture in the American tropics: Forms, measures, and recent research. In *Maya Subsistence,* edited by Kent V. Flannery. New York, Academic Press.

Flores Mata, G., J. Jiménez López, X. Madrigal Sánchez, F. Moncayo Ruiz, and F. Takaki Takaki
1971 *Tipos de Vegetación de la República Méxicana,* México, D. F.

Gliessman, Stephen R.
1979 *Some ecological relationships of traditional agroecosystems in the lowland humid tropics of southern Mexico.* Paper presented at the XLIII International Congress of Americanists, Vancouver.

Harrison, Peter D.
1977 The rise of the *bajos* and the fall of the Maya. In *Social Process in Maya Prehistory: Studies in Memory of Sir Eric Thompson,* edited by Norman Hammond. London, Academic Press.
1978a Bajos revisited: Visual evidence for one system of agriculture. In *Pre-Hispanic Maya Agriculture,* edited by Peter D. Harrison and B. L. Turner II. Albuquerque, Univ. of New Mexico Press.
1978b So the seeds shall grow. In *Pre-Hispanic Maya Agriculture,* edited by Peter D. Harrison and B. L. Turner II. Albuquerque, Univ. of New Mexico Press.
INIREB (Instituto Nacional de Investigaciones sobre Recursos Bióticos)
1976 *Estudio Ecológico de la Región de Balancán-Tenosique.* Mimeograph available from author.
Lambert, J. D. H., and J. T. Arnason
1979 Drained fields in the New River floodplain and their agricultural potential—Past and present. Ms. on file, Department of Biology, Carleton University, Ontario.
Lundell, Cyrus L.
1937 The vegetation of the Petén, *Carnegie Institution of Washington; Publication* 478. Washington, D.C.
Martínez Hernández, Juan (editor)
1929 *Diccionario de Motul: Maya–Espanōl.* Atribuido a Fray Antonio de Ciudad Real y Arte de lengua Maya por Fray Juan Coronel. Merida, Yucatán, Compañía Tipográfica.
Miranda, Faustino
1958 Estudios acerca de la vegetación. In *Los Recursos Naturales del Sureste y su Aprovechamiento,* Volume II, pp. 213–271. Mexico, Instituto Mexicano de Recursos Naturales Renovables.
Nielsen, U.
1974 Description and performance of the forestry radar altimeter. *Forest Management Institute Information Report* FMR-X-59. Ottawa.
Olson, Gerald W.
1974 *Field Report on Soils Sampled Around San Antonio in Northern Belize (British Honduras).* Cornell Agronomy Mimeo 74-23.
Orozco-Segovia, Alma D. L., and Stephen R. Gliessman
1979 The Marceño in flood-prone regions of Tabasco, Mexico. Paper presented at the XLIII International Congress of Americanists, Vancouver.
Pohl, Mary
1977 Hunting in the Maya village of San Antonio Río Hondo, Orange Walk District, Belize. *Journal of Belizean Affairs* 5:52–63.
Puleston, Dennis E.
1977a The art and archaeology of hydraulic agriculture in the Maya Lowlands. In *Social Process in Maya Prehistory: Studies in Memory of Sir Eric Thompson,* edited by Norman Hammond. New York, Academic Press.
1977b Experiments in prehistoric raised field agriculture: Learning from the past. *Journal of Belizean Affairs* 5:36–43.
1978 Terracing, raised fields and tree cropping in the Maya Lowlands: A new perspective on the geography of power. In *Pre-Hispanic Maya Agriculture,* edited by Peter D. Harrison and B. L. Turner II, Albuquerque, University of New Mexico Press.
Puleston, Dennis E., and Mary Pohl
1980 Models for the development of Maya raised field agriculture. In *Man and Landscape in the Maya Lowlands,* edited by Mary Pohl, in press.
Richards, P. W.
1966 *The Tropical Rainforest: An Ecological Study.* Cambridge, Cambridge Univ. Press.
Siemens, Alfred H., and Dennis E. Puleston
1972 Ridged fields and associated features in southern Campeche: New perspectives on the Lowland Maya. *American Antiquity* 37(2):228–239.

Siemens, Alfred H.
1977 Some patterns seen from the air. *Journal of Belizean Affairs* 5:5–21.
1978 Karst and the pre-Hispanic Maya in the southern lowlands. In *Pre-Hispanic Maya Agriculture,* edited by Peter D. Harrison and B. L. Turner II. Albuquerque, Univ. of New Mexico Press.
1981 Oriented raised fields in Central Veracruz, in press.

Thompson, J. Eric S.
1970 *Maya History and Religion.* Norman, Univ. of Oklahoma Press.
1974 Canals of the Río Candelaria Basin. Campeche, Mexico. In *Mesoamerican Archaeology: New Approaches,* edited by Norman Hammond, pp. 297–302. Austin, Univ. of Texas Press.

Turner II, B. L.
1974 Prehistoric intensive agriculture in the Mayan Lowlands. *Science* 185:118–124.

Turner, B. L., II *et al.*
1980 Maya raised-field agriculture and settlement at Pulltrouser Swamp, Northern Belize. *Report of the 1979–80 University of Oklahoma–National Science Foundation Pulltrouser Swamp Project,* Clark University, Worcester, Massachusetts.

Wilford, John Noble
1980 Maya canals found by radar. *The New York Times* June 3, p. C3.

Wright, A. C. S., D. H. Romney, R. H. Arbuckle, and V. E. Vial
1959 Land in British Honduras. *Colonial Research Publications* 24, London.

9

The Origin of Raised Fields near San Antonio, Belize: An Alternative Hypothesis

Pierre P. Antoine,[1] *Richard L. Skarie,*[2] *and Paul R. Bloom*

Introduction

Systems of intensive agricultural production among the ancient Maya are characterized by Puleston (1978) as terraces, kitchen-gardens, tree cropping, and raised fields. Sizeable acreages of the latter have been reported in the Maya Lowlands, especially in northern Belize (Olson 1975; Puleston 1977; Siemens and Puleston 1972). In 1977, Puleston invited the authors of this article to examine further the problem of the origin of raised fields near San Antonio, Belize and to conduct soil fertility studies aimed at verifying his experimental model of Maya agricultural practices in riverine environments. The present work considers only the origin of the raised fields.

Puleston was not entirely convinced that all the raised fields that have been reported are of human origin. In a review article (1978), he suggests that some fields may in fact be gilgai, resulting from the expansion of montmorillonitic clays. He also points out that of the large number of fields that have been located on aerial photographs, excavations sufficient to confirm their identification as human artifacts have only been carried out at El Tigre on the Candelaria River in Campeche, Mexico and at San Antonio on the Hondo River in northern Belize. These excavations suggested to Puleston that "the fields were initially built up

[1]Present address: National Agronome Institute of Yangambi, Yangambi, Zaire.
[2]Present address: Box 29, Rt. 1, Audobon, Minnesota 56511.

ISBN 0-12-259780-X

out of floodplain sediments, and that at some later date, they were converted (by the Maya) to laboriously constructed limestone marl platforms. The limestone was brought from still extant quarries on the uplands'' (Puleston 1978). More recent excavations of two raised fields near San Antonio indicate to the authors that Puleston's model for their formation may be incorrect. The origin of the observed strata is readily explained by geological processes without hypothesizing any human intervention. Possible use of the fields by the Maya cannot be ruled out, however, and the ''canals'' between the fields might possibly be human artifacts.

Physical Setting

San Antonio is located on a secondary channel of the Hondo River that together with the main channel, form Albion Island. Because the karst topography of the drainage basin acts as a buffer to runoff waters, the level of the Hondo remains relatively constant throughout the year (Siemens 1978). Daily tidal fluctuations in stage attest to the extremely low elevation of the river at San Antonio. The floodplain near the village is drained by a network of waterways which surround convex landforms of variable size (possibly 0.1–0.3 ha). Each ''field'' is raised about 30 to 40 cm above the level of the waterways and the river. The waterways, referred to by Puleston as canals, are oriented in a somewhat rectilinear pattern with respect to the river.

Moving away from the floodplain, the land around San Antonio is a low-lying karst platform with elevations less than 20 m. Elevations exceed 40 m near the center of Albion Island, where topography is controlled by fairly resistant limestone bedrock. Exposures of soft limy material known locally as *sascab* are fairly common in upland areas.

Two fields, located in a swampy area south of San Antonio, were selected by Puleston for excavation by one of the authors of the present work (R. L. S.). The first field is about 100 m. south of the village and was previously cleared of forest vegetation by Puleston. This experimental field had also been capped with a layer of *sascab* (Figure 1) and a layer of canal sediments as he believed the Maya to have done in the original construction of the field (Olson 1975; Olson 1979; Puleston 1978). The second site is located about 100 m southwest of the experimental field and remained in its natural (abandoned) state.

Methods

On each of the two fields selected by Puleston, a test pit of about 1 m^2 was dug to a depth of about 2 m. Materials deeper than 2 m were examined using a soil probe. Because most of the strata were below the water table (about 40 cm) both pits had to be bailed frequently. The exposed profiles were described

FIGURE 1. *Test pit at site 1, experimental field reconstructed by Puleston, with* sascab *visible at the top of the profile. Note the darkened layers near the middle of the profile and the very dark peats at the bottom of the pit. Depth intervals are 10 cm with 20 cm at the original surface.*

according to standard pedological procedures, and samples were collected from each horizon for later analysis by the soil-characterization laboratory.

Particle-size analyses were performed by the pipette method after the organic matter, soluble salts, and calcium carbonates were removed (Soil Conservation Service 1972). Organic carbon was determined in the mineral soils by using a LECO carbon furnace (Allison *et al.* 1965) or by wet oxidation with $K_2Cr_2O_7$ (Walkley and Black 1934). Organic matter in the peaty samples was determined by weight loss after 16 hours at 450°C. Carbonate content was measured using 6 N HCl, according to the method described by the Soil Conservation Service (1972).

X-ray diffraction analysis was performed on finely ground whole-soil samples and some clay fractions (Whittig 1965). All samples were pretreated with sodium citrate and dithionite solutions. Clay samples were analyzed after saturation with magnesium ion (air dried, glycerol solvated, and heated to 550°C). The peat sample for radiocarbon dating was pretreated twice with 1 N HCl to destroy carbonates and was extracted twice with 0.1 M $Na_4P_2O_7$ to remove mobile humic materials. This latter treatment was used to minimize the influence of carbon exchange with the humic matter in the river water.

Examination of Strata from Test Pits

Tables 1 and 2 list the physical and chemical data of the strata observed in the two test pits. Disregarding the layers applied by Puleston (horizons 1a and 1b), the sequences of horizons of the two profiles are remarkably similar. The organic surface layer is underlain by about 20 cm of heavy clay, the lower limit of which corresponds roughly to the depth of the water table. The clays are underlain by approximately 1 m of layered silty materials which contain significant amounts of carbonates, especially in the lower portion. Gypsum is a major component of these materials and mollusk shells commonly occur. Beneath the silts are several layers of sapric peat which is highly decomposed. A sample taken from the upper horizon of the peat (horizon 9 of profile 2) yielded a radiocarbon date of 3510 ± 185 B.P.[3] This date is the average age of the horizon, but the horizon is thin (7 cm), and the date of burial is likely within several hundred years, or less, after 3500 B.P. The next lower unit below the peat consists of heavy clays much like those observed near the surface and probably reflects a similar depositional environment.

The organic-matter content of each horizon was determined in order to detect any formerly exposed surfaces where plants had grown for an extended period and/or where organic-laden sediments might have been applied by the Maya. These data were of special interest for the silty materials where darkened horizons were hypothesized to be former agricultural surfaces (Figure 1, Figure 2:horizon 2.7). If the dark horizons were actually buried surfaces, they would appear as bulges in the organic-matter profile. We note in Tables 1 and 2 however, a typical pattern of decreasing organic matter with depth. This trend continues until the peat layers are approached, where the values sharply increase. The darker color observed in horizons 1.5, 1.6, and 2.7 apparently are not related to organic-matter content (note the extremely low values), and the only buried surface that can be identified from the data is the buried peat.

Mineralogical data show that the clays are predominantly 2:1 interlayer clays with poorly defined mica-smectite, vermiculite-mica and/or chlorite-vermiculite clays, plus some montmorillonite and mica. These clays have a limited capacity to expand, which is reflected in the pressure faces observed on the surfaces of peds in the upper clay layers. There was, however, no visible field evidence of vertisol activity that could result in gilgai formation. The silty layers overlying the peat are mostly gypsum and/or calcite (Table 1). The *sascab* applied by Puleston is not limestone marl, but largely gypsum with a very small calcium carbonate content.

[3]Data based on Libby half-life (5,570 years) for C-14.

Table 1
Raised Fields near San Antonio, Belize: Physical and Chemical Data for Site 1

Horizon	Depth (cm)	Texture class	Sand[c] (%)	Silt[c] (%)	Clay[c] (%)	$CaCO_3$ (%)	Organic matter (%)	X-ray minerology
1a[a]	+8–+19	Sapric	—	—	—	—	52	—
1b[a]	0–+8	Silt loam	14	70	16	5	0.76	Gypsum
1.1	0–1	Sapric	—	—	—	—	48	2:1 clays[b]
1.2	1–5	Clay	0.8	10	89	5	14.2	2:1 clays
1.3	5–23	Clay	5.3	12	83	19	4.10	2:1 clays
1.4	23–54	Silt loam	43	53	4	16	0.41	Gypsum, 2:1 clays
1.5	54–73	Loam	41	37	22	12	0.40	Gypsum, calcite, 2:1 clays
1.6	73–101	Silt loam	36	63	2	18	0.81	Gypsum, calcite, 2:1 clays
1.7	101–147	Silt loam	1	66	18	70	1.59	Calcite, gypsum, 2:1 clays
1.8	147–155	Silty clay loam	20	45	35	76	8.60	Calcite, gypsum, 2:1 clays
1.9	155–165	Sapric	—	—	—	—	55	2:1 clays
1.10	165–175	Peaty	—	—	—	—	14.6	Gypsum, 2:1 clays
1.11	175–231	Peaty	—	—	—	—	—	—
1.12	231–286	Clay	3	7	90		2.56	2:1 clays

[a] Material applied by D. Puleston.
[b] Two:one clays refers to a mixture of poorly defined interstratified clays containing mica-smectite, vermiculite-mica and/or chlorite vermiculite, plus some vermiculite, mica and/or montmorillonite.
[c] Percentage determined after removal of organic matter and $CaCO_3$.

Table 2
Raised Fields near San Antonio, Belize: Physical and Chemical Data for Site 2

Horizon	Depth (cm)	Texture class	Sand[a] (%)	Silt[a] (%)	Clay[a] (%)	$CaCO_3$ (%)	Organic matter (%)
2.1	0–9	Sapric	—	—	—	—	56
2.2	9–15	Clay	1	12	86	1	29.0
2.3	15–26	Clay	5	8	87	2	2.98
2.4	26–34	Clay	9	21	70	44	2.41
2.5	34–61	Silty clay loam	14	59	27	11	0.36
2.6	61–84	Silt loam	21	55	25	26	0.44
2.7	84–103	Silt loam	16	58	26	7	0.55
2.8	103–126	Silt loam	17	57	26	39	1.31
2.9	126–143	Sapric	—	—	—	—	38
2.10	143–187	Sapric	—	—	—	—	61
2.11	187–210	—	—	—	—	—	1.67
2.12	210–255	Clay	3	0	97	—	1.00
2.13	255–285	Clay	6	1	93	—	1.02
2.14	285–305	Clay	6	4	90	—	3.22

[a] Percentage determined after removal of organic matter and $CaCO_3$.

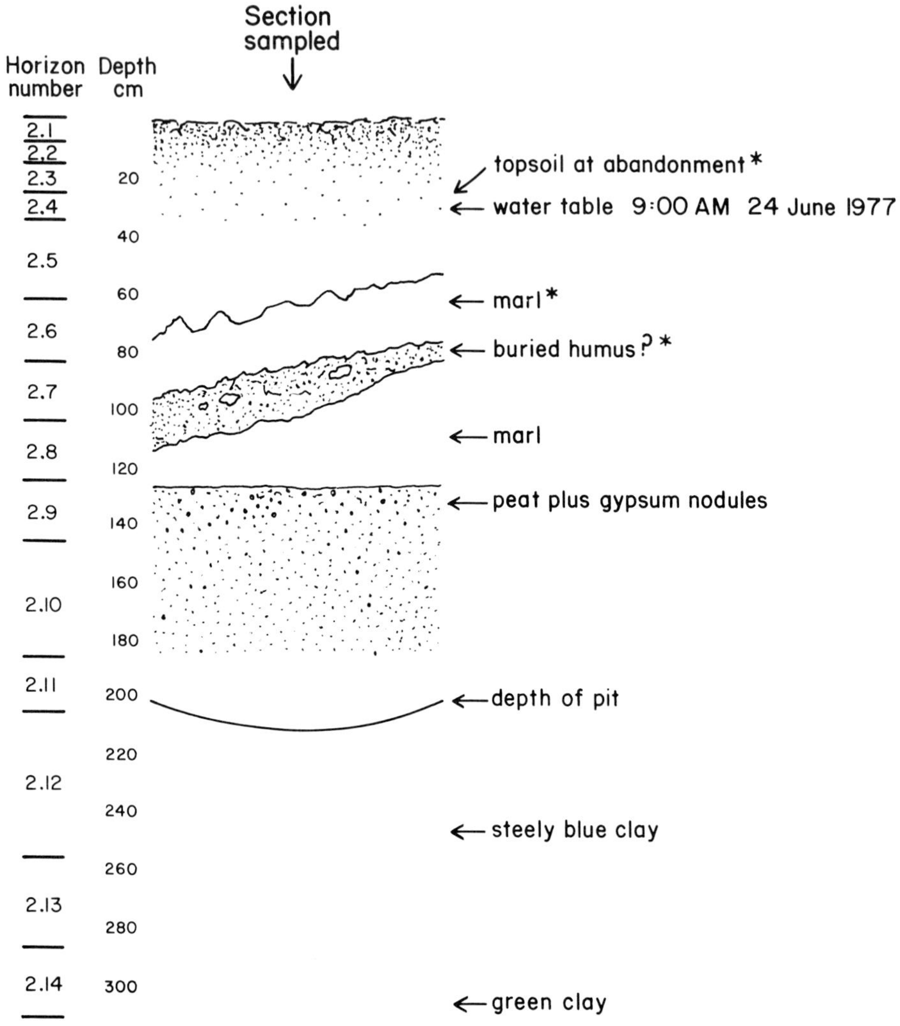

FIGURE 2. *Diagram and notes for south face of test pit at site 2. Adapted from Puleston's field notes (77-2-78). *, Laboratory evidence shows these suppositions to be incorrect.*

Discussion

Puleston's interpretation of the strata (personal communication) can best be understood in reference to his field diagram and notes, which are presented in Figure 2. The marl layer (2.8) immediately overlying the peat was seen as an initial attempt by the Maya to build up the field surface and enhance drainage for agriculture. The darkened layer (2.7) was interpreted as a former surface horizon that was covered by successive applications of *sascab* (2.6, 2.5), possibly in response to increased frequency of flooding. Horizon 2.4 was considered the topsoil at the time of abandonment by the Maya, and the overlying clays (2.3, 2.2) were considered postabandonment flood deposits.

An alternative approach is to consider all the strata as natural deposits and to seek to interpret them in light of the recent geologic history of the area. There is good evidence that the area has undergone environmental change, which would be expected to result in the sequence of horizons observed. Environmental change is indicated by the presence of a buried peat at a meter or more below the present water table. Peat of the type observed is an accumulation of residues from plants growing in direct contact with the atmosphere; therefore, these buried layers must represent a formerly exposed surface. Since the water table closely reflects the level of the river, the peats must have formed when the river was at least 1 m below its present elevation. As mentioned previously, the river stage is subject to tidal fluctuation and is ultimately controlled by sea level. The rise in river level must therefore be the result of a rise in sea level with respect to the land surface. This could be accomplished by a global rise in ocean levels, which occurred as glacial ice melted after the Pleistocene. Such a rise in the base level of the river would disrupt the presumed steady state and render impossible the transport of the quantity of sediment being supplied to the stream. A phase of aggradation would therefore begin and continue until the river had adjusted to its new base level. It is during this period of aggradation that the peats were most likely buried by the silty sediments observed in the test pits. As the floodplain was built up with respect to the surrounding land, less sediment would enter the river, and only fine particles would be transported. The river is apparently now in a phase where only clay-size particles are being deposited during floods.

REGIONAL IMPLICATIONS

The hypothesis outlined above is strongly supported on a regional level by geologic research that has been carried out in the coastal areas of northern Belize. Because of the extremely low elevation of the San Antonio sites, their depositional history would be expected to be closely related to that of nearby coastal areas. Investigating Holocene sediments at 128 stations of northern coastal Belize, High (1975) has identified a "regular and persistent sequence" of strata consisting of terrigenous basal clay underlying fibrous mangrove peat, which in turn is overlain by differentiated carbonate mud and sand. High points out that the deposition of these materials coincides with post-Pleistocene rises in sea level.

Characterizing the depositional environments, High states that the basal clay unit was most likely deposited on a grass-covered inland meadow when the land surface was a few feet above sea level. A minimum age of 3,000 to 4,000 years is given for the basal clays. The next unit is described as a dark, red-brown, massive, fibrous peat with an average thickness of about 0.3 m. High points out that this unit was probably accumulated when the land surface was very nearly at sea level, and the peat therefore records the latest flooding of the area due to a rise in sea level. As water levels increased to the point where peat accumulation was precluded, a period of deposition of carbonate materials began and continued until the rate of sea-level rise decreased about 2,500 years ago. High characterizes the carbonate unit as cream-colored calcareous muds or fine-grained skeletal sands, with shell debris in the upper portions and relatively homogeneous calcareous mud in the low part.

The stratigraphic units described by High near the coast are most likely counterparts of the silt, peat, and lower clay layers observed at the San Antonio sites. The strata observed in the tests pits are most likely the result of a rise in sea level that began, according to High, about 3,000 to 4,000 years ago. The observed date of the peat (3500 B.P.) corresponds well to these proposed dates.

POSSIBLE ROLE OF THE MAYA

Against the evidence presented here, the likelihood that the Maya were instrumental in the deposition of any of the materials observed in the test pits seems small indeed. They may have had an indirect role in the deposition of the more recently deposited clays by accelerating erosion through deforestation (Olson 1979).

There is evidence that the Maya were active at San Antonio during the aggradation phase of the river. Puleston (1977) found a piece of worked timber in a canal on the Hondo River which is dated at about 3100 B.P. The presence of this artifact in a canal, however, does not affect the authors' interpretation of the origin of the materials beneath the fields. A natural origin of the fields does not preclude their possible use by the Maya, and the canals may indeed be human artifacts, reflecting an attempt to drain swampy areas for agriculture. Puleston (1978, and personal communication) hypothesized that organic-matter-laden canal sediments might have been dumped on adjacent fields for the dual purpose of cleaning the waterways and supplying nutrients to crops. The low organic-matter content of the silty horizons, however, seems to indicate that these horizons were not modified in this way.

Summary and Conclusions

The origin of the strata observed beneath raised fields near San Antonio must be considered within the context of the recent geological history of the low-lying portions of northern Belize. The stratigraphic sequence of basal clays, peat, silts high in carbonates and gypsum, and clay cap are most likely the result of post-Pleistocene flooding due to a global rise in sea level. The basal clays were probably deposited in an environment similar to that of the present in which the upper clays are accumulating, i.e., relatively constant sea level and land surface well above the water level during most of the season. The peats and the silts are apparently the result of a fairly rapid rise in sea level which began about 4000 B.P. and continued until about 2500 B.P. Peat accumulation occurred during the initial stages of flooding and was followed by silt deposition as water levels increased further. The upper clays represent very recent deposition (since 2500 B.P.) that took place after the Hondo River had more or less achieved a steady state with respect to its new base level.

The Maya were apparently active in the area during the periods of silt and clay deposition, but their role in this process was probably quite small. While erosion may have been accelerated by deforestation activities, massive silt and clay accumulation on the Hondo floodplain would have occurred even without any such practices. To presume that any of the materials observed beneath the raised fields were deposited directly by the Maya is not consistent with the geological and pedological data presented here.

Puleston's model of the Maya using the fields for agriculture by dredging canals for improved drainage to provide plant nutrients would appear to deserve further consideration. However, the idea of Maya construction of the fields studied at San Antonio should be ruled out, and similar presumptions for other sites should be scrutinized carefully with geomorphologic fieldwork.

References

Allison, L. E., W. B. Bollen, and C. D. Moodie
1965 Total carbon. In *Methods of Soil Analysis* (Part 2), edited by C. A. Black. Madison, Wisconsin, American Society of Agronomy.

High, L. R., Jr.
1975 Geomorphology and sedimentology of Holocene coastal deposits, Belize. In *Belize Shelf—Carbonate Sediments, Clastic Sediments, and Ecology,* edited by K. W. Wantland and W. C. Pusey III, pp. 53–96. Tulsa, American Association of Petroleum Geologists.

Olson, G. W.
1975 *Study of Soils in the Sustaining Area Around San Antonio in Northern Belize.* Cornell Agronomy Mimeo 75–1. Cornell University.
1979 The bitter harvest of the ancient Maya. *Garden* 3(1):26–29.

Puleston, D. E.
1977 The art and archaeology of hydraulic agriculture in the Maya Lowlands. In *Social Process in Maya Prehistory: Studies in Memory of Sir Eric Thompson,* edited by Norman Hammond. New York, Academic Press.
1978 Terracing, raised fields, and tree cropping in the Maya Lowlands: A new perspective on the geography of power. In *Pre-Hispanic Maya Agriculture,* edited by Peter D. Harrison and B. L. Turner, pp. 225–245. Albuquerque, Univ. of New Mexico Press.

Siemens, A. H.
1978 Karst and the Pre-Hispanic Maya in the southern lowlands. In *Pre-Hispanic Maya Agriculture,* edited by P. Harrison and B. L. Turner, pp. 117–145. Albuquerque, Univ. of New Mexico Press.

Siemens, A. H., and D. E. Puleston
1972 Ridged fields and associated features in southern Campeche: New perspectives on the Lowland Maya. *American Antiquity.* 37(2):228–239.

Soil Conservation Service
1972 *Soil Survey Laboratory Methods and Procedures for Collecting Soil Samples.* U.S. Department of Agriculture Soil Survey Investigations Report No. 1.

Walkley, A., and I. A. Black
1934 An examination of the Degtjareff method for determining soil organic matter and a proposed modification of the chromic acid titration method. *Soil Science* 37:29–38.

Whittig, L. D.
1965 X-ray diffraction techniques for mineral identification and mineralogical composition. In *Methods of Soil Analysis,* Part 1, edited by C. A. Black. Madison, WI, American Society of Agronomy.

IV
Maya Subsistence in the Postclassic, Colonial, and Modern Eras

10

The Plant World of the Sixteenth- and Seventeenth-Century Lowland Maya

Joyce Marcus

Introduction

ARCHAEOLOGICAL research of the past decade has added greatly to our understanding of ancient Maya agricultural techniques. Such discoveries as raised fields (Siemens and Puleston 1972), diversion canals, terracing (Turner 1979), and tilled fields below ashfalls (Zier 1980; Sheets, see Chapter 2) have increased our knowledge of HOW the Maya grew their crops. However, we still have relatively little information on the full range of plant species that were used, in one way or another, by the ancient Maya.

For this reason, I have decided to concentrate my efforts on the period A.D. 1566–1696. It was during this period that European eyewitnesses gave us our first documentary evidence of how the Lowland Maya classified, named, grew, and used the rich variety of plant species known to them. Because some of the Maya plant names have remained virtually the same up to the present date, it is often possible to connect even the sixteenth-century terms to their scientific (or Latin) counterparts. This renders a whole series of modern ethnobotanical studies appropriate as an interpretive framework for the sixteenth- and seventeenth-century documents.

In still other cases, it is clear that the word used in the ancient document is a loan from Nahuatl, from Arawak or one of the other Caribbean languages, or from Spanish. Some of these plants, while important to the present-day Maya, are Postclassic or more recent introductions; in other cases, the Spanish authors simply employed a term with which they were more familiar, due to their prior contact with the Aztec or the Indians of the Antilles. For example, such widespread terms as *maíz, maguey, ají, mamey,* and *pitahaya* are Arawak words introduced into Mesoamerica by the Spaniards.

ISBN 0-12-259780-X

In this Chapter, I will attempt to do the following. First, I will present the raw data on plants used during the sixteenth and seventeenth centuries in two different areas of the Lowland Maya region: (1) the area on both sides of the upper Usumacinta drainage (the so-called Lacandón area), and (2) the northern part of Yucatán. My primary source for the Usumacinta area will be the Cholti vocabulary collected by Morán in the middle of the seventeenth century and compiled in 1695 (Morán 1695 [1935]); other sources on the Cholti include Avendaño y Loyola (1696 [1917]), Villagutierre Soto-Mayor (1701 [1933]), Means (1917), Thompson (1938), and Hellmuth (1977). Primary sources for Yucatec Maya are the Motul dictionary (dating to the sixteenth or seventeenth century [Martínez Hernández 1929]), the *Relaciones de Yucatán* from 1579–1581, Fray Diego de Landa (Tozzer 1941) and the San Francisco dictionary (Michelon 1976). An extremely valuable interpretive framework for Yucatec plant classification appears in Barrera Marín, Barrera Vásquez, and López Franco (1976).

All the plants mentioned in the documents from these two regions will be divided into four categories:

1. plants grown in the domestic field, called *col* in Yucatec and *chol* in Cholti;
2. fruit-bearing trees grown in the orchard, called *pacal* in Yucatec;
3. trees or other plants of ritual or economic importance grown in perennial fields (often communally worked in, with the fruit being divided later), called *makan kab col* in Yucatec;
4. root crops.

In the course of this section of the paper, I will note similarities and differences between the plants known to the Cholti speakers and those known to the Yucatec, and will also consider those plants regarded as "famine foods." Since some of the latter were root crops, I will briefly discuss the (largely unresolved) question of the role of root crops among the Lowland Maya.

Second, I will consider the sizes of the various kinds of Lowland Maya fields, reconstructing them from sixteenth- and seventeenth-century documents with the aid of modern ethnographic sources and relevant archaeological data. Third, I will consider some "ethnoscientific" aspects of aboriginal Maya plant terms. Fourth, I will present the native classification of the soils and habitats of the region. Fifth and last, I will consider some apparent continuities in Maya agriculture from the sixteenth to the twentieth centuries.

The Sixteenth- and Seventeenth-Century Sources

Tables 1–12 list the plants that appear in the Motul dictionary, the *Relaciones de Yucatán*, the Morán vocabulary, and other sources. One is immediately struck by the considerable variety of plants used by the Maya, a

Table 1
Sixteenth- and Seventeenth-Century Crops Grown in a Yucatec Field (col)[a]

Common name	Maya name	Scientific name	Comments and/or translations
Maize	*Ixim*	*Zea mays* L.	General term for maize grains, kernels off the cob
	Zac ixim	*Zea mays* L.	Literally, "white maize"; a big-kernel maize with a six-month growing cycle
	Peeu ixim[b]	*Zea mays* L.	Literally, "small" or "early" maize; a small, yellow-kernel maize which ripens in 40 days
	Xacin	*Zea mays* L.	Black and white kernels of maize intermixed
Beans	*Buul*	*Phaseolus* spp.	A general term employed for beans
	Buul	*Phaseolus vulgaris* L.	Small, black beans
	Ib	*Canavalia* (?)	"*Como faba, favilla*"
Squashes	*Kum, kuum*	*Cucurbita* spp.	General term for squashes
	Peeu kum	*Cucurbita moschata* (Duch.) Duch. ex Poir.	Small, early squashes
	Zaatay kum	(?)	"Squashes without seeds"
	ɔol	*Cucurbita moschata*	Green, squat squash
	Ca	*Cucurbita* sp.	White squash
Chile	*Ic*	*Capsicum* spp.	General term for chile
	Yax ic	*Capsicum annuum* L.	"*Axí*" or "*ají*," 'green chile'
	Bolol	*Capsicum annuum* L.	A large chile
	Xubala	*Capsicum* sp.	Type of chile known as a very "hot" variety
Tomato	*Ppac*	*Lycopersicon esculentum* Mill.	General term for tomato

[a]Sources: Motul dictionary (Martínez Hernández 1929); San Francisco dictionary (Michelon 1976).
[b]*peeb* or *kan kan nal mehen chac chob:* a maize that matures in 90 days (Michelon (ed.) 1976:294).

Table 2
Sixteenth-Century Crops Grown in a Yucatec Field[a]

Common name	Maya name	Scientific name
Corn	*Yxim, ixim*	*Zea mays* L.
Beans	*Bul, buul*	*Phaseolus* spp.
Squashes	*Ruum, rum*	*Cucurbita* spp.
Chile	*Yc*	*Capsicum* spp.
Tomato	(?)	*Lycopersicon* sp. (?)

[a]Source: *Relaciones de Yucatán,* Volumes I and II.

Table 3
Sixteenth- and Seventeenth-Century Fruit-bearing Trees in Yucatán (ah ichil che)[a]

Common name	Maya name	Scientific name	Comments and/or translations
Avocado	*On*	*Persea americana* Mill.	
Hogplum	*Abal*	*Spondias* spp.	"Ciruela"
	Abalac	*Spondias* (?)	*Abal silvestre,* "wild abal"
Anona	*Zaop*	*Annona purpurea* Moc. & Sessé ex Dunal (?)	*Anona morada* (?)
	Op	*Annona reticulata* L.	*Anona colorada*
	Poox	*Annona cherimola* Mill. (?)[b]	
Chicozapote	*Ya, yaa*	*Manilkara zapota* (L.) van Royen	
	Zaya	*Manilkara zapota* (L.) van Royen	
	Zac ya	(?)	Literally, "white *zapote*"
Pitahaya	*Uo*	*Lemaireocereus* spp.	
Papaya	*Put*	*Carica papaya* L. (L.) H.B.K.	
Nanche, nance	*Chi, chij*	*Byrsonima crassifolia* or *Malpighia glabra* L.	
Pinuelas	*Cham*	*Bromelia karatas* L.	
Tuna, nopal	*Pakam*	*Opuntia* spp.	
Guayaba	*Pichi*	*Psidium guajava* L.	
Physic nut[c]	*Ppih*	*Jatropha curcas* (?)	"Avellana de esta tierra; fruta purgativa," filbert, hazel nut
(?)	*Kulim*	(?)	"Ciruela pasa de esta tierra"; dried plum (?)
Achiote	*Kuxub*	*Bixa orellana* L.	Annetto seed, arnotto tree, arnatto tree
Cacao	*Chacau haa*[d]	*Theobroma cacao* L.	
Guázima	*Pixoy*	*Guazuma ulmifolia* Lam. (?)	
Cocoyol	*Tuk*	*Acrocomia mexicana* Karw.	

[a]Sources: Motul dictionary (Martínez Hernández 1929); San Francisco dictionary (Michelon 1976).
[b]The description of this fruit in the Motul dictionary—"fruta grande y espinosa, especie de anonas"—makes one think of the guanábana, *Annona muricata.*
[c]Source: (Standley 1930:329).
[d]The Lacandón term for cacao is *šau* (Tozzer 1907:21).

variety that is frequently ignored by writers who emphasize maize at the expense of other species. An exception to this pattern was Morley (1946:156), who noted the value of beans as the second most important food crop, indicating that "in ancient times beans must have contributed a large part of the protein intake of every Maya, as they still do today"; he also enumerated various varieties of squashes, pumpkins, sweet potatoes, tomatoes, *chayote, chaya, jícama, zapote colorado, 'mamey',* avocado, papaya, several species of *anona,* guava, *ciricote (kopte), nanche,* and breadnut fruit (*ox, Brosimum alicastrum*) as being very important items in the modern Lowland Maya diet. Roys (1931), Lundell (1937,

Table 4
Sixteenth-Century Fruit-bearing Trees in Yucatán[a]

Common name	Maya name	Scientific name	Comments and/or translations
Avocado	*On, hon*	*Persea americana* Mill.	
Hogplum	*Aval, abal*	*Spondias* spp.	General terms for hogplum
	Çabacabal	*Spondias purpurea* L. var.	Purple hogplum
	Nucabal	*Spondias* sp.	Greenish hogplum
	Yxhoven	*Spondias purpurea* L.	Reddish hogplum
	Yxrranabal	*Spondias lutea* L. (?)	Yellow hogplum
	Yxchiabal	*Spondias purpurea* L. (?)	Green hogplum
Anona	*Op, rop, oy*	*Annona reticulata* L.	
(Sweetsop)	*Kulumuy*[b]	*Annona squamosa* L. (?)	
	Culu	*Annona squamosa* L. (?)	
Zapote blanco	*Choch, chocho*	*Casimiroa edulis* Llave & Lex.	White *zapote*
Chicozapote	*Ya*	*Manilkara zapota* (L.) van Royen	
Pitahaya	*Huon*	*Lemaireocereus* sp.	
Papaya	*Put*	*Carica papaya* L.	
Nanche	*Chi*	*Malpighia glabra* L.	
Zapote colorado	*Haz*	*Pouteria sapota* (Jacq.) H. E. Moore & Stearn	*"Mamey"*
Zapote amarillo	*Canizte*[c]	*Lucuma salicifolia* H.B.K. (?)	
Chaya	*"Chaya"*	*Cnidoscolus aconitifolius* (Mill.) I. M. Johnst. (?)	
Ramón	*Ox*	*Brosimum alicastrum* Sw.	
Cocoyol	*Tuk*	*Acrocomia mexicana* Karw.	
Guaya	*Uayam*	*Talisia olivaeformia* H. B. K. Radlk. (?)	
Bonete	*Cunche, kunche*	*Leucopremna mexicana* (A.D.C.) Standl.	
Cuajilote	*Cat*	*Parmentiera aculeata* (H.B.K.) L. Wms.	
Roble	*Bec*	*Ehretia tinifolia* L. (?)	
Guayaba	*Piche*	*Psidium guajava* L.	

[a] Source: *Relaciones de Yucatán,* Volumes I and II.
[b] *Dzalmuy.*
[c] *Canistel* is the term employed in Cuba and Tabasco (Barrera Vásquez 1937:20).

1939), and others interested in Lowland Maya agriculture also have commented on the variety of crops and fruits—wild, tended, and cultivated.

A COMPARISON OF THE CHOLTI AND YUCATEC AREAS

There are some expected differences between the plants grown in Yucatán and in the Cholti area. For instance, in the dry scrub and thickets of northern Yucatán, *nopales* and *pitahayas* were grown and are mentioned in the Yucatec documents, while no such entries are encountered in the Cholti sources for the

Table 5
Sixteenth- and Seventeenth-Century Yucatec Plants or Trees of Ritual and Economic Importance[a]

Common name	Maya name	Scientific name	Comments and/or translations
Tobacco	*Kuz, kutz*	*Nicotiana tabacum* L.	
Cotton	*Tanam*	*Gossypium* spp.	
Copal incense	*Pom*	*Protium copal* Engl. in DC.	
Maguey	*Yax ci*	*Agave sisalana* Perr.	Literally, "blue-green maguey"; this was used for its fiber, and to produce fermented beverages
Pitarrilla	*Balche*	*Lonchocarpus longistylus* Pitt.	
Cacao	*Chacau haa*	*Theobroma cacao* L.	Chocolate

[a]Sources: Motul dictionary (Martínez Hernández 1929); San Francisco dictionary (Michelon 1976).

Table 6
Sixteenth-Century Yucatec Plants or Trees of Ritual and Economic Importance[a]

Common name	Maya name	Scientific name
Maguey	*Qui*	*Agave* spp.
Cacao		*Theobroma cacao* L.
Copal incense	*Pom*	*Protium copal* Engl. in DC.
Cotton		*Gossypium* spp.
Wax		
Honey		
Tobacco		*Nicotiana tabacum* L.

[a]Source: *Relaciones de Yucatán,* Volumes I and II.

Table 7
Sixteenth- and Seventeenth-Century Yucatec Root Crops[a]

Common name	Maya name	Scientific name	Comments and/or translations
Camote	*Iz*	*Ipomoea batatas* (L.) Lam.	"Sweet potato" vine
Yuca, cassava	*ɔin*	*Manihot esculenta* Crantz (?)	
Jícama cimarrona	*Cup*	*Calopogonium coeruleum* Benth.	"Una raíz que se come en tiempo de hambre"
Jícama	*Chicam, xicam*	*Pachyrrhizus erosus* (L.) Urb.	"Es una raíz que se cria debaxo tierra como el nabo"

[a]Sources: Motul dictionary (Martínez Hernández 1929); San Francisco dictionary (Michelon 1976).

Table 8
Sixteenth-Century Yucatec Root Crops[a]

Common name	Maya name	Scientific name
Camote	*Iz*	*Ipomoea batatas* (L.) Lam.
Caçabe, cassavi, cassava	*ɔin*	*Manihot esculenta* Crantz
Jícama, gícama, xícama	*Chicam*	*Pachyrrhizus erosus* (L.) Urb.
(?)	*Macal*[b]	*Dioscorea alata* L. (?)[c]
Gícama cimarrona	*Cup*	*Calopogonium coeruleum* Benth.
(?)	*Veez*	(?)
Contrayerba (?)	(Cabal?) *hau*	*Dorstenia contrajerva* L. (?)

[a]Source: *Relaciones de Yucatán,* Volumes I and II.

[b]Roys (1931:262) states, "This, of course, is an Old World importation, but the term *macal* designated a native plant originally." In the *Relaciones de Yucatán* (Vol. XI:263) we read of "a root which they call *macal* and which directly resembles the root of a lily. These are eaten boiled, because when they are raw they have a milk and take the skin from the mouth and burn it." Roys goes on to say that this *macal* might be *Xanthosoma violaceum* Schott.

[c]Not native to the New World (Standley 1930:229).

sixteenth- and seventeenth-century Usumacinta region. In spite of these regional differences, the emphasis in both areas on wild and tended tropical fruit trees is clear, and the words for the vegetable crops grown together in the field (*col, chol*) are very similar. Within the Yucatec area, there are many similarities between the plants listed in the Motul dictionary and those given in the various *Relaciones de Yucatán.* However, there are also significant differences in detail, completeness, content, and meaning. Additionally, Fray Diego de Landa's sixteenth-century work on northern Yucatán (Tozzer 1941) provides some important information.

Table 9
Sixteenth- and Seventeenth-Century Crops Grown in a Cholti Field (chol)[a]

Common name	Maya name	Scientific name
Maize	*Ixim*	*Zea mays* L.
Beans	*Bul*	*Phaseolus* spp.
Squashes	*Chum*	*Cucurbita* spp.
Ayote	*Chum*	*Sechium edule* (Jacq.) Sw. (?)
Pepita de ayote	*Caquil*	*Sechium edule* seed (?)
Chile	*Ich*	*Capsicum* spp.
Tomato	*Paac*	*Lycopersicon esculentum* Mill.
(?)	*Pix*	(?)

[a]Source: (Morán [mss. 1695] 1935).

Table 10
Sixteenth- and Seventeenth-Century Fruit-Bearing Trees in the Cholti area[a]

Common name	Maya name	Scientific name
Avocado	*Hun*	*Persea americana* Mill.
Anona	*Tzulmui*	*Annona squamosa* L. (?)
Coyol tree	*Yu*	*Acrocomia mexicana* Karw.
Coyol fruit	*Map*	
Palma (corozo)	*Tuch*	*Orbignya cohune* (Mart.) Dahlgr. ex Standl.
Jocote	*Lum*	*Spondias* sp. (?)
Zapote colorado	*Haaz*	*Pouteria sapota* (Jacq.) H. E. Moore & Stearn
Sonzapote	*Tzocotz*	*Licania platypus* (Hemsl.) Fritsch
Guayaba	*Pata*	*Psidium guajava* L.

[a] Source: (Morán [mss. 1695] 1935).

Table 11
Sixteenth- and Seventeenth-Century Cholti Plants or Trees of Ritual and Economic Importance[a]

Common name	Maya name	Scientific name
Cotton	*Tinam*	*Gossypium* spp.
Tobacco	*Cuctz*	*Nicotiana tabacum* L.
Cacao grande	*Uaalcab*	*Theobroma cacao* L.
Cacao	*Uchel*	*Theobroma cacao* L.
Copal incense	*Pom*	*Protium copal* Engl. in DC.
Pitchpine or *ocote*	*Tahte*	*Viguiera* sp.
Ramón	*Ahx*	*Brosimum alicastrum* Sw.
Achiote	*Quivi*	*Bixa orellana* L.

[a] Source: (Morán [mss. 1695] 1935).

Table 12
Sixteenth- and Seventeenth-Century Cholti Root Crops[a]

Common name	Maya name	Scientific name
Camote, batata	*Iz iz*[b]	*Ipomoea batatas* (L.) Lam.
Camote	*Iz*	*Ipomoea batatas* (L.) Lam.
Yuca	*Tzin*	*Manihot esculenta* Crantz (?)
Turma de tierra	*Ome*	*Ipomoea batatas* (L.) Lam. (?)

[a] Source: (Morán [mss. 1695] 1935).
[b] A comma should have appeared in Morán's dictionary separating *iz, iz;* then *camote* would refer to the first *iz* and *batata* would refer to the second *iz*.

Of maize, Landa (Tozzer 1941:195) stated, "the seeds which they have for human sustenance are of a very good maize of many varieties and colors and they gather a great deal of it and make granaries and keep it in underground places for the barren [sterile, or drought] years."[1] The *Relaciones de Yucatán* (Vol. XIII:30) emphasized *posol* 'a small ball of cooked maize', which was carried by the farmer on trips to his field and for hunting so that he could "sustain" himself; it was prepared by dissolving the ball of maize in water.

The Motul dictionary also gives some of the varieties of corn with their different growing seasons: the large, white corn that had a six-month growing season (*zac ixim*) and the small, yellow corn that could be harvested in only 40 days (*peeu ixim*) (Martínez Hernández 1929:218,766).

The ethnobotanical data on twentieth-century Yucatán include two varieties of maize, which probably correspond to *zac ixim* and *peeu ixim,* as well as varieties not mentioned in the Motul dictionary. Barrera Marín *et al.* (1976) provide the folowing data:

1. *Nalt'el, Hunalt'el, and K'ayt'el:* These are all fast-growing varieties of maize with small cobs and small kernels, having a growing cycle of seven weeks. These varieties would seem to correspond to the *peeu ixim* in the Motul dictionary.
2. *Xnuknal, xk'an-nal, and k'inal:* These varieties have large cobs and kernels, with some varieties requiring five months to complete the growing cycle. These probably correspond to the *zac ixim* entry in the Motul dictionary.

These authors also list eight other varieties of maize not mentioned in the Motul dictionary.

1. *Chakchob:* This variety of maize has reddish kernels.
2. *Chik'ints'ono'ot:* This variety has a long growing season and has blue kernels.
3. *Ek'chob:* This variety has dark red, almost black kernels.
4. *Sahum:* This variety has yellow kernels.
5. *Saktux:* This variety has white kernels that are dented, serrated, or have dentate markings.
6. *Xbelbakal:* This variety of maize has a peculiar cob; its middle section has only two pairs of kernel rows.
7. *Xchunga', xunga',* and *xt'up:* This variety takes four months to grow.
8. *Xt'up'nal:* These varieties have very small kernels and the cycles can vary from 2½, to 3, to 3½ months.

[1]Some have suggested that Landa is referring to the lateral-chambered *chultunes* encountered for the most part in the Petén. Supporting Landa's statement that maize could be stored underground are data from Alta Verapaz that indicate SMOKED maize was stored underground for an entire year (Viana *et al.* [1574] 1955:21–22; Reina and Hill 1980:77). The terms *xux cab* or *xux cab haaltun* are given in the Motul dictionary for a dry silo or cistern where maize is stored.

A number of similarities can be seen between these just mentioned varieties and the Lacandón maize varieties recorded at the turn of the century (Tozzer 1907:51)

1. *sakšim* or *šnuknal* 'a large, white-kerneled corn';
2. *tšaktšotš* or *tšakšnuknal* 'a large red variety';
3. *tšaktšikin ɔonot* 'a small red corn';
4. *qanšim* 'a yellow corn';
5. *tšikinɔonot* 'a blue corn'.

Unfortunately, the diverse terms for maize colors, sizes, and lengths of the growing seasons are not given in as great detail for the sixteenth century, although Landa and the authors of the Motul dictionary and various *relaciones* were aware of the diversity and importance of maize: corn on the cob, the cob itself, or the ear of corn (*nal*); corn off the cob (*ixim*); corn in dough and liquid form, *atole (zaa)* and *posole (koyem, k'eyem);* the beverage of maize, cacao, and water (*zaca*); and many other methods of maize preparation.

As Thompson (1938:597) has noted, Landa makes no mention of tortillas, although he does describe in detail many other methods of corn preparation. Also, Thompson noted that the Manche Chol apparently did not know how to make tortillas in the sixteenth and seventeenth centuries. Rather, the use of *posole,* tamales, and a variety of corn beverages appears to characterize the Maya of early Posthispanic times and probably applies to aboriginal times as well.

Significantly, there are notably few *comales* in the Classic Maya sites of the Petén, and even when they are found, they may indicate the practice of roasting cacao, squash seeds, and so forth. For example, the modern Maya of San Antonio, Southern Belize (the probable descendants of the Mopán Maya) roast dry cacao beans on a small pottery *comal* known as *šok* (Thompson 1930:186).

The larger *comal* (now used for making tortillas) is called *šumutš* in San Antonio today, while *šamatš* is the term employed by the modern Maya of San José on the shores of Lake Petén-Itzá (Thompson 1930:37). The Yucatec term *xamach* corresponds to the Petén-Itzá term (Martínez Hernández 1929:916; Michelon 1976:394). While it is possible that the sixteenth-century Maya had two different types of *comal* (one for tortillas and one for cacao), we cannot verify this because we only have one term for *comal.*

The term *uah,* which today is glossed 'tortilla', was originally translated by the Spaniards as *pan* or 'bread'. However, today, those compounds including *wa* primarily refer to tamales: *snawa* is *tamal, buuliwa* refers to tamales with beans in the middle, and *tutiwa* refers to tamales with squash seeds at the center (Thompson 1930:99–100). Thus, Colonial Spanish references to 'bread' may refer to tamales or dough balls rather than to tortillas.

THE FIELD (*Col*) AND THE ORCHARD (*Pacal*)

One of the fundamental contrasts recognized by the Lowland Maya for the last five centuries has been between the artificially maintained field (where maize, beans, squashes, chiles, and other plants were grown) and the forest wilderness that surrounds it. The wilderness of untended flora was *k'aaxil, 'silvestre', 'de la selva'*. In cross-cultural terms, this was a reasonable equivalent for the Zapotec suffix *quijxi,* 'wild', 'of the *monte*', which was employed in a similar context (Marcus and Flannery 1978:69).

For the tended rectangle of cultivated plants, the Lowland Maya reserved the term *col* or *chol,* a word which apparently functioned both as a noun and as a verb. For example, in the sixteenth-century Motul dictionary, *col* was defined as "to prepare a field, to clear land for planting", while *colbil* referred to the field itself (Martínez Hernández 1929:197). In the Morán dictionary, the summer cornfield was defined as *yaxchol* and the winter cornfield as *pulchol.* Sometimes the terms for forest and field could be combined, as in the Yucatec expressions *che kol, tah k'aax,* "to clear forest for the first time, burning off the vegetation [for planting]," or *u kaaxil col,* "the forested part of the *milpa* that is not planted" (Martínez Hernández 1929:500).

Desirable fruit-bearing trees were spared during this clearing process, and still other fruit trees were planted in orchards called *pacal (pakal).* These orchards seem to have been smaller than the *col* and were located near houses and residences, where the fruit trees would provide shade as well as "protected" food, especially in times of famine. Such may have been the niche of the ramón tree, *ox* in Maya, which was studied by Puleston in the 1960s (Puleston 1968a, 1968b; Folan *et al.* 1979).

In addition to the diversity of plant species we encounter in the ethnohistoric documents, it is clear that the Maya maintained several widely spaced fields and several types of orchards. In particular, the orchards suggest an agricultural strategy which, in effect, created an artificial rain forest. One of the differences between fields and orchards mentioned in the documents was the *density* of trees maintained, rather than their species. When other plants were planted in an orchard, they had to be shade-tolerant varieties.

Not only did the Maya maintain several kinds of fields, they planted two or three crops a year. For the Petén, for example, Avendaño y Loyola (1696: 37 recto) reports that the Maya planted maize, beans, chiles, and "other seeds" two or three times a year. We have already seen that the Morán dictionary has entries for both summer and winter cornfields. There is also contemporary evidence for multicropping in the Petén (Culbert, Magers, and Spencer 1978).

THE "MIX" OF CULTIVATED PLANTS

The ancient Maya *col* or *chol* did not fit our Western notions of a 'cornfield'; rather, it was a multispecies garden composed of a mixture of different crops. In this respect it more closely resembles geographer David Harris' (1972) notion of vegeculture, a form of agriculture that is more stable ecologically because its species diversity more closely approximates the complexity of natural vegetation.

Such a pattern still survives. In Yucatán, for example, one can still find the term *xaak'-wi'nal* used for a mixture of seeds of various genera (maize, beans, and a variety of squashes, in some cases) that are precombined and planted at the same time (Barrera Marín, *et al.* 1976:41). In addition to maize, a typical Yucatec field might include *xkolibu'ul* (a special variety of *Phaseolus* grown with maize) and three cucurbits (*xka', xkokok'uum,* and *xkalis'k'uum*) all growing together. Lundell (1933:68) also notes that besides corn, a variety of beans, squashes, chiles, camotes (*Ipomoea* spp.), and tomatoes were planted on fields ranging in size from 1 to 4 ha.

FAMINE FOODS OF THE LOWLAND MAYA

An important aspect of Maya ethnobotany was their knowledge of "famine foods," those items that could be used when the most common crops failed. As it happens, these included a number of wild roots, root crops, wild trees, and tree crops.

There are at least eight plants specifically referred to as "famine foods" in various documents from the sixteenth and seventeenth centuries in Yucatán. They are given in Table 13.

In the prophecies recorded in the books of Chilam Balam, particularly the Chilam Balam of Chumayel (Roys 1933), a few crops are consistently associated with drought, subsequent famine, and misery. For example, one passage in the Chilam Balam de Chumayel (Roys 1967:103–104) provides information on some of the foods listed in Table 13.

Ox	*u*	*uah*	*ox*		*yaal;*
Ramón	their	"bread"	ramón	[their]	drink
cup	*u*	*uah*	*cup*		*yaal;*
Jícama cimarrona	their	"bread"	jícama cimarrona	[their]	drink
la	*cu*	*hantic*	*la*	*cu*	*yukic*
that	which	they eat	that	which	they drink
Xbatun	*chimchimchay*	*cu*	*hantic.*		
Xbatun	chimchimchay	which	they eat.		

These things were present here where misery settled . . .

Thus, it is clear that when the regular crops failed, several plants assumed greater prominence, both in terms of nutrition as well as cosmology. In the *Relaciones de Yucatán* (Julian 1581:299) there is information about *chimchimchay* (a spiny variety of *Cnidoscolus aconitifolius*) which is said to have been boiled and eaten when the crops failed. *Ramón* was also boiled and eaten, or ground up to make "bread," while the root of the *jícama* was eaten raw (Santillana 1581:262). The *zapote blanco,* the *bonete* or 'early fig' (Palomar and Chi 1579:61), and the pods and seeds of the *guanacaste* (Sarmiento Figueroa *et al.* 1579:34) are all mentioned as foods which enabled the Maya to sustain themselves in times of hunger during the dry season.

Table 13
Sixteenth- and Seventeenth-Century "Famine Foods" in Yucatán

Maya name	Common name	Scientific name	Food part
Ix-batun, Babtun	Unidentified	Unidentified	Root
Cup, kup	*Jícama cimarrona*	*Calopogonium coeruleum* Benth.	Root
Chooch	*Zapote blanco*	*Casimiroa edulis* Llave & Lex.	Fruit
Kunche, kumche	*Bonete*	*Leucopremna mexicana* (A.D.C.) Standl.	Fruit
Pich	*Guanacaste*	*Enterolobium cyclocarpum* (Jacq.) Griseb.	Fruit
Tonton-citam	"Peccary genitals"	Unidentified	Root crop
Ox	*Ramón*	*Brosimum alicastrum* Sw.	Fruit, seeds
Chimchimchay, Chichimchay	Unidentified	*Cnidoscolus aconitifolius* (Mill.) I. M. Johnst.; also, *C. chayamansa* McVaugh	Leaves

Standley (1930:363) says that the *kunche* is a tree 12 m in height with a fruit "15 cm long or more, 5 angled, pendent, green or yellow—the fruit varies greatly in shape. It is usually eaten cooked or as a salad, and also made into *dulces.*" In the sixteenth century, *kunche* was said to be "useful to the natives, because in years of scarcity they make a food and drink of it [with] which they sustain themselves" (Palomar and Chi 1579:59).

The Motul dictionary says that the root of the *babtun* was eaten by the Indians in times of famine. Although we can not be certain what plant it is—it is described as having broad leaves and bearing certain *mazorcas,* which were eaten by pigs—we can be sure of its close association with famine.

Another famine food, the *cup* or *jícama cimarrona,* assumes great prominence in Maya cosmology. Roys (1931:226) states that the *cup* was practically a "symbol for famine" in the prophecies in the Chilam Balam books.

The *ramón* fruits ripen during the dry season from March through May, "thus affording the people food during the period when they probably needed it most, for as at the present time, the corn supply may often have been low or exhausted at that time" (Lundell 1933:72). In fact, we can suggest that these foods (root crops, fruits, and leaves) associated with famine were important precisely because they served to sustain and to supplement the diet during the dry season and during times of crop failure.

One of the famine crops of the Maya was the tuber *Pachyrrhizus erosus,* called *chicam* in Yucatán. This is clearly a loan word from Nahua, where the same tuber was called *xicamatl,* present-day *'jícama'.* Since this word appears only in the ancient Yucatec documents, and not in the Petén or Usumacinta area, it would be logical to suspect that it was introduced into Yucatán with the arrival of Nahua speakers during the Postclassic period. The implication would be that the Nahua introduced both the root crop and its name relatively late in Lowland Maya history.

I personally suspect this interpretation is correct in this case, but I would like to add a word of caution. The Maya sometimes gave perfectly good Maya names to introduced plants. A case in point would be the term *haaz,* which in 1581 was the Yucatec Maya term for *zapote colorado* (Bracamonte 1581:109). By the time the Motul dictionary was written, however, the term *haaz* had already been applied to the banana, an Old World import. Since it then became necessary to distinguish between the banana and the red *zapote,* the latter became *chacal haaz*—literally, the 'red banana'. This is perhaps the opposite of what some might have predicted—the imported plant has ended up with a good Maya name, and the indigenous plant now requires a modifier.

This term has persisted to the present day, such that the botanist Standley (1930:235) still gives *haaz* for both the *plátano* banana and the *guineo* banana (*Musa* × *paradisiaca* L.). In Yucatán today the *zapote colorado* is still called *chakalha'as,* while *ha'as* alone refers to both types of banana (Barrera Marín, Barrera Vásquez, and López Franco 1976). The only clue to the foreign nature of these species is the fact that *M.* × *paradisiaca* is sometimes modified as *sakha'as,* possibly 'false or white *ha'as*', which is perhaps a reminder that it was not an original member of the *ha'as* family.

This use of a perfectly good Maya term for a foreign plant has implications for the introduction of root crops into the Maya region as well. It appears that many of these crops were introduced either from the Old World or from South America via the Antilles. Some still have Arawak or Carib names, but even those with "Maya" names may have been redesignated in relatively recent times. The fact is that, given the present state of our knowledge, it is virtually impossible to make a convincing case that ANY of these root crops are of great antiquity in the Maya area. There are so many wild species of *Manihot* and *Xanthosoma* native to Mesoamerica that it seems almost inevitable that some were eaten as wild famine foods throughout the entire history of the area. Their cultivated forms, however, may have been introduced from the Antilles in the sixteenth century by the Spaniards, or during the Postclassic period by non-Maya speakers or traders.

For example, *Manihot esculenta* (cultivated manioc) does NOT occur in its wild form in the Maya area. Rogers (1963) feels that the genus *Manihot* had at least two geographic centers of speciation. *Manihot esculenta* and related species are found in lowland tropical portions of South America and Central America, and he suggests that the cultivars have hybridized with local native species in each of the geographical centers. Interestingly, the most widespread names of *M. esculenta (yuca, mandioca, boniata, cassava, cassavi, casabi)* are derived from Arawak or Carib languages.

Since the genus *Manihot* includes from 100 to 200 species (Rogers 1963:47), finding *Manihot* spp. in many places in the tropical lowlands of the Western Hemisphere is not at all surprising. However, we still must return to the unresolved questions: How early was *M. esculenta* raised in the Maya area? How important was *M. esculenta* in relationship to the staples of corn, beans, avocado, chiles, squashes, etc.? Where were its original centers of domestication?

The 'white yam' (*Dioscorea alata* L.), now called *macal* by the Maya, is thought to be a native of southern Asia, introduced into tropical America by early slaves (Standley 1930:229). Interestingly enough, in the Motul dictionary and other early Yucatec dictionaries, the word *macal* does not refer to a root crop at all; thus, it appears that the term was reassigned to an introduced crop. Did we not know that *Dioscorea* was imported, we might guess from the term employed that it was just as indigenous as maize.

Complicating the picture is the fact that the Maya today employ the term *xmacal* for *Xanthosoma yucatanense* Engl., the 'malanga' of Cuba. This might suggest that *macal* originally referred to the genus *Xanthosoma,* and was later extended to include the introduced *Dioscorea alata* L. However, as mentioned previously, for the early part of the sixteenth century, we have no indication that *macal* ever referred to a root crop. It may, however, have referred to some kind of edible wild root.

After a rapid survey of the foods the Maya associated with famine, one is impressed with the prominence of root crops and collected wild roots. In addition, some "tended" or "protected" fruit trees were important precisely because they bear fruit during the dry season. Thus, dry season foods such as *ramón* replaced maize in times of famine (Roys 1967:122,134) and constituted a type of 'bread', as did the *cup.* From the available ethnohistorical documents for the sixteenth and seventeenth centuries, however, it is clear that the Maya preferred maize and the other plants of the *col.* Only when maize and these other items were unavailable—during the dry season in some years, or during periods when the maize crop failed—did they rely on root crops or tree crops.

Since famines seem to be fairly common in northern Yucatán—for example, in 1648, yellow fever afflicted many Indians, and this was followed by death from famine for five consecutive years (1650–1654)—it is not surprising that root crop consumption looms large in the early Postconquest Yucatecan documents. However, our task is to reconstruct the Prehispanic diet. Although ethnohistorical sources may aid us in providing an interpretive framework, it is absolutely necessary for us to have the carbonized plant remains themselves for the time periods in question. No amount of documentary information can substitute for evidence from the Classic period or before. Wherever we have such data, it appears that maize and other seed crops in the *col* were more important than root crops in a normal year.

The Size of the Sixteenth- and Seventeenth-Century Fields

How large were the fields of cultivated plants grown by the sixteenth- and seventeenth-century Maya? At present, this question cannot be answered for the

Petén, but the available Yucatec data make it possible to produce a rough approximation of several ancient field sizes in that region.

Yucatec fields apparently were rectangular (and more often than not, square). The Maya calculated field size in terms of total circumference, rather than by area as we would today. Transects or *brechas* (Maya, *holche*) were cleared in the forest to facilitate the laying out of fields with "measuring strings." The specialists who carried out such measurements were called *ah ppiz k'aan* (Martínez Hernández 1929:796; Roys 1967:65,74).

One of the smaller units of land measurement in the sixteenth century was translated by the Spaniards as a *braza.* This was probably the distance between fingertip to fingertip of a man standing with both arms outstretched. Since 12 brazas were approximately equal to 20 m (see Figure 1), we could reconstruct the braza as roughly 1.66 m. The relevant Maya terms were *zaptah (zaaptah) 'medir a brazas'* and *hun zap (zaap)* 'una braza' (Martínez Hernández 1929:227; Michelon 1976:425,431).

The next standard unit was called *k'aan* in Yucatec Maya. It has been defined as the "medida de un cordel con que los indios miden sus milpas, llamado mecate entre españoles" (Martínez Hernández 1929:494). Thus the *k'aan,* or *mecate* in Spanish (derived from the Nahuatl word for string, *mecatl*), refers both to the lineal measurement of a field and to the instrument employed. The *k'aan* was a square some 12 brazas on a side, or 48 brazas in total circumference.

The term *k'aan* or *mecate* is still employed in parts of Yucatán[2] for a field 20 m on a side, that is, 80 m in circumference, or 400 m^2 in total area (Barrera Marín, *et al.* 1976:31). The sixteenth-century Maya of Yucatán expressed this as *hun kaan ti can çapal che,* still referring to a square 12 brazas on a side and 48 brazas in circumference (Martínez Hernández 1929:494). These same Maya also had a smaller field, *hun kaan tah ox çapal che,* which was 9 brazas on a side; such a field would equal 223.2 m^2.

As one might expect with a vigesimal system, the next unit was 20 times as large as a *k'aan.* This unit, the *hun uinic col* or *hun (n)ac col,* has been defined as the "field sown by a married man" (Martínez Hernández 1929:412; Michelon 1976:159); it was a piece of land 240 brazas on a side, or 960 brazas in circumference. In AREA, however, such a field would have a surface 400 times the size of a 12- × 12-braza field. Thus, the field sown by a married man would equal 8,000 m^2 or 0.8 ha (Figure 1).

One important reference to the size of the Maya field that has created some discussion over the years was made by Diego de Landa (1900:322), who stated:

> Suelen de costumbre sembrar para cada casado con su muger medida de CCCC piés, lo qual llaman *humvinic* medida con vara de XX pies, XX en ancho y XX en largo.

[2]For example, the Piste cemetery is decribed as exactly one *mecate* or *k'aan* in area (Steggerda 1941:15).

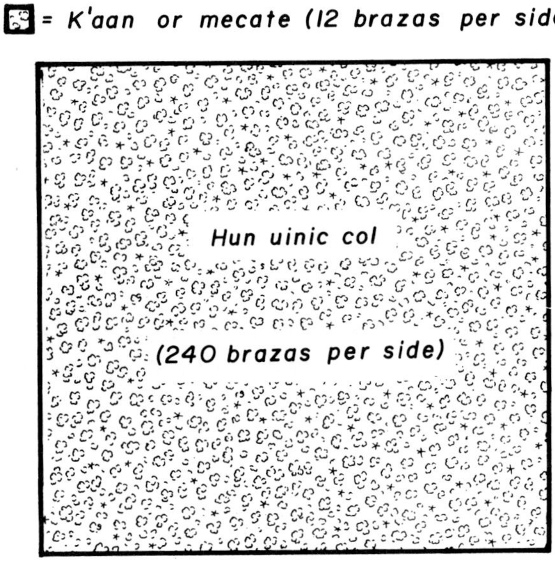

FIGURE 1. *Two units of land measurement recognized by the sixteenth-century Yucatec Maya: the* k'aan = *400* m^2 *and the* hun uinic col = *8,000* m^2.

Brinton (1882:27) had considerable difficulty in believing Landa's statement, as we can see from his comments:

> The agrarian measure *uinic* or *hun uinic* 'one man' contained 20 *kaan,* each 24 yards (*varas*) square. One *kaan* was estimated to yield two loads of corn, and hence the calculation was forty loads of the staff of life for each family. Landa's statement that a patch 20 feet square was assigned to a family is absurd on the face of it.

Still another transcription of Landa's passage was made by O. F. Cook (1919:12), who provides us with the following:

> They follow the custom of sowing for each married man and his wife an area 400 feet square, which they call *hun uinic,* measured with a stick 20 feet long, 20 sticks in breadth, and 20 in length.

Cook states that Landa was discussing a piece of land some 400 times as large as Brinton had supposed, and Cook concludes that the field was 160,000 square feet or over 49,230 m^2. Unfortunately, it now appears that both Brinton and Cook have erred, the former underestimating and the latter overestimating the size of the *hun uinic col.* Both the Motul and San Francisco dictionaries state that the *hun uinic col* is 20 *k'aanob* or 20 *mecates* in size, making it some 8,000 m^2.

There are perhaps at least two possible explanations for this confusion: (1) Landa might have intended to write the word *k'aan* instead of *hun uinic,* with each "*pie*" then being equal to about 1 m; however, even so, the area of a *k'aan* (400 m^2) would not have been large enough to support a married man and his wife, as Brinton noted. (2) Each of Landa's "*pies*" was equal to 20 m, as strange as that may seem. Given the definitions in the Motul and San Francisco dictionaries, as well as the passage from Landa, the equation of 20 m = 1 *pie* is the only one that makes sense in terms of the amount of land needed by a small family.

Archaeological evidence useful for reconstructing the size of ancient Maya fields has rarely been collected. One exception to this is the island of Cozumel, which was apparently covered with rectilinear plots of land delimited by stone walls that apparently date to the Late Postclassic period (Freidel and Leventhal 1975:61; Sabloff *et al.* 1974). Freidel (1976:220) suggests that these walls extend over an area of at least several square kilometers. Although these field walls (especially at the site of Aguada Grande) were previously noted by Sanders (1955:196), he expressed some doubt as to the antiquity of these agricultural units. However, given the recent reports of similar field walls in the eastern part of the Yucatán peninsula (e.g., Xelha, Coba, and Tancah), as well as their small size when compared to modern fields, it does seem likely that these units were utilized in Prehispanic times (Freidel 1976:222). Where the plots have been mapped, they generally range from less than 0.1 ha to just over 1.0 ha (see Figure 2). In Table 14, I have given the possible relationship of a *k'aan* and its multiples to the metric system so that Freidel's data can be considered in those terms.

A word of warning, however: we should not expect perfect correspondence between ancient and metric units, because (today, at least) the measuring string can vary slightly from town to town, and farmer to farmer. For example, Steggerda (1941:94) measured 15 of these strings belonging to men from Piste and Xocenpich, Yucatán and found that the strings had an average length of 21.5 m, while Redfield and Villa Rojas (1934:43) supply the figure of 21 m for a present-day *mecate* in Chan Kom.

The modern farmer in northern Yucatán still divides his field into *mecates,* marking each corner of each *mecate* with a pile of stones (Steggerda 1941:94). This activity may correspond to the sixteenth- and seventeenth-century terms *ppic tun,* "mojón de término y lindero de heredad" (Martínez Hernández 1929:795; Michelon 1976:313) and *multun,* "mojón de término; monte de piedras, cerro hecho a mano" (Michelon 1976:246). As for the rough field walls of loose stones, the Maya term was *cot,* 'enclosure of loose stone' (Michelon 1976:68), or *ticin cot,* 'wall or enclosure of dry-laid stone without *barro*' (Martínez Hernández 1929:201).

Another subject of great importance is the potential yield of these agricultural plots, with or without walls. Although one should ideally calculate the yield of such fields in terms of the whole complex of plants grown in the same field, the data on modern field productivity in northern Yucatán are unfortunately given in terms of maize alone. The average yield of corn per *mecate* (0.04 ha) in 1931 in Chan Kom was 0.8 of a *carga* (one carga = approximately 42 kg), or 33.6 kg. For the years 1932–1934, the average yield was 0.65 of a *carga* or 27.3 kg. (Redfield 1950:55). Higher yields are given by Kempton (cited in

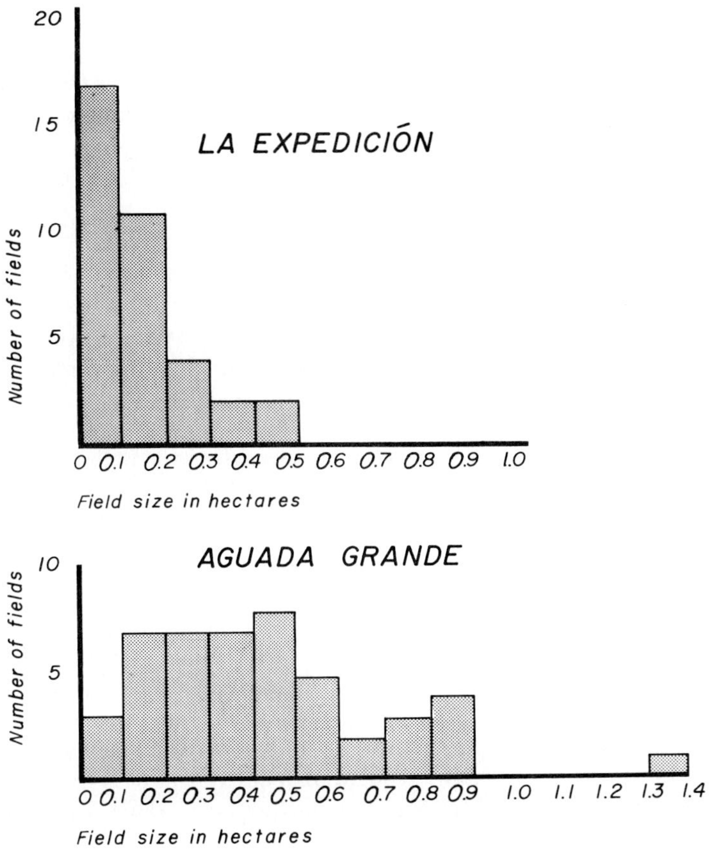

FIGURE 2. *Postclassic stone-walled field sizes for two sites on Cozumel Island (redrawn from Freidel 1976: Table 6).*

Steggerda 1941:117), who states that 1 − 1.5 cargas per *mecate* were expected for first-year crops, while half that amount was expected for second-year crops. The daily consumption of (dry) maize in Piste was given as an average of 1.43 lb (.65 kg), while 1.23 lbs (.55 kg) was the average for Chichimila, Yucatán, (Steggerda 1941:127). The Maya would therefore have required perhaps 35 *mecates* of land to feed a family of five for one year. The archaeological picture indicates that single fields this large were rare—only one mapped field at Aguada Grande, Cozumel, was this large, encompassing 1.4 ha (35 *mecates*).

Table 14
Possible Relationships of a K'aan and Its Multiples to the Metric System

K'aan:	1	2.5	10	20	30	35
Size (ha):	0.04	0.1	0.4	0.8	1.2	1.4

Thus, for the most part, the ancient fields delimited by stone walls do not correspond to the unit a family of five would need to support itself for a year. This is not too surprising, since from the ethnohistorical sources, we know that Maya families maintained more than one plot of land. For example, Landa (1900:323) states, "siembran en muchas partes por si una faltare supla la otra." There are good reasons behind this pattern of spreading one's crop through several fields: the separation of fields reduces the impact of localized pests, such as corn-borers, leaf-cutting ants, and various mites (Wiseman 1978:75), and has the function of promoting long-term agricultural stability. The plots of land planted by farmers also tend to be located in slightly different habitats (Reina 1967); thus, as Landa indicated, if one field fails, another will provide. Additionally, we must keep in mind that the Maya farmers were communal laborers, the sixteenth-century term for a field worked in common being *mul colbil* (Martínez Hernández 1929:642).

> The Indians have the excellent custom of helping one another in all their work. At sowing time those who have no one to do this work band together in groups of 20, more or less, and all together they do the share of each individual, and they do not stop until each man's piece has been done. The land today is held in common, so that he who first stakes out a claim is given possession of that piece of land (Landa 1900:323).

Just how many different fields the average Maya farmer worked is not known. A *hun uinic col* might have served as the principal field, but it was evidently supplemented by a range of smaller fields, some measuring a *k'aan* or two. We might expect in-village fields to be smaller than fields located some distance away from the settlement. The sixteenth-century term *tancabal* was given as "el corral, herreñal, o pertenencia que siembran los indios que está junto y alrededor de su casa" (Martínez Hernández 1929:838). This entry refers to pieces of land located *tan cah,* "in the middle of the town." Another term referred to the milpa which was set aside to support the village church (*tancabal col,* quiñón o milpa de la cruz del pueblo). One might surmise that these church lands were analogous to those formerly sown and maintained for the Maya *batab,* the so-called 'cacique'. Roys (1939:44–45) reports that the sixteenth-century Yucatec town was obliged to cultivate a milpa of 60 *mecates* for the *batab;* this land was called *u hanal batab,* 'the *batab's* food' (Martínez Hernández 1929:642).

Maya Sixteenth- and Seventeenth-Century Plant Categories

TREES

Brown (1979) has reconstructed six hypothetical developmental stages through which he feels the Maya ethnobotanical classification passed. Like many other Mesoamerican Indian groups, the Maya had a single word which meant "plant," "tree," or "wood." All such terms in the various Maya dialects are ultimately descended from the same proto-Maya stem (Kaufman 1969), and in the sixteenth and seventeenth century, were pronounced *che* or *te*. For example, in the seventeenth-century dictionary for the Cholti, Morán (1695 [1935]) glossed 'tree' as *te*, but added, "otros dicen *che*." To be more precise, the word was pronounced *te* in Chol, Cholti, Chontal, Huastec, and Chicomuceltec, and *che* in Yucatec, Lacandón, Mopán, and Itzá.

In this repect, the Maya resembles some ancient Otomanguean languages which also possessed a single word for "plant," "tree," and "wood," such as the sixteenth-century Zapotec *yaga* and the sixteenth-century Mixtec *yutnu* (Marcus and Flannery 1978:68).

Various trees of economic importance to the Maya had *te* or *che* suffixes, as in the following list:

1. *balamte* a species of chocolate (literally, 'jaguar tree'), *Theobroma cacao* L.
2. *balche* *Lonchocarpus longistylus* Pitt., the bark of which was mixed with honey and water to produce a fermented beverage often employed in rituals (Sarmiento Figueroa 1579:45)
3. *cibche* (literally 'wax tree'), *Myrica mexicana* Willd., which provided wax for burning after the fruits were boiled
4. *chacte* (literally 'red tree'), *Caesalpinia platyloba* S. Wats., the red wood of which was used for dye and for roof beams
5. *canizte* *Pouteria campechiana* (H.B.K.) Baehni, the sweet, yellow fruit of which was similar to the *chicozapote,* whereas in size it was similar "to the yolk of a roasted egg" (Palomar and Chi 1579:58)
6. *kikche* (literally 'rubber tree'), *Castilla elastica* Sessé
7. *kuche* (literally 'sacred tree'), *Cedrela mexicana* M. Roem., a cedar often used for carving sacred images (Marcus 1978:180)
8. *pomolche* *Jatropha gaumeri* Greenm., of which Avendaño y Loyola said, "this produced a fruit of the same form as the hazel nut of Spain, as well in the shell as in the kernel, color, smell, and taste" (Means 1917:110)
9. *tahte* the pitch pine tree (*Viguiera* sp.), used as torches for night journeys
10. *yaxche* (literally, 'first tree', 'new tree', 'blue-green tree'), *Ceiba pentandra* (L.) Gaertn., which served as a great shade tree for the ancient Maya (Palomar *et al.* 1581:85).

HERBS

The Morán dictionary supplies us with the terms *xucul,* "verdolagas" and *cacul,* "yerba en general". No specific terms for "grass" or "vine" AS LIFE FORMS are listed, although Morán gives one word which may since have been redefined in that direction. This is the term *ac,* which in 1625, referred to 'savanna', 'a plant of the savanna', or 'a type of straw used to thatch roofs'. Note that in Table 15, variants of this term are now used to mean 'vine' or 'grass' in twentieth-century Maya dialects. We may also be suspicious of the relationship between Morán's *xucul* and the twentieth-century term *su'uk,* 'grass'; this could be another term that has changed in meaning since the sixteenth century.

If we turn now to the Motul dictionary of the sixteenth-century Yucatán peninsula (Martínez Hernández 1929), we again encounter *ac,* "a plant with which they thatch houses." In the Motul dictionary, however, we find an entirely different word for 'herb in general', *xiu,* which survives in twentieth-century Yucatán as *xiw* or *xiu,* 'herbaceous plant' (see Table 15). Here is our first example of a regional difference within the Lowland Maya area which can be attributed not to linguistic drift, but to acculturation: the Nahua-speakers who entered Yucatán in the tenth or eleventh centuries A.D. from the central highlands of Mexico had evidently introduced the Nahua term *xiuitl,* 'herb' (Molina 1571:170), which went on to become an important loan word (and family name) in the northern Yucatec Maya region. Interestingly, it seems not to have penetrated the Highland Chiapas (Tzeltal, Tzotzil) Maya area, where a different term—*wamal,* also probably a loan word—is used instead (Table 15). The success of these various loan words leads one to wonder whether all ancient Maya dialects really had a category distinguishing "herbs" as a separate life form.

When "vine" became a life form is equally hazy. The Motul dictionary lists the term *kan* as both 'snake' and 'vine'—certainly a reasonable analogy—and *kan (il)* continues to be used as 'vine' in modern Yucatec. On the other hand, the Tzeltal term for 'vine' is *ʔak',* suggesting a close relationship to *ʔak* 'grass', and possibly indicating a rather recent distinction between 'vine' and 'grass'.

PLANT COLOR CATEGORIES

Below the level of the general life form, the Maya relied strongly on color as a way of classifying plants. In this respect they differed sharply from the ancient Zapotec, for whom color was much less important than taste and general physical resemblance to other plants (Marcus and Flannery 1978:73), and whose modern descendants use color only at the lowest and most specific level of their classification (Messer 1978).

The importance of color categories is already clear in the incomplete and haphazard word lists of the sixteenth and seventeenth centuries, such as the Motul dictionary (Martínez Hernández 1929) and the *Relaciones de Yucatán.* The red *Plumeria* was called *chac nicte,* the white *Plumeria* was called *zac nicte.* The yellow *Spondias* was *kan abal;* the black *Croton* was *ek balam.* In modern Yucatec, where the collection of plant names has been more intensive and systematic, two-fifths of the 350 plants reported by Barrera Marín *et al.* (1976) have names that begin with the terms red (*chak),* yellow (*k'an),* blue-green (*ya'ax*), white (*sak*), or black (*ek'*). Similarly, in modern Tzeltal, 76 of the 237 specific plant names collected by Berlin *et al.* (1974) are formed by color attributives.

Table 15

Continuity and Change in Basic Maya Plant Categories between the Sixteenth and Twentieth Centuries

Sixteenth century Yucatec[a]	Seventeenth century Cholti[b]	Twentieth century Yucatec[c]	Twentieth century Tzeltal[d]
Che 'tree, wood'	*Te, che* 'tree, wood'	*Che'* 'tree, woody plant, shrub, wood'	*Teʔ* 'tree'
Xiu 'herb'	*Cacul* 'herb'	*Xiw* 'herbaceous plant'	*Wamal* 'herb'
Ak 'vine, tongue, green and fresh'	*Ac* 'paja para cubrir casa'	*Ak'* 'vine'	*ʔAk'* 'vine'
Zuuc 'grass, herb, hay'	—	*Su'uk* 'grass'	*ʔAk* 'grass'
Xucúl 'verdolagas'	*Xucul 'verdolagas'*		

[a]Source: Motul dictionary (Martínez Hernández 1929).
[b]Source: (Morán [ms. 1695] 1935).
[c]Source: (Barrera Marín, Barrera Vásquez, and López Franco 1976).
[d]Source: (Berlin, Breedlove, and Raven 1974).

These color terms were originally more than descriptive adjectives. The colors were related to the four great world directions (or quadrants) and the center of the universe and were tied to a belief system in which four 'lightnings' or *chacob* displayed different attributes or qualities, each associated with a different color, tree, and direction (or quadrant). The *chac* of the east was associated with red and with rain, the *chac* of the north was associated with white and with cold, the *chac* of the south was associated with yellow and with wind, and the *chac* of the west was associated with black and with sickness and death. The center of the Maya cosmos was apparently blue-green. While the color-attributive system of twentieth-century Yucatán and Highland Chiapas is probably only a pale reflection of the rich Precolumbian system, it would be worthwhile to examine old dictionaries to evaluate an intriguing possibility: that the ancient Maya believed many (if not most) major classes of plants came in red, yellow, white, and black varieties.

Maya Classification of Soils and Environmental Features

From the sixteenth- and seventeenth-century sources it is also possible to obtain the native Maya terms for some soil types (*luum*) and environmental features. The Yucatecan soil types were as follows (Michelon 1976:223):

1. *ɔu luum* 'good soil'
2. *ek luum* 'good soil' (literally 'black soil')
3. *noth luum* 'bad soil'
4. *yukucnac luum* 'wet or moist soil'
5. *cheh luum* 'rocky soil'
6. *buy luum* 'sterile soil'

The Motul dictionary (Martínez Hernández 1929) provides us with additional terms for Yucatán in the sixteenth century:

1. *puz luum* 'dry soil without stones'
2. *xib luum* 'sterile or depleted soil'
3. *nothocnac luum* 'depleted, impoverished soil'
4. *tzekel luum* 'poor soil for planting; very rocky soil'

By way of comparison, Steggerda (1941:238) supplies us with the modern Maya terms employed in Yucatán:

1. *ek luum* 'black soil'; best for growing corn
2. *chich ek luum* 'black soil with stones'; also considered good for planting corn
3. *kan luum* 'good soil for corn'
4. *yax kax* soil color is between red and black; tall bush grows on it

5. *chac luum* 'red soil'; not good for milpa
6. *tzekel luum* 'shallow soil; does not support tall bush
7. *apa luum* 'pockets of good soil surrounded by rocky soil'

One of the factors affecting the Maya in their selection of a piece of land for cultivation was the presence of high bush or vegetation, because this was seen as an indicator of good soils and sufficient moisture. Low vegetation usually indicates poorer soil quality, less moisture retention, or that the land has been used to produce corn (and other crops) for many years and, therefore, the soil is nutrient-depleted.

For the northern portion of the Yucatán peninsula the soils, as noted by Landa and others, are very shallow, and are often confined to depressions or pockets in the limestone plain. There are some areas, such as the Chenes zone, where the soils are notably deeper. In general, the soils of northern Yucatán are reddish where drainage is good to excellent, and reddish-brown to gray in silted-in areas such as *aguadas.* In the more densely forested area to the south (in southern Campeche and Quintana Roo), two physiographic zones—the uplands and the lowlands—are characterized by two major soil groups (Lundell 1934:263). Upland soils are often black (corresponding to the ancient Maya *ek luum),* while the lowlands have soils that are often "compact, sticky, grayish to black in color, cracking extensively during the dry period" (Lundell 1934:264). The wooded swamp soils are sometimes designated as the "*akalche* series," using the native Maya term.

The sixteenth-century Yucatec Maya also recognized a number of environmental features of significance to their subsistence. Some of those features are given in the Motul dictionary (Martínez Hernández 1929) and in the San Francisco dictionary (Michelon 1976) as follows:

I. Coastal formations
   A. Brackish lowland areas
      ukum 'lagoon'
      chiib 'salt springs'
      u chuchil taab 'salt pan'
   B. Upland areas
      pay 'beach'
      nicab } 'headland'
      ecab }
II. Inland Formations
   A. Flooded areas or water sources
      chi haa general term for 'bank or edge of a body of water'
      akal 'swamp'
      akalche 'wooded swamp'
      acaan 'calm lake'
      acan haa 'puddle, pond'

chen 'cistern, well'
emelbil chen 'walk-in well'
actun chen 'cave with water'
ɔonot 'cenote, waterhole'
pek 'artificial reservoir or pond'
yakalil cay 'fish reservoir or pond'
yoc haa 'river'

B. Open grasslands or plain
chakan 'open grassland'
pik chakan 'savanna'

C. Denser vegetation
kaax 'forest of trees'
chen che 'woods'
tzuc 'small or low woods'
poc che 'grove of trees'

D. Cultivated areas
col 'planted field'
chol pakal 'garden'
pakal 'orchard'

Continuity and Change: The Impact of Nahua and Arawak

Most Mesoamericanists are aware of the profound changes in the native cultures of Mesoamerica brought about by the arrival of the Spaniards. A great deal less attention has been given to the modifications in Maya culture brought about by interaction with non-Maya peoples such as the Toltec, Aztec, Lenca, and various Carib, Taino, or Arawak groups before the Spanish Conquest. When archaeologists have discussed the "influences" of these various groups on the Maya, they have usually concentrated on traits or single elements (e.g., in ceramics, architecture, and art style) rather than searching for the nature of the interaction, the processes involved, and the impact such groups might have had on Maya ideology, cosmology, and plant classification.

NAHUA IMPACT

We have already mentioned the introduction of the Nahua term *xiuitl,* which was adopted by the Yucatec Maya as *xiu,* 'herb'. Another Nahua word which appears prominently in most Maya languages is *cacauatl,* 'cacao'. In the Motul dictionary, cacao is given as *chacau haa,* which seems to be a fusion of Nahuatl and Maya—the ancient Maya term may be preserved in the Cholti words *uchel,* 'cacao', or *uaalcab,* 'large cacao' (Morán 1695).

Another introduction already mentioned for Yucatec is *chicam,* from the Nahua *xicamatl.* However, Barrera Marín *et al.* (1976) believe that Nahua influence can even be seen in a series of deeper structural changes in Yucatec.

While Nahua is similar to Maya in lacking a "unique beginner," or single term for the plant kingdom, there are basic classificatory differences. For example, Maya tends to have more GENERIC terms than Nahua, modifying these according to color symbolism, world directions, and number. Nahua, on the other hand, tends to have more terms at the SPECIES level, and these more closely resemble Linnean classification. This is frequently achieved by the use of prefixes and suffixes—for example, the prefix *tlal,* 'short', or 'low to the ground', or the suffix *tic,* which means approximately the same thing. Barrera Marín *et al.* (1976:488–489) argue that the Nahua system has been added to the Maya in Yucatán, and that both coexist today in twentieth-century Yucatec. For example, the Maya term *kabal* or *kamba(l)* is now used as a prefix analogous to the Nahua *tlal,* as can be seen in the following example using the "milkweed" genus, *Asclepias:*

1. in Nahua, *cuauh ayotli,* 'tree' + 'squash' (*Jacaratia mexicana);* add *tlal* and you have: *tlalayotli (Asclepias linaria)*
2. in Maya, *k'uumche,* 'squash' + 'tree' *(Jacaratia mexicana);* add *kabal* and you have: *kabalk'uumche' (Asclepias curassavica)*

Barrera Marín *et al.* (1976:488) go on to note that *kabal* and *kamba(l)* are prefixed with greatest frequency to generic names that are NOT prefixed by color terms. In fact, unlike the color prefixes, the use of *kabal* or *kamba(l)* changes the generic meaning greatly. For example, *muk* is *Celtis,* but *kabal muk* is *Rauwolfia; chunup* is *Clusia,* while *kabal chunup* is *Portulaca; pich* is *Enterolobium,* while *kamba pich* is *Desmanthus.*

However, the prefix *kabal* is never used to modify basic cultivated crops; to indicate that the latter are 'low to the ground', one uses instead the prefix *mehen.* Examples of 'short' or 'low to the ground' staple plant foods would be *mehen nal* ('low maize'), *mehenbu'ul* ('low beans'), *mehenxtohk'u (Datura stramonium,* or 'jimson weed'), and *mehenchi'ikam* ('low jícama').

Those plants that take *mehen* rather than *kabal* or *kamba(l)* are as follows (Barrera Marín *et al.* 1976:490):

1. *bu'ul Phaseolus*
2. *ik Capsicum*
3. *is Ipomoea*
4. *kakaw, xaw Theobroma*
5. *chiikam Pachyrrhizus*
6. *kat Parmentiera*
7. *cup Calopogonium*
8. *k'uum Cucurbita*
9. *(ah)nal/(ix)si'im Zea*
10. *on Persea*
11. *pichi' Psidium*
12. *poox Annona*

13. *put* *Carica*
14. *p'ak* *Lycopersicon*
15. *siisbik* *Vanilla*
16. *ts'iim* *Manihot*
17. *k'uuts* *Nicotiana*
18. *taman* *Gossypium*
19. *chi'* *Malpighia*
20. *homa'* *Crescentia* and *Lagenaria*
21. *kopo'/hu'un* *Ficus*

ARAWAK AND ISLAND CARIB IMPACT

Another source of linguistic change in plant classification was the introduction of terms from the Arawak, the first New World Indians encountered by the Spaniards. Columbus also made contact with the Arawak in the Bahamas, in northern Cuba, and in northern Hispaniola during 1492 and 1493. On his second voyage of 1493 to 1496, Columbus explored the Greater Antilles and the Virgin Islands.

The Antilles have traditionally been viewed as an area that witnessed three broad waves of cultural "influence" (Steward 1948:23)

1. the *Ciboney,* hunters and gathers believed to have come from Florida
2. the *Arawak,* Circum-Caribbean people coming from South America
3. the *Carib,* tropical forest people from the interior of South America

At the time of the Spanish Conquest, the Ciboney inhabited parts of Cuba and Haiti, while the Arawak occupied the rest of the Greater Antilles, with the Carib populations moving in during the Postclassic period.

Most Mesoamericanists are probably unaware that many of the plant terms we think of as Mesoamerican were actually borrowed by the Spaniards as they passed through the Greater Antilles. The terms were then introduced by the Spaniards into Mexico and Central America. Some of these introduced terms are provided in Table 16.

INTRODUCED OLD WORLD PLANTS

During the 450 years of contact since the Spanish Conquest, a considerable number of Old World plants has been introduced. Although some of these nonindigenous plants have Spanish or Hispanicized names, the number of plants introduced since the sixteenth century THAT HAVE RECEIVED MAYA NAMES is impressive. For example, for the Old World castor bean (*Ricinus communis* L.), the Maya use *k'och* or *xk'och,* while for the indigenous guárumo (*Cecropia obtusa* Trécul.), they employ xk'ooch or *xk'oochle.* In order to distinguish between the castor bean and the guárumo, the Maya of today use the prefix *k'aaxil* ('wild', 'of the monte') for *Cecropia.* Also, all introduced citrus trees have received the prefix *paka'al,* 'tended', 'cultivated', 'planted'.

One aspect of this linguistic evolution is that the Maya, as well as the

Table 16
Arawak Plant Terms Introduced by the Spaniards into Mexico and Central America

Arawak term	Plant
Mahiz (Dominican Republic) *Maisi, majisi* (Cuba) *Mají* (Haiti)	Maize
Axí *Ají*	Chile pepper
Caçabí *Cacabe* (Dominican Republic) *Cassaví*	Bitter manioc
Yuca *Mandioca*	Sweet manioc
Papaya (Cuba)	Papaya
Batata, bathata (Haiti)	*Convolvulus batatas*
Maguey (Cuba)	*Maguey*
Guanábana (Dominican Republic)	*Guanábana*
Guayaba (Dominican Republic)	Guava
Anona	*Annona* spp.
Mamey	*Zapote colorado*
Chirimoya	*Chirimoya*
Tabaco	Tobacco

Spanish, classificatory system of plants has been altered to accommodate the new crops, the new terms for those plants, and the relationships that these items had in relationship to other plants. Maya, as spoken today, contains a fusion of the original Maya system and the tenth- or eleventh-century Nahua system, as well as Aztec, Arawak, and Spanish plant terms.

Summary and Conclusions

An examination of sixteenth- and seventeenth-century documents for the Lowland Maya reveals a pattern of plant use and classification which shows both (a) extraordinary continuity and (b) some aspects of significant change.

In the realm of change, we have seen that the plant vocabulary of the period reflects at least four different phases of Maya history. The first of these was an indigenous Maya phase, in which the concept of tree, plant, or wood had been encoded, and color terms were used to distinguish specific plants within generic categories. In the next phase, perhaps as early as the Toltec migrations to Yucatán in the A.D. tenth and eleventh centuries, the Nahua concept of *xihuitl*, 'herb', was introduced to Yucatec, where it became *xiu*. In addition, it seems that the Maya began to use *kabal* or *kambal* to indicate low-growing plants, perhaps as an analogy to the Nahua affixes *tlal* or *tic*. During this period, new plants such as the jícama were introduced along with their Nahua names, with the result that Yucatec (in contrast to the Cholti dialect spoken in the Usumacinta and western Petén areas) began to show a fusion of Maya and Nahua classificatory schemes.

At a still later date, new cultivated plants (some of which had their ultimate origin in South America) were introduced from the Antilles, bringing their Arawak or Carib names with them. This process was accelerated by the Spaniards, who brought still more Arawak plants and plant terms with them when they arrived in Yucatán. Indeed, it was the Spaniards who made such Arawak terms as *cacique, maíz, maguey, mamey, anona,* and *guayaba* widespread in Mesoamerica.

Finally, the Spaniards introduced Old World plants to the Maya. Some of these brought Old World names with them, but others, intriguingly enough, were given perfectly good Maya names—even when those names had to be taken away from indigenous plants already known to the Maya for centuries.

In the realm of continuity, the sixteenth- and seventeenth-century data reveal a pattern of plant use, some aspects of which can be traced backward in time to the Late Classic period and forward to the twentieth century. I refer to a pattern in which each Maya family maintained a 20 × 20 m garden (Smith and Cameron 1977) in which a mixture of 3 to 10 vegetable crops was grown, while cultivated trees were dispersed throughout the village, and still another set of tree crops was 'tended' rather than fully cultivated. Evidence for the antiquity of this system can be seen at the Late Classic site of Coba, where Folan *et al.* (1979) have recovered data that indicate a concentration of cultivated trees within the community. The outskirts of Coba revealed very few fruit trees, while most of the ceremonially and economically important trees were located near the site center and associated with vaulted high-status structures which are assumed to have once housed the nobility. Some of the trees occurring in great numbers near the site center were *ramón, copal, balche,* and *guayas.* In fact, Folan *et al.* (1979:700) found that 96% of the *balche* trees and 91% of the *copal* trees were in the site center and associated with the administrative nobility.

As for tracing this pattern forward in time, we need only turn to the work of Cyrus Lundell, one of the first scholars to emphasize the heterogeneity of crops grown in the southern lowlands as well as the importance of terracing, which supposedly involved the investment of great labor. Lundell (1933:73) notes that he and P. W. Schufeldt had reached the conclusion that many areas in the forest of southern Campeche which were delimited and divided by stone walls were actually agricultural plots, and that these tracts were reserved for intensive cultivation.

In a village covering approximately 5 ha, Lundell (1933) encountered nine families, eight of whom lived off the land. Lundell discusses the garden associated with every house, the fruit trees scattered in the villages, the fields of each family, and the perennially planted field.

1. Each family had a garden enclosure behind the house (now referred to as the kitchen garden). These gardens included:

cacao (*Theobroma cacao*)
cotton (*Gossypium*)
avocado (*Persea americana*)
chile (*Capsicum annuum*)
chicozapote (*Manilkara zapota*)
chayote (*Sechium edule*)
tomato (*Lycopersicon esculentum*)
tobacco (*Nicotiana tabacum*)
introduced plants

2. Dispersed throughout the center of the village were various fruit trees, such as:

anona (*Annona* sp.)
guayaba (*Psidium guajava* L.)
siricote (*Cordia dodecandra*)
caimito (*Chrysophyllum cainito*)

3. The fields contained a mixture of crops, such as maize, beans, squashes, chiles, and tomatoes. *Zapote* and *ramón* (*Brosimum alicastrum*) trees were spared "for the value of their fruit as well as for shade."

4. The perennial field combined tree crops and herbs that were often communally tended (Thompson 1930; Lundell 1933:68). These would include *zapote colorado, ramón, guaya, zapote, anona,* cacao, and avocado.

I conclude that of all the various forms of Maya agriculture, this type, with its great species diversity closely approximating that of nature (Harris 1972), was the most stable over long periods of time. Indeed, it has survived until the present day, while the raised fields and water diversion systems of the Classic period (Harrison and Turner 1978) have disappeared. Future investigators should make a concerted effort to find out if those more intensive and sophisticated systems were examples of "monocrop" or commercial agriculture, which is far less stable than the cultivation of the *col* or *pacal.* Should this turn out to be the case—for example, should the raised fields and other intensive systems turn out to have been reserved for commerical cropping of such items as cotton and cacao—it will certainly have implications for the Maya collapse. In this case, I have to conclude that it was only the most sophisticated and intensive type of Maya griculture that collapsed; the oldest, simplest, and most ecologically stable type is still with us.

Acknowledgments

I would like to thank several people who aided me in the preparation of this chapter: Evon Z. Vogt for obtaining various copies of manuscripts from the Tozzer Library, Harvard University; C. Earle Smith, Jr. for greatly aiding me in the identification of various plants and their botanical nomenclature; Al Siemens for suggesting I investigate the Maya classification of soils and habitats; F. E. Smiley for his preparation of Figures 1 and 2; and Denny Puleston for getting me (and other Mayanists) to take a more active interest in Maya agriculture and ecology.

References

Avendaño y Loyola, Andrés de
1696 *Relación de las dos Entradas que Hize a la Conversión de los Gentiles Itzaez y Cehaches.* Ms. copy in Tozzer Library, Harvard Univ., Cambridge.

Barrera Marín, Alfredo, Alfredo Barrera Vásquez, and Rosa María López Franco
1976 Nomenclatura Etnobotánica Maya: Una interpretación taxonómica. *Colección Científica* 36 (Ethnology). Instituto Nacional de Antropología e Historia, Mexico, Centro Regional del Sureste.
Barrera Vásquez, Alfredo
1937 Mayismos y voces Mayas en el Español de Yucatán. *Investigaciones Lingüísticas* IV(1–2):9–35.
Berlin, Brent, Dennis E. Breedlove, and Peter H. Raven
1974 *Principles of Tzeltal Plant Classification: An Introduction to the Botanical Ethnography of a Mayan-Speaking People of Highland Chiapas.* New York, Academic Press.
Bracamonte, Hernando de
1581 Relación de Tequite. In *Colección de Documentos Inéditos Relativos al Descubrimiento, Conquista y Organización de las Antiguas Posesiones Españolas de Ultramar,* Vol. XI. Relaciones de Yucatán I:103–115. Madrid, Sucesores de Rivadeneyra (1898).
Brinton, Daniel Garrison
1882 Maya chronicles. *Library of Aboriginal American Literature, No.* 1. Philadelphia.
Brown, Cecil H.
1979 Growth and development of folk botanical life forms in the Mayan lanuage family. *American Ethnologist* 6(2):366–385.
Cook, Orator F.
1919 The size of Maya farms. *Journal of the Washington Academy of Sciences* 9(1):11–14.
Culbert, T. Patrick, Pamela C. Magers, and Mara L. Spencer
1978 Regional variability in Maya Lowland agriculture. In *Pre-Hispanic Maya Agriculture,* edited by Peter D. Harrison and B. L. Turner II, pp. 157–161. Albuquerque, Univ. of New Mexico Press.
Folan, William J., Laraine A. Fletcher, and Ellen R. Kintz
1979 Fruit, fiber, bark, and resin: Social organization of a Maya urban center. *Science* 204:697–701.
Freidel, David A.
1976 Late Postclassic settlement patterns on Cozumel Island, Quintana Roo, Mexico. Unpublished Ph.D. dissertation, Department of Anthropology, Harvard Univ.
Freidel, David A., and Richard M. Leventhal
1975 The settlement survey. In *A Study of Changing Pre-Columbian Commercial Systems: The 1972–1973 Seasons at Cozumel, Mexico,* edited by Jeremy A. Sabloff and William L. Rathje. *Monographs of the Peabody Museum, Harvard University, No.* 3:60–76. Cambridge.
Harris, David R.
1972 Swidden systems and settlement. In *Man, Settlement and Urbanism,* edited by Peter J. Ucko, Ruth Tringham, and G. W. Dimbleby, pp. 245–262. London, Duckworth.
Harrison, Peter D., and B. L. Turner II (editors)
1978 *Pre-Hispanic Maya Agriculture.* Albuquerque, Univ. of New Mexico Press.
Hellmuth, Nicholas M.
1977 Cholti-Lacandón (Chiapas) and Petén-Ytzá agriculture, settlement pattern and population. In *Social Process in Maya Prehistory: Studies in Honour of Sir Eric Thompson,* edited by Norman Hammond, pp. 421–448. New York, Academic Press.
Julian, Alonso
1581 Relación de los Pueblos de Tetzal y Temax. In *Colección de Documentos Inéditos Relativos al Descubrimiento, Conquista y Organización de las Antiguas Posesiones Españolas de Ultramar,* Vol. XI. Relaciones de Yucatán I:292–307. Madrid, Sucesores de Rivadeneyra (1898).
Kaufman, Terrence
1969 Teco—A new Mayan Language. *International Journal of American Linguistics* 35:154–174.

Landa, Fray Diego de
1900 Relación de las cosas de Yucatán. In *Colección de Documentos Inéditos Relativos al Descubrimiento, Conquista y Organización de las Antiguas Posesiones Españolas de Ultramar,* Vol. XIII, pp. 265–411. Madrid, "Sucesores de Rivadeneyra".

Lundell, Cryus L.
1933 The agriculture of the Maya. *Southwest Review* 19:65–77.
1934 Preliminary sketch of the phytogeography of the Yucatán peninsula. In *Contributions to American Archaeology,* Vol. XI, No. 12. *Carnegie Institution of Washington, Publication* 436:255–321. Washington, D.C.
1937 The vegetation of the Petén. *Carnegie Institution of Washington, Publication* 478. Washington, D.C.
1939 Plants probably utilized by the Old Empire Maya of Petén and adjacent lowlands. *Papers of the Michigan Academy of Sciences, Arts, and Letters* 24:37–56. Ann Arbor.

Marcus, Joyce
1978 Archaeology and religion: A comparison of the Zapotec and Maya. *World Archaeology* 10(2):172–191.

Marcus, Joyce and Kent V. Flannery
1978 Ethnoscience of the sixteenth-century valley Zapotec. In *The Nature and Status of Ethnobotany,* edited by Richard I. Ford, *Anthropological Papers No.* 67:51–79. Museum of Anthropology, Univ. of Michigan, Ann Arbor.

Martínez Hernández, Juan (editor)
1929 *Diccionario de Motul: Maya–Español.* Atribuido a Fray Antonio de Ciudad Real y Arte de lengua Maya por Fray Juan Coronel. Mérida, Compañía Tipográfica Yucateca, S.A.

Means, Philip A.
1917 History of the Spanish conquest of Yucatán and of the Itzas. *Papers of the Peabody Museum, Harvard University,* Vol. 7. Cambridge.

Messer, Ellen
1978 Zapotec plant knowledge: Classification, uses, and communication about plants in Mitla, Oaxaca, Mexico. In *Prehistory and Human Ecology of the Valley of Oaxaca,* Volume 5, Part 2, edited by Kent V. Flannery and Richard E. Blanton. *Memoirs of the Museum of Anthropology, University of Michigan No.* 10. Ann Arbor.

Michelon, Oscar (editor)
1976 Diccionario de San Francisco. *Biblioteca Linguistica Americana* Vol. II. Graz, Austria, Akademische Druck-u. Verlagsanstalt.

Molina, Alonso de
1571 *Vocabulario en lengua Castellana y Mexicana y Mexicana y Castellana,* facsimile edition. Biblioteca Porrua 44. Mexico, D. F., Editorial Porrua (1977).

Morán, Fray Francisco
1695 Arte en lengua Cholti. (Copy in Peabody Museum Library, Harvard Univ., Cambridge). (1935).

Morley, Sylvanus G.
1946 *The Ancient Maya.* Stanford, Stanford Univ. Press.

Palomar, Martín de, and Gaspar Antonio Chi
1579 Relación de la ciudad de Mérida. In *Colección de Documentos Inéditos Relativos al Descubrimiento, Conquista y Organización de las Antiguas Posesiones Españolas de Ultramar,* Vol. XI. Relaciones de Yucatán, Vol. I:37–75. Madrid, "Sucesores de Rivadeneyra" (1898).

Palomar, Martín de, Don Juan Peche, and Juan Cumci de Landa
1581 Relación de Motul. In *Colección de Documentos Inéditos Relativos al Descubrimiento, Conquista y Organización de las Antiguas Posesiones Españolas de Ultramar,* Vol. XI. Relaciones de Yucatán I:75–88. Madrid, "Sucesores de Rivadeneyra" (1898).

Puleston, Dennis E.
1968a *Brosimum alicastrum* as a subsistence alternative for the Classic Maya of the central southern lowlands. Unpublished M.A. thesis, Department of Anthropology, Univ. of Pennsylvania.

1968b New data from Tikal on Classic Maya subsistence. Paper presented at the 33rd Annual Meeting of the Society for American Archaeology, Santa Fe.

Redfield, Robert

1950 *A Village that Chose Progress: Chan Kom Revisited.* Chicago, Univ. of Chicago Press.

Redfield, Robert, and Alfonso Villa Rojas

1934 Chan Kom: A Maya village. *Carnegie Institution of Washington, Publication* 448. Washington, D.C.

Reina, Ruben E.

1967 Milpas and milperos: Implications for prehistoric times. *American Anthropologist* 69:1–20.

Reina, Ruben E., and Robert M. Hill II

1980 Lowland Maya subsistence: Notes from ethnohistory and ethnography. *American Antiquity* 45(1):74–79.

Relaciones de Yucatán

1898–
1900 In *Colección de Documentos Inéditos Relativos al Descubrimiento, Conquista y Organización de las Antiguas Posesiones Españolas de ultramar.* 2nd series, Volumes XI (I) and XIII (II). Madrid.

Rogers, David J.

1963 Studies of *Manihot esculenta* Crantz and related species. *Bulletin of the Torrey Botanical Club* 90(1):43–54.

Roys, Ralph L.

1931 The ethno-botany of the Maya. *Middle American Research Series, Publication No.* 2. Tulane University, New Orleans.

1933 The book of Chilam Balam of Chumayel. *Carnegie Institution of Washington, Publication* 438. Washington, D.C.

1939 The titles of Ebtun. *Carnegie Institution of Washington, Publication* 505. Washington, D.C.

1967 *The Book of Chilam Balam of Chumayel.* Norman, Univ. of Oklahoma Press.

Sabloff, Jeremy A., William L. Rathje, David A. Freidel, Judith Connor, and Paula L. W. Sabloff

1974 Trade and power in Postclassic Yucatán: Initial observations. In *Mesoamerican Archaeology: New Approaches,* edited by Norman Hammond, pp. 397–416. Austin, Univ. of Texas Press.

Sanders, William T.

1955 An archaeological reconnaissance of northern Quintana Roo. *Carnegie Institution of Washington, Department of Anthropology, Current Report No.* 24:179–222. Washington, D.C.

Santillana, Pedro de y Gaspar Antonio

1581 Relación de Quinacama o Moxopipe. In *Colección de Documentos Inéditos Relativos al Descubrimiento, Conquista y Organización de las Antiguas Posesiones Españolas de Ultramar,* Vol. XI, Relaciones de Yucatán I:251–265. Madrid, "Sucesores de Rivadeneyra" (1898).

Sarmiento Figueroa, Diego

1579 Relación de los pueblos de Popola y Sinsimato y Samiol. In *Colección de Documentos Inéditos Relativos al Descubrimiento, Conquista y Organización de las Antiguas Posesiones Españolas de Ultramar,* Vol. XIII. Relaciones de Yucatán II:41–49. Madrid, "Sucesores de Rivadeneyra" (1900).

Sarmiento Figueroa, Diego *et al.*

1579 Relación de la ciudad de Valladolid. In Colección de Documentos Inéditos Relativos al Descubrimiento, Conquista y Organización de las Antiguas Posesiones Españolas de Ultramar. Vol. XIII. Relaciones de Yucatán II:3–40. Madrid, "Sucesores de Rivadeneyra" (1900).

Siemens, Alfred H., and Dennis E. Puleston

1972 Ridged fields and associated features in southern Campeche: New perspectives on the Lowland Maya. *American Antiquity* 37(2):228–239.

Smith, C. Earle, Jr., and Marguerita L. Cameron
1977 Ethnobotany in the Puuc, Yucatán. *Economic Botany* 31:93–110.
Standley, Paul C.
1930 Flora of Yucatán. *Field Museum of Natural History Publication* 279, *Botanical Series* Vol. 3. Chicago.
Steggerda, Morris
1941 Maya Indians of Yucatán. *Carnegie Institution of Washington, Publication* 531. Washington, D.C.
Steward, Julian H.
1948 The Circum-Caribbean tribes: An introduction. In *Handbook of South American Indians,* Volume 4, edited by Julian H. Steward, pp. 1–41. Smithsonian Institution, Bureau of American Ethnology, Bulletin 143, Washington, D.C., Government Printing Office.
Thompson, J. Eric S.
1930 Ethnology of the Mayas of southern and central British Honduras. *Field Museum of Natural History Publication* 274, *Anthropological Series,* Vol. 17, No. 2. Chicago.
1938 Sixteenth and seventeenth century reports on the Chol Mayas. *American Anthropologist* n.s. 40:584–604.
Tozzer, Alfred M.
1907 *A Comparative Study of the Mayas and the Lacandones.* New York, Macmillan.
Tozzer, Alfred M. (editor)
1941 Landa's relación de las cosas de Yucatán: A translation. *Papers of the Peabody Museum of American Archaeology and Ethnology, Harvard University,* Vol. XVIII. Cambridge.
Turner, B. L. II
1979 Prehispanic terracing in the central Maya Lowlands: Problems of agricultural intensification. In *Maya Archaeology and Ethnohistory,* edited by Norman Hammond and Gordon R. Willey, pp. 103–115. Austin, Univ. of Texas Press.
Viana, Francisco Prior de, Lucas Gallego, and Guillermo Cadena
1574 Relación de la provincia de la Verapaz hecha por los religiosos de Santo Domingo de Cobán, 2 de diciembre de 1574. *Anales de la Sociedad de Geografía e Historia de Guatemala* 28:18–31 (1955).
Villagutierre Soto-Mayor, Juan de
1701 Historia de la conquista de la provincia de el Itzá, reducción y progresos de la de el Lacandón y otras naciones de Indios bárbaros de la mediación de el reyno de Guatemala, a las provincias de Yucatán en la América septentrional. Primera parte. Madrid. (2nd edition: Guatemala, *Biblioteca "Goathemala" de la Sociedad de Geografía e Historia,* Vol. IX. 1933).
Wiseman, Frederick M.
1978 Agricultural and historical ecology of the Maya Lowlands. In *Pre-Hispanic Maya Agriculture,* edited by Peter D. Harrison and B. L. Turner II, pp. 63–115. Albuquerque, Univ. of New Mexico Press.
Zier, Christian J.
1980 A Classic-period Maya agricultural field in western El Salvador. *Journal of Field Archaeology* 7:65–74.

11

Agriculture and Trade in the Colonial Period Southern Maya Lowlands

Grant D. Jones

Introduction

UNTIL recently the Postclassic period was all but ignored in the archaeological study of the Southern Maya Lowlands. However, recent research in this direction is now on the increase, and early results suggest that this region was of more importance following the so-called "collapse" of Classic Maya society (Culbert 1973) than had long been assumed. It is by now apparent, in fact, that during the Postclassic, certain areas of the Southern Maya Lowlands were characterized by high population densities, stratified polities, specialized agriculture, complex systems of interregional exchange, and the construction of large-scale architecture (Bullard 1970, 1973; Chase 1979; Cowgill 1963; Johnson 1979; Pendergast 1977; Rice and Rice 1979b).

Continuing investigation of the Postclassic Southern Maya Lowlands will, of course, depend primarily upon archaeological research. However, since the Spanish conquest of this region was on the whole a far more gradual process than in areas of Yucatán to the north, the use of ethnohistorical evidence from the sixteenth and seventeenth centuries will be of major importance in the interpretation of the Postclassic period (see, for example, Jones *et al.* 1981). The Lake Petén Maya were not conquered until 1697, and other areas remained essentially independent of Spanish control for nearly two centuries. While the documentation for much of the period is only partially known (Jones 1979a), there is a substantial body of information that can increase our knowledge of native social and political organization, systems of agriculture, networks of trade

ISBN 0-12-259780-X

relations, and ideology. Analysis of this information, however, must proceed in light of increasing evidence that although there were striking continuities in certain aspects of native life, there were also strong influences throughout the region from areas that were directly influenced by strong colonial control, in particular northern Yucatán. Even the central Petén, seen by the Spanish as the last frontier of Christendom, was deeply affected by persons and events in centers of colonial control.

Given the complex nature of the continuities and changes that characterized the Postclassic period Southern Maya Lowlands, it would obviously be misleading to infer directly the form and substance of precontact native economic and sociopolitical systems from a study of the Colonial period evidence. I believe, however, that it may be possible to infer from this evidence a generalized model that may account for certain broad processes of integration that continued to characterize the Southern Maya lowlands from the time of contact until the 1697 Itzá conquest. The discussion that follows therefore suggests that continuities may be discovered in the ethnohistorical record that will deepen our knowledge of the Postclassic period, but that such continuities should for the present be sought at the level of broad hypotheses concerning economic, political, and social integration and not at the narrow level of ethnographical particulars.[1]

In the following pages, I shall first outline the specific historical processes characterizing the first two centuries of conquest as these affected the population of the Southern Maya Lowlands. It appears that the net effect of these events was twofold. On the one hand, certain precontact trade relations, in particular those comprising valued agricultural products, were greatly weakened as a result of Spanish colonial policy. On the other hand, newly established trade relations revived and maintained long-standing relations between the "frontier zone" Southern Maya Lowlands and northern Yucatán. These relations were stimulated in part by substantial population movements from centers of colonial control to the "frontier zone." We discover that such economic relations among groups in the frontier zone provided the material basis for political unifications that in turn prevented any long-term success by the Spanish to conquer and administer the region as a whole. These systems of exchange, while serving as the very foundation of frontier-zone political relations, operated quite independently of Spanish control. Their relative autonomy from forces of external expansionary control seems to suggest that it would be incorrect to assume that long-distance trade of elite agricultural products must always be associated with the expansion of imperial power and the growth of large-scale stratified polities.

[1]Nicholas Hellmuth of the Foundation for Latin American Research generously provided me with copies of documents from the Archivo General de Indias, Seville. Robert R. Kautz and Anthony P. Andrews made valuable suggestions for the clarification of this material.

Space limitations prevent a review of the potential uses of the known ethnohistorical data for the ethnographical reconstruction of the Colonial-period central Maya Lowlands. Hellmuth (1971, 1977) reviewed this problem, but reached much more optimistic conclusions concerning the adequacy of the known record than did the present author in a discussion of the subject (Jones 1979a).

This historical review attempts to demonstrate that throughout the Colonial period, agricultural production remained far more than a subsistence enterprise. The evidence suggests that apparent demand for certain highly valued agricultural products, in particular cacao, continued to stimulate native entrepreneurial activity and the elaboration of native-controlled systems of interregional exchange. This observation is not intended to deny completely the long implicit assumption that the Southern Maya Lowlands remained unconquered because of the sheer ideological intransigence of the inhabitants. However, it is important to note that this ideological resistance, which remained a constant source of Spanish irritation, was but one aspect of a remarkable system of interregionally articulated Maya activity. This sytem was characterized by the Maya-controlled network of long-distance exchange, by the continuous movement of anti-Spanish refugees from northern Yucatán into the Southern Lowlands, and by the formation of Maya political alliances that reinforced the Maya ability to maintain systemic independence from Spanish meddling and colonial control. Ritual activity, as we shall see, remained nonetheless an important element in the ideological expressions of this independence.

Following this historical discussion, I shall return to a more specific consideration of patterns of agricultural production. Finally, I shall attempt to relate the Colonial period model developed here to certain theoretical questions of importance to the broader study of the Postclassic period Southern Maya Lowlands.

The Southern Maya Lowlands in Colonial Times

Several years ago, J. Eric S. Thompson (1977) proposed the existence in colonial and recent times of a "Chan Maya" region roughly corresponding geographically to most of present-day Belize and the district of Petén, Guatemala (see Figure 1). This first major statement on Colonial period regionality in the Southern Maya Lowlands suggested that the Yucatec-speaking "Petén Maya, the Mopan Maya, the Cehach, the Chinamita, and the Yucatec-speaking Lacandon should be constituted a subgroup, related rather closely to the Yucatec Maya but attached with considerably looser bonds to the Putun and Chol-speaking groups to their west, south, and southeast" (1977:3). Further, Thompson took the controversial position that the ancestors of the so-called Chan Maya might well have occupied the same region during the Classic period (1977:39).

This regional delineation will serve to identify what I regard as the Southern Maya Lowlands during the Colonial period. However, it is important to note that Thompson's identification of the Chan Maya was ultimately based upon ahistorical factors of cultural distribution, whereas the region as he defined it was actually the result of significant historical processes beginning some time before Spanish contact and continuing through the Colonial period. The following discussion is based on evidence that these processes included the appearance of

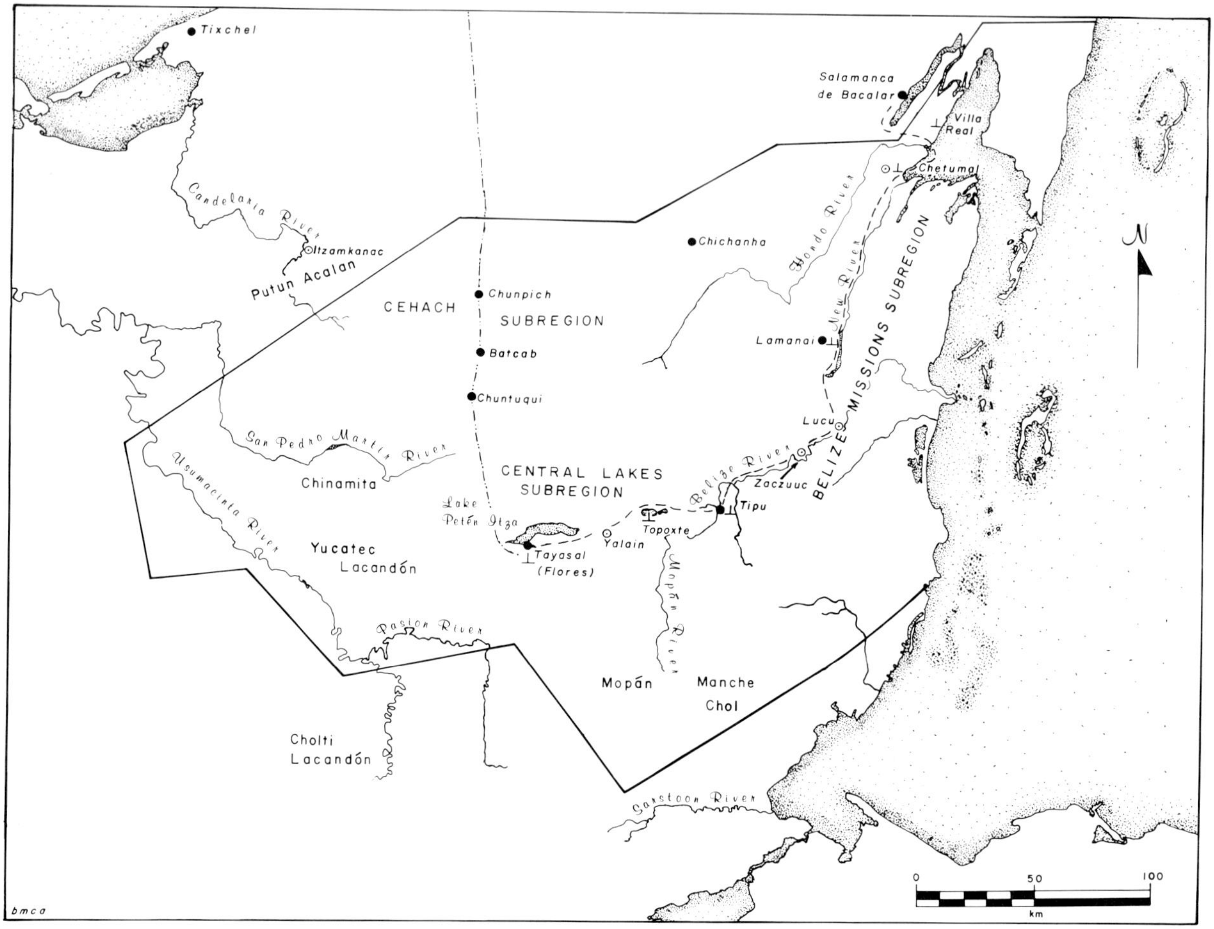

FIGURE 1. *The Southern Maya Lowlands during the sixteenth and seventeenth centuries. The Chan Maya region (Thompson 1977) is indicated by the boundary line. ⊥, Archaeological sites; ●, settlements; ⊙, approximate location of settlements; ———, approximate boundary of the area; — — —, approximate Maya—Spanish route from Bacalar; —· ·—, approximate route of Camino Real.*

an unknown number of migrants from northern Yucatán into the central Petén area at least as early as the mid-fifteenth century, the establishment of these migrants as elites in a new or revolutionary political order around Lake Petén and possibly Lake Yaxhá, the depopulation of the entire region after Spanish contact due to disease and warfare, the migration of many more thousands of Maya from northern Yucatán to the region during the sixteenth and seventeenth centuries, the often temporary establishment of Spanish missions along the fringes of the region and deep into central Belize, and the reestablishment of Maya control over the Belize missions in the early seventeenth century.

Throughout the Colonial period, the northern frontier of the Chan region was an open one, far more significant in terms of exchanges of people, ideas, and goods than the frontiers with Chontal/Chol-speaking neighbors to the south and west. This openness, coupled with the fact that the Chan region remained a poorly known frontier zone in the Spanish system for many years, was a major stimulus for agricultural diversity, interregional trade, and political interaction until the conquest of the Lake Petén Maya in 1697. In the following discussion, I outline some of the evidence that appears to support this assertion, sketching the principal roles played by each of several major subregions in this large sphere of interaction.

In the interest of historical clarity, a group outside the Chan region must be introduced; this group, the Putun Acalán Maya, controlled much of the trade in elite agricultural goods up to the time of Spanish contact. With the decline of this trade during the sixteenth century, the Itzá of Lake Petén and their neighbors came into increasing colonial prominence. I refer to these groups here collectively as the central lakes subregion. The Belize missions subregion, extending from around Bacalar on the north to Tipu in western Belize on the south, gradually strengthened the anti-Spanish posture of the central lakes subregion through the former area's economic role as intermediary between the Petén and northern Yucatán. Finally, we see that the Cehach subregion, located northwest and north of Lake Petén, although it also played the role of economic intermediary between the Petén and northern Yucatán, ultimately failed to function as a buffer for the central lakes subregion due in large measure to its own economic weakness. Cacao, in particular, a critical element in the economy of the Belize Missions subregion, was largely absent, as were other elite agricultural products, in the Cehach subregion.

THE PUTUN ACALÁN

Among the best known of Lowland Maya groups, the so-called Putun Acalán had long been important in the coastal movement of goods between northern Yucatán and the Tabasco Chontal cacao producers to the west. These great traders, whose homeland settlements were located around the town of Itzamkanac in the vicinity of the Candelaria River (see Figure 1), also exchanged goods with their immediate southern neighbors, the Cehach, and the groups of the central lakes subregion. These trading activities extended as far south as the eastern cacao-producing areas of Guatemala and as far east as the important cacao region of Chetumal (Scholes and Roys 1948:82, 86). Thompson, in an influential article, attempted to relate the Putun Acalán to evidence for politically expansionary trading peoples active throughout the Lowlands from Late Classic through Postclassic times (Thompson 1970:3–47).

The Putun Acalán homeland was itself productive, yielding for Spanish tribute demands large amounts of maize, beans, squash seeds, chile, cotton, calabashes, honey, copal, canoes, and paddles (Scholes and Roys 1948). These items were apparently an important aspect of their total trading activities. Acalán cacao production was apparently limited to local consumption, although along with other luxury goods, including slaves at the time of contact, it appears that they controlled the cacao trade for the entire Yucatán Peninsula.

Beginning in 1571, however, most of the Acalán population was relocated by Spanish colonial authorities to the coastal area around Tixchel, south of Campeche. During the years that followed, the extent of Putun Acalán influence in the long-distance trade of elite agricultural products to Yucatán from points south declined dramatically. By the end of the sixteenth century, this influence was limited to the movement of nonlocal goods between northern Yucatán, Chiapas, and the central lakes subregion. Only a few relatively wealthy Acalán merchant–traders survived into the early seventeenth century (Scholes and Roys 1948:246–247). The effect of the economic decline of the Putun Acalán was to stimulate, beginning in the late sixteenth century, the development of entrepreneurial agricultural and trading activities in the Belize missions subregion. I will return to these developments later in this discussion.

There should also be mention of the so-called "eastern Acalán" southwest of Lake Petén and south of the Usumacinta and lower Pasión Rivers (Thompson 1970:27–38). These "Cholti-Lacandón" were seen by Thompson as mixed descendants of the Candelaria River Putun Acalán and local Chol-speaking Maya (1970:37). Although we may doubt that this "mixture" was the result of Late Classic period Putun invasions, as Thompson maintained, it is probable that the eastern Acalán were not closely related in a sociopolitical or economic sense to other groups of importance in the Chan Maya region. It is important to note this in light of recent comparisons by Nicholas Hellmuth of the late seventeenth century eastern Acalán at their principal town of Nuestra Señora de los Dolores (or Sac Balam, its proper Cholti name) with the inhabitants around Lake Petén (Hellmuth 1971, 1977). While the Sac Balam Cholti are of major ethnohistorical interest (see discussion by Marcus in Chapter 10), I have omitted them from this discussion due to their apparent relative isolation from the historical events that gave form and substance to the interrelated subregions of the Chan Maya region.

THE CENTRAL LAKES SUBREGION

There is little doubt that at the time of Spanish contact the politically dominant peoples of the Southern Maya Lowlands were those of the central lakes subregion. Principal among these were the so-called Itzá, whose capital town of Tayasal was probably located on the present island of Flores in Lake Petén-Itzá (Jones *et al.* 1981). The Itzá claimed to be the descendants of an important Yucatecan people who abandoned their homes in northern Yucatán, perhaps during the fifteenth century around the time of the collapse of Mayapán (López de Cogolludo 1688:Bk. 9, Ch. 14). During Colonial times, they maintained shifting political alliances with groups to their south and to their immediate west and north.

Descriptions of Hernán Cortés's great march through Itzá territory in 1525 indicate that at that time the Itzá rulers maintained strong trade relations all the way from Acalán to the north to at least as far south as the Sarstoon River (Cortés 1976:243–245; Jones 1979c). Much of the trade to the south seems to have been in cacao, a product highly valued by the Itzá nobility throughout the Colonial period but one that apparently did not grow well in the central Petén region. It appears that their southern allies provided the Itzá with a supply of cacao that freed them from dependence on the Putun Acalán traders. However, it is not clear whether or not the Itzá in turn participated in wider cacao trade with northern Yucatán.

It is possible that "Itzá" peoples had controlled the town of Topoxte on Lake Yaxhá as late as 1525, and it may be that we are beginning to discern a widespread late Postclassic occupation throughout central Petén and central and northern Belize that in some way is linked to Itzá expansion. It is possible that at the time of contact the territory north of Lake Petén was open to the extent that the movement of people and goods between Lake Petén and northern Yucatán was regular, perhaps even intense. This movement continued during Colonial times (Farriss 1978), and by the late seventeenth century, notwithstanding early losses from European-introduced diseases, the flight of Maya from northern Yucatán may well have augmented the Contact period population of central Petén significantly.[2]

The Itzá and their allies resisted Spanish conquest until their final conquest in 1697. During the intervening period, the Spanish gradually attempted to weaken Itzá influence throughout the region. From the northwest, the mid-sixteenth-century removal of the Putun Acalán traders from their inland location around Itzamkanac to the coastal town of Tixchel was followed by intensive missionary activities in the Cehach area, to the immediate north of Itzá territory (Scholes and Roys 1948). From the south, the reduction of Verapaz was followed in the 1670s by missionization activities in the Manche Chol and Mopán regions (Bunting 1932; Thompson 1972). Finally, from the northeast, the pacification and missionization of Belize by the late sixteenth century was followed by intense efforts to seek the conversion of the Itzá and their submission to Spanish colonial rule. By the late seventeenth century, these efforts had led, however, to only a partial encirclement of the central Petén lakes region, for after 1636, the Belize missions region remained relatively independent of Spanish control. The conquest of the Itzá in 1697 was the final step in the gradual destruction of much of the Itzás' political and economic control over their formerly vast sphere of influence. However, it was the Belize missions subregion, to which we now turn, that may have borne the major responsibility for having drawn out the long process of Itzá conquest until the end of the seventeenth century.

[2]Avendaño y Loyola's descriptions of the Lake Petén Maya in 1696 suggest that by that date, population densities in the several island settlements had reached levels of overcrowding. While his estimate of a population of 24,000 for these settlements may have been an exaggeration (1696:42v.), a figure even half this large would suggest a remarkably high total when combined with the numerous recorded mainland communities (see Jones 1979c:88).

THE BELIZE MISSIONS SUBREGION

This area is defined by a string of secular Spanish missions established during the late sixteenth century from Bacalar, along the coast of Chetumal Bay, up the Hondo and New Rivers, and overland to the south along the Belize River (Jones 1979b). The last of these missions was located at the town of Tipu, believed to be located at the site of Negroman on the Macal or eastern branch of the Belize River (Scholes and Thompson 1977; Jones 1979b). Most of this area falls roughly into Roys' province of Chetumal, and it includes Thompson's "Maya of Tipu" (Roys 1957:159–165; Thompson 1977:8–10).

The roots of the Belize missions subregion may be traced to the brutal conquest of the Chetumal–Bacalar region in 1544, following Alonso D'Avila's unsuccessful attempt in 1531 to reduce the people of the Chetumal region and the neighboring Uaymil province (Chamberlain 1948:99–127, 232–236). At the time of contact, Chetumal is believed to have been an important agricultural and trading center, partially controlled by a Putun Acalán elite (Scholes and Roys 1948:385, 321, 83). Conquest, however, left Chetumal abandoned and towns and crops destroyed. Famine and disease, coupled with subsequent flight of many of the survivors to more remote regions, including the central lakes subregion of Petén, left the Bacalar–Chetumal area "to a large degree depopulated" (Chamberlain 1948:236). Salamanca de Bacalar was founded in 1544, but the town's presence did not inhibit the growing flight of fugitives from Bacalar and northern Yucatán through the forests to the "Itzá gentiles" (López de Cogolludo 1688:Bk. 4, Ch. 16). In late 1546, the entire region, from eastern Yucatán (Sotuta–Cupul) in the north to the Bacalar region in the south, broke out in rebellion against Spanish rule. This event, certainly sparked by the 1544 conquest of Chetumal–Bacalar, effectively delayed the missionization of the Belize region for a number of years.

By 1582, however, secular missionaries had established 22 *visita* stations administered by the *cura* of Bacalar. At least 9 of these were located south of the mouth of the Río Hondo, in the present territory of Belize. These missions were small and remote, weak centers of Spanish influence in a vast sea of rebellious local and refugee Yucatec Mayas. However, even though their location encouraged flight to pagan regions in order to escape tribute and *doctrina,* Bishop Gregorio de Montalvo rejected the usual solution of forced reduction of the scattered population in a single central town. To do so, he significantly observed, would have forced the population to abandon their cacao orchards (Scholes *et al.* 1936–1938, II:81, 117).

The establishment of the missions in Belize may have been pursued for two related ends. First, the region lay adjacent to the hostile Itzas, and its river system provided a major point of entry for contact with the central lakes subregion. Second, since the region produced cacao of especially fine quality, its economic potential may have stimulated the establishment of secular controls for the collection of tribute.

From the first detailed account of the Belize missions subregion, including Tipu, in 1618, it is apparent that the bulk of the inhabitants were Yucatec refugees from points north all the way to Cozumel and the Campeche–Mérida area (López de Cogolludo 1688:Bk. 9, Ch. 7). The Franciscans Bartolomé de Fuensalida and Juan de Orbita journeyed to Tipu with the intention of evangelizing the Itzás on Lake Petén. Their descriptions indicate that Mayas from northern Yucatán controlled Tipu both politically and economically. The Spanish alliance with these entrepreneurial leaders was short-lived. Later, Fuensalida and Orbita were forced to depart from Tayasal without having dented the strength of Itzá paganism, and signs of underground cults at Tipu were soon uncovered and the supposed perpetrators strongly punished (López de Cogolludo 1688:Bk. 9, Ch. 12). These and other events appear to have led to the rebellion of the entire Belize missions region as well as areas north of Bacalar in about 1636. Towns were deserted as the population moved south toward the "forests of Tipu . . . which are the closest to the Itzá gentiles" (López de Cogolludo 1688:Bk. 11, Ch. 12).

The effect of this uprising was to seal off the Belize missions from all Spanish control throughout most of the remaining years of the seventeenth century (López de Cogolludo 1688:Bk. 11, Chs. 13–14; Scholes and Thompson 1977:52–64). Not until 1695 was direct Spanish contact at Tipu reestablished. The long intervening period of anticolonial hostility appears to have been characterized by a political alliance of the Tipu region with the Itzá leadership of Tayasal in what amounted to a resurgence of Itzá religious and political influence (Jones 1979b). There is thus little doubt that the Belize missions subregion played a major role in the survival of independent Maya polities in the Southern Maya Lowlands until the end of the seventeenth century.

Central to this long-term role of the Belize missions subregion was the late sixteenth-century resurgence of cacao production in Belize at a time when Putun Acalán trading activities were in a state of decline. Cacao, which had been a major crop at Putun-controlled Chetumal, continued to be produced in the late sixteenth century around the south end of Lake Bacalar, possibly along Chac Creek, which flows from the lake to the Río Hondo. By that time, however, cacao was purchased by merchants from Mani in northern Yucatán, who carried it overland for later resale (Roys 1943:52, 1957:164). This seems to indicate that Yucatán merchants, perhaps themselves of Putun affiliation, had already begun to take up the slack provided by the demise of the Acalán trading system.

This possibility becomes especially clear when it is discovered that during the late sixteenth and seventeenth centuries, cacao was being produced on a significant scale in the Belize settlements. As early as 1618, Fuensalida and Orbita found at Lucu on the Belize River:

> much *achiote* [anatto], which is the best that is known in all New Spain: very good fat cacao that produces a deep color and by itself is of good flavor—[and] vanillas that they call *cizbiques,* [which are] very good and fragrant for chocolate [beverage] (López de Cogolludo 1688:Bk. 9, Ch. 6).

Once settled in Tipu, the priests were treated to "much kindness and charity," being provided with, "for their sustenance, even more than necessary, for as they raised much cacao, they were rich and wealthy" (López de Cogolludo 1688:Bk. 9, Ch. 7). At that town, they learned that the *maestro de capilla,* who had moved to Tipu from Hekelchacán, a trading town north of Campeche (Scholes and Roys 1948:245), was a hard working and wealthy man, having planted, "by his own hand," an orchard of 8,000 cacao trees (López de Cogolludo 1688:Bk. 9, Ch. 7). In 1641, when Fuensalida and his party attempted to recontact the then rebellious leaders of Tipu, they found a cacao orchard at Chantome on the Belize River. Further upstream at Zaczuc (Zaczuuz), they camped in another cacao orchard belonging to the cacique of that settlement. There they were visited by emissaries from Tipu who brought them a welcoming gift of cacao, vanillas, and some prepared chocolate; these were noted as gifts appropriate for a visitor "whom they know should be respected" (López de Cogolludo 1688:Bk. 11, Ch. 3).

While the Itzá also drank chocolate and presented it to honored guests on a routine basis (López de Cogolludo 1688:Bk. 9, Ch. 8; Avendaño y Loyola 1696:28v), various lines of evidence suggest that they were not themselves large producers of cacao (Avendaño y Loyola 1696:37r). With their early sixteenth-century dependence on cacao orchards far to the south disrupted by Spanish activities in the Verapaz and Mopán areas, it is highly probable that the Itzá and their neighbors next turned to the Belize missions subregion producers for a significant portion of their cacao supply (see Villagutierre Soto-Mayor 1701:Bk. 2, Ch. 3).

In addition, the Itzá traded woven clothing made from their own cotton and dyes with the inhabitants of the Tipu area, from whom it was reported that they received axes and machetes (Avendaño y Loyola 1696:37r). That manufactured iron tools were in considerable demand in the central lakes subregion is indicated by reports that on the eve of the 1697 conquest, axes, machetes, and knives (as well as salt and various trinkets) were presented by the Spanish as gifts to the Itzá. In addition, Itzás hired as road builders were also to be paid in machetes and axes (Ursua y Arizmendi 1697). Such regular Spanish contact was of a very late date, however, and it is likely that the Tipu planter–traders, whose contacts with northern Yucatecan sources were well established, were major suppliers of manufactured tools to the Itzá and their neighbors for much of the colonial period. It should be recalled in this context that the Maya god Ek Chaua was the patron of merchants and the god of cacao (Thompson 1970:306–307); to these beneficiaries Scholes and Roys also added cacao planters (1948:57). Ek Chaua's responsibilities in Belize must have been especially heavy.

It is, nevertheless, doubtful that these economic relations alone would have maintained a balanced political alliance between these two subregions, for the Tipu area clearly had the upper hand in terms of the value of its various economic activities. The critical long-term factor in the maintenance of this balance was probably the potential military protection offered by the Itzá to the Tipu planter–merchants against continuing threats of Spanish intrusion. The presence of armed Itzá in Tipu territory in 1641, (López de Cogolludo 1688:Bk. 11, Chs. 13–14) associated with strong Itzá religious influence and intermarriage between Tipu and Itzá elites throughout the seventeenth century (Jones 1979b) strongly suggests that these economic ties were balanced by such political contingencies.

THE CEHACH SUBREGION

Northwest of Lake Petén, extending into southeast Campeche, was the so-called Cehach region, sometimes known as Mazatlán after the large town of that name (Scholes and Roys 1948:128). Cehach may not have comprised a political entity but was more likely the general designation for a buffer zone between Acalán and the colonial Yucatec to their north on the one hand and the Petén lakes region on the other. In a sense, then, the Cehach region served in colonial times much the same role that was served by the Belize missions subregion: that is, the role of a strategic intermediary in the long struggle for the maintenance of Itzá independence in the face of colonial expansion.

When Cortés passed through Acalán on his way to Cehach territory he met two Acalán merchants returning from Cehach, where they had been trading salt for clothing (Cortés 1976:238). During the second half of the sixteenth century, relocated Acalán merchants from Tixchel on the southern Campeche coast were engaged in trade with northern Yucatán, bringing from there salt, cloth, knives, machetes, and axes, which they traded with apostate fugitives in the Cehach area, who supplied them with beeswax, honey, copal, and other forest products (Scholes and Roys 1948:245). However, with the collapse of the Putun Chontal influence along the coast during the seventeenth century, due to population loss and a growing dominance of Yucatec Maya, the character of this trade changed.

By the early seventeenth century, the inhabitants of the Cehach area appear to have been trading directly between northern Yucatán and the central lakes subregion in the absence of the Acalán coastal trading system. By the end of the seventeenth century, they, like the Belize towns, traded manufactured tools for Itzá clothing. However, in contrast to the Tipu area, the Cehach failed to play a critical political role in Itzá affairs. This, I suggest, was due to the absence of critical agricultural products in this region. The Cehach area was unsuitable as an alternative source of cacao following the decline of Putun Acalán trade, whereas Belize provided ideal growing conditions for the crop. Cacao production, coupled with its role as trader of Yucatecan tools for Itzá cloth, provided the Belize missions subregion with the economic basis for considerable political independence and strength, whereas the Cehach region languished as a zone of hunted, missionized subsistence producers.

SUMMARY

During the Colonial period, both the Putun Acalán and the Itzá lost their formal control over the trade of cacao and other elite goods due to Spanish conquest activities. It is suggested that the demand for such items in northern Yucatán continued through the eighteenth century, and that Yucatán planter–entrepreneurs established agricultural operations in the Belize missions subregion as a response to this continuing demand. The Itzá and their neighbors continued to produce cloth goods for export to northern Yucatán, where it may be assumed that such items were in demand for tribute payments and for use by a dwindling native elite. These goods reached their northern destinations through middlemen in the Cehach and Belize missions regions, who in turn supplied iron tools for agricultural purposes to central Petén. In this exchange network, the Belize entrepreneurs had the upper hand, for only they were able to export cacao and other valuable crops in return for large-scale importation of iron tools.

The great revolt of 1636 in the Belize missions region was almost certainly carried out in order to maintain economic as well as sociopolitical independence from Spanish control. This independence was maintained through increasingly strong political ties between communities around Tipu and the Itzá. This Tipu–Tayasal alliance, founded upon economic independence and a dedication to anti-Spanish resistance, withstood Spanish conquest efforts until the end of the seventeenth century. Missions, the usual colonial manifestation of Spanish frontier activity, were disallowed, and an anti-Christian religious cult spread from the central lakes region throughout the cacao-producing settlements of Belize during the seventeenth century. The final conquest of the Itzá, completed in 1697, was pursued, not through the hostile territory of Tipu, but rather through the thoroughly weakened, Christianized Cehach region.

Agriculture and trade, however, were only part of this process of interregional articulation. Had it not been for the movement of northern Yucatecans into the southern Maya Lowlands throughout colonial times, continuing Precontact patterns of population movement, the alliances that articulated this region both internally as well as with northern Yucatán would have been far weaker due to the absence of open systems of information exchange and personal interaction. One is struck by the rapidity with which information was communicated and the degree to which knowledge was shared throughout what one might call, following Freidel (1979), a Lowland Maya interaction sphere. The relatively open large-scale movement of people, I suggest, was a key factor in the coherence of these systems of interaction.

Patterns of Agricultural Production

While the aim of this chapter is to explore the broader ramifications of agricultural production, it would be misleading to leave the reader with the impression that production of crops for export was practiced in the absence of production for subsistence and local use. In this section, I shall therefore present a very brief sketch of the known forms of agricultural production in the Colonial period southern Maya Lowlands. A more detailed discussion of specific crops, as well as the utilization of natural flora and fauna, may be found in a useful article by Hellmuth (1977).

There appear to have been two principal forms of agriculture practiced in the Southern Maya Lowlands during colonial times. Swidden cultivation was virtually ubiquitous throughout the region. Arboriculture in the form of cacao plantings and mixed orchards was also widely distributed, possibly varying more widely from region to region than did swidden plots in terms of the number and variety of cultivated plants. In addition, there is less firm evidence for intensive cultivation along low-lying lakeshores.

SWIDDEN CULTIVATION

The terms *milpa* and *milpería* are frequently found in Spanish descriptions (López de Cogolludo 1688:Bk. 19, Ch. 13; Avendaño y Loyola 1696:33r, map). I believe that all of these were swidden plots, although from the wide variety of crops grown, it may be assumed that there were several types of plots in accordance with a specific repertoire of crops.

While the Spanish maintained a selfish interest in these swidden plots for their own maize needs (especially during the building of the Camino Real to the Lake Petén area during the famine that followed the 1697 Itzá conquest), they provided substantial information that indicates the diversified nature of the crops grown in the swidden plots. The following Lake Petén example is typical of such descriptions. While as "shopping lists" these contain noncultivated products as well as crops that were more likely grown by other means (e.g., cacao and vanilla), the listings are not at all unlike the diversified intercropped milpas found in the region up to this day (see, for example, Thompson 1930:184–195).

> I have seen the corn harvest, and the Indians say that when they make a new clearing they build a house in it, and the milpa lasts for twenty years without ceasing to give two harvests per year. I have seen in these maize, squash, beans, chiles, pineapples, tobacco, sugar cane, plantains, sweet potatoes, chayotes, cochineal, and cotton, from which the Indian women weave extraordinary and fine quality white and colored fabrics and other things (Artiga 1699).

Various references to the harvesting of two or three crops of maize per year suggest the presence of temporally intensive cultivation techniques during the Colonial period (Villagutierre Soto-Mayor 1701:Bk. 8, Ch. 14; Bk. 10, Ch. 12; Avendaño y Loyola 1696:10v, 37r). It is possible that this was a form of consecutive planting in environmentally distinct zones in order to offset the danger of failure of the principal crop, as described by Reina for contemporary Maya swiddening in the Lake Petén area (1967:1). I have observed similar practices in northern Belize, where unpredictable rainfall and the consequent danger of drought and flooding require a similar insurance strategy.

True double cropping of maize, however, has been reported for the contemporary Poptun region in Petén as well as elsewhere in the Maya Lowlands

(Culbert *et al.* 1978:158–159). We cannot discount the possibility that such practices were more widely utilized during the Colonial period. The wide variety of cultigens reported, coupled with remarkably high population estimates for the Lake Petén settlements (see footnote 2 on page 281), may also suggest the presence of short fallow intercropped plots—or "intensive milpas," in Wiseman's designation (1974:84). The data that are presently at my disposal, however, do not confirm this possibility.

There is little evidence concerning the relative size of these plantings or their locations vis-à-vis permanent settlements. In the case of the central lakes subregion we may state with certainty that the community of Yalain east of the lake (possibly at Lake Macanché) contained the dwellings of individuals of Itzá affiliation who produced crops consumed by the residents of the settlements at Lake Petén. In other cases, it is clearly stated that small shelters were built in milpas that were situated at some distance from the farmer's village; harvests could be stored in these temporary buildings (Avendaño y Loyola 1696:42r; Villagutierre Soto-Mayor 1701:Bk. 10, Ch. 9). Such practices are still common in many areas today.

ARBORICULTURE

Quite apart from forms of swidden cultivation, which we may assume was universally practiced throughout the Colonial period, there is strong evidence for the intensive cultivation of orchard tree crops. Of these crops cacao, discussed previously, was by far the most important.

Avendaño y Loyola was clearly struck by the great many fruit orchards that he passed on his way through southern Campeche and into Cehach territory as well as in the Itzá agricultural area near Yalain (1696:3v, 5v, 10v, 14r, 51r). In Campeche and Cehach, he reported what he considered to be plantings of oranges, lemons, coconut palms, *nanche, guazuma,* and various unnamed fruit trees. Some cacao was grown near Yalain (Villagutierre Soto-Mayor 1701:Bk. 10, Ch. 10). Unfortunately, there are few other sources that mention orchard production other than cacao. This omission is not surprising in view of the fact that few modern ethnographic studies in the Maya Lowlands pay notice to the wide range of fruit trees cultivated in mixed-crop orchards near villages or planted in village *solares* (a notable exception being Thompson 1933:184–195). Such mixed orchards are commonly found today in various parts of Belize and in contemporary central and southern Quintana Roo.

The orchard is of special interest as a form of cultivation that implies by its relative permanence the practice of private landownership as well as the existence of rewards for entrepreneurial behavior (see Press 1975:53). The degree to which orchard crops other than cacao were grown on a significant scale in the Southern Maya Lowlands during Colonial times is not yet clear, however. If there were, in fact, orchards larger than required by the needs of an individual household—and Avendaño y Loyola appears to describe such larger plantings—we would expect to find orchard production in the hands of a relative few, perhaps wealthy entrepreneurial individuals. Such could be expected even where fruits are being produced for local distribution. This may have been the case at Yalain, the Itzá agricultural community, where significant local social stratification could well have been associated with orchard production for local markets. In the case of cacao-growing communities such as Tipu, where the product was intended for export to district markets, the emphasis on wealth differentiation between producer and nonproducer would likely have been stronger.

OTHER FORMS OF CULTIVATION

While it is little more than speculation, there is some possibility that low-lying lakeshores in the Petén might have been used for purposes of intensive cultivation. Cortés's descriptions of "*labranzas*" along the southwestern end of Lake Petén (Cortés 1976:241) suggests such a possibility. Conditions along the southern side of Lakes Yaxhá–Sacnab might also have been suitable for such practices. Various crops could have been grown in such contexts. Cotton, given its importance as an item for export in manufactured cloth, would have been a likely candidate.

Another single reference states that the savanna grasslands south of Lake Petén were utilized to plant "large *milperías,* in which two consecutive harvests a year are grown; and the ears and grains of corn are extremely thick" (Villagutierre Soto-Mayor 1701:Bk. 8, Ch. 12). Rice and Rice (1979a:23) have noted that these savannas are limited agriculturally due to high soil acidity, low fertility, and an unpredictable annual water regimen. In their view, it is more likely that planting was limited to the adjacent upland soils. In any event, there may have been Colonial period settlements in the savanna areas. Perhaps, as suggested by Mary Pohl for earlier times, the settlers of this region may have been specialized hunters or game caretakers associated with ritual and elite consumption of meat (Rice and Rice 1979a:24).

Implications of the Model

The Colonial period southern Maya Lowlands, I have suggested, must be understood in the context of a wider interregional sphere of trade and population movement. Colonial period events external to the region deeply affected the substance of this trade, the role of particular parties in the wider system of exchange, and the political alliances that maintained the stability and continuity of this wider system. It is nonetheless significant that such a system, albeit altered in a particular sense from that of precontact times, continued to operate for nearly two centuries following the conquest of Yucatán. Central to this continuity, I have suggested, was the open nature of the northern frontier of the southern Maya Lowlands; for the continuous ongoing southward movement of anti-Spanish "refugees" into Belize, and thus the Petén, maintained the flow of both information and personnel required for the effective operation of an interregional exchange system.

It is primarily in the systemic interaction of the principal variables identified—agricultural production, interregional and intraregional trade, population movement, and political alliance—that we find a useful level of comparison and analogy at which the Colonial period data may lead to an understanding of Postclassic Maya economic and sociopolitical processes. While a satisfactory consideration of such analogies would require separate treatment, I believe that several issues emerge from this discussion that should be identified here as subjects for future consideration.

THE ADAPTABILITY OF LONG-DISTANCE TRADING NETWORKS

We have seen that Spanish pressures rapidly destroyed the presumably longstanding Putun Acalán control over interregional trade well before the end of the sixteenth century. On the other hand, the rapidity with which new networks were established by the planter–merchants of Belize behooves observers to recognize that systems of exchange may be established as rapidly as they decline. That such alternative "underground" systems came into existence in the face of a system of pervasive colonial control makes this phenomenon even more striking. Postclassic studies should therefore recognize that, in the case of exchange systems, external political events should be viewed as key elements in the rapid reorientation of interregional exchange relations.

THE ECONOMIC BASIS OF POLITICAL ALLIANCE

The establishment and maintenance of interregional political alliances during the colonial period were imbedded in the protection of mutually beneficial economic ties. That such alliances are both fragile and flexible is seen as a direct reflection of the conditions of trade and exchange. Such wider conditions, as maintained above, are influenced both by economic and political factors at the level of interregional interaction, but local political systems appear to be highly responsive to specific economic factors. The "underground" character of trade during the Colonial period suggests that exchange may continue in the presence of relatively weak or declining centralized control, although both production and trade of cash crops and elite goods were apparently controlled by elite minorities who were also influential in political affairs. It should also be noted that intraregional exchange relations were also reinforced by religious and ritual ties; such ties, however, seem to have appeared subsequent to the establishment of strong economic and political interdependence.

Such an analysis suggests that Postclassic research should continue to seek evidence of the interrelations between local economic specialization, systems of exchange, and centers of sociopolitical activity. Evidence of shared ideological content over wide regions may indeed suggest the presence of unanimity of higher purpose, but the roots of such unanimity should be understood in terms of systems of mutual economic and political interest.

POPULATION MOVEMENT

The significance of population movement in wider systems of exchange has already been discussed. It should be reemphasized, however, that the Colonial- and Independence-period (e.g., Caste War) pattern of rapid and large-scale movement of people was probably typical of precontact times as well. The demographic study of the Southern Maya Lowlands should, I believe, be open to the proposition that a major characteristic of Lowland Maya prehistory is to be found in such massive patterns of long-distance population movement.

ECONOMIC BEHAVIOR AND POLITICAL INSTABILITY

The model presented here emphasizes the role of individual decision-makers in the establishment and maintenance of exchange systems. It is, in fact, at the level of individual choice that we see the crystallization of political alliance and ritual sharing that seals the effectiveness of systems of production and exchange. We should recognize that such systems may be predicated, not on the prior existence of stable, permanent, highly stratified polities that independently manipulate production and trade, but rather on the collective interaction of political elites who manipulate conditions of political instability in order to further their individual economic ends. The unsettled conditions of both the Postclassic- and Colonial-period Southern Maya Lowlands stimulated the activities of such potential elites, who in turn were the formulators of systems of exchange and political alliance that resulted in patterns of interaction in which their own positions became increasingly dominant. Such a view, I believe, is a useful alternative to the static conception that has long pervaded the study of the political context of economic production and exchange in traditional Maya studies.

References

Artiga, Gabriel de
1699 *Testimonio de Gabriel de Artiga.* Archivo General de Indias, Guatemala 151. Seville.

Avendaño y Loyola, Andrés de
1696 *Relación de las entradas que hize a la conversión de los gentiles Ytaex.* Original Ms. in Newberry Library, Chicago.

Bullard, William R.
1970 Topoxte: A Classic Maya site in Peten, Guatemala. *Peabody Museum of Archaeology and Ethnology, Monographs and Papers in Maya Archaeology* 61:245–307.
1973 Postclassic culture in central Petén and adjacent British Honduras. In *The Classic Maya Collapse,* edited by T. Patrick Culbert, pp. 221–242. Albuquerque, Univ. of New Mexico Press.

Bunting, Ethel-Jane W.
1932 From Cahabon to Bacalar in 1677. *Maya Society Quarterly* 1:112–119.

Chamberlain, Robert S.
1948 The conquest and colonization of Yucatan, 1517–1550. *Carnegie Institute of Washington, Publication* 509. Washington, D.C.
Chase, Arlen
1979 Regional development in the Tayasal–Paxcaman zone, El Petén, Guatemala: A preliminary statement. *Cerámica de Cultura Maya* 11:87–120.
Cortés, Hernan
1976 *Cartas de Relación,* 9th edition. Mexico, Editorial Porrua.
Cowgill, George L.
1963 *Postclassic period culture in the vicinity of Flores, Petén, Guatemala,* 2 vols. Unpublished Ph.D. dissertation, Department of Anthropology, Harvard Univ.
Culbert, T. Patrick (editor)
1973 *The Classic Maya Collapse.* Albuquerque, Univ. of New Mexico Press.
Culbert, T. Patrick, Pamela C. Magers, and Mara L. Spencer
1978 Regional variability in Maya Lowland agriculture. In *Pre-hispanic Maya Agriculture,* edited by Peter D. Harrison and B. L. Turner II, pp. 157–162. Albuquerque, Univ. of New Mexico Press.
Farriss, Nancy M.
1978 Nucleation versus dispersal: The dynamics of population movement in Colonial Yucatán. *Hispanic American Historical Review* 58:187–216.
Freidel, David A.
1979 Culture areas and interaction spheres: Contrasting approaches to the emergence of civilization in the Maya Lowlands. *American Antiquity* 44(1):36–54.
Hellmuth, Nicholas M.
1971 Some notes on the Ytzá, Quejache, Verapaz Chol and Toquegua Maya: A progress report on ethnohistory research conducted in Seville, Spain, June–August 1971. Ms. on file, Foundation for Latin American Research, Guatemala, C.A.
1977 Cholti-Lacandón (Chiapas) and Petén-Ytzá agriculture, settlement pattern and population. In *Social Process in Maya Prehistory: Studies in Honour of Sir Eric Thompson,* edited by Norman Hammond, New York, Academic Press.
Johnson, Jay K.
1979 Postclassic Maya site structure of Topoxte, El Petén, Guatemala. Paper presented at the 78th Annual Meeting of the American Anthropological Association, Cincinnati.
Jones, Grant D.
1979a Ethnohistoric patterns and research needs. Paper presented at the Annual Meeting of the Northeastern Anthropological Society, Henniker, New Hampshire.
1979b Lamanai in ethnohistorical perspective. Paper presented at the XLIII International Congress of Americanists, Vancouver.
1979c Southern Lowland Maya political organization: A model of change from Protohistoric through Colonial times. *Actes du XLIIIe Congrès International des Américanistes, Congrès du Centenaire* (Paris, 2–9 September 1976) 8:83–94. Paris.
Jones, Grant D., D. Rice, and P. Rice
1981 The location of Tayasal: A reconsideration in light of Petén Maya ethnohistory and archaeology. *American Antiquity* 46(3)530–547.
López de Cogolludo, Diego
1688 *Los Trés Siglos de la Dominación Española en Yucatán o sea Historia de esta Provincia,* fifth edition, 2 vols. Graz, Austria, Akademische Druck- u. Verlagsanstalt (1971).
Pendergast, David M.
1977 Royal Ontario Museum excavation: Finds at Lamanai, Belize. *Archaeology* 30:129–131.
Press, Irwin
1975 *Tradition and Adaptation: Life in a Modern Yucatan Maya Village.* Westport, Greenwood Press.

Reina, Ruben E.
1967 Milpas and milperos: Implications for prehistoric times. *American Anthropologist* 69:1–20.
Rice, Prudence M., and Don S. Rice
1979a Home on the range. *Archaeology* 32:16–25.
1979b The Postclassic at Macanché and Topoxté, El Petén, Guatemala. Paper presented at the 78th Annual Meeting of the American Anthropological Association, Cincinnati.
Roys, Ralph L.
1943 The Indian background of Colonial Yucatan. *Carnegie Institution of Washington, Publication* 548. Washington, D.C.
1957 The political geography of the Yucatan Maya. *Carnegie Institution of Washington, Publication* 613. Washington, D.C.
Scholes, France V., and Ralph L. Roys
1948 The Maya Chontal Indians of Acalan–Tixchel: A contribution to the history and ethnography of the Yucatan Peninsula. *Carnegie Institution of Washington, Publication* 560. Washington, D.C.
Scholes, France V., and J. Eric S. Thompson
1977 The Francisco Pérez *probanza* of 1654–1656 and the *matrícula* of Tipu (Belize). In *Anthropology and History in Yucatán,* edited by Grant D. Jones, pp. 43–68. Austin, Univ. of Texas Press.
Scholes, France V., Carlos R. Menéndez, J. Ignacio Rubio Mañé, and Eleanor B. Adams (editors)
1936–1938 *Documentos para la Historia de Yucatán.* I. 1550–1561. II. La iglesia en Yucatán, 1560–1610. III. Discurso sobre la constitución de las provincias de Yucatán y Campeche. Mérida, Compañía Tipográfica Yucateca.
Thompson, J. Eric S.
1930 Ethnology of the Mayas of southern and central British Honduras. *Field Museum of Natural History, Publication* 274, *Anthropological Series* 17 (2). Chicago.
1970 *Maya History and Religion.* Norman, Univ. of Oklahoma Press.
1972 *The Maya of Belize: Historical Chapters since Columbus.* Belize, Benex Press.
1977 A proposal for constituting a Maya subgroup, cultural and linguistic, in the Petén and adjacent regions. In *Anthropology and History in Yucatán,* edited by Grant D. Jones, pp. 3–42. Austin, Univ. of Texas Press.
Ursua y Arizmendi, Martín de
1697 Testimonio de Martín de Ursua y Arizmendi. Archivo General de Indias, Guatemala 151. Seville.
Villagutierre Soto-Mayor, Juan de
1701 Historia de la conquista de la provincia de el Itzá, reducción y progresos de la de el Lacandón. *Biblioteca "Goathemala" de la Sociedad de Geografía e Historia,* Vol. 9. Guatemala, Tipografía Nacional (1933).
Wiseman, Frederick M.
1978 Agricultural and historical ecology of the Maya Lowlands. In *Pre-hispanic Maya Agriculture,* edited by Peter D. Harrison and B. L. Turner II, pp. 63–116. Albuquerque, Univ. of New Mexico Press.

12

The Traditional Role of Women and Animals in Lowland Maya Economy

Mary Pohl and Lawrence H. Feldman

Introduction

RESEARCH on the economy of the ancient Maya has focused heavily on agriculture. The question of which subsistence techniques supported Maya civilization has been a major point of discussion. The recent discovery of the great variety and sophistication of farming methods actually used by these Indians has generated much excitement among archaeologists.

One might well ask what excited the ancient Maya. Above all, they were absorbed by ritual and ceremony. They used their agricultural produce to feed animals that were raised for sacrifice. Sacrificial blood was essential for rain and the fertility of crops.

In addition to ceremonialism, trade and tribute were significant factors in the Maya economy, especially in the Postclassic and Colonial periods. Indian overlords demanded animals, together with such commodities as corn, beans and textiles. The Spaniards appropriated this tribute system after they conquered the native elites. Such produce was also bartered in local villages and taken to the markets.

This paper spans the Late Classic period through the Colonial era. Most of the data comes from scattered references in Spanish historical treatises and dictionaries, as well as from tribute records. Fauna can be traced back into the Prehistoric period through ancient art and bones recovered from archaeological sites.

Recent research demonstrates that Maya women have traditionally provided deer and peccaries for sacrifice, taken dogs to market, and paid tribute with fowl. Women, and their economic domain, have been essential to the maintenance of Maya culture and civilization.

ISBN 0-12-259780-X

Ritual Feasts

THE CUCH CEREMONY

Deer and peccaries were very closely associated with agriculture in the Maya mind. This association was no doubt based on the habits of these animals. Deer browse on second growth around cultivated fields, and peccaries eat the crops themselves. Populations of such game will increase with the spread of agriculture through a tropical forest.

One of the central agricultural rituals of the Maya ceremonial cycle featured deer and peccary characters. A Late Classic period polychrome vessel from San Agustín Acasaguastlán, middle Motagua, Guatemala, (Smith and Kidder 1943: Figure 43b) shows this ritual. To the left (Figure 1), a deer impersonator is being pulled away by a man carrying a sacrificial axe. A bone, a symbol of sacrifice, projects from the forehead of the deer impersonator. No doubt he is about to be dispatched.

The center of attention is a "float" composed of two elements. The first is a sacred tree growing out of a shell with a human face. Behind, a bearded peccary head lies in the jaws of a serpent (Taube, personal communication 1981).

The scene on the San Agustín vase is related to that on the famous Calcehtok polychrome (Figure 2). Men brandishing spears are shown removing the antlers of a stag. Red spots at the base of the antlers suggest the blood involved in this operation. The stag wears a blanket with a crossed-bone design, and a vulture hovers overhead. On the right, the sacred tree appears again, here with the anthropomorphic features of a god at its base. Above the god's ear is perched the three-dotted sign of the frog or toad. The branches of the tree are actually water lilies. A snake with a blue tail is curled around the trunk. These are all traditional Maya symbols for water, rain, sacrifice, and agricultural security (Thompson 1970). This is a sacred tree of abundance.

This ritual is repeated on page 40 of the Postclassic period Madrid Codex (Figure 3). The hornless stag is tied up while the spear sacrificer stands by. At the bottom a jaguar howls as a woman prepares a sacrificial meal. Above her is the dead stag, lying on a sky band.

The ceremony involving the planting of the sacred tree, the domination of the stag and the presentation of the peccary head is analogous to the bullfight practiced all over the Maya area today (Bricker 1973; Vogt 1969, 1976; Redfield and Villa 1962; Villa 1945; Tozzer 1907; Girard 1962, 1966). Close examination reveals that the modern bullfight is not truly Spanish in character. The fiesta is very similar to the ritual shown in Precolumbian paintings except that the bull and pig introduced by the Spaniards have been substituted for the aboriginal deer and peccary characters (Pohl 1979). Apart from these minor changes, the Maya have persisted in the celebration of their ancient rite.

The present-day ceremony is the central fiesta of the Maya calendar. This festival is a rite of desanctification. The Chortí of eastern Guatemala believe that the spirit of agricultural fertility has resided in the maize kernels since the crops

FIGURE 1. *Prehistoric ritual depicted on Late Classic period polychrome vessel from San Agustín Acasaguastlán, middle Motagua, Guatemala (from Smith and Kidder 1943).*

FIGURE 2. *Late Classic period Calcehtok vase showing ancient "Deerfight" (Reprinted from* The Ancient Maya, *Third Edition by Sylvanus Griswold Morley; revised by George W. Brainerd, with the permission of the publishers, Stanford University Press. Copyright © 1946, 1947, and 1956 by the Board of Trustees of the Leland Stanford Junior University.)*

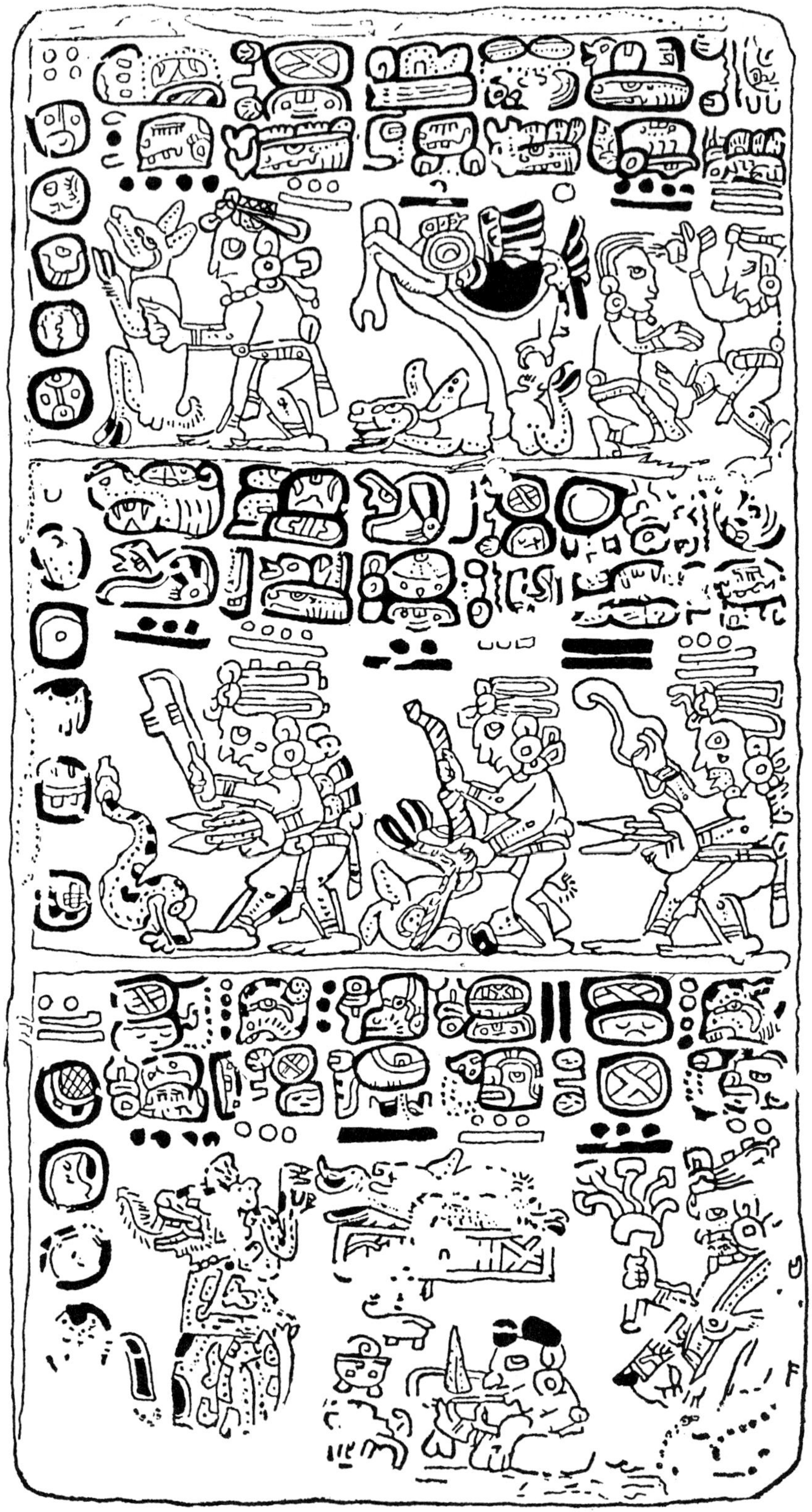

FIGURE 3. *The binding and sacrifice of a hornless stag portrayed in the Postclassic period Madrid Codex (from Villacorta and Villacorta 1930).*

were consecrated the previous year. The deities must be allowed to return to the sky where they rest (Girard 1962:307–308). The lassoing of the bull symbolizes the closing of the agricultural cycle, just as the tying of the stag must have in prehistoric times. Once the bull is overcome, great communal feasts celebrating agricultural prosperity can take place.

The climax of the present-day bullfight is the Dance of the Pig's Head. The pig's head accompanies the transfer of the "cargo" (*cuch* in Maya), responsibility for the welfare of the community in the coming year (Redfield and Villa 1962:157; Villa 1945:130–131). The cargo transfer is a most solemn event. Like the modern rite, the ancient fiesta, which is here called the *cuch* ceremony, must also have held great significance for the Maya. Many prehistoric paintings depict this festival.

The Cakchiquel Maya believe that two deer pull the brilliant sun across the sky on short days while two peccaries draw the sun on long days (Stoll in Thompson 1970:370). This surviving folk tradition suggests that the deer and the peccary have traditionally personified different seasons of the year. The animals appear to have symbolized the concept of renewal in the calendar round. For this reason they must have seemed characters appropriate for the aboriginal *cuch* drama, an allegorical rite about the continuity of life.

Peccary (*Dicotyles*) and particularly white-tailed deer (*Odocoileus virginianus*) bones are common at most Classic and Postclassic period ceremonial centers (Pohl 1976). Perhaps the Maya raised animals especially for their elaborate ceremonies. At Seibal, excavators uncovered a relatively large, walled structure resembling a pen (Tourtellot, personal communication 1974). Two fragments of antler tine occurred in the associated refuse.

The faunal remains provide further evidence for the proposed connection with the fertility cult. Deer bones have frequently been found in caves and cenotes (Savage 1978; Pollock and Ray 1957). The Maya were still practicing such rituals in early Historic times. It was the chance discovery of a deer sacrifice in a cave near Maní that sparked the terrible Inquisition in Yucatán in 1562 (López de Cogolludo 1688, I:410–411).

Pictures of the New Year ceremony in the Dresden Codex (Figure 4), together with the distribution of fauna at archaeological sites (Pohl 1976; Hamblin 1978), indicate that turkey sacrifices came to be required in the Postclassic period. The ocellated turkey (*Meleagris ocellata*) is native to the Yucatán Peninsula. Domestic turkeys (*Meleagris gallopavo*) were present on Cozumel Island in Postclassic times (Hamblin 1978, 1980); these birds must have been imported from somewhere further north in Mexico.

The ocellated turkeys do not occur naturally on Cozumel; the islanders must have brought them from the mainland. Perhaps the Indians tamed these wild turkeys. Bones representing at least four immature individuals suggest that the Maya captured young animals to be raised in captivity or stole eggs from nests for hatching (Hamblin 1980). Landa (Tozzer 1941:202) describes the latter practice. One suspects that the inhabitants of Cozumel would have been

FIGURE 4.

FIGURE 5.

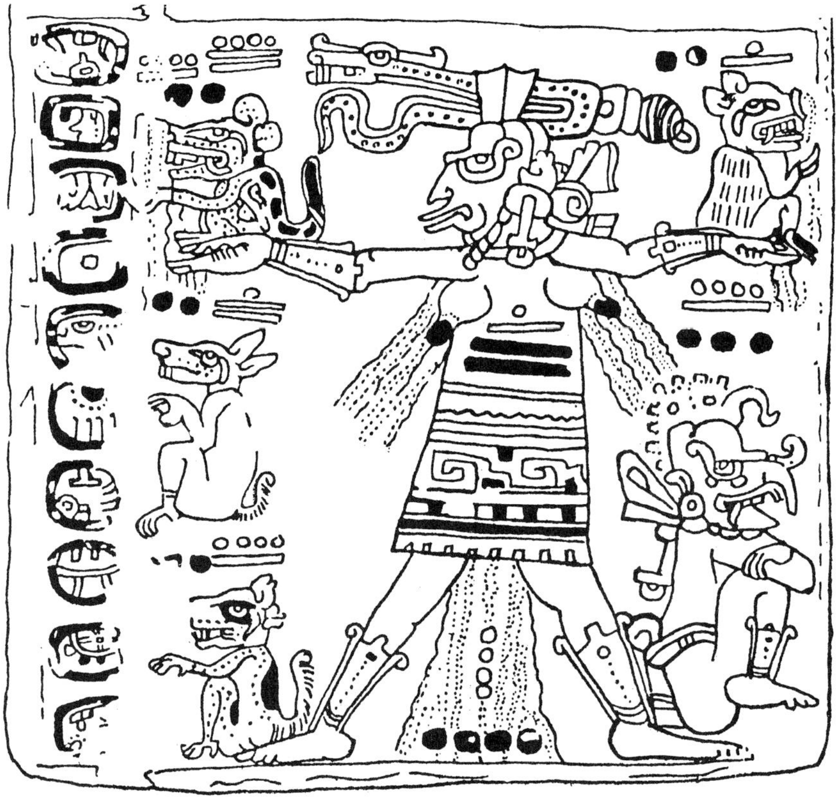

FIGURE 6.

FIGURE 4. *A deer haunch and turkey offered to the sacred tree in the Postclassic Dresden Codex (from Villacorta and Villacorta 1930).*

FIGURE 5. *The rain god planting in the company of a dog (Madrid Codex from Villacorta and Villacorta 1930).*

FIGURE 6. *Female fertility goddess with deer, peccary, jaguar, and dog in the Madrid Codex (from Villacorta and Villacorta 1930).*

particularly anxious to raise their own flocks since the birds were not available locally. Ocellated turkeys are very difficult to raise, however. This fact may explain the appearance of northern domestic turkeys on the island.

The Cozumel Maya may have tended turkeys in 5 to 15 m stone enclosures that archaeologists found at some sites (Hamblin 1980). Testing revealed that the soil inside the rings differed from that outside. The characteristics of the soil within the rings were consistent with the hypothesis that animal droppings had been deposited there.

The large numbers of turkey bones from Postclassic Mayapán were identified as wild ocellated turkey (Pollock and Ray 1957). Although no soil tests were conducted, stone rings found at the site may also have been pens. Since only a single bone was from an immature turkey, one might conclude that the birds were sent to the center, perhaps as tribute, rather than raised on the premises.

The Maya also used dogs in the year renewal ceremonies. In the Madrid Codex, the rain god, accompanied by a dog, plants corn (Figure 5). In the culmination of this sequence (Figure 6), the rain god and a dog, along with a deer, peccary, and jaguar, surround a huge female deity with water streaming from her body. This fertility goddess with a snake in her hair may be an alternative form of the sacred tree encircled by a serpent.

In sixteenth century Yucatán, Bishop Landa reported that during Uayeb rites preceding Muluc years, old women danced with pottery dogs, which had bread on their backs. The women sacrificed a little virginal dog with a black back to ward off calamity in the coming year (Tozzer 1941:145).

Although the Uayeb rites may have been introduced into the Maya area from Mexican sources at a fairly late date (Proskouriakoff and Bricker, personal communications 1979), we do know that dogs were associated with agricultural rituals at least as early as the Classic period. Quantities of dog teeth were found in Actun Polbilche (Savage 1978; Pendergast 1974), a cave that was probably used for rain ceremonies during Late Classic times. Dog bones were also abundant in cenote fauna from Postclassic Mayapán (Pollock and Ray 1957).

The archaeological record demonstrates that dogs were raised in very great numbers in Precolumbian times (Wing and Steadman 1980; Olsen 1978; Savage 1978; Pollock and Ray 1957; Pohl 1976; Hamblin, personal communication 1978). The faunal data indicate that the Maya had a larger and a smaller variety. Large, yellow and small, spotted dogs are depicted in Late Classic period art.

Ethnohistorical manuscripts devote considerable attention to dogs. The seventeenth-century Vienna Dictionary of Yucatec Maya (Lejón 1625) contains eight entries on dogs. This linguistic document lists a *perro* (*pek*) and a *perrito de falda* (*ixchan chan pek*). These may be the large and small dogs detected archaeologically. The Vienna Dictionary (Lejón 1625) further defines both *tzotzom in pek* 'short haired' and *ixbil ahbil* 'hairless' dogs. The San Francisco

Dictionary (Michelon 1976) lists *holom* 'a dog without a tail'. We do not know how many different breeds the Maya actually had. The ancient art shows that the dogs most often used for blood sacrifices were the black and white spotted ones.

THE SIGNIFICANCE OF RITUAL SACRIFICES

The use of animals for ritual offerings and for feasting was enormously important to the Maya. The redistributive feasts accompanying ceremonials were significant factors in patterns of food consumption. Priests stationed in the communities of Tecauto, Tepacan, Cuçal, and Chalante reported that meat was largely consumed at fiestas in the sixteenth century (Relaciones de Yucatán 1898–1900, I:244, 271). López de Cogolludo (1688, I:228, 235, 296) indicates that this custom was observed throughout Yucatán.

Animals would be carefully nurtured in preparation for a ritual event:

> so great is the confluence of persons attending any of these festivities, and if one could tell the multitude of turkeys eaten on that day, it would be difficult to believe, as they raise them all year for that day (López de Cogolludo 1688, I:296).

Trade and Tribute

TRIBUTE

In addition to raising animals for feasts, the Maya had to produce foods, including fowl, for the payment of tribute. Early Colonial tax records suggest that tribute was the primary means of resource mobilization used by native elites in the Postclassic period. The Spaniards took over this method of taxation in the Historic era. Tribute both supplied food and fueled long-distance trade.

According to these tax records (Paso y Troncoso 1939), in 1549 to 1551, 26,812 chickens and turkeys were received from Campeche, Yucatán, and those portions of Quintana Roo that had been conquered. This figure appears to represent slightly less than one bird per household. The sheer numbers of birds are nevertheless staggering. A substantial quantity of food was garnered by this means.

Beekeeping figured prominently in the economy of northern Yucatán. Honey and wax were valuable products of the area. During the same years, the Spaniards took in 2,182 *arrobas* (11-kg units) of wax and over 2,035 *arrobas* of honey (Paso y Troncoso 1939).

TRADE

Barter was a very common method of conducting business in Maya villages, especially before the Spaniards introduced coinage. Prestations of produce were also used to affirm kin ties. The Spaniards refer to these transactions as *regalos* 'gifts'. Both fowl and dogs were used for this purpose (Villagutierre Soto-Mayor 1701:242, López de Cogolludo 1688, I:228, 240).

Fowl

The Yucatec Maya used chickens introduced by the Spaniards for sale, for gifts and for sustenance for the infirm (López de Cogolludo 1688, I:228). These Indians continued to use native turkeys for sacrifices. Even today, this distinction in function is maintained in native communities in Yucatán (Bonfil Batalla 1962) and in northern Belize (Jones, personal communication 1978).

The Maya raised animals for specifically designated, special purposes: feasts, trade, and tribute. The Maya attitude towards their fowl amazed the Spaniards:

> they are of such nobility that even if they had many fowl and needed them for their illnesses and had the money for other things, they would rather let themselves die than kill a chicken or spend a penny on food and if any bird is taken or killed they weep as though their father or mother had died (Relaciones de Yucatán 1898–1900, II:193–194).

One must note that the economic conditions, and specifically the patterns of rearing fowl, that characterized the northern Yucatán Peninsula were not the same as those found in other areas inhabited by Maya speakers. As an example, the Chortí town of San Juan Ermita, located near the archaeological site of Copán, was prosperous in 1741. Long life spans are recorded; some villagers were in their 80s. Yet, only 7% of the families of this rural community raised poultry (Anonymous 1741).

The Chortí of southeastern Guatemala rendered just 896 fowl in taxes during the same period that the residents of Campeche, Yucatán, and Quintana Roo contributed over 26,000 animals (Cerrato *et al.* 1549–1551; Paso y Troncoso 1939). Chontal Maya of Acalán—Tixchel and communities located in Tabasco paid 1,376 birds in 1553 (Anonymous 1570–1571). These figures demonstrate the extent to which the northern Yucatán Peninsula was a center for the production of fowl.

Dogs and Pigs

Dogs were customarily raised in the houses of the Maya (Ximénez 1967:66). López de Cogolludo (1688, I:240) mentions the construction of pits for this purpose. Presumably pits were designed for larger numbers of dogs than could be fitted into the family house.

When they first arrived, the Spaniards ate dogs, but they conveyed negative attitudes towards this meat. In the sixteenth century, Landa noted the Maya custom of eating dogs: "Now I think they are ashamed and consider it mean to eat them. They say that they have a good taste" (Tozzer 1941:203). By the eighteenth century, Ximénez (1967) said that he had not seen any native dogs either in highland Guatemala or anywhere else in New Spain.

Once introduced by the Spaniards, the pig came to assume some of the economic functions of the dog. The sixteenth-century Motul Dictionary of Yucatec Maya (Martínez Hernández 1929) defines *mac ex keken tu cuchil* as *encerrad los puercos en su corral.* Pigs were evidently corralled around the house as they are today. This was the area where dogs had been raised.

In contrast to dogs, pigs were perfectly acceptable to the Spaniards. Pigs had proven useful to the Maya, too. Pigs would yield large quantities of fat. The Motul Dictionary (Martínez Hernández 1929) has an entry for pig fat, *manteca de puerco—u tzatz keken.*

Prior to the introduction of the pig, the Maya must have been fairly limited in the amount of fat that they could obtain. They fattened up dogs with corn. In their orchards, they grew avocados, which Landa (Tozzer 1941:200) described as "fatty" and possessing the "taste of butter." The Motul Dictionary (Martínez Hernández 1929) lists the *uo* frog as providing fat and grease, *unas ranas de mucho unto y manteca, buenas de comer.* Pigs are better sources of fat. Present-day Maya claim that one of the main reasons for raising pigs is for their lard (Marshall 1976).

López de Cogolludo (1688, I:220–229) observed that pigs did well in Yucatán, while cattle, sheep, and goats had proven difficult to raise. In the eighteenth century, pigs were very numerous. They formed part of a flourishing, illicit export trade with Cuba. Lard was sent to Havana in jars. In Valladolid, a seasoning called *enchilado* was applied to pork to preserve it so that it could be shipped (X. de C. 1766).

In this century, local pig marketing has been greatly aided by the availability of trucks (Marshall, personal communication 1979) and of refrigerators in meat markets. Pig rearing has become a profitable business for villagers. The profession is for the most part dominated by women (Marshall 1976).

Pigs were also used in ritual sacrifices soon after they were introduced. Testimony given in the Inquisition of 1562 indicates that deer, pigs, and dogs were offered at pagan ceremonies, even in church at the foot of the cross (Scholes and Adams 1938:96). The Maya considered the cross an alternative form of their sacred tree. Such sacrifices may have been related to the traditional Maya *cuch* ritual previously described.

The pig was not adopted everywhere. Eighteenth-century Guatemalan census data for the Chortí area report that households had some poultry but no pigs (Anonymous 1741).

The Economic Role of Maya Women

The Spaniards admired the industriousness of Maya women. Landa wrote:

> They are great workers and good housekeepers, since on them depends the more important and the most work for the support of their houses, the education of their children, and the payment of their tribute. And in spite of all this, if there is need for

it, they sometimes carry a greater burden, cultivating and sowing their supplies. They are good managers, working at night in the moments which remain to them from their housework, and going to market to buy and sell their little articles. They raise fowls for sale and for food—both the Castilian and the native breeds; they also raise birds for their own pleasure, and for the feathers from which to make their fine clothes (Tozzer 1941:127).

In the late seventeenth century, Spaniards described the Chiapas Cholti of Nuestra Señora de los Dolores de Lacandón (Sac Balam) thus:

having occupied their houses, those Spaniards that resided in the town [of Sac Balam] considered [that the Lacandones in fact] lived rationally like human beings because they [did] not have more than one wife, who each assisted and applied herself with care to the work of the milpas and the sown places of maize, chile, and beans, in which they plant pineapples, platanos, potatoes, jicamas, jocotes, zapote trees, and other fruit trees. . . . And all raise chickens . . . the most abundant [of which were] turkeys. . . . We found in the village many troops. . . . They killed them by twisting their heads and [by] putting a foot over the turkey and pulling [the head] off. . . . And later they threw them into a fire to burn off the feathers. Deplumed, they washed them and put [them] to cook (Hellmuth 1977:426).

The ethnohistorical data indicate that Maya women tended fowl. Landa observed that the houses were the domain of women (Tozzer 1941:127). Ximénez (1967:66) said that dogs were raised in the houses. Women probably also raised the dogs, much as women now tend pigs (Marshall 1976).

According to Landa, Maya women raised deer:

and they raise other domestic animals, and let the deer suck their breasts, by which means they raise them and make them so tame that they never go into the woods, although they take them and carry them through the woods and raise them there (Tozzer 1941:127).

Other ethnohistorical sources mention the custom of farming deer. The Motul Dictionary (Martínez Hernández 1929) defines *ah may* as *venadillo pequeño criado en casa* 'a little deer raised in a house'. Ximénez (1967:57) also cites the practice of taming deer in the highlands.

The idea that women raised deer for rituals in prehistoric times may explain the unusual character of cattle ranching in Yucatán, which emerged in the mid-seventeenth century (Farriss 1979, personal communication 1981). Cattle herding was confined to the *cofradía,* an institution that embodied the corporate community and was supported by communal labor. In the Maya view, the Virgin and the saints owned the cattle, and the animals supported religious worship. The Maya used the cash to purchase hundreds of beeswax candles that they needed for ceremonies. They also used bulls in bullfights and consumed large quantities of beef at the accompanying fiesta banquets. This practice of cattle ranching, which came to be controlled by men, lasted until the late eighteenth century when the Catholic church intervened and auctioned off the *estancias.*

The ethnohistorical data indicate that the principal businesses of Yucatec women were wax production and cloth production (X. de C. 1766). The beehives were cared for by women, although everyone participated in the collection of the wax. Eighteenth-century wills from the community of Tekanto, located between Mérida and Valladolid, demonstrate a marked matrilineal emphasis in the inheritance of hives (Thompson 1978:176).

In this paper, the economic role of women has been traced through the animals they raised because faunal evidence is available for the prehistoric period, as well as for the historic era. We must point out that the most significant work women performed was to produce cotton cloth, which they did at home on their backstrap looms (Farriss, personal communication 1981). Sixteenth-century observer Ciudad Real described the *mantas* as "almost as delicate as fine Dutch linen" (Noyes 1932:311). The early Spanish tax records for northern Yucatán demonstrate the importance of textiles in the economy. From 1549 to 1551, the Spaniards received more than 47,813 woven *mantas* in tribute (Paso y Troncoso 1939). Generally, each household was responsible for providing 1 *manta*. The figures on goods contributed by women, consisting of wax, honey, fowl, and cloth, can be compared with those for which men were probably primarily responsible. During the very same time period, the Spaniards received 693 *fanegas* (bushels) of maize, over 121 *fanegas* of beans, 223 *fanegas* of salt, and over 118 *arrobas* of fish. Women's produce, together with salt, supported the Spanish export trade; the agricultural surplus fed the local Spaniards primarily through urban markets (Farriss 1979).

At the time of the Conquest, the economy of the Yucatec Maya of northern Yucatán, now the modern Mexican states of Yucatán, Campeche and Quintana Roo, was different from that of the Chontal Maya of Tabasco. From 1549 to 1551, the Chontal tribute payment consisted of 224 fowl, 400 *mantas,* 300 *fanegas* of maize, 8 *fanegas* of beans, 200 *xiquipiles* (units of 80,000 beans) of cacao, 2 jars of honey, and a small number of chiles. Despite the differences between the Chontal and Yucatec Maya areas, the Maya Lowland region as a whole was distinctive for the lack of economic specialization among communities.

The economy of Yucatán was a primitive agrarian structure based mainly on tribute in various guises before the late eighteenth century (Farriss 1979). Women provided the main source of money for the family. By the early eighteenth century, cash advances were made for fixed quotas of beeswax and cotton cloth (García Bernal in Farriss 1979). The rural Maya were largely self-sufficient, however, and most people were isolated from what market activity existed. Nevertheless, women's ability to sell and particularly to barter meat locally for goods and services, though an apparently minor endeavor, may have been a significant source of independence as it is in Indian villages today (Marshall 1976).

In the late eighteenth century, Yucatán began to participate in external markets, particularly in Veracruz and Cuba (Farriss 1979). Indian women around Valladolid were probably furnishing many of the pigs, which figured

FIGURE 7. *Elite women shed blood at an accession ritual that took place at Bonampak during the Late Classic period. The man on the steps holds a spear. A sacrificial victim is being offered in the adjacent panel (Ruppert* et al. *1955).*

prominently in the export trade (X. de C. 1766). Market opportunities for women would have increased at this time. Lack of efficient transportation to market places in cities must have placed restrictions on pig production, however.

Eighteenth- and early nineteenth-century wills and bills of sale from Tekanto list neither pigs nor fowl. This fact suggests that local village transactions occurred primarily through kin ties and barter, as described by the earlier Spanish sources (see p. 302). One might conclude that the animals were considered an integral part of the house compound, over which women presided, rather than the property of individuals, as were beehives.

Certain elite women held key political positions in Maya society and performed ritual functions at sacred events (Figure 7), notably during the Classic period (Proskouriakoff 1961; Marcus 1976; Schele 1978). The prehistoric art and ethnohistorical documents suggest that most women were assigned second-class status however (e.g., Tozzer 1941:97). The majority of the goods they produced were appropriated. Nevertheless, Maya women may have derived a measure of economic leverage from the goods they produced for sale and for barter.

Maya women have been limited in their pursuit of economic activities, but they have traditionally been quick to take advantage of the opportunities that have been available to them (see also Stavrakis 1979). This characteristic is not confined to rural Indian women. An analysis of dowries and wills from seventeenth- and eighteenth-century Guadalajara and Puebla has demonstrated that many Hispanic urban women derived economic independence through small-scale businesses, such as shopkeeping and moneylending (Lavrin and Couturier 1979).

Conclusions

The Maya have traditionally cast their concerns for agricultural prosperity in zoomorphic metaphors. Petitions for rain and fertility have taken the form of dramas featuring animal characters. A portion of each harvest was set aside to feed the dogs, fowl, deer, peccaries, and pigs that were to shed the blood necessary for continued economic viability.

The consumption of animal flesh was the high point of communal feasts that took place at Maya fiestas. Poorer people ate meat only at these festivals. Maya women have traditionally raised the animals for the ritual celebrations.

At least as early as the Postclassic period, Maya women were responsible for providing tribute payment. One of the main categories of tribute was fowl. Women have also used meat to barter for goods and services.

The ethnohistorical documents quoted here demonstrate that Maya women did a great deal more than raise animals. They have worked in the fields and tended fruit trees. They have produced textiles, one of the most valuable commodities of the Maya Lowlands. Women have historically formed the keystone of the Maya economy.

Acknowledgments

Olga Stavrakis and Dennis Puleston provided Mary Pohl with a home base in the Río Hondo Project. Observations on animals and the Maya were made from this vantage point. This study of the traditional role of Maya women was aided by comparison with Marion Marshall's (1976) data on present-day Indian women in Belize. The analysis of the Precolumbian origins of the Maya bullfight was initiated by Victoria Reifler Bricker's theory concerning the ritual replacement of the stag by the bull. Library research was aided by grants to Mary Pohl from the Newberry Library and the Penrose Fund of the American Philosophical Society. Cecelia Klein's comments proved helpful in the writing of this chapter. Lourdes Grindal translated passages from López de Cogolludo and the Relaciones de Yucatán quoted in the text. Jack Draisey worked on the Bonampak mural illustration.

References

Anonymous
1741 *Nueva Cuenta y Padrón de los Tributarios del Pueblo de San Juan Ermita, Jurisdicción de Chiquimula.* Archivo General de Centro América. Manuscript A3.16, expediente 41010, legajo 2823.

Anonymous
1570–1571 *Antón García contra Feliciano Bravo, escribano, y Juan Vásquez y Juan de Monserrate.* Archivo General de Indias Justicia 250, ff. 1885–2255*v*.

Bonfil Batalla, G.
1962 Diagnóstico sobre el hambre en Sudzal, Yucatán. *Instituto Nacional de Antropología e Historia, México, Serie Investigaciones Antropológicas* 11.

Bricker, V. R.
1973 *Ritual Humor in Highland Chiapas.* Austin, Univ. of Texas Press.

Cerrato, A., Pedro Ramírez, and Alonso Zurita
1549–1551 *Tasaciones de los Naturales de las Provincias de Guatemala.* Archivo General de Indias, Guatemala 128.

Farriss, N.
1979 *Landed estates in Colonial Yucatán: Some observations on Spanish poverty and Indian autonomy.* Paper presented at the XLIII International Congress of Americanists, Vancouver.

Girard, R.
1962 *Los Mayas Eternos.* Mexico, Libro Mex Editores.
1966 *Los Mayas.* Mexico, Libro Mex Editores.

Hamblin, N.
1978 *Isla Cozumel archaeological avifauna.* Paper presented at the 43rd Annual Meeting of the Society for American Archaeology, Tucson.
1980 *Animal utilization by the Cozumel Maya: Interpretation through faunal analysis.* Ph.D. dissertation, Department of Anthropology, University of Arizona. Ann Arbor, University Microfilms.

Hellmuth, N.
1977 Cholti-Lacandón (Chiapas) and Petén-Ytzá agriculture, settlement pattern, and population. In *Social Process in Maya Prehistory,* edited by Norman Hammond, pp. 421–448. New York, Academic Press.

Lavrin, A., and E. Couturier
1979 Dowries and wills: A view of women's socioeconomic role in colonial Guadalajara and Puebla, 1640–1790. *Hispanic American Historical Review* 59:280–304.
Lejón, D.
1625 *Bocabulario de Mayathan por su Abeseario* (Vienna Dictionary). Ms. in the National Library in Vienna, Austria. From microfilm in the Library of Pomona College, Claremont, California.
López de Cogolludo, D.
1688 *Los tres Siglos de la Dominación Española en Yucatán o sea Historia de esta Provincia,* 2 vols. Graz, Akademische Druk-u. Verlagsanstalt, (1971).
Marcus, J.
1976 *Emblem and State in the Classic Maya Lowlands.* Washington D.C., Dumbarton Oaks.
Marshall, M. L.
1976 *A pig is a gold tooth.* Unpublished M.A. thesis, Department of Anthropology, Univ. of Minnesota.
Martínez Hernández, Juan (editor)
1929 *Diccionario de Motul: Maya—Español.* Atribuido a Fray Antonio de Ciudad Real y Arte de lengua Maya par Fray Juan Coronel. Mérida, Compañía Tipográfica Yucateca, S.A.
Michelon, Oscar (editor)
1976 *Diccionario de San Francisco.* Biblioteca Linguistica Americana, Vol. II. Graz, Akademische Druck-u. Verlagsanstalt.
Morley, S. G.
1946 *The Ancient Maya.* Stanford, Stanford Univ. Press.
Noyes, E., (editor and translator)
1932 Fray Alonso Ponce in Yucatán, 1588. *Tulane University, Middle American Research Series, Publication* 4.
Olsen, S. J.
1978 Vertebrate faunal remains. In *Excavations at Seibal, Department of Petén, Guatemala,* edited by G. R. Willey. *Harvard University, Peabody Museum of Archaeology and Ethnology, Memoirs* 14.
Paso y Troncoso, F. del, comp.
1939 *Epistolario de Nueva España,* Vol. 5, 1547–1549. México, Antigua Librería Robredo, de José Porrúa e Hijos.
Pendergast, D. M.
1974 Excavations at Actun Polbilche, Belize. *Royal Ontario Museum, Archaeology Monograph* 1.
Pohl, M. E. D.
1976 *Ethnozoology of the Maya: An analysis of fauna from five sites in Petén, Guatemala.* Unpublished Ph.D. dissertation, Department of Anthropology, Harvard Univ.
1979 *The Maya bullfight.* Paper presented at the XLIII International Congress of Americanists, Vancouver.
Pollock, H. E. D., and C. E. Ray
1957 Notes on vertebrate animal remains from Mayapán. *Carnegie Institution of Washington, Current Reports* 41.
Proskouriakoff, T.
1961 Portraits of women in Maya art. In *Essays in Precolumbian Art and Archaeology,* edited by S. K. Lothrop *et al.,* pp. 81–99. Cambridge, Harvard Univ. Press.
Relaciones de Yucatán
1898–1900 *Colección de Documentos Inéditos Relativos al Descubrimiento Conquista y Organización de las Antiguas Posesiones Españolas de Ultramar.* 2nd series, Vols. 11 and 13, Madrid.
Redfield, R., and A. Villa R.
1962 *Chan Kom: A Maya Village,* (2nd ed.) Chicago, The Univ. of Chicago Press.

Ruppert, K., J. E. S. Thompson, and T. Proskouriakoff
1955 Bonampak, Chiapas, Mexico. *Carnegie Institute of Washington Publication* 602.
Savage, H.
1978 Faunal findings in cave sites in Belize. Paper presented at the 43rd Annual Meeting of the Society for American Archaeology, Tucson.
Schele, L.
1978 Genealogical documentation on the tri-figure panels at Palenque. In *Tercera Mesa Redonda de Palenque,* Vol. IV, edited by M. G. Robertson, pp. 41–70. Monterey, California, Pre-Columbian Art Research Center and Herald Printers.
Scholes, F. V., and E. B. Adams (editors)
1938 *Don Diego de Quijada, Alcalde Mayor de Yucatán, 1561–1565.* Mexico, Antigua Librería Robredo.
Smith, A. L., and A. V. Kidder
1943 Explorations in the Motagua Valley, Guatemala. *Carnegie Institution of Washington, Contributions to American Archaeology* 19.
Stavrakis, O.
1979 *The effect of agricultural change upon social relations and diet in a village in northern Belize, Central America.* Unpublished Ph.D. dissertation, Department of Anthropology, Univ. of Minnesota.
Thompson, J. E. S.
1970 *Maya History and Religion.* Norman, Univ. of Oklahoma Press.
Thompson, P.
1978 *Tekanto in the eighteenth century.* Ph.D. dissertation, Department of Anthropology, Tulane University. Ann Arbor, University Microfilms.
Tozzer, A. M.
1907 *A Comparative Study of the Mayas and the Lacandones.* New York, Macmillan.
1941 Landa's relación de las cosas de Yucatán. *Papers of the Peabody Museum of American Archaeology and Ethnology, Harvard University,* 18.
Villa R., A.
1945 The Maya of east central Quintana Roo. *Carnegie Institution of Washington, Publication* 559.
Villacorta C., J. A., and C. A. Villacorta
1930 *Codices Mayas: Dresdensis-Peresianus-Tro-Cortesianus.* Guatemala, Tipografía Nacional.
Villagutierre Soto-Mayor, Juan de
1701 Historia de la conquista de la provincia de el Itzá. *Biblioteca "Goathemala" de la Sociedad de Geografía e Historia* 9 (1933).
Vogt, E. Z.
1969 *Zinacantán: A Maya Community in the highlands of Chiapas.* Cambridge, Massachusetts, Belknap.
1976 *Tortillas for the Gods: A Symbolic Analysis of Zinacanteco Rituals.* Cambridge, Massachusetts, Harvard Univ. Press.
Wing, E. S., and D. Steadman
1980 Vertebrate faunal remains from Dzibilchaltún, Yucatán. In *Excavations at Dzibilchaltún, Yucatán,* edited by E. W. Andrews IV and E. W. Andrews V. Tulane University, Middle American Research Institute, Publication 48.
X. de C., F.
1766 *Extracto de la Descripción Política y Geográfica de las Provincias de (Campeche) y (Yucatán) hecha en al Año de 1766 . . . por Orden del Sor.* D. Josef de Galvez, Mérida. Ms. in the British Museum. From W. E. Gates' photo in the Newberry Library, Chicago.
Ximénez, F.
1967 Historia natural del reino de Guatemala. *Sociedad de Geografía e Historia de Guatemala, Special Publication* 14.

13

The Contemporary Role of Women in Lowland Maya Livestock Production

Marion Marshall Nimis[1]

Introduction

DATA collected in northern Belize indicate that women play an important role in household production economics by rearing animals in the backyards of their houses for food, festivals, profit, and security. This research revealed the extent of women's involvement in livestock production and suggested that women have long been active in this area.

The Maya woman's animals provide her with a resource that is hers to deploy, giving her a measure of independence and providing security in the face of sudden calamity. Money from sale of livestock, meat, or eggs provides the Maya woman with an income to buy other household necessities or luxury items which confer personal and public status. With the exception of their livestock, women have few alternative financial resources, and none of similar magnitude.

Meat is critical in many ways to the efficient functioning of village life; it is part of the village barter system in that it is a product that is exchanged for goods, favors, and services. When an animal is butchered, meat is given to close friends, relatives, and coreligionists provided they, in turn, reciprocate. The Maya perceive meat to be important in their diet, and home-produced meat is useful when meat is scarce, because an animal from a woman's backyard can be slaughtered to tide the family over.

In Belize, private and public festivals of various kinds feature festive dishes containing meat. This meat is reared, prepared, cooked, and then donated or sold by village women. These festivals form the backbone of village social life.

[1]Present address: 801 Iowa West, St. Paul, Minnesota 55117.

ISBN 0-12-259780-X

In the 70s, however, the situation changed. The numbers and types of domestic animals were affected by the changing economic structure of northern Belize. The rapid expansion of sugar-cane cultivation produced a competitor for corn. Land and labor formerly used for corn production were diverted into cane production. Two years of drought, a hurricane, and the switch to cane resulted in a scarcity of corn. Women livestock producers felt the pinch and one strategy that they adopted was the rearing of animals that did not depend on corn for feed. Women also began other forms of entrepreneurial activity made possible by the influx of money from cane.

Women adapting to new challenges using traditional skills is nothing new. Mary Pohl (see Chapter 12) suggests that in the past, women reared indigenous animals, and later, colonial imported animals with objectives similar to those they currently hold. This trend continues today, with Maya women adopting recently introduced animals such as sheep and goats and employing these animals in traditional ways.

Methods

This study of the Maya woman's role in livestock production began in 1973 under the auspices of the Río Hondo Project, and continues into the present (1981). Data were collected for the most part from one village in northern Belize. However, villages in central and southern Belize were studied for comparison. The basic elements and goals of animal husbandry were found to be much the same throughout the country, although private and public festivals reveal geographic and ethnic differences.

The duration of the research proved fortuitious. Changes could be observed in all aspects of people's lives with the rapid expansion of sugar cane production in the north in 1975. Women's strategies vis-à-vis their animals began to change as corn became scarcer. Lack of corn and an outbreak of hog disease contributed to a decline in livestock numbers, particularly pigs. Between 1973 and 1975, pig numbers decreased by 50%, and more people went out of the business of hog rearing than entered the field.

This trend has reversed itself today, as people become accustomed to having money from cane. Corn farmers have begun planting as much corn as they did prior to the cane boom. Livestock numbers have returned to former levels with women using money from cane to buy imported animals and, when necessary, animal feed.

Traditional Methods of Animal Production

Lowland Maya women raise a variety of animals in their backyards—most commonly pigs, turkeys, chickens, and ducks. Less common animals occasionally reared include deer (*Odocoileus virginianus*), peccaries (*Dicotyles tajacu*) (Figure 1), chachalacas (*Ortalis vetula*), and various species of parrots, pigeons, and turtles. The former group comprise part of a planned economic and survival strategy; women calculate how many animals they will need and for what purpose, leaving a few extra for insurance against calamities. The less commonly raised animals are haphazardly acquired, usually found as young orphans in the bush during hunting expeditions, and taken home. Sometimes a woman walking through the *monte* 'bush' will find eggs in a nest, carry them home, and place them under her hens. These will be hatched and raised like chickens, to eat or sell later. Women are clearly ready to seize every opportunity to make money, but this system operates more as a cash or food bonus and will not be described at length here.

PIG PRODUCTION

The pig is the most important of the backyard animals to the village household. Villagers describe the pig as belonging to one of two types: a *de raza* (exotic),

FIGURE 1. *A peccary kept by a northern Belize household.*

or a *malishe* or *local* (nonexotic). Outsiders descriptively, although unkindly, call them "razorbacks" or "greyhounds," referring to their often gaunt appearance. Although very slow growing, local pigs are small and hardy and can survive difficult times when feed is scarce.

A household typically has four or five pigs: a sow for breeding, a replacement gilt, and two or three barrows (castrated males) for fattening. On the occasion of her marriage, the young wife is traditionally given a small female pig to start her herd. After two to three litters of pigs, the new wife's herd is established, and the original pig will be sold before her physical appearance declines sufficiently to affect her price.

The system of small-scale pig rearing could best be described as one of benign neglect, with villagers making little effort to maximize production. At sunrise, pigs are set loose to begin their hunt for food and water. In addition to what they find on their own, pigs are fed household scraps and spoiled corn. Occasionally a pig's diet may be supplemented with feed concentrates, but this is rare because it is scarce and expensive. At dusk, pigs are rounded up by their owners and corralled in *chiqueros* (crude but adequate, dirt floor pigsties).

Women do not control or record the mating of their sows and gilts, and as a result, do not know when they are due to farrow. Thus pigs often farrow in the bush with resultant loss of offspring. Pigs are allowed to nurse until weaned by the sow and are not treated for worms or vaccinated against prevalent diseases. Selection of males to be retained for breeding appears to be random although color is sometimes a criterion.

POULTRY PRODUCTION

Individual flocks of turkeys and chickens are maintained free-range style by almost every family. Two dozen chickens, a dozen or so turkeys, and occasionally a few ducks comprise the average household flock. Poultry are fed twice a day with rice husks or spoiled corn, and peck for grubs and seeds in neighboring yards. Usually a big pan of water suffices for several days. Flocks are checked at feeding time to see whether individual birds are missing. If this is the case, an immediate search is mounted because foxes, dogs, and other people are natural predators. Women shut their flocks in at night to protect them.

Raising turkeys is time-consuming and risky because they are notoriously difficult to raise. Poults are extremely susceptible to chills and must be rescued from the rain. Women often have to search for their turkeys at night because the birds fall asleep wherever dusk falls and cannot find their way home.

Chickens, conversely, are quite easy to rear as long as there is enough food. Women prefer to take only those eggs needed for household use, leaving the rest to hatch.

HOUSEHOLD PRODUCTION ECONOMICS

It appears that Maya women are maximizing their productive activity by producing livestock because it represents the highest return for the inputs involved. The largest of these inputs are women's time and the cost of animal feed, because women do not invest money in veterinary care, equipment, or land, and only very rarely in boar stud fees ($2.50 U.S. per service).[2] The only specialized building is the lean-to pigsty which is constructed of local materials or odds and ends at minimal cost ($5.00) by the woman or her relatives.

The output is primarily pigs and chickens, and, to a lesser extent, turkeys and chicken eggs. The sale of livestock provides money that can be used for purchasing other inputs into future household production or consumer goods that increase the standard of living of the household. In addition, meat from the livestock is bartered for goods and services that are useful to the household or improve community welfare.

THE TIME INPUT

The time input can vary enormously, depending on the number of animals being reared, and whether they are to be fattened for sale or retained for breeding. An unusually large herd of 15 or more pigs being fattened will require 1½ hours of work per day. Daily care involves feeding three or four times, putting water into containers (sawn-off tires or tin cans), and herding the pigs into the bush to eat grasses and roots. This includes time spent checking the pigs, rounding them up, and shutting them in at night. Fowl do not involve additional labor because they are fed and watered with the pigs.

A smaller herd of three or four pigs for breeding will take only 30 minutes of work per day; they are fed once or twice and allowed to scavenge. In any event, women do not invest all this time themselves but enlist their children's help to feed and water the animals.

The opportunity cost involved in village women's time is minimal, since apart from small sums of money to be made from the seasonal sale of such items as homemade sweets or breads, *recado* (red spice paste), or garden produce, most women have no alternative forms of employment. Some villages do have a few women specialists, however, such as the *yerbatera* or *curandera,* herbalist–healer, and the *comadrona,* midwife, who make larger amounts of money on an intermittent basis. In addition, quarrying and road building in the north generated jobs for some women, for example, making sandwiches or laundering clothes for work crews. But these opportunities are only open to the few, whereas more than two thirds of all village women produce livestock.

Above all, women can raise livestock without leaving their homes, freeing them to keep up with household tasks. Backyard animals, particularly pigs, adapt well to the daily household routine; they appear at mealtimes to garner leftovers but do not loiter around the house (Figure 2). Women can complete household chores such as food preparation and cleaning while broadcasting handfuls of corn for their livestock. Young pigs and babies may be formula-fed, in which case women prepare bottles for each at the same time.

[2]Prices are based on 1974–1975 data and are included for comparison only. U.S. equivalent figures are quoted for Belizean dollars.

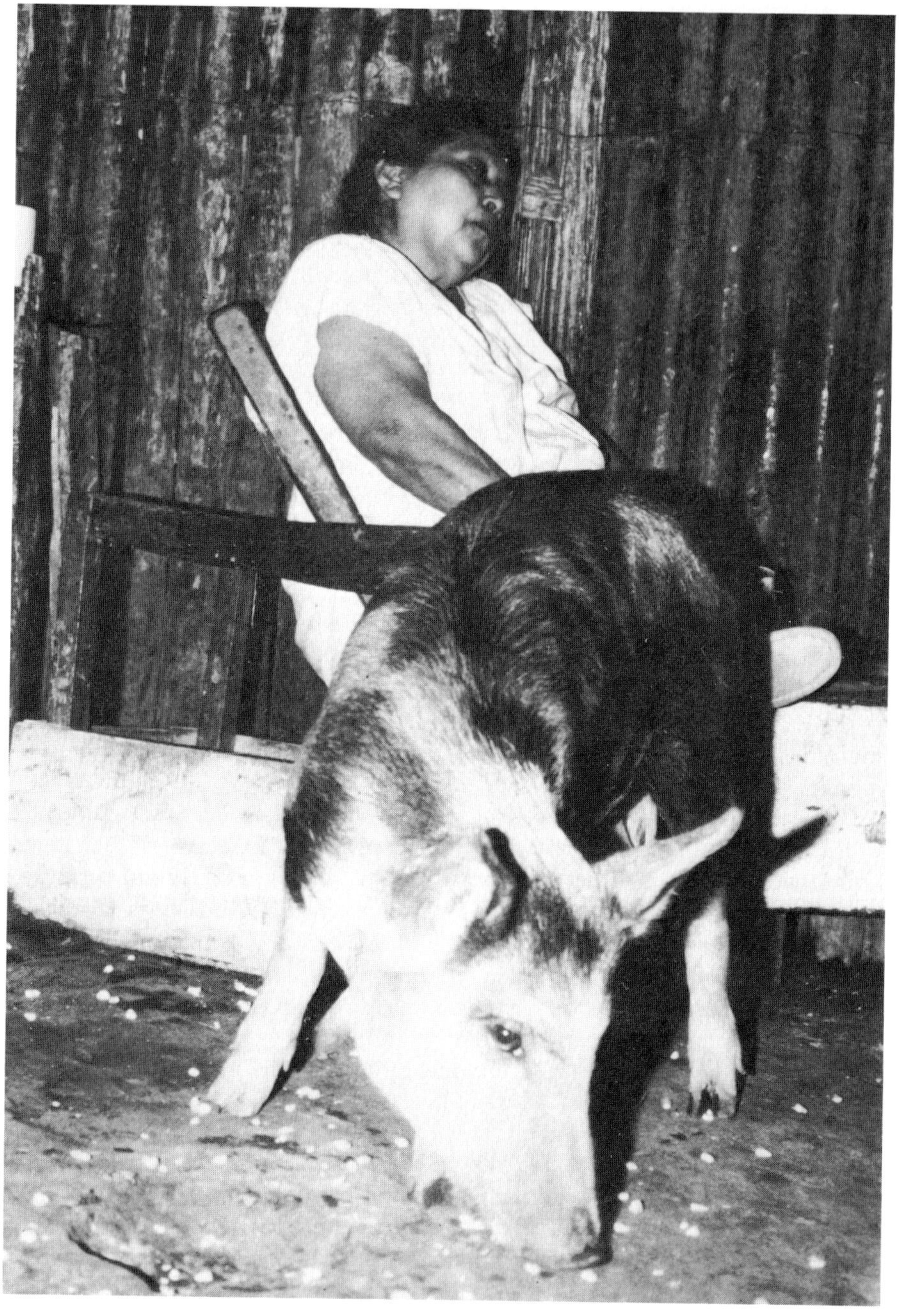

FIGURE 2. *A domestic pig eats broadcast corn kernels while her owner relaxes.*

THE FEED INPUT

The other major input is feed; but corn is traditionally inexpensive to produce, and natural phenomena guarantee a certain proportion of wastage in the crop that may go entirely unused if not fed to livestock. Women are intuitively choosing their best option by converting this feed into meat for postponed consumption and/or sale.

Men's productive contribution to animals is the time they invest in growing corn. However, corn is a delicate crop, and a successful harvest depends on a large number of variables, such as rainfall and local pests. Corn production, although not considered to be as intensive as raised-field agriculture, is labor intensive; rent for land is minimal ($.10 per *mecate* [506 m^2]), and wages for hired labor are negligible. Corn yields are typically 1½ *cargas* (68 kg approximately) per *mecate* but of this, 25% may be lost to birds, raccoons, drought, or disease. Additional spoilage often takes place during storage when rats, weevils, and other vermin attack the crop. This *desperdicio* (spoiled, blighted portion) is not saleable but ideally suited for animal consumption.

RETURNS FROM A PIG

Women realize their highest return from a pig that is sold *al bruto* (alive) (Figure 3). Unless an emergency arises, pigs are usually sold when they weigh 45–55 kg. At $.94/kg, this amounts to the tidy sum of $42.50 to $52.00 or more. When pigs are butchered, villagers are obligated to participate in ritual exchanges of meat, which reduces their profit by $7.50 to $10.00 as the case may be. This is not a real loss, however, for recipients of meat are obligated to return meat for meat when they, in turn, slaughter their animals.

Lard is another important product yielded in addition to meat. Local pigs are lard-type animals, and a fattened *capado* 'barrow' weighing 63 kg will yield approximately 14.5 kg of *manteca* 'lard'. Lard is the preferred cooking fat and must, otherwise, be purchased at $.73/kg.

The money from pig sales is used to purchase other commodities which cannot be produced by the household, such as coffee ($1.20/170 g),[3] flour ($.18/kg), onions ($.25/kg), or a whole month of grocery bills ($40.00 approximately) in the case of a large pig. Women's or children's needs for shoes, dress material, and used school books can be met with pig-sale money. Other small pigs, or corn to feed remaining pigs, may be purchased to keep the pig cycle going. Women also settle medical bills or repay money borrowed from women neighbors with this income.

Women use pig sales to make long-term investments in the form of luxury status items for themselves and their children; gold teeth, necklaces, earrings, and bracelets are common purchases of this kind. Their trips across the border to buy these prestigious items and to visit relatives are funded by pig sales. Men benefit from pig sales in that they are the recipients of purchased food items,

[3]This is equivalent to a 6-oz jar. Prices quoted are approximations and vary regionally.

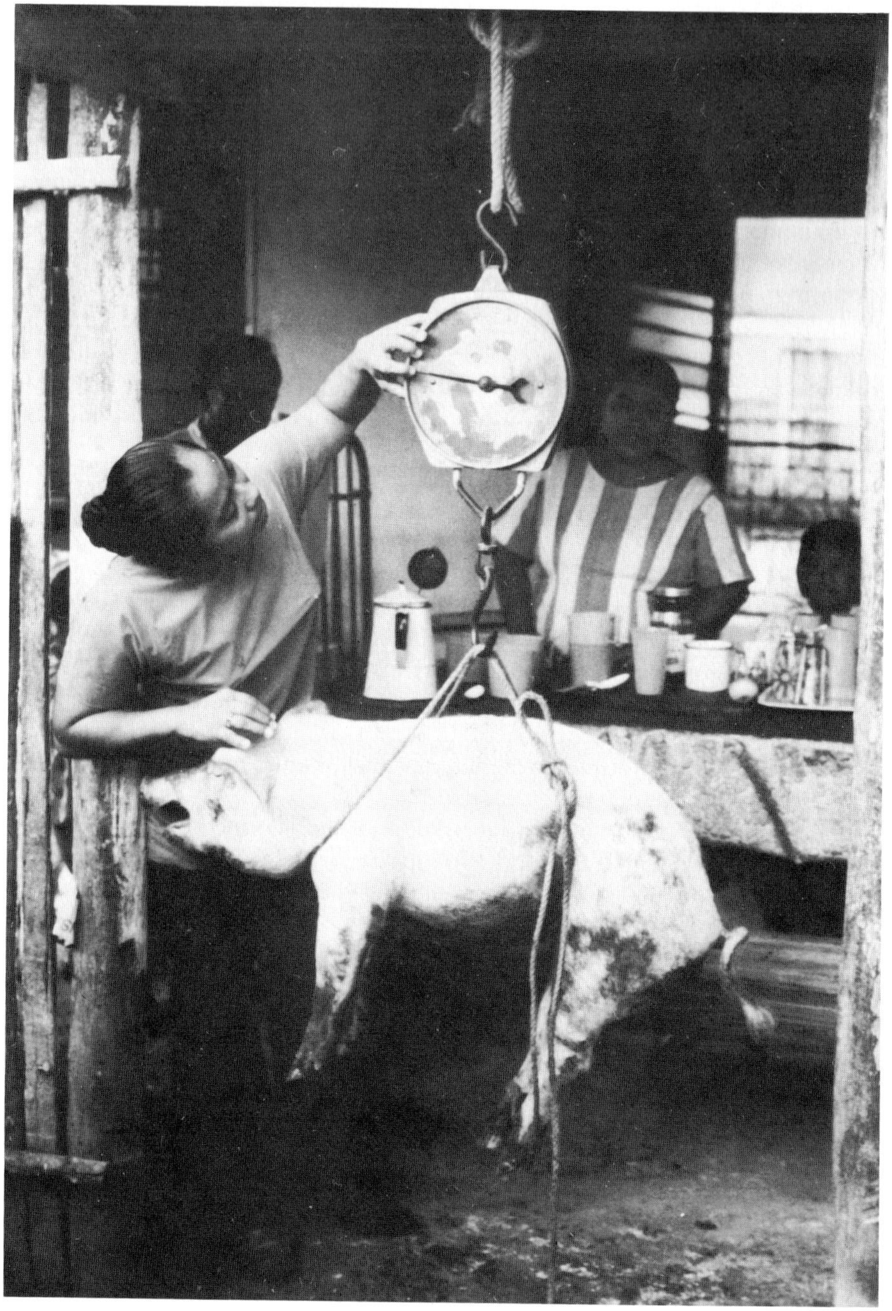

FIGURE 3. *The sale of a live pig.*

and their wives occasionally buy them tobacco or corn seed for planting with these funds.

RETURNS FROM OTHER LIVESTOCK

Women realize smaller returns from the sale of other livestock; however, the input is also smaller. Turkeys are not sold since they are mainly used in ceremonies and only yield \$.55/kg at best. Chickens sell for \$.80/kg and eggs for \$.04 each, and some women specialize in poultry production by raising large flocks of several dozen birds and selling chickens and eggs on a small but constant scale. Women use chicken eggs as everyday currency in villages—an egg being proffered for whatever small item a women wants. In much the same way, women in the United States during the Depression supplemented the family income by selling eggs. In the north, ducks are not sold and are being phased out of production because they are hard to raise and difficult to sell. Picking the feathers to prepare ducks for the table is a dreadful task that women say they hate. In the lowland villages of southern Belize, ducks are still very plentiful, and it is turkeys that are rare. Indeed, ducks fulfill all functions that turkeys serve in the north, being retained exclusively for household use.

THE BARTER SYSTEM

Although more common 20 years ago, pig meat, or a small pig, is still bartered for such goods as *palos* 'wooden posts', house roof materials, cooked stews, a bed (several small pigs in this case!) and other items. Services—for example, roof mending, crop planting, babysitting, truck rides, or the loan of a scale—may also be exchanged for pieces of meat. As previously stated, meat is traded for meat in reciprocal village exchanges that operate rather like loans, one family giving meat one week on condition that a similar portion of meat is repaid at a later date. If this is not forthcoming, then that family may be excluded from the system in the future.

In southern Belize, women reward men for their labor through feasts, not unlike the feeding of neighborhood threshing crews on U.S. farms before widespread use of the combine. Dinners are commonly given for *mozos* 'male work groups' who cooperate to help a man plant or *tumbar* 'clean' his fields. Men may also join forces to build a relative's house or mend his roof. A man's wage labor costs \$2.50/day, and perhaps 20 men spend a full day clearing a man's field.

The farmer's wife provides meat sufficient for the group. Seven turkeys or ducks, a few chickens, or a small pig will be needed for an average group of 10 to 12 men. Women also invest considerable time preparing and cooking the meat. Five or six wives and daughters will help clean and prepare the fowl for *escabeche* (onion–pepper stew), or stew a pig to be eaten with tortillas. Women spend all day in this activity, rising at dawn to boil water and butcher animals and staying up until the last man has finished his supper. When the *mozo* moves on to the next man's field, it is another wife's turn to provide the feast. The average woman provides four such dinners a year.

THE RISK FACTOR IN LIVESTOCK PRODUCTION

Livestock production is not a venture entirely without risk. Severe drought or hurricanes may destroy the corn crop completely, forcing women to purchase expensive feed or to butcher pigs en masse. Disease is certainly a risk in rearing all animals. Chickens are afflicted with a number of diseases such as fowl typhoid, Marek's disease, and chicken pox. Normally the entire flock is at risk. Amongst other hazards pigs are subject to a cyclical disease, locally called *la peste,* which is apparently a form of hog cholera. Outbreaks occur irregularly every year in one area or another, often due to the illicit traffic in pigs, which are ferried surreptitiously across the river in dugout canoes. This disease results in 100% mortality in nonimmune pigs, but women face this unavoidable hazard philosophically. Indeed, it is not a complete write-off, because the government has a compensation scheme to repay villagers whose suspect animals have been slaughtered.

Contemporary Festivals

Conspicuous consumption of meat marks all important life-cycle events in the Maya Lowlands as it does in other parts of the world. Livestock provide meat for private family ceremonies which enhance household solidarity and status. Meat for feasts given at public festivals, dances, and soccer games, where village prestige, agricultural prosperity, or community welfare are at stake, is also produced by women. These major festivals necessitate a large investment of livestock.

It is the custom to decide the fate of a particular pig or turkey from the moment it is born. A pig may be set aside to fatten for Christmas tamales, while another may be reserved to make *pib*[4] for a daughter's upcoming feast day. Turkeys might be designated for a wedding to make *relleno* (a black stew cooked with pork meat and eggs) or to cook *escabeche* to feed relatives who attend a child's baptism.

FAMILY CELEBRATIONS

Pigs, turkeys, or chickens are used for family feasts, depending upon the importance of the occasion and the number of people attending. Pig or turkey meat is most common for baptism, confirmation, Christmas, and wedding feasts. Three turkeys may be slaughtered and cooked for a large confirmation gathering. As many as 50 chickens can be used in addition to turkeys for wedding and Christmas feasts when more than 100 people are to be fed, including friends from out of town. Female kin from both sides provide poultry and labor in the event of a large wedding.

[4]*Pib* is a dish made from chunks of pork, that are smeared with red seasoning, covered with banana leaves, and roasted in the ground.

Chickens are customarily served at birthdays and wakes, although a small pig may be substituted in place of chicken for a birthday meal. Two meals are served after a villager dies. The first, three days after the death, is a rice with cinnamon dish, and the second, nine days after the death, is a turkey or chicken stew.

Finados 'day of the dead' is celebrated in November. Prayers are said for dead relatives and people who come to share family prayers are fed either *escabeche, relleno,* or tamales. Five chickens or more are often cooked for this gathering.

The most important family feast is given for the patron saint of the household. Some families have their own saints who offer protection and family security. Women pray to their saints at altars in their houses if sickness or misfortune strikes. A pig is butchered and roasted, and food is shared with participants at the family thanksgiving held to honor the saint.

VILLAGE FESTIVALS

The festival of *Señor de Esquipulas* is celebrated in January during the slack season before planting begins to ensure a good harvest. A 9-day novena is recited and homemade sweets are distributed. *Relleno* is served on the tenth day; a plate is sent to each family participating in the ritual.

Each village has its *patrón* 'patron saint' who is thought to be in charge of village well-being and prosperity. *Pib* is cooked and the pig's head is decorated with ribbons and placed on a platter with flags. A procession forms during which a man dances with the platter while another man teases and angers him. A dance may be held, and women sell pig meat to purchase rum and Coke for the celebrants. People may be charged $.75 admission to help defray costs.

An informal and seasonal soccer game forms the social focus of the village every other Sunday in summer. Young men compete vigorously and everyone gathers to watch. It is the village's obligation to provide the visiting players with a meal. Women supply poultry to make tamales or perhaps a stew, which they donate or sell to the visitors to make some cash.

Personal Independence and Family Security

Livestock production provides women with personal independence and their families with a measure of economic security. In an emergency, animals provide women with the food or money necessary to sustain the family. Village women cannot amass even modest sums of money, and conventional banks are not utilized. Without their livestock women would be dependent on their husbands or their own kin, both of whom have prior commitments for their financial resources. Village animals belong to the women because they invest their time and skill to produce them.

The multipurpose pig is the most valuable animal in the backyard and is described variously as *una alcancía* 'a larder or savings account', or *dinero que anda* 'walking money'. This large "piggy bank" keeps the woman's "savings" intact until needed because small amounts cannot be withdrawn little by little!

A pig is a prized possession in northern Belize as it is elsewhere in the world for the poor and hungry. Women demonstrate high regard for their animals, often drawing a comparison between pigs and children: "pigs give money; children give people trouble." Women, who are on the front line when it comes to satisfying hungry dependents, be it children or livestock, say "everything is always hungry." Indeed, most of the activity in the house and yard centers around "hunting and gathering," with children constantly clamoring for handouts.

The pig is afforded privileges denied other livestock, which attests to its importance in the backyard hierarchy. Favorites, usually given names and special tidbits, are permitted to sleep in the kitchen when children, dogs, and poultry are booted out. People even tell tales about their pigs, exalting their bravery or their beauty and productivity. This emotional attachment to their animals goes beyond the utilitarian, although when the time comes for butchering, the animal is dispatched without sentiment.

Women as Entrepreneurs

THE CASH CROP UPHEAVAL

The introduction of sugar cane in the early 1970s caused a dramatic change in village life in northern Belize. This attractive and valuable cash crop competed with corn for land and labor and won temporarily. In 1973, there was a rapid increase in the world price of sugar due to widespread crop failures in the sugar beet harvest elsewhere. The price of cane in northern Belize rose from $6.50 a ton in 1973 to $28.00 in 1975, and fierce competition for cane licenses, required by the sugar processing factory, began. Pressure on land intensified, and *milpas* 'corn fields' crept ever closer to villages. Corn became a scarce commodity.

The rising price of corn threatened women's livestock production. The going price for good corn increased from $2.50 a *carga* in 1972 to $14.50 in 1975. Even spoiled corn could be sold for a fourth of the price. This inflationary situation was mirrored in the price of all basic food commodities. Without sufficient corn, women could no longer feed animals on a comparable scale. Pig, turkey, and chicken numbers declined significantly. *¿Por qué queremos animales si no hay maíz?* 'Why do we want animals if there is no corn?'.

NEW LIVESTOCK OPPORTUNITIES

Women are responding to the challenge by exploring new opportunities. Pigs, turkeys, and chickens are nonruminants which compete with people for corn. Women have begun producing other livestock, such as sheep and goats, which are grass-eating ruminants and do not require corn. Children lead these animals out to pasture, tethering them along grass verges and common land.

Caribbean and Lebanese people have popularized curried goat meat to serve at dances, and Maya women have followed suit.

Although Maya men have begun diversifying their cane money into dual-purpose (meat and milk production) cattle, women have not yet entered this field. Most probably, the initial investment is too great and the return too uncertain for women to embark on this venture. Milk is, in any event, not a prized commodity to the Lowland Maya. Male status and prestige may be involved in rearing large animals.

Pigs and chickens have become more expensive commodities due to high corn prices, and sales reflect this increase. Young pigs are currently sold by weight rather than for a fixed price. Chickens and eggs bring in more money, and chickens are being substituted for turkeys in feasts. Some women buy chickens in bulk from the Mennonites and transport them to the village. There they clean and pluck them, and sell them for $1.65/kg to earn a handy profit.

Conclusion

Women are quick to exploit new economic opportunities. The cane bonanza in northern Belize has bought those women able to take advantage of it both the time and money to invest in other activities. Some have started small grocery stores; others operate soft-drink businesses or are in the liquor trade. A few women are cane farmers, using the money from cane to open bank accounts in town. With this money, these women are able to buy commodities such as furniture, clothing, and household necessities, which, in the recent past, were purchased with proceeds from the raising of pigs. Pigs are nonetheless still retained for meat and lard by these wealthy women.

Not all women, however, participate in these business ventures, personal preference and chance playing as large a part as ever in these matters. Yet, the majority of village women continue to rear animals, and it is an indication of the value of livestock that women are loath to abandon the *costumbre* 'habit' of raising animals, in spite of both rising prices and the increasing market orientation of northern Belize. The financial and other benefits from this long-term tradition are such that women actively seek new avenues to develop in livestock production. The Maya women's perception is: "*Solo de los animales vivimos nosotros*" 'we live only by raising animals'.

Acknowledgments

While the focus of my study is on the CONTEMPORARY role of Maya women in livestock production, Mary Pohl, through her ethnohistorical and archaeological approach to this subject, has provided a much needed background against which the contemporary roles can be viewed. Olga Stavrakis and Dennis Puleston provided assistance throughout the project. The Nimis family helped in the preparation of the manuscript for this chapter.

14 Experiences in Traditional Hydraulic Agriculture

Arturo Gómez-Pompa, Hector Luis Morales, Epifanio Jiménez Ávilla, and Julio Jiménez Ávilla

Introduction

LAND and resource planning in tropical regions of the world have been difficult for various reasons, some of which are

1. the lack of knowledge about the tropical environment
2. the scarcity of scientific research on the natural resources of the tropics
3. the lack of systematized information on specific types of land and resource uses for different ecological zones
4. the shortage of scientific and technical personnel trained to work within the existing ecological and socioeconomic systems who could help develop viable solutions for regional planning problems

These deficiencies have led to the introduction of technologies developed in extratropical countries, where ecology as well as socioeconomic and political systems are markedly different from those of tropical nations. Agricultural development programs in many of these countries stress high production at the lowest possible cost.

Consequently, basic food production has notably increased at costs competitive in the world market. This type of agriculture, characterized by the utilization of machinery and chemical inputs throughout the entire agricultural process from planting to final packaging, has spectacularly revolutionized agriculture and is, therefore, referred to as the "green revolution." However, the emphasis on mechanized labor in this type of agriculture has displaced countless agricultural workers to the cities (Dahlberg 1979).

ISBN 0-12-259780-X

In Mexico, this form of agriculture has been eagerly accepted by government, industry, and agronomical academia and has been implemented in large areas of the country that can be irrigated. Agricultural investigation has been oriented at improving this type of agriculture through the development of new crop varieties, fertilizer, and pesticide formulations and by the construction of irrigation works and large hydrologic installations. As a result, there exist within Mexico agricultural areas where the operation and efficiency are very similar to that found in the industrialized countries in which this type of agriculture originated.

However, in spite of the successes of these special areas, we have to admit that unfortunately, it has not been possible to implement this form of agriculture throughout Mexico. Industrialized agriculture does not generate sufficient employment to meet the job demands of the growing rural work force. This means that even though the profits of high-yield, irrigated systems, employing modern agricultural techniques are high, the majority of the population lacks the necessary income to buy the food produced by these systems or the grains imported by our country. An even more serious shortcoming of these systems is that a large portion of the basic grains produced in Mexico is destined for livestock fattening and not for human consumption. Worse still, certain irrigated areas are used to produce livestock forage.

Alongside high-technology, industrialized agriculture, one often finds another type of agriculture known as "traditional rural agriculture." While difficult to define, this form of agriculture exhibits varying degrees of efficiency due to the specific production techniques employed and the limited resources available to the rural farmer. Traditional rural agriculture, which is practiced by the majority of farmers in Mexico, is characterized by the following:

1. It is employed in areas where the main source of water for crop production is precipitation.
2. It is practiced on the worst soil types in the country.
3. Its main objective is the production of food for the family unit, rather than for the marketplace.
4. The industrialized agricultural technologies that have been tried by rural farmers were introduced in a disorderly, random fashion, and little effort was made to inform rural farmers about the advantages and disadvantages of these new methods.
5. Traditional agricultural techniques are based on centuries of empirical experimentation and knowledge.
6. Traditional rural agriculture is extraordinarily diverse, both in the number of species cultivated per unit area and in the techniques used for production.
7. The various techniques used evolved independently over many centuries in different regions of the country and among different ethnic groups. In comparison, the methods of industrialized agriculture are similar wherever the system is employed.

Considering that both types of agriculture presently cooccur in Mexico, our country today is faced with the problem of defining the best strategy for developing its agricultural resources. Obviously, this problem is aggravated by a rapidly growing population and its need for food and other agricultural products, that, presently, cannot be satisfied by the combined production of traditional and industrialized agriculture.

Several decades ago, a decision was made to introduce industrialized agriculture through government-sponsored programs into several tropical areas in southeastern Mexico. Unfortunately, many of these programs, due to many of the reasons already discussed, were not as successful as had been hoped (Barkin 1978).

In addition, we might add that due to environmental characteristics, the soils found in a hot, humid climate are quite different from those found in a temperate one. Furthermore, because of the great biological diversity of the tropics, industrialized agricultural systems must be able to cope with new diseases and insect infestations, but thus far, no adequate and efficient control techniques have been developed.

However, in spite of the problems and failures that have occurred, this type of agriculture continues to be introduced into tropical areas in the hope that scientific and technological advancements will eventually solve these problems. Nevertheless, the problem of creating jobs for millions of rural workers will still remain.

As a result of this policy, enormous areas of tropical forest have been destroyed. Later, these areas often are abandoned as the production from intensive agriculture declines. Forest land clearing, cultivation, and abandonment indirectly result in increased erosion and in the contamination of waterways by fertilizers and biocides, which are applied in large amounts to increase the productivity of tropical soils.

The current solution for using these large areas, once covered by lush tropical forest, is to turn them into grasslands for extensive cattle grazing. However, numerous studies have documented the inefficiency of such grazing systems from ecological, economic, and social points of view.

The Balancán–Tenosique Plan

The modern tropical *chinampas* story began with an invitation to study the biotic resources of the Balancán–Tenosique region in the state of Tabasco. We were invited to participate in a study aimed at formulating an ecologically sound development strategy for the area. The Balancán–Tenosique Plan was one of many plans instituted for the development of agriculture and animal husbandry in the hot humid tropics of Mexico.

Our research involved studies on the community types, flora, vegetation, climate, and soils of the region (INIREB 1976). Based on these investigations we hoped to make suggestions for ways to reorient the plan.

One fact to remember is that the Plan had already been underway for several years when we were invited to participate. By this time, most of the economically valuable forest species had been harvested, the remaining vegetation had been clear-cut, and the search for appropriate agricultural technologies for the region had not been successful.

Considering the past history of the area and the results of our various research projects, we recommended that a large part of the area should be reforested using several species of useful native trees. One species, which had been abundant in the zone and which we recommended, was the *ramón* (*Brosimum alicastrum*). Our studies had demonstrated its adaptability to a variety of soils and climates, its rapid growth, the utility of its leaves for forage and its fruits, particularly the seeds, for human and animal food, as well as the commercial potential of its wood (Pardo and Sánchez 1977). In other words, we suggested that the area should be reforested and used for agrosilviculture. It was precisely this suggestion that led to more studies on *B. alicastrum* as we began to recognize its ecological and economic importance.

Researchers at our institute conducted several studies to learn more about the distribution of *B. alicastrum* and to verify the nutritional value of its seed and the characteristics of its wood. The results of these studies were very encouraging, and we began to promote the dissemination of information about the advantages of this species—especially its potential as a species to be used in reforestation.

We even began to urge the commercialization of its seed. Today, partly through the efforts of our investigators, nurseries and groves of *B. alicastrum* may be found in many states of the republic. We hope that in the near future it will once again be an important tree of the Mexican tropics. To further this goal, several studies are underway on varietal selection, population dynamics, predation, and the taxonomy of *B. alicastrum.* Without a doubt, Dennis Puleston's work on this species was an inspiration and great stimulus to our studies (Puleston 1968).

Surprisingly, our conclusions on the best way to undertake tropical silviculture, are precisely those which were surely discovered by our ancestors in Mesoamerica. I am convinced that *B. alicastrum* was a protected species, selected and cultivated by the ancient cultures. In one study (Barrera *et al.* 1977), we point out that *B. alicastrum,* like many other fruit trees presently dominant in the forests of humid tropical Mexico, was linked to agriculture, family gardens, and to the profound knowledge of the characteristics of the species these ancient cultures protected. Through this process of protective management, the highly productive varieties we have today were selected. It is not surprising that cultures as advanced as those that domesticated beans, chile, squash, cacao, corn and other plants were also capable, using the same techniques, of domesticating tree species with economic value. The Maya, in fact, practiced a mixed tropical agrosilviculture that even today does not exist in any other tropical country.

Returning to the Balancán–Tenosique Plan, agricultural recommendations for this devastated region were also needed. We found that a large part of the area was covered by swamps (Lot *et al.* 1976), in spite of the major drainage works undertaken there.

The area remained inhospitable, unproductive, and neglected. There appeared to be mainly two agricultural alternatives for this area: to raise crops either on small areas of alluvial soils during the flood-free period or on some of the recently drained swamp soils. After examining the area and talking to local farmers, it was apparent that large-scale cultivation on these soil types was feasible but the amount of such land was rather small. This left us with the option of suggesting uses for the swamp itself. A study of the local fauna was conducted to discover its potential for development (Reyes 1978). In addition, samples of aquatic vegetation, water, and mud from the swamps were analyzed (Quiroz 1976). These data on the ecology of the swamps in the Balancán–Tenosique region led us to believe that experimental chinampas could be established in the area for the following reasons (Gómez-Pompa and Venegas 1976):

1. Various genera, and even species, of aquatic plants found in the swamps were also found in the chinampas of Mixquic, near Mexico City (Venegas 1978).
2. Furthermore, analysis of the mud indicated that it had several characteristics in common with the mud from the canals in Mixquic and, thus, could be used in the first phase of chinampa agriculture, the construction of seedling beds.

Given the large area covered by the swamps and the availability of funding from the Federal government, we felt that a chinampa experiment would be well worth our efforts.

Several experimental chinampas were built in early 1976 in a swampy area drained by the San Pedro River (Figures 1 and 2). The results of this project are discussed by Gómez-Pompa (1978) and Gómez-Pompa *et al.* (1976), but I would like to emphasize here that a *chinampero* 'a chinampa farmer' from Xochimilco contracted especially for this project was in complete charge of site selection and chinampa construction, and chose which crops to plant.

The idea of building chinampas in the tropics seemed reasonable from several points of view:

1. In a few months the results of the experiment were visible (Figure 3) in the form of harvestable *Manihot,* radishes, lettuce, cabbage, squash, rice, corn, watermelon, alfalfa, different varieties of chile, carrot, turnip, melon, tomato, cucumber, coriander, parsley, swiss chard, beans and others.
2. The work was done using manual farm labor (Table 1). This meant that the technique was appropriate for swampy areas since resident landless farmers could supply the labor needed.
3. The canals could be used to raise animals (fish and turtles) for human consumption.

FIGURE 1. *For the construction of the chinampas in San Pedro, alternate layers of mud and plant materials (*Typha *mainly) were used.*

FIGURE 2. *The vegetation adjacent to the swamp provided the plant materials for the chinampa construction.*

FIGURE 3. *Several crops were produced only a few weeks after initiation of the work.*

Table 1
Comparative Data on the Work Involved in the Construction of Two Chinampas Using Manual Labor

Site	Initial water depth (cm)	Initial height of the soil above the water level after construction (cm)	Width of the canals (m)	Number of layers of mud and organic matter used (mainly *Typha*)	Man hours to construct (100 m^2)
San Pedro Balancán, Tabasco (*Typha* swamp)	20	20	1	3 + 2	210
La Mancha, Veracruz (*Typha* swamp)	15	40	2	3 + 2	320

4. Most importantly, the experiment could demonstrate a new technique for making swamps agriculturally productive. Up to this time, complete drainage was the most common way to bring swampy areas into agricultural production.

In a few months, news about the successful transference of an indigenous agricultural technique from the altiplano of Mexico to the humid tropics had spread throughout the region, and also, via the press, to distant organizations (PIMSA 1976). In this way, the experiment became known in ecological and agronomic institutions throughout Mexico. A short time after the presentation of the initial results, the chinampas of San Pedro Balancán (although the extent of the cultivated area was only 1,276 m^2) were perhaps the experimental agricultural sites most visited by technicians, farmers, and professors, not only from the state of Tabasco, but also from other parts of Mexico and abroad.

The most important outcome of our study was that the idea of chinampa agriculture spread and was further tested not only by our own investigators, but also by other investigators, farmers, and government organizations.

A discussion, in more or less chronological order, of the more outstanding experiments that were begun after our San Pedro study and the present status of these investigations follows.

Experiment in El Espino, Tabasco

The officials of the Secretaría de Recursos Hidráulicos, the organization that had financed the San Pedro study, felt that the importance of our findings, combined with the inaccessibility of the San Pedro chinampas, made it desirable to conduct a similar study closer to the capital of Tabasco, Villahermosa. There, demonstration chinampas could be seen by high-level officials, who frequently visit the city, as well as by the then presidential candidate, who was scheduled to campaign in the area. An experiment, employing the same methodology as was used in San Pedro, was conducted in a place called El Espino near the city of Villahermosa. Since the study had to be completed quickly with whatever information was available locally, chinampa raising began immediately in August 1976. We decided, based on information from local farmers, that the height of the chinampas should be several centimeters higher than the maximum flood height expected for that year. The experiment was carried out by many of the same people who had worked on the San Pedro chinampas. Nursery beds were started, but precisely at the time when the seedlings were ready to be transplanted to permanent chinampa plots, an exceptionally severe cyclone occurred. It inundated a large part of the low sections of Villahermosa as well as the chinampas, which had just been completed after a few weeks of intensive labor. The experiment at El Espino attracted the attention of government officials and technicians who had been following the progress of the project, some of whom were enthusiastic supporters as well as others who were more skeptical. Unfortunately, at the same time that the disaster occurred, the term of President Luis Echeverría ended and, with it, financing for the chinampa project at the Instituto de Investigaciones sobre Recursos Bióticos (INIREB) in Tabasco. Consequently, we were not able to repeat the experiment at El Espino.

The unsuccessful experiment at El Espino was documented by a social scientist (Maier 1979), who had been contracted by the Secretaría de Recursos Hidráulicos to evaluate the possible socioeconomic impact of large-scale chinampa agriculture in the Villahermosa area. Unfortunately, her report focused mainly on the aborted experiment at El Espino, missing the more important issue of chinampa agriculture as a new alternative for utilizing the tropical swamps.

The College of Tropical Agriculture

The director of the College of Tropical Agriculture in Cárdenas, Tabasco, encouraged by our efforts in San Pedro, decided to undertake a joint study with us in the swamps near the school. His idea was to use the experimental chinampas as a teaching model for young agronomists specializing in tropical agriculture. According to an agreement between INIREB and the director of the college, one of our chinamperos was commissioned to work with professors of the college in selecting an experimental chinampa site. Since the goal of this experiment was different from that of our previous experiments we employed a tractor to aid in the chinampa raising process. However, during the construction of the chinampas, bad weather struck again, and we were forced to suspend work until conditions improved. Fortunately, during our work there, we encountered great enthusiasm on the part of two of the professors, Dr. S. Gliessman and Dr. R. García, who had followed our different experiments closely and understood the importance of the agricultural technique we were promoting. The chinampas in Cárdenas, like those in San Pedro and El Espino, were visited by investigators from various institutes as well as by government officials and farmers. Fortunately, the experiment begun at the college, though suspended for a while, was later continued by professors of the college (Gliessman *et al.* 1978). They developed very imaginative designs to experiment with diversified agricultural production units in which the chinampa system formed an integral part.

The Cultural Institute of Nacajuca

The Cultural Institute of Nacajuca, a church-administered private organization, is located in Nacajuca, a town near Villahermosa. Its objective is to give poor young farmers training in agricultural and animal husbandry techniques. Having read and heard about our chinampa experiments, the director of the institute, Mother Muriel, and one of the professors, Ramiro Sánchez, invited one of our chinamperos to visit the institute and explore the possibility of setting up a chinampa experiment in the swamps nearby with some of their students. Our technician spent time at the institute teaching the students the principles of the chinampa technique. As a result, chinampas were raised at the Cultural Institute of Nacajuca. Through the work and enthusiam of Mother Muriel, Professor Ramiro, and their students, these chinampas grew in size and attracted the attention of various people, including the governor, who had already had contact with our chinampa experiments in San Pedro when he was the Secretario de Recursos Hidráulicos. When he visited the Institute at Nacajuca and saw the chinampas and the enthusiasm of the students and professors, he offered his complete support to expand the project. He loaned them a dredge to open more canals and thus enlarge the experimental area. Governor Rovirosa also told them about the fish culture tanks he had seen during his recent visit to China and suggested that they should also experiment with this technology. Following his suggestion, the institute began work combining both types of production techniques—chinampas with canals and fish culture tanks with crops planted along the edges. These experiments continue today at the Institute in Nacajuca, and as a result, many young farmers are being trained to use these agricultural methods.

The Camellones Chontales

Governor Rovirosa, cognizant of the potential advantages of constructing chinampas in the swamps of Tabasco and following suggestions made in the reports on our studies in San Pedro and El Espino, decided to begin an extensive program using all the modern engineering techniques available. The region where the Cultural Institute of Nacajuca is located, and which is inhabited by the Chontal Indians, was selected as the construction site. The Instituto Nacional Indigenista of Tabasco, headed by an energetic sociologist, Lic. Andrés López Obrador, undertook the program, which was subsequently funded by the federal government (López Obrador 1978). Dredges were brought in, and in a relatively short time, 40 ha were raised. By now 100 ha should be completed. The large platforms (Figure 4), 20 × 100 m, were raised much to the surprise of the Chontal Indians who will use this new land for agricultural production (Figure 5). The Camellones Chontales program thus solved two problems at the same time. It provided agricultural land for the Chontals and also tested this method of bringing swamplands into agricultural production on a large scale.

Curiously, the word chinampa was never mentioned in connection with the Camellones Chontales program of the Instituto Nacional Indigenista. Nevertheless, it is obvious that this project was based on the chinampa technology. In any case, the project is in full operation and apparently is successful, both from the point of view of yield as well as in the number of species cultivated on these large platforms.

However, there have been problems with the program. A dredge cannot

FIGURE 4. *The use of a dredge for the Camellones Chontales speeded the construction process of large raised fields.*

FIGURE 5. *View of the Camellones at a very early construction stage.*

select which sediments it raises from the swamp bottom. Often clays of low fertility and organic sediments that were not nutrient-rich wound up on the top of the platforms. Several months following the initiation of the program, our institute was asked to evaluate the work and to suggest how the project could be improved. The results of our studies (Morales *et al.* 1978) led us to suggest a new design for the platforms and a management regime for the organic matter and the aquacultural projects. We also suggested that the farmers who were ultimately going to use the platforms should be more involved in the process of platform construction and crop selection. Some of our suggestions were adopted, others were not.

Although it is too soon to predict the final outcome of this program, we can say that it is in operation today, and that plans are being made to construct more *camellones* in other areas of the state of Tabasco.

The Lagoon of Tecocomulco

An investigator and a collaborator from our institute studying the aquatic vegetation of a high-altitude lake (2,500 m above sea level) in the state of Hidalgo (Lot and Novelo 1978), were approached by local fisherman and farmers in 1977. They asked for our suggestions as to how they could better use their available natural resources, and how they could save the lake from a proposed drainage project. Up to that time, the lagoon had been used primarily for fishing and occasionally for duck hunting by sportsmen. Since one of the investigators was familiar with chinampa technology, he prepared a slide presentation about chinampas and showed it to the local farmers. They expressed great interest in the chinampa technique, particularly since there were no vegetable gardens in the area, and the industrial city of Sahagún was nearby. They decided to try a pilot chinampa project to see if this technique was possible in their area. We suggested that they construct one or two experimental chinampas for agriculture and aquaculture (Figure 6) and use the results from these to plan a larger project.

At their own expense, they hired a chinampero from Mixquic to help them raise the chinampas and advise them about cultivation. Local officials supported the project, and within a few months, they began to see the favorable results of high vegetable yields, which were rapidly sold locally. Soon additional farmers raised new chinampas; in a relatively short period of time, a large area was under cultivation, and the canals were planted with fish and vegetables, which were consumed locally as well as sold in Ciudad Sahagún. Later, competition led them to form a cooperative to sell the produce in Sahagún. In fact, a large part of the vegetables eaten by the workers of Sahagún come from the chinampas of Tecocomulco.

These chinampas are in operation today and investigators from our institute continue to study the lagoon, the canals, and the agricultural production of the chinampas and to offer assistance and advice to the local farmers.

FIGURE 6. *In Tecocomulco, Hidalgo, aquaculture in the canals was an important aspect of the chinampa development project.*

Chinampas of Laguna de La Mancha

Given the need for more information about chinampas, we decided to raise experimental chinampas (Figure 7) in a swampy area within our biological field station, El Morro de La Mancha (Novelo 1978), a salt water lagoon north of the city of Veracruz. This type of swamp, located near a body of salt water, is common in the state of Veracruz. A small experimental chinampa in this area would not only serve as a teaching center for the dissemination of this methodology in the coastal region, but also would provide our investigators with a site, near our laboratories, in which to carry out more basic studies on the ecology of chinampas. This experiment has been quite important since it has provided useful information which can be employed in other projects utilizing the chinampa technology. Small-scale scientific investigations on nutrient cycling, organic productivity, and chinampa efficiency have been conducted at El Morro de La Mancha, and the station is visited by groups of students, professors, farmers, and investigators who conduct various types of research in the region, including studies on chinampa agriculture.

Based on our work at El Morro de La Mancha, different aspects of chinampa technology are being tested in various communities throughout the state. These studies form part of a larger project within our institute to develop a model for an integrated self-sufficient farm.

FIGURE 7. *Chinampas in the La Mancha lagoon region of Veracruz. These are research educational units constructed in our biological station.*

Conclusion

These are the most outstanding efforts in the modern use of chinampa techniques; other efforts in different parts of Mexico are now underway. In the future, our institute will continue teaching, promoting, and disseminating intensive traditional hydroagricultural techniques, thereby trying to improve the use of these resources and the condition of life in farm communities with limited economic resources. Frequently, we receive requests for technical assistance from people living in areas in which we have conducted studies as well as from others who have learned of our projects from other sources. These people want to know how to manage their natural resources using the only capital they possess: human labor.

Acknowledgments

This work is a contribution to the Man and the Biosphere Program of UNESCO (MAB). We wish to acknowledge the following organizations for their financial support: UNESCO, the government of the State of Tabasco, the government of the State of Veracruz, the former Secretaría de Recursos Hidráulicos, and the Secretaría de Educación Pública. We wish to express our gratitude to Dr. Joann Roskoski for the English translation of the manuscript. Our deepest appreciation is to the campesinos of the swamplands who worked to raise the experimental chinampas.

References

Barkin, A.
1978 Desarrollo regional y reorganización campesina. In *La Chontalpa como Reflejo del Problema Agropecuario Mexicano.* México D.F., Editorial Nueva Imagen.

Barrera Marín, A., A. Gómez-Pompa, and C. Vázquez Yanes
1977 El manejo de la selva por los Mayas. *Biótica* 2(2):47–60. Xalapa, Veracruz.

Dahlberg, K. A.
1979 *Beyond the Green Revolution.* New York, Plenum Press.

Gómez-Pompa, A.
1978 Vino nuevo en odre viejo. *Mazingira* 5:49–55. London, Pergamon Press.

Gómez-Pompa, A., and R. Venegas
1976 La chinampa tropical. *INIREB Informa* 5:1–4. Xalapa, Instituto de Investigaciones sobre Recursos Bióticos.

Gómez-Pompa, A., E. Jiménez, A. Orozco, and J. Jiménez.
1976 La chinampa tropical. In *Estudio Ecológico de la Región de Balancán–Tenosique.* Xalapa, Veracruz, Informes del Instituto de Investigaciones sobre Recursos Bióticos.

Gliessman, S., R. García, and M. Amador
1978 *Módulo de Producción Diversificada: Un Agroecosistema de Producción Sostenida para el Trópico Húmedo de México.* Cárdenas, Tabasco, Colegio Superior de Agricultura Tropical.

Instituto de Investigaciones sobre Recursos Bióticos (INIREB)
1976 *Estudio Ecológico de la Zona de Balancán–Tenosique.* Xalapa, Veracruz, Informes del Instituto de Investigaciones sobre Recursos Bióticos.

López Obrador, A. *et al.*
1978 Camellones chontales: Proyecto para la explotación de zonas pantanosas. *Proyecto Coplamar* 2:1–176, México, Instituto Nacional Indigenista.

Lot, A., F. Menéndez, A. Novelo, J. I. Calzada, and F. J. Saldívar
1976 La vegetación de la primera etapa de Balancán–Tenosique. In *Estudio Ecológico de la Zona Balancán–Tenosique, Tabasco.* Xalapa, Veracruz, Informes del Instituto de Investigaciones sobre Recursos Bióticos.

Lot, A. and A. Novelo
1978 Laguna de Tecocomulco, Hidalgo. *Guías Botánicas de Excursiones en México.* México, Sociedad Botánica de México.

Maier, E.
1979 *Chinampa Tropical: Una Primera Evaluación.* México, Centro de Ecodesarrollo.

Morales, H. L. *et al.*
1978 *Estudio Ecológico y del Medio Ambiente en los Camellones Chontales de Nacajuca, Tabasco.* Xalapa, Veracruz, Informes del Instituto de Investigaciones sobre Recursos Bióticos.

Novelo, A.
1978 La vegetación de le estación biológica El Morro de La Mancha, Veracruz. *Biótica* 3(1):9–23. Xalapa, Veracruz.

Pardo, E., and C. Sánchez
1977 *Brosimum alicastrum* (ramón, capomo, ojite, ojoche), recurso silvestre tropical desaprovechado. *Cuaderno de Divulgación del Instituto de Investigaciones sobre Recursos Bióticos.* Xalapa, Veracruz.

PIMSA
1976 Se harán producir los pántanos. *Diario de Xalapa,* June 5, Xalapa, Veracruz. (The same news appeared in several newspapers of Mexico).

Puleston, D. E.
1968 Brosimum alicastrum *as a subsistence alternative for the classic Maya of the central southern lowlands.* Unpublished M.A. Thesis, Department of Anthropology, Univ. of Pennsylvania.

Quiroz, A.
1976 Los suelos de la región Balancán–Tenosique, Tabasco y su relación con la vegetación. In *Estudio Ecológico de la Zona de Balancán–Tenosique Tabasco.* Xalapa, Veracruz. Informes del Instituto de Investigaciones sobre Recursos Bióticos. (Also published as a Thesis, School of Sciences, Universidad Nacional Autónoma de México, 1977).
Reyes, C. P.
1978 La fauna silvestre en el plan Balancán–Tenosique. *Cuadernos de Divulgación del Instituto de Investigaciones sobre Recursos Bióticos.* Xalapa, Veracruz.
Venegas, R.
1978 Las chinampas de Mixquic. Thesis., School of Sciences, Universidad Nacional Autónoma de México, México.

V
Overview

15

Maya Subsistence: A Commentary

George A. Collier

THERE is a certain sensuous pleasure to be had in the study of agriculture, a pleasure we shared for three days in Minnesota. There, and in the pages of this volume, we have been cultivating images of Maya farming so vivid that we can all but feel them. Payson Sheets' fossil seedlings are temptingly pluckable; the furrows of his cornfields undulate under foot. In the same vein, we feel empathetically with our soles the remains of raised fields as Denny Puleston, Alfred Siemens, or David Freidel trudge or slog through them. We are all awash in the sensations of these physical features, even when we view them remotely as through Peter Harrison's views from above.

From these virtually tangible experiential understandings of Maya agriculture, we harvest more than a kernel of truth, but it is not the whole truth. Agriculture is more than corn and other cultigens in fields razed or raised. It also entails a social system for deploying human labor and its product. Our problem is that whereas the physical features of Maya agriculture seem nearly within our grasp, how the Maya organized themselves in relation to agriculture tends to elude us. Our understanding is as incomplete as our comprehension of Raymond Matheny's highland walk-in wells would be if we ignored how settlement creates a catchment around them. We center our attention on Maya fields and cultigens as though they were at the heart of Maya social systems, as recent scholarship suggests. But in doing so we must not disregard social determinants of Maya agriculture.

The authors have done much to call attention to how social systemic factors affect tropical agriculture in the Maya area at present, or have done so in the recent past. Arturo Gómez-Pompa lucidly depicted how commercial agribusiness, particularly the ranching of cattle for export to the world market, devastates contemporary tropical agriculture. He showed us the power shared by vested economic interests, key political officials, and the state for deciding whether projects of experimental tropical agriculture are to succeed or fail. Grant Jones pleaded for recognition of how broad networks of political alliance and trade determined the essential characteristics of agriculture in the Colonial-era Petén.

ISBN 0-12-259780-X

Discussions at Minnesota also highlighted the need for us to think about tropical agriculture and the poverty of today's tropical peasantries at this systemic level. Should we not attribute poverty to the need for peasantries to produce for sale rather than for subsistence because of their dependence on the market for goods no longer available locally? Must we not examine the displacement of human subsistence for that of herbivores and omnivores, such as cows and pigs, that are destined for others' dinner plates? In all these instances we have sensed how political economy encompasses and penetrates agricultural hinterlands.

Equally important, though very difficult to achieve, is an appreciation of how the Maya organized production at a level somewhere above the field and below the state and marketplace. For example, ritual scheduling could have entered into regulating competition over intensely cultivated farmlands. Similarly, Joyce Marcus's depiction of the patterned utilization of diverse cultigens from the sixteenth-century Yucatec garden, field, and forest identifies settlement as an important organizational element of Maya agriculture. Barbara Voorhies considers a similar mechanism of order in her discussion of how the Maya would have had to spread themselves through a thin network in order to collect tropical forest products efficiently. Nonetheless, we have much to learn about such fundamentals for understanding Maya agriculture as property and the organization of labor.

Property enters in as one means by which elites appropriate the product of others' labor in agrarian societies. The advances the authors have reported in their understanding of Maya cultigens and techniques of cultivation are substantial, but their archaeological evidence tells us little about prehistoric Maya property relations and less about how these affected agriculture. Ethnographical analogy indicates the important role property can play in tropical agriculture. Elites control the fertile Coatzacoalcos River levees at Michael Coe's San Lorenzo site today, and Kent Flannery points out that a state institution, the school, commands an allotment of regularly productive levee land there for its support. Lack of levee access probably forces San Lorenzo peasants to labor for elites at wages drawn from the sale of levee cash crops in a market economy. But these consequences of ownership are so tied to contemporary market economy that we risk gross anachronism if we extrapolate from them back to prehistoric ownership of levees, raised fields, gardens, or *milpas*. Perhaps Pedro Carrasco's (1976) reconstruction of how central Mexican elites appropriated commoners' labor on office land is the least anachronistic analogy for us to consider for the Maya. We should also reflect on what Carmack (1976) and others' reconstructions of Maya stratification may tell us about property in the organization of agriculture.

We have read a good deal about Maya labor in these pages, mostly with respect to the labor investment that hydraulic engineering may have required. The estimates range from zero under Richard Skarie's model of the engineering to hundreds of million "man" days under William Denevan's! The gross magnitude of labor, however, concerns me less than the question of how the Maya recruited and deployed it. In this regard, the attention drawn by Mary Pohl and

Lawrence Feldman, and Marion Marshall Nimis to the taming and managing of animals by Maya women reminds us that the division of labor by sex must form part of our analysis and that kinship and domestic organization will figure prominently in the organization of Maya labor when we understand it. Domestic laborers, probably women, seem likely to have first cooked up and served food generating every kilocalorie ultimately expended in the construction and utilization of the Maya agricultural infrastructure.

Here ethnographical analogy may be of some value despite its limitations. For example, the prevalence of Maya patterns of bridewealth and inheritance lead me to suggest that these may have influenced the organization of labor for production in somewhat the same way as they have brought the contemporary Tzotzil, under certain conditions, to organize farming production within localized descent groups. Among the contemporary Tzotzil, bridewealth not only indemnifies a girl's family for the "cost" of raising her but, in so far as young grooms borrow bridewealth from kin, the custom also indebts juniors to their elders, enabling the latter to stave off eventual fission of the household by keeping young couples at work to repay their debt. This is how Tzotzil farmers build up efficient field and kitchen operations. Withholding inheritance of the means of production (e.g., land, pack animals, and tools) also counteracts fission of the family in the domestic cycle. As a result, family groups endure as localized multigenerational units of production and consumption. The conditions that bound this state of affairs seem to be land sufficiently circumscribed such that it is not a free good available to rebellious juniors, yet not so circumscribed as to prevent the emergence of specialized alternatives to farming, which might enable juniors to repay debts other than by working at home.

These questions regarding the social organization of Maya agriculture are easier for me to pose than for the authors to answer. I regret our not having Denny Puleston around to help us answer them. I did not have the good fortune, before now, to know Denny other than through his writing. Perhaps those of us who did not know him can grasp his individuality best with reference to what he evoked in others. Through the authors' presentation of their research and their accounts of how Denny affected it, I sense who Denny was, and is, as vividly as if we had just met face-to-face. It is clear to me that the readers of this volume will as well.

References

Carmack, Robert M.

1976 La estratificación quicheana prehispánica. In *Estratificación Social en la Mesoamérica Prehispánica,* edited by Pedro Carrasco *et al.* pp. 245–277. Mexico, D.F., Instituto Nacional de Antropología e Historia.

Carrasco, Pedro

1976 Los linajes nobles del México antiguo. In *Estratificación Social en la Mesoamérica Prehispánica,* edited by Pedro Carrasco *et al.,* pp. 19–36. Mexico, D.F., Instituto Nacional de Antropología e Historia.

Appendix 1
Dennis E. Puleston: A Tribute[1]

Frank C. Miller

FOR nine years, Dennis Puleston was a vital force in the Department of Anthropology. The first colloquium that he gave here foreshadowed the impressive contribution that he was to make within a few short years. The topic was settlement patterns and subsistence of the ancient Maya. His presentation carried all the contours of the Puleston trademark: imaginative hypotheses, ingenious use of data (including, in this case, experimental results), and superb color slides. The effect was stunning. Over the next few years, we were gratified to witness the growing acclaim with which Dennis' work was received.

Perhaps the best way to recognize the extent of his scholarly contribution is to quote colleagues in other universities who evaluated Denny's work when he was being considered for tenure. For example:

> Puleston's work on agriculture . . . [has] given us a new and potentially very productive perspective on Maya subsistence. He has not avoided larger questions of the growth and decline of Mesoamerican civilization. Because of his ideas and his involvement with field archaeology that is not just digging, he has been criticized as undisciplined and something of a bushwhacker. I would contend that his contributions are scholarly and stimulating, and that the unconventional problems he has tackled are on the intellectual frontiers rather than in the safe traditional areas of ceramics and temple architecture. He may be wrong, but he is asking the right questions. Since his propositions often depend on ethnographic analogy and a knowledge of extant subsistence systems, he also represents that integration of cultural and archaeological approaches so basic to American anthropology. I think he has carved out a distinctive and influential role for himself.

[1]The following remarks are from a Memorial Service held at the University of Minnesota on July 12, 1978.

ISBN 0-12-259780-X

Another colleague wrote,

> Denny is one of the two or three most productive and stimulating scholars in the field of Maya studies. . . Every one of his papers is a major breakthrough. . . . It is very rare in the field of anthropology today to find a scholar about whom one can say this. I think in 20 years Denny will probably be the leading scholar in Maya studies, with a reputation comparable to that of the late Sir J. Eric Thompson.

That wayward bolt of lightning in Yucatán has left a large vacant space in archaeology and in this department.

More than most scholars, Dennis Puleston reached people in other disciplines. The remarks here today by Professors Lukermann and Wright are testimony to his interdisciplinary influence. That influence was apparent two years ago, here in the Campus Club, at a conference on the transfer of agricultural technology. After dinner one evening, Dennis showed slides and talked about the entire range of his interests in Mayan subsistence: his early work on ramón nuts in Tikal as well as his recent reconstructions of ancient agriculture on ridged fields in Belize. Represented in the audience was a broad spectrum of agricultural and social scientists—possibly the largest group of that all-too-rare combination ever assembled in this university. Many people in both camps were impressed with the scope of his ideas and his intuitive grasp of a holistic perspective; he had a finely honed conception of the systemic nature of the phenomena with which he was dealing. The production people in agriculture—the agronomists, soil scientists, and others—were particularly taken with his ability to fit the pieces of the puzzle—ecology, technology, social structure, and culture—together into a coherent picture.

If I may paraphrase Eric Wolf's remark about peasant agriculture, anthropology is a way of life, not simply a way to make a living. The discipline demands, more than most vocations, a full integration of work and life. Most of us struggle to pull it off; to Denny, it seemed to come effortlessly. His research was a reflection of his adventuresome self, and he pursued archaeology as enthusiastically as he embraced life.

The character of this man had generous portions of two distinctive human qualities: a rapport with children and a love for picnics. His curiosity and delight in the world had an unspoiled, childlike aspect, and he liked to look at things in new ways. These qualities were reflected in his relationships with children, especially his own. They also inspired another of his projects: the quest for the ultimate picnic. I remember when he got up in the middle of the night to start barbecueing an entire goat over an open fire. I can assure you that it was delicious—but perhaps one must be a Middle Americanist to appreciate that delicacy.

Since Olga shared Denny's adventuresome spirit, their traditional Easter breakfasts were notable occasions. A huge makeshift table almost filled the living room. One year, as we sipped vodka laced with fresh lemon peel and contemplated Olga's spectacular Easter bread towering in the center of the table, we could glance up at the ceiling and see a strip of paper one foot wide and sixteen feet long: Denny's transection of settlement sites and ramón trees at Tikal.

We honor the memory of Dennis Puleston: imaginative scholar, stimulating colleague, loving husband and father, and above all, a lovable human being. I think that we shall never see another like him. We are left with his work and with many precious images of his life. Denny went on creating vivid pictures until the end. Olga quoted a marvelous one from his journal: Denny on that crazy inner tube going into a dark cave without a lantern and speculating about Mayan cosmology. Then the final image: our friend on top of the big pyramid at Chichén Itzá, enjoying the company of his children and no doubt delighted to watch the approaching thunderstorm. How much we wish that he had come down from there alive.

Appendix 2
The Role of Ramón in Maya Subsistence

Dennis E. Puleston[1]

Introduction

IN recent years, anthropologists have focused increasing attention on the process by which cultures have attained the status of statehood and civilization. Environmental factors appear to have been of considerable importance. Time after time, the combination of semiarid environments and fertile river valleys appear to have provided the essential ingredients for the development of agricultural systems dependent on large-scale irrigation and strong central governments to control them. Early developments in the Indus, Hwang Ho, Tigris–Euphrates, and Nile valleys provide classic examples. With minor modifications this explanation has been applied to Prehispanic civilizations of the New World, including the Valley of Mexico where lakes, rather than rivers, provided the principal water resource.

Despite the broad application of the hydraulic hypothesis, there have been some very interesting exceptions. Perhaps the most notable of these is that provided by the Classic Maya civilization which achieved its greatest development in the northern Petén of Guatemala (A.D. 300–900). Here the combination of dense tropical forests along with the peripheral distribution of rivers seems to provide an environmental antithesis of what might be expected to produce civilization on the basis of the other examples.

The apparent inconsistency has not gone unrecognized. A. V. Kidder (1950:6) in his introduction to the Uaxactún excavation reports wrote "I still feel that the unbroken Petén forests would have been an almost prohibitively difficult environment for pulling oneself up, so to speak, by one's own bootstraps." J. Eric S. Thompson in his *Rise and Fall of Maya Civilization* (1954:26) writes, "To me, one of the greatest mysteries is why Maya culture should have reached its

[1]Deceased.

ISBN 0-12-259780-X

greatest peak in this region so singularly lacking in natural wealth, where man, armed only with stone tools and fire, had everlastingly to struggle with the unrelenting forest for land to sow his crops." More recently, Lowe (1971:237) has offered the following statement on the Maya heartland. "With little doubt this is the least desirable environment for human occupation in Mesoamerica."

The image of determined agriculturalists beating back the relentless jungle with stone tools so that a civilization could rise and prosper for a time is intriguing, but hardly satisfying. The historian Toynbee (1947) attempted to provide a rational explanation for the Maya exception with the suggestion that it was the very adversity of the lowland environment that provided the stimulus for their incredible success in an environment that was outwardly so hostile and difficult. Rathje (1971), following what is ultimately a very similar reasoning, has suggested that the ancient Maya, made up for environmental deficiencies by cleverly working out a means of expertise in religion.

It is my intention here to suggest that our view of the relationship between ancient Maya culture and its environment, particularly with regard to subsistence practices, has been totally wrong. Perhaps heavily biased by our own agricultural heritage, western archaeologists have been extremely slow to question long-accepted basic assumptions about the Maya. Far from being "the least desirable environment for human occupation in Mesoamerica," the tropical forests of the Maya Lowlands, in fact, seem to have offered certain specific resources which, because they were utilized skillfully, permitted the rise of a state society, which was sustained by one of the highest regional population densities in the preindustrial world. The key to this success appears to have been the utilization of the seed crop produced by a single tree species, *Brosimum alicastrum* Sw. This essentially unknown tree, with the common names of breadnut or *ramón* is of such staggering potential it is difficult to imagine how the magnitude of its significance has escaped more than passing notice until the initiation of our investigations of the tree began at Tikal in 1967.

Slash-and-Burn Agriculture

The synonomy of Maya civilization and maize fields cut out of tropical forests has been one of the essential truisms of Maya culture throughout time. It is a fact, however, that as Meighan *et al.* (1958:132) point out, "even in areas of known archaeological development such as Mesoamerica, the interpretation of a site as representing an agricultural economy is often a mere assumption, not an inference from anything in the archaeological picture." The assumption that slash-and-burn maize cultivation provided the subsistence base for ancient Maya civilization is the keystone for the supporting arch of an entire superstructure of secondary assumptions and hypotheses, cultural reconstructions, and elaborate evolutionary schemes that have been developed over a period of more than a hundred years.

At this point, I intend to remove that keystone and present the evidence and the barest outlines for the implications of a dramatically different structure. I begin with a review of the evidence that has traditionally been used to sustain the assumption of maize agriculture for the ancient Maya. The most frequently cited items include

1. the overwhelming importance of maize to postconquest and modern Maya populations (Morley 1946),
2. the frequent appearance of maize motifs and "maize gods" in ancient Maya iconography (Thompson 1954),
3. the dispersed nature of ancient Maya residential settlement patterns, presumably the result of the land requirements of slash-and-burn agriculture,
4. the discovery of maize cobs in the excavation of Maya sites like Tikal and Uaxactún, and
5. the ubiquitous appearance of *mano* and *metate* fragments, presumably used for the grinding of maize at ancient Maya sites all over the Maya Lowlands (Rathje 1971).

Taken together, these separate pieces of evidence might appear to provide a substantial basis for the assumption of a primary role for maize. The problem arises, however, when we consider the long-range liabilities and limitations of slash-and-burn agriculture in the tropical forest environment. It is these considerations that lie at the root of several decades of frustrating discussion and debate about Maya subsistence, the collapse of Classic civilization (ca. A.D. 850), and slash-and-burn agriculture in general. Though slash-and-burn agriculture has traditionally been viewed as a wasteful and destructive form of agriculture (Leach 1959:64), it recently became fashionable "to blame poor returns on the soils and to describe shifting cultivation as a wise adjustment to environmental conditions" (Carter 1969:9). Now the tide has begun to turn again against slash-and-burn agriculture in all but those situations where population densities are low. The arguments for the potential of slash-and-burn agriculture for large and relatively densely settled areas have been no more cogently argued than by Dumond (1961). Despite this, however, there are critical problems that he does not address. I will examine these briefly now.

For the most part, the difficulties of slash-and-burn agriculture are linked to the effects of open-field cultivation on tropical soils. Upland forest soils in the vicinity of the Classic Maya site of Tikal are characteristically thin and, like other tropical limestone soils, heavily dependent on a rapid recycling of nutrients in order to prevent loss of them. An intensive survey of soils around Tikal reveals that where nutrients have been kept under forest, fertility is high. As part of a dynamic system that includes the forest that grows on the nutrients, however, they are subject to marked changes when the forest cover is stripped away and burned. One of the important first steps in slash-and-burn agriculture is the burning of trees and shrubs after cutting. During this process somewhere between 227 and 408 MT of organic matter per ha may be destroyed to bring nutrients—stored above the ground in tree trunks, stems, and leaves—down into the soil; 270–410 kg of fixed nitrogen alone may be released into the atmosphere and lost from a single acre (Gourou 1966:32–33). Soil fertility is thus temporarily lifted, but at a tremendous cost to the forest–soil system as a whole. The full effect of the high temperatures produced by burning on soil is poorly understood, so I will not go beyond this point here; but it is clear that completion of burning does not terminate destruction. As shown in studies like that of Likens *et al.* (1969), the removal of forest cover, even without burning, is highly detrimental. They found that clear-cutting of a New Hampshire forest greatly accelerated nutrient loss by terminating the uptake of nutrients by plants and increasing the quantity of drainage water passing through the system, which had the effect of flushing nutrients out in solution. Of all nutrient losses, that of nitrate was the highest, increasing from less than 1 mg/liter before cutting to more than 50 mg/liter after cutting. Foliage, a continuous supply of leaf litter, and extensive networks of fine roots also perform the vital function of breaking the impact of falling rain and preventing erosion. On the New Hampshire watershed, the loss of particulate matter was increased ninefold by cutting down trees and shrubs. There is no reason to suppose that these factors would be any less significant in the tropical lowlands where rainfall is 1,500–2,000 mm.

In the tropics, foliage performs the additional function of protecting soils from higher levels of solar radiation, which raises soil temperatures, which in turn increases the volatilization of many nutrients and retards humus formation. The critical temperature for humus formation appears to be in the range of 25°–26°C. Above this temperature, humus decomposition exceeds the rate of its formation with a loss of 17–29 kg of humic nitrogen per degree rise in temperature per ha per annum (Gourou 1966:22). June and July daytime temperatures of 7 *milpa* soils in the vicinity of Tikal ranged from 28°–32°C with an average of 29°C. A similarly measured sample of 20 soils under forest averaged 26°C. Clearly, soils in the Maya Lowlands are very near the critical level for humus formation and, once cleared of forest vegetation, appear to move well above it.

The effect of some of these factors is diminished somewhat once milpa crops (including the broad-leafed cucurbits and maize) begin to grow, but there is little doubt that rapidly declining yields on continuously cropped land is significantly augmented by elevated soil temperatures. In fact, measurements of soil fertility in comparative plots of milpa and forest soils at Tikal indicate dramatic declines in organic matter, nitrates, and soluble salts, confirming earlier studies carried out by Ursula Cowgill (1961).

Another contributor to nutrient loss is crop removal. Since the Maya do not practice manuring or use fertilizers on slash-and-burn fields, nutrients, including phosphorus and magnesium (which are high in corn and beans), represent a significant drain on the system when they are not replaced.

In the tropics, where soils tend to be shallow and thus have small reserves, the cumulative detrimental effects to field agriculture can be partially negated by fallowing the land. Ursula Cowgill (1962:279), on the basis of interviews with 40 modern Maya farmers living in the vicinity of Lake Petén, estimates that a stable slash-and-burn agriculture could be carried out with a four-year fallow after a single crop. For long-term considerations, this may be too short. The British Honduras Land Use Survey team found that in areas where population pressures were not high, preferred fallowing periods were in the range of 8 to 15 years (Wright *et al.* 1959:217). Here lies the crux of the problem. The fallowing requirement for slash-and-burn agriculture reduces the overall carrying capacity to a level that is grossly inconsistent with estimates of prehistoric settlement density based on prehistoric settlement densities. On the basis of her data, Cowgill (1962) estimates an average production of 1,620 kg of maize per ha on first-year plots. With a minimal 4-year fallow, the average yield per ha for a full 5-year cycle would be 324 kg/ha/year. Two harvests from the same piece of land provide even less (306 kg/ha/year) because of the necessity of extending the fallow. It is estimated on the basis of present techniques and currently used varieties of maize that 30–75 people/km^2 can be sustained by maize agriculture in the Petén (Sanders and Price 1968; Cowgill 1962). With 4-year fallows, this means a family of 6 would require from 8 to 20 ha of good agriculture land within a reasonable walking distance of home.

This brings us to consideration of one of the more puzzling inconsistencies in the traditional models for ancient Maya society. The combination of fallowing and a poorly developed system of transport would appear to make it most efficient to keep settlements small and compact. It is this hamlet pattern that characterizes nonindustrial Maya settlement in Yucatán today. Classic Maya settlements, however, were large and relatively dispersed in a pattern, which is exactly the converse of what would be expected (Puleston 1973). In the central 16 km^2 of Tikal, there were apparently more than 1,900 contemporaneously occupied houses in Late Classic times (Haviland 1969). In a situation where ease of transport would seem to be vital for the maintenance of a densely populated region, we find the largest and seemingly most permanent centers in the heartland where navigable rivers do not occur at all.

It has been around this seemingly impossible situation that for so many years, debate and earnest speculation has surged. As might be imagined, there has been no shortage of explanations as to why the collapse of Classic Maya civilization might have occurred. Hypotheses involving exhausted soils and erosion have appeared more frequently than any other for more than 60 years (Cook 1909; Morley 1920; Cooke 1931; Ricketson and Ricketson 1937; Meggers 1954; Cowgill 1962; Sabloff and Willey 1967; Willey and Shimkin 1971).

In many cases, the arguments were so well taken it seemed difficult to rationalize the existence of the Classic Maya for any period of time at all, to say nothing of a collapse.

"We will take the position here that the breakdown came, not necessarily because of an inadequate subsistence base alone, but more importantly, because the 'sociological imperatives' of the subsistence as reflected in Maya milpa agriculture were such that the maintenance of a class-structured state organization was, while not impossible, extremely difficult" (Altschuler 1958:193). Betty Meggers (1954), with a realization of the impossibility of the situation, postulated that Classic Maya civilization could not have been indigenous to the lowlands but must have been brought in full blown, only to begin a decline that must have started almost immediately. W. R. Coe (1957), in a reply, was without an alternative, but pointed out that this hypothesis was totally inconsistent with the available archaeological data, which indicated a gradual and orderly growth over a long period of time. A body of literature has recently grown up around the question of whether or not residential structures were occupied contemporaneously. Sanders (1962), claiming that they were not, has proposed that 75% of all the residential groups must have been abandoned during the peak occupation of the Late Classic period (A.D. 550–830) Haviland (1970:191–192) has demonstrated fairly conclusively that the situation was otherwise.

Thus, though practically every essential element in what amounted to a model of ancient Maya ecology had been examined and questioned (including the carrying capacity of maize, prehistoric settlement density, the contemporaneity of occupation, and the amount of labor actually needed for the construction of the great architectural centers), the model was still unworkable, exhibiting grave internal inconsistencies. Settlement densities were much higher and seemingly more stable than could be expected. The material achievements were simply too great. Somewhere there was a flaw. Despite the impossibility of the situation, there was one basic assumption that had never been seriously questioned. This was the assumption of a central role for some form of slash-and-burn cultivation of maize. In fact, it was not until Bronson (1966) proposed the hypothesis that root crops played a major role in Classic Maya subsistence that serious consideration was given to any alternative. In favor of his argument were the much greater yields of root crop per unit area in comparison to that of maize. The assumption of slash-and-burn cultivation with all its liabilities, however, remained unchallenged. The low nutritional value of root crops and unfavorable soil conditions for potentially one of the most important of these, manioc, have been indicated as problems (Cowgill 1971). The limitations of open-field slash-and-burn agriculture are still unresolved, and without any specific archaeological evidence in support of a primary role for root crops, the hypothesis remains just that. I will now present the case for a second alternative to maize, the fruit-producing tree *Brosimum alicastrum* Sw. or ramón.

The Ramón Survey

It was at this point that our attention was drawn to the ramón. Three features made the ramón stand out: (1) it showed a close association with sites, (2) it was an edible staple, and (3) it was storable. Over the years, various archaeologists and botanists including Lundell (1937), J. E. S. Thompson (1930), and O. F. Cook (1921) have noted the physical association of the ramón tree with Classic Maya site areas. Typical are comments such as those of Bullard (1960), who in the course of his trail survey of the northeast Petén observed a "striking correlation between the presence of Maya ruins and groves of the ramón 'breadnut' tree . . . throughout the survey." Though the fruit of this tree contains a large edible seed, preferred by wild animals and commonly used by the Maya today when other food resources fail, the association was never investigated further. Lundell alone suggested that these trees might be relic populations of a Maya cultigen, though even at that, he did not question the role of maize. Others, including Thompson (1930) and Higbee (1948), while indicating that the edible fruit might have been used, suggested that the tree (along with other fruit-producing species) was simply left standing when encountered in the course of clearing for milpa, the primacy of which again was left unquestioned.

My own investigation of the ramón began with the intention of examining in detail associations of several tree species with ancient Maya ruins as noted by Lundell (1937). In 1967, with the assistance of Jeffrey Parsons and Richard Blanton, I completed four ½-km wide settlement survey maps, which extended 12 km north, south, east, and west from Tikal. We were in an ideal position to quantify the suggested association and, by this means, possibly to identify fruit trees that had been cultivated in association with residences. The ramón seemed to fall in a special category because it produced an edible seed that would be more amenable to storage than would the products of the more than 50 softfruited species. It might seem that the outcome of this survey must have been self-evident at this point, but it was not. The density of the forest, along with the necessity of carefully examining foliage in order to separate out 1 tree species from the more than 200 others that occur in the area, made it impossible to generalize about ramón distribution outside of the site nucleus, which was the only place its abundance had been recognized.

Having decided to work with the ramón, our first objective was to test quantitatively the reality and extent of the relationship between ramón trees and Maya ruins. I was anxious to discover if dense concentrations of the tree were limited to the nucleus of major temples, pyramids, and "palace" structures within a kilometer or two of the site center, or if indeed it extended into the 5–6 km radius of primarily residential settlement within the earthworks system that surrounded this nucleus. Of the four strips, we selected the south one for our investigation since it offered the broadest range of terrain and settlement combinations, including a good sample of elevated, well-drained forest that was lightly settled and far from the site epicenter.

Our survey technique was basically quite simple; it involved the mapping of all ramón trees that (1) occurred on a 100-m-wide strip that extended down the center of the 12-km-long settlement survey strip, and (2) had a diameter of 5 cm or more. (The survey was carried out by my brother, Peter O. Puleston, with the assistance of Elias Contreras, who assisted in tree identification.) A total of 1985 trees were mapped on the 12-km-long strip. The broader but overlapping settlement survey strip produced a total of 739 structures. The survey data were broken up into ½-km-long sections, and the number of trees and house platforms in each were tabulated. Application of the standard product-moment correlation formula (Puleston 1973:274) produced a high 0.86 correlation between trees and structures that was significant at the 0.01 level. The distribution of the trees is a function of terrain only insofar as settlement is influenced by this variable. Between 6.5 and 10 km out, the trees are comparatively scarce despite the presence of high well-drained ground. This high degree of correlation was considerably greater than we had anticipated, and suddenly drew into focus the idea that we were probably dealing with the descendants of an ancient Maya cultigen that had been grown in the vicinity of residences. Possible alternative explanations for the association, at best, appeared to be unlikely.

One of these—the possibility that the mounds themselves offered a preferred microhabitat for the ramón trees—was examined. In fact, the collapsed-building microhabitat does appear to be partially responsible for the frequency of the trees in the ceremonial nucleus of Tikal, where the rubble mounds are more than 2 m high. Outside this hub of large collapsed palaces and temples, however, where low house platforms predominate, this factor seems to lose its importance since trees do not occur with any higher frequency on mounds than they do in surrounding areas. Soil samples taken at 500-m intervals along the strip were also examined to see if there might be a generally higher level of some nutrient, such as nitrates or phosphorus, in the area of higher settlement densities, such as that which might have been produced by former occupation. The results were completely negative and strongly suggestive of the conclusion that whatever differences may have existed in the past had long since been obliterated by factors relating to slope and drainage. Finally, the possibility that the trees moved into cleared land ahead of other species at the time of abandonment was eliminated by observation of the fact that the species is not typical of the secondary growth vegetation found on abandoned milpas today (Lundell 1937:46), probably because of the poor dispersal capabilities of the heavy seeds. In summary, I would agree with Lundell, who wrote, regarding the ramón, "we may assume that the dominance on Maya sites is due to an initial advantage occurring to the species through its presence in large numbers when the places were abandoned" (Lundell 1937:10).

Productivity

On the basis of these data then, it seems highly probable, if not certain, that at the time of Tikal's abandonment in the ninth century, ramón trees were growing in large numbers around Maya houses. If such was the case, it is unlikely that much maize was growing there, since maize requires as much sun as it can get and does not grow well in situations where incomplete clearing leaves the plants in shade for part of the day. Why would valuable land be sacrificed to trees? In a situation where food-producing land must have been at a premium, such a sacrifice on such a grand scale would only be made if there were some advantage to be derived from it. I will now turn to the question of ramón productivity.

Short acquaintance with the tree is all that is necessary to bring one to the realization that it is a heavy producer. The ground beneath the trees during the fruiting season is literally covered with small round seeds from which the soft pericap is quickly eaten by insects. In 1967, we collected 32.6 kg from beneath a single tree. While González (1939) reveals that a large tree can produce up to 60 kg, Martínez (1936:100) reports that in humid areas a medium-sized tree can yield 75 kg of edible seed annually. Since fruit trees are often quite variable in what they produce from year to year, however, data on a single tree for one season would have to be considered insufficient for calculating yields per unit area.

In order to circumvent this problem, I set up a grid on a 900-m^2 plot of forest floor at Tikal. This plot was divided into 100 3-m^2 subplots from which a sample of 25 was randomly selected for systematic collection and weighing of the seed fall during the fruiting season. This was done over a period of three years, during which time the plots yielded an average of 1,763 kg/ha/year. This was despite the fact that the trees were untended and in full competition with other non-food-producing species that crowded around them.

As indicated above, maize under the best of conditions and minimal fallowing periods can yield little more than an average of 324 kg/ha/year. The trees then have a demonstrable ability to produce more than five times as much food per unit of land area as maize.

It seems likely that these figures probably fall short of the full potential of this tree. Proper spacing would probably do much to increase the yields of individual trees. In Yucatán and Campeche, where the ramón is grown for its foliage (which is used as a green fodder for dairy cattle), a spacing that would allow 100–125 trees/ha is advocated (González 1939:222). This not only allows the trees to produce a broader and denser crown, resulting in a maximum production of leaves and fruit, but further permits intercropping of smaller garden and root crops between the trees. In a good year, such a stand of trees might produce 5,680–9,090 kg of edible seed per ha. Maya families in Yucatán, who depend on a diet that may be 80% maize, consume 1,090–1,727 MT of this staple per year (Steggerda 1941:130; Hester 1954:166; Cowgill 1962:277; Reina 1967). Clearly, under normal conditions, ½–1 ha of ramón trees would be more than enough to sustain a family on a permanent basis.

Nutrition

Available studies indicate that the nutritional value of the seeds is high. In several important respects, it appears to be superior to maize. Ramón seed compares favorably with maize in respect to content of protein, calcium, iron, and the vitamins A, B_2, and niacin. Closer investigation reveals that the protein found in ramón is also of higher quality, containing greater amounts of the essential amino acids lysine, arginine, tryptophane, and valine than maize. Particularly significant is the high value for tryptophane since this amino acid is generally deficient in plant proteins. Its low level of availability in maize and beans is responsible for one of the principal deficiencies in modern diets throughout Middle America. All the available evidence suggests that ramón seed is a nutritionally acceptable and probably superior staple in comparison to maize. There is no evidence to suggest that it harbors any harmful properties. It has long been a dietary supplement throughout the Maya area though this fact has not often been recorded. Humans have lived essentially exclusively on the fruit for as long as 15 days without any sign of ill effect (González 1939). Experimental work in Campeche has demonstrated that ramón forage actually increases milk production in cattle by 1.5–2.0 liters/day in animals which normally produce 8.0 liters/day on regular forage (González 1939:222).

Labor

Slash-and-burn agriculture as practiced in the Maya Lowlands today is essentially a year-round task. As Reina (1967) has noted, the modern maize farmer of the Petén region "just manages to 'break even' all his life by expending a maximum amount of physical energy and by planning carefully." A breakdown of the labor requirements into 15 separate tasks reveals that a typical household invests 2,000–3,000 man-hours in the maintenance of a wet-season maize field alone (Carter 1969:135). When we take into account the comparative inefficiency of stone tools for the felling of bush, this figure must be increased. Experiments carried out by Saraydar and Shimada (1971) indicate that as much as 5.1 times as many calories are needed to cut wood with a stone axe as with a steel one.

Assuming then that 2,000–3,000 man-hours is a minimal figure, what labor is required to produce an equivalent quantity of ramón seed? In an established grove, it is clear that the onerous task of land clearing is completely eliminated. With the elimination of land clearing, weeding becomes unnecessary. Planting, along with the attendant and worrisome questions of timing, disappears. Because the crop is harvested within hailing distance of house transport, labor costs are brought to the absolute minimum. On the basis of experiments carried out in Tikal in 1973, I have determined that a woman and 2–3 children, working at a normal pace, can harvest 455 kg of ramón seed in 25 hours, which means that a total of 60–95 hours would be required to supply a year's worth of food for an average family. Assuming ramón was the staple then, as maize is now, a family's full subsistence complement of 1,364 kg could be collected with an average input of 1 to 1.5 hours/day during the main fruiting season of 7 to 10 weeks.

The significant factor here is that no measurable input is required by males. For reasons that are perhaps unique in the annals of human history, adult males may well have been released from essentially all subsistence activities. It is doubtful that their liberation gave them cause to celebrate, for almost certainly it was this tremendous manpower resource that raised up the architectural monuments which bring visitors to the Maya Lowlands from all over the world even today. I suggest that it is unlikely that these were constructed by teams of happy farmers who convened at the great centers in a fit of seasonal religious ecstasy to build temples so their crops would grow. Careful excavation reveals that even the small temples and palaces of Tikal were methodically put together by skilled (and, by implication, full-time) specialists that included stonecutters, plasterers, masons, lime burners, wood hewers, painters, and vast numbers of porters, attendants, and priests. In view of the harsh and often discouraging struggle that modern steel-wielding *milperos* must sustain in order to survive today, it seems unlikely that their forebears could have accomplished so much more without utilizing some quite dramatically different adaptation.

Settlement Patterns

The distinctiveness of the relationship the ancient Maya had with their environment is revealed nowhere more strongly than in their settlement patterns. In comparison with modern Maya settlements and even those of Postclassic times, as at Mayapán, residential settlement is remarkably dispersed. A typical plaza group at Tikal is surrounded by a vacant space of about 1 ha, which works out to an average of 0.6 ha per residential structure (Puleston 1973:197).

Traditionally, the characteristic dispersal of plaza groups has been attributed to the land requirements of slash-and-burn agriculture, but the evidence indicates fairly clearly that 1 ha falls far short of what is needed. Cowgill's data (1962:276) indicate that at least 5.4 ha of good land are needed to provide the 1,735 kg of maize per year necessary for permanent support of a modern family of six persons. This limitation of space makes it far more likely that these areas were used as kitchen gardens. Sanders (1973) has suggested the presence of an infield—outfield situation which would remove maize cultivation to peripheral areas beyond the limits of dense settlement. It was on the basis of this assumption that in 1965 we began what was called the Tikal Sustaining Area Project. The explicit goal of this project was the identification of an agricultural sustaining area that would be recognized by large unoccupied areas that could presumably be devoted entirely to food production. The site limits of Tikal turned out to be easier to recognize than had been anticipated when we discovered the remains of a defensive earthworks system (Puleston and Callender 1967) that encloses an area of approximately 120 km^2. Beyond these limits, however, we were surprised to discover that settlement density, while it did decline significantly, did not reach a level that permitted these settlements to be self-sustaining by slash-

and-burn agriculture—much less provide food resources for the estimated 65,000–80,000 occupants of the area within the earthworks. For the "intersite area" outside the earthworks, the total amount of land available per structure in Classic times is calculated to be 3.54 ha. If *tintal* and *escobal bajo* areas are removed, the figure falls to 1.62 ha. Clearly, if these peripheral areas were agricultural sustaining areas, a system a good many more times productive than slash-and-burn agriculture must have been used. This is not to say that maize was not cultivated in these areas—it is very likely that it was—but rather that it contributed little to the caloric intake of the population as a whole.

References

Altschuler, Milton
1958 On the environmental limitations of Mayan cultural development. *Southwestern Journal of Anthropology* 14:189–196.

Bronson, Bennet
1966 Roots and the subsistence of the ancient Maya. *Southwestern Journal of Anthropology* 22:251–279.

Bullard, William R.
1960 Maya settlement pattern in northeastern Petén, Guatemala. *American Antiquity* 25:355–372.

Carter, William E.
1969 *New lands and old traditions: Kekchi cultivators in the Guatemalan lowlands. Latin American Monograph No. 6.* Gainesville, Univ. of Florida Press.

Coe, William R.
1957 Environmental limitations on Maya culture: A reexamination. *American Anthropologist* 59:328–335.

Cook, Orator F.
1909 Vegetation affected by agriculture in Central America. *U.S. Department of Agriculture, Bureau of Plant Industry, Bulletin* 145. Washington, D.C.
1921 Milpa agriculture: A primitive tropical system. *Annual Report of the Smithsonian Institution* 1919. Washington, D.C.

Cooke, C. Wythe
1931 Why the Mayan cities of the Petén district, Guatemala were abandoned. *Washington Academy of Sciences* 21(13):283–287. Baltimore.

Cowgill, Ursula, M.
1961 Soil fertility and the ancient Maya. *Transactions of the Connecticut Academy of Arts & Sciences* 42:1–56.
1962 An agricultural study of the southern Maya Lowlands. *American Anthropologist* 64:273–286.
1971 Some comments on *Manihot* subsistence and the ancient Maya. *Southwestern Journal of Anthropology* 27:51–63.

Dumond, Donald E.
1961 Swidden agriculture and the rise of Maya civilization. *Southwestern Journal of Anthropology* 17:301–316.

González Pérez, Arturo
1939 El ramón o capomo. *Boletín Platanero y Agrícola* 2(12):221–222.

Gourou, Pierre
1966 *The Tropical World: Its Social and Economic Conditions and Its Future Status,* 4th ed. translated by S. H. Beaver and E. D. Laborde. New York, Wiley.

Haviland, William A.
1969 A new population estimate for Tikal, Guatemala. *American Antiquity* 34:429–433.
1970 Tikal, Guatemala and Mesoamerican urbanism. *World Archaeology* 2(2):186–198.
Hester, Joseph A.
1954 *Natural and cultural bases of ancient Maya subsistence economy*. Unpublished Ph.D. dissertation, Department of Anthropology, Univ. of California at Los Angeles.
Higbee, Edward C.
1948 Agriculture in the Maya homeland. *Geographical Review* 38:457–464.
Kidder, Alfred V.
1950 Introduction. In *Uaxactún, Guatemala: Excavations of 1931–1937* by A. Ledyard Smith. *Carnegie Institution of Washington, Publication* 588. Washington, D.C.
Leach, Edmund R.
1959 Some economic advantages of shifting cultivation. *Proceedings of the Ninth Pacific Science Congress.* 7:64–66. Pacific Science Association.
Likens, Gene E., F. Herbert Bormann, and N. M. Johnson
1969 Nitrification: Importance to nutrient losses from a cut-over forested ecosystem. *Science* 163:1205–1206.
Lowe, Gareth W.
1971 The civilizational consequences of varying degrees of agricultural and ceramic dependency within the basic ecosystems of Mesoamerica. In *Observations on the Emergence of Civilization in Mesoamerica,* edited by Robert F. Heizer, John A. Graham, and Carl W. Clewlow, Jr, pp. 212–248. *Contributions of the University of California Archaeological Research Facility, No.* 11. Berkeley.
Lundell, Cyrus L.
1937 The vegetation of Petén. *Carnegie Institution of Washington, Publication No.* 478. Washington, D.C.
Martínez, Maximo
1936 *Plantas útiles de Mexico,* 2nd ed. México, Ediciones Botas.
Meggers, Betty J.
1954 Environmental limitation on the development of culture. *American Anthropologist* 56:801–824.
Meighan, Clement W., David M. Pendergast, B. K. Swartz, and M. D. Wissler
1958 Ecological interpretation in archaeology: Part I. *American Antiquity* 24:131–150.
Morley, Sylvanus G.
1920 The inscriptions at Copán. *Carnegie Institution of Washington, Publication* 219. Washington, D.C.
1946 *The Ancient Maya.* Stanford, Stanford Univ. Press.
Puleston, Dennis E.
1973 *Ancient Maya settlement patterns and environment at Tikal, Guatemala: Implications for subsistence models.* Unpublished Ph.D. dissertation, Department of Anthropology, Univ. of Pennsylvania.
Puleston, Dennis E., and Donald W. Callender, Jr.
1967 Defensive earthworks at Tikal. *Expedition* 9(3):40–48.
Rathje, William L.
1971 The origin and development of Lowland Classic Maya civilization. *American Antiquity* 36:275–285.
Reina, Ruben E.
1967 Milpas and milperos: Implications for prehistoric times. *American Anthropologist* 69:1–20.
Ricketson, Oliver G., and Edith B. Ricketson
1937 Uaxactún, Guatemala, Group E, 1926–1931. *Carnegie Institution of Washington, Publication* 477. Washington, D.C.
Sabloff, Jeremy A., and Gordon R. Willey
1967 The collapse of Maya civilization in the southern lowlands: A consideration of history and process. *Southwestern Journal of Anthropology* 23:311–336.

Sanders, William T.
1962 Cultural ecology of the Maya Lowlands, part 1. *Estudios de Cultura Maya* 2:79–121.
1973 The cultural ecology of the Lowland Maya: A reevaluation. In *The Classic Maya Collapse*, edited by T. Patrick Culbert, pp. 325–365. Albuquerque, Univ. of New Mexico Press.
Sanders, William T., and Barbara J. Price
1968 *Mesoamerica: The evolution of a civilization.* New York, Random House.
Saraydar, Stephen C., and Izumi Shimada
1971 A quantitative comparison of efficiency between a stone axe and a steel axe. *American Antiquity* 36(2):216–217.
Steggerda, Morris
1941 Maya Indians of Yucatán. *Carnegie Institution of Washington, Publication No.* 531. Washington, D.C.
Thompson, J. Eric S.
1930 Ethnology of the Mayas of southern and central British Honduras. *Field Museum of Natural History, Publication* 274, *Anthropological Series* 17(2). Chicago.
1954 *The rise and fall of Maya civilization.* Norman, Univ. of Oklahoma Press.
Toynbee, Arnold J.
1947 *A study of history.* Abridgment of Vols. I–IV by D. C. Somervell. London, Oxford Univ. Press.
Willey, Gordon R., and Demitri B. Shimkin
1971 The collapse of Classic Maya civilization in the southern lowlands: A symposium summary statement. *Southwestern Journal of Anthropology* 27(1):1–18.
Wright, A. C. S., D. H. Romney, R. H. Arbuckle, and V. E. Vial
1959 Land in British Honduras: Report of the British Honduras Land Use Survey Team. *Colonial Research Publication* 24. London, Her Majesty's Stationery Office.

Index

STUDIES IN ARCHAEOLOGY

Consulting Editor: Stuart Struever

Department of Anthropology
Northwestern University
Evanston, Illinois

Charles R. McGimsey III. **Public Archeology**

Lewis R. Binford. **An Archaeological Perspective**

Muriel Porter Weaver. **The Aztecs, Maya, and Their Predecessors: Archaeology of Mesoamerica**

Joseph W. Michels. **Dating Methods in Archaeology**

C. Garth Sampson. **The Stone Age Archaeology of Southern Africa**

Fred T. Plog. **The Study of Prehistoric Change**

Patty Jo Watson (Ed.). **Archeology of the Mammoth Cave Area**

George C. Frison (Ed.). **The Casper Site: A Hell Gap Bison Kill on the High Plains**

W. Raymond Wood and R. Bruce McMillan (Eds.). **Prehistoric Man and His Environments: A Case Study in the Ozark Highland**

Kent V. Flannery (Ed.). **The Early Mesoamerican Village**

Charles E. Cleland (Ed.). **Cultural Change and Continuity: Essays in Honor of James Bennett Griffin**

Michael B. Schiffer. **Behavioral Archeology**

Fred Wendorf and Romuald Schild. **Prehistory of the Nile Valley**

Michael A. Jochim. **Hunter-Gatherer Subsistence and Settlement: A Predictive Model**

Stanley South. **Method and Theory in Historical Archeology**

Timothy K. Earle and Jonathon E. Ericson (Eds.). **Exchange Systems in Prehistory**

Stanley South (Ed.). **Research Strategies in Historical Archeology**

John E. Yellen. **Archaeological Approaches to the Present: Models for Reconstructing the Past**

Lewis R. Binford (Ed.). **For Theory Building in Archaeology: Essays on Faunal Remains, Aquatic Resources, Spatial Analysis, and Systemic Modeling**

James N. Hill and Joel Gunn (Eds.). **The Individual in Prehistory: Studies of Variability in Style in Prehistoric Technologies**

Michael B. Schiffer and George J. Gumerman (Eds.). **Conservation Archaeology: A Guide for Cultural Resource Management Studies**

Thomas F. King, Patricia Parker Hickman, and Gary Berg. **Anthropology in Historic Preservation: Caring for Culture's Clutter**

Richard E. Blanton. **Monte Albán: Settlement Patterns at the Ancient Zapotec Capital**

R. E. Taylor and Clement W. Meighan. **Chronologies in New World Archaeology**

Bruce D. Smith. **Prehistoric Patterns of Human Behavior: A Case Study in the Mississippi Valley**

Barbara L. Stark and Barbara Voorhies (Eds.). **Prehistoric Coastal Adaptations: The Economy and Ecology of Maritime Middle America**

Charles L. Redman, Mary Jane Berman, Edward V. Curtin, William T. Langhorne, Nina M. Versaggi, and Jeffery C. Wanser (Eds.). **Social Archeology: Beyond Subsistence and Dating**

Bruce D. Smith (Ed.). **Mississippian Settlement Patterns**

Lewis R. Binford. **Nunamiut Ethnoarchaeology**

J. Barto Arnold III and Robert Weddle. **The Nautical Archeology of Padre Island: The Spanish Shipwrecks of 1554**

Sarunas Milisauskas. **European Prehistory**

Brian Hayden (Ed.). **Lithic Use-Wear Analysis**

William T. Sanders, Jeffrey R. Parsons, and Robert S. Santley. **The Basin of Mexico: Ecological Processes in the Evolution of a Civilization**

David L. Clarke. **Analytical Archaeologist: Collected Papers of David L. Clarke. Edited and Introduced by His Colleagues**

Arthur E. Spiess. **Reindeer and Caribou Hunters: An Archaeological Study**

Elizabeth S. Wing and Antoinette B. Brown. **Paleonutrition: Method and Theory in Prehistoric Foodways.**

John W. Rick. **Prehistoric Hunters of the High Andes**

Timothy K. Earle and Andrew L. Christenson (Eds.). **Modeling Change in Prehistoric Economics**

Thomas F. Lynch (Ed.). **Guitarrero Cave: Early Man in the Andes**

Fred Wendorf and Romuald Schild. **Prehistory of the Eastern Sahara**

Henri Laville, Jean-Philippe Rigaud, and James Sackett. **Rock Shelters of the Perigord: Stratigraphy and Archaeological Succession**

Duane C. Anderson and Holmes A. Semken, Jr. (Eds.). **The Cherokee Excavations: Holocene Ecology and Human Adaptations in Northwestern Iowa**

Anna Curtenius Roosevelt. **Parmana: Prehistoric Maize and Manioc Subsistence along the Amazon and Orinoco**

Fekri A. Hassan. **Demographic Archaeology**

G. Barker. **Landscape and Society: Prehistoric Central Italy**

Lewis R. Binford. **Bones: Ancient Men and Modern Myths**

Richard A. Gould and Michael B. Schiffer (Eds.). **Modern Material Culture: The Archaeology of Us**

Muriel Porter Weaver. **The Aztecs, Maya, and Their Predecessors: Archaeology of Mesoamerica, 2nd edition**

Arthur S. Keene. **Prehistoric Foraging in a Temperate Forest: A Linear Programming Model**

Ross H. Cordy. **A Study of Prehistoric Social Change: The Development of Complex Societies in the Hawaiian Islands**

C. Melvin Aikens and Takayasu Higuchi. **Prehistory of Japan**

Kent V. Flannery (Ed.). **Maya Subsistence: Studies in Memory of Dennis E. Puleston**

Dean R. Snow (Ed.). **Foundations of Northeast Archaeology**

in preparation

Charles S. Spencer. **The Cuicatlán Cañada and the Rise of Monte Albán**

Steadman Upham. **Polities and Power: An Economic and Political History of the Western Pueblo**

Vincas P. Steponaitis. **Ceramics, Chronology, and Community Patterns: An Archaeological Study at Moundville**

Michael J. O'Brien, Robert E. Warren, & Dennis E. Lewarch (Eds.). **The Cannon Reservoir Human Ecology Project: An Archaeological Study of Cultural Adaptations in the Southern Prairie Peninsula**